The MIT Press
Cambridge,
Massachusetts,
and London,
England

**THE
OPEN
HAND**
**Essays
on
Le Corbusier**

**THE
OPEN
HAND**

**Essays
on
Le Corbusier**   edited by Russell Walden

Copyright © 1977 by
The Massachusetts Institute of Technology

This book was set in Univers by DEKR Corporation printed on
R&E Book by Murray Printing Company and bound in G.S.B. #9
by Murray Printing Company in the United States of America.

Library of Congress Cataloging in Publication Data
Main entry under title:

The Open hand.

Includes index.
1. Jeanneret-Gris, Charles Édouard, 1887–1965—
Addresses, essays, lectures. 2. Architecture,
Modern—20th century—Addresses, essays, lectures.
I. Walden, Russell.
NA1053.J4063   720'.92'4   76-40046
ISBN 0-262-23074-7

See! I am tired of my wisdom,
like a bee that has collected too much honey,
I need hands which stretch out for it.

I should like to give it away and
distribute it until the wise among men
become happy again in their foolishness,
and the poor happy in their riches.

Pleine main j'ai reçu
pleine main je donne.

Over this passage on page 8 of his 1908 French translation of Nietzsche, *Thus Spoke Zarathustra,* Le Corbusier wrote in 1961, "La main ouverte."

Le Corbusier, *Le Poème de l'angle droit.*

Contents

This foreword is perhaps paradoxical, because I am writing it before I have read the book. It would not have been possible to write an afterword in the same way. But a foreword can be an anticipation of the book itself. And from the introduction by Russell Walden, and especially from my conversation with him, I feel I can visualize this book.

It is very difficult to understand Le Corbusier fully. I knew him very well for thirty years; I worked with him. And yet sometimes I have the impression, ten years after his death, that I am still discovering him. In order to understand him, one has to discover him. And in order to discover him, one has to look for him.

Great credit is due to Russell Walden, for he has set out to look for Le Corbusier with fifteen or so different personalities, so that this search, and this discovery, may be contradictory in its findings. Thus the rich content of this book will raise questions, stimulate reactions, and thereby further research, further discoveries.

One should not be afraid of contradictions. Le Corbusier is so rich a personality that he reconciles contraries. If one is not content simply to read his books, but if one studies all his projects, of which only a few have been realized, one will find such a wealth of ideas, thoughts, intentions, feelings, wishes, endeavors, and even desires that one swings from one extreme to another, from one position to its very opposite, and finally one is projected beyond to a point where the contraries are no longer op-

Foreword

posed but convergent, where a unity is found. Le Corbusier evades classifications; he perplexes the classifiers. He embraces contraries, refuses dilemmas, reduces oppositions, and builds his thought on an integrated whole, on a totality.

I am by no means sure that the term *utopian* can be applied to Le Corbusier. In a utopian thinker, the artist takes second place to the inventor. Le Corbusier stands on that thin line that separates the ideal from the utopia. He knows how to judge the degree of perfection it is possible for him to achieve, and he does not go beyond this. I believe that Le Corbusier is first of all a realist, but by the power of his creative energy he leads this realism toward an ideal. The *Unité d'habitation,* the Radiant City, are first of all thoughts in terms of what people are today, as individuals, families, and societies.

All Le Corbusier's architecture and urbanism are based on a vision of social structures. But he is not resigned to them as they exist. He measures how far he can lead these social structures toward an ideal that is possible.

The first two motivating ideas of the *Unité d'habitation* are simple and objective: first, to protect individuals and families from all outside intrusion or disturbance. To do this, he set out to design a dwelling in which the family should not see or hear their neighbors, and therefore should neither be seen nor heard by them. Second, he sought to reconcile this protection of privacy with the collective life, to resolve the individual/society dilemma by integrating the dwelling units into a community—what he called the vertical village.

Those who claim that the high-rise or tower blocks, the scourge of our present age, are the result of Le Corbusier's ideas, are fools. For these large blocks do not fulfill either of his two conditions. Families are grouped together indiscriminately. These blocks simply contain a number of dwelling units, and therefore families, in a juxtaposition that is only an arithmetical addition and not an integration into a community. They do not create a collective nucleus, a village, a *unité*, so the society is destructured and destroyed.

For Le Corbusier, the dwelling unit is the shell, the matrix. He has a profound understanding of the fact that the need to have an identity, to be oneself, which every individual feels, necessitates both the opportunity of being alone and of being protected from other people and the possibility to think oneself part of a group, to be recognized by others, and to recognize oneself in a habitat, in a *unité,* in an architecture.

In order to understand Le Corbusier, one must dig deep and must understand, even feel beyond the words his real intentions, his secret desires. His famous saying: "The house is a machine for living in" has brought him much criticism. Many people failed to understand it; some did not want to understand it. Yet "let us get it firmly into our heads that a chair is a machine for sitting in. A house is a machine for living in. . . . A tree is a machine for bearing fruit. A plant is a machine for bearing flowers and seeds. . . . A heart is a suction pump." Now, this quotation is not from Le Corbusier, but from Frank Lloyd Wright.[1]

[1] Lecture at Princeton in 1930. Quoted by Michel Ragon in *Histoire mondiale de l'architecture et de l'urbanisme,* vol. 2, Tournai (Belgium), 1971.

I do not understand why some writers contrast Le Corbusier's architecture, which they call functionalist, with Frank Lloyd Wright's, which they call organic. Le Corbusier forbade the use of the word *functionalism* in his office. He hated the word. He thought it a stupidity to believe that a functional form is necessarily beautiful.

And it is easy to find nonfunctional forms in his work! I was criticized by him several times when I said to him "it's more logical" or "it's more rational." His creation of architectural forms goes beyond reason and logic. In him, the artist always comes first, before the inventor and the organizer. Le Corbusier can only be grasped within the process of his creating, for it is a continuing process. The organization of form is subjected to all the functional requirements, but it then goes beyond them in order to attain the plastic and the emotional. Le Corbusier's creating is a continuum that passes from the logical and from the rational to the nonrational and aesthetic state of thought. He then attains what he calls "the ineffable space."

Through this organizing continuum Le Corbusier tries to create organisms. He wants to create living forms. "Making architecture is making a creature."[2]

[2] Le Corbusier, *Le Poème de l'angle droit*, Paris, 1955.

Le Corbusier's architecture, led thus to the extreme edge of his thought, reduces the complicated to the simple, chaos to order, all directions to the vertical and to the horizontal, all lines to the right angle, all the noises of space to spatial music.

His architecture is built on an immense human hope of solidarity and complementarity, instead of opposition between men. The ultimate lesson of Le Corbusier to his followers lies beyond architecture: to build oneself. To make a man of oneself.

This wish is contained in the idea of the open hand.

André Wogenscky
Fondation Le Corbusier, Paris
December 1975

I wish to thank the following contributors for permission to reproduce their work: Paul Turner, Mary Patricia May Sekler, Maurice Favre, Brian Brace Taylor, Charles Jencks, Anthony Sutcliffe, Robert Fishman, Martin Purdy, John Winter, Maxwell Fry, Jane Drew, Madhu Sarin, and Stanislaus von Moos.

Collectively, these contributors express their thanks to the following people who have helped this project in a variety of ways: François Faessler, Irene Grill, Curé Louis de Montmollin (deceased), Irene von Moos, Isabelle Morillion, Rudolf Arnheim, Fernand Donzé, Emily Romney, Laurence Wylie, Costantino and Ruth Nivola, Eduard Sekler, Pierre-Max Wasem, Amos N. Wilder, James Ackerman, John Coolidge, Francette and Henri Gray, Kerstin Rääf, Pierre Emery, Pierre Hirsch, Max du Bois, Henri Frugès, the Kunstmuseum at Basel, the Director of the Basler Nachrichten, the Bibliothèque de La Chaux-de-Fonds, the Swiss Embassy in London, Thomas and Philipp Speiser, Wolfgang Bessenich, Willy Boesiger, Gordon Davies, Christian Gimonet, Silvia Sutton, Ise Gropius, Kenneth Frampton, Stanford Anderson, Alan Colquhoun, Jacques Michel, Valerie Winter, Heidi Weber, J. Perez y Jorba, Louis Michel, the Director of the Maison de la Culture at Firminy, Abbé André Belaud (deceased), Abbé René Bolle-Reddat, Glauco Gresleri, Roger Banks, Alan Jones, Leo Davies, Igor Kolodotschko, Madeline Jay, and Narindar Lamba.

Acknowledgments

On my own behalf and that of several of the contributors, I should like to express our deep gratitude to André Wogenscky, President of the Fondation Le Corbusier, Paris, for permission to work on original material held in the archives and for approval to publish this material. We are most grateful to him for generously providing a Foreword to *The Open Hand*. We are indebted to Françoise de Franclieu, archivist at the Fondation Le Corbusier, for her tireless support of our research.

I should also like to thank the Birmingham School of Architecture, which held a two-day symposium on Le Corbusier in October 1973.

To my friend Dr. Dennis Wood, I wish to express my thanks for his criticism of the book from its inception.

Finally, and above all, I thank my wife, Helen Walden, for the innumerable hours she has spent in typing and translating French archive material and for her invaluable thoroughness in checking the manuscript.

Russell Walden
Birmingham, England

Pleine main j'ai reçu
pleine main je donne.

L-C

Figure 1
Le Corbusier's sketch of the Open Hand symbol at Chandigarh. (Photograph courtesy of
Maison de la Culture at Firminy and Archives Fondation Le Corbusier.)

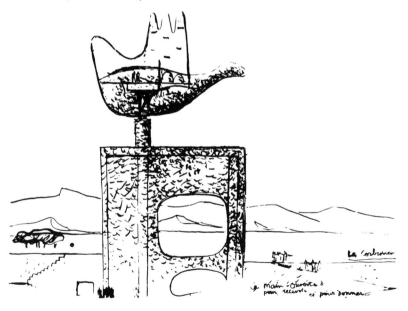

One might not like the personality or the architecture of Le Corbusier—indeed, in the transatlantic correspondence between critics Lewis Mumford and Frederic Osborn, Mumford called him "a menace."[1] Osborn regarded him as "godlike,"[2] as "fundamentally stupid," as "a pernicious influence," with the "controversial manners of a ranting political columnist," and said that as a "pseudo-sociologist-economist he is a babbling baby."[3] Yet no one can look at twentieth-century architecture without considering Le Corbusier very seriously—even in his demythologized form.

For architects who have an individual approach to design in modern architecture, and for scholars whose experiences are sufficiently broad to appreciate the difficulties involved, it is time to look objectively at the work of one of the important architectural masters.

In this book, under the symbol of the Open Hand (Fig. 1), the enigmatic figure of Le Corbusier is examined. In organizing this collective endeavor, I have been conscious of the fact that genius evades classification. Neither have I forgotten Maxwell Fry's timely warning to those "who hope by pecking over the remains of the great—the diaries, letters, reported conversations, photographs, and so on—that they will be permitted to pierce to the heart of the mystery that makes men great." It was not simply for fun that Le Corbusier went to the trouble of preserving the historical evidence from his office: working drawings, models, sketches, job dossiers, letters, *carnets* or notebooks, spanning the period from 1914 to 1964. Obviously, as a man with human problems and an architectural message to preserve, he hoped for some form of intelligent and patient reassessment from history. Indeed, if one takes the divergent poles of universal acclaim and hostility as representing the extremes of response which his work has always aroused, it is time, now that he and his period are no longer with us, to begin to set the record straight. Moreover, if his achievement is ever to be seen clearly, then serious commitment to reassessing it is essential.

Progress toward a comprehensive view of Le Corbusier's work, in the words of Eduard Sekler of Harvard, will "take the sustained efforts of many individuals to chart it and to make its full comprehension possible. While treatments in exhibitions and books no doubt will continue to give impressive evidence of the scope and richness of Le Corbusier's achievement, an increase in genuine understanding of his contribution will only follow from studies in depth of individual works."[4]

Conscious of this need, I have carefully arranged the contributions to capture the multiplicity of interpretations current among Le Corbusier scholars. Thus, the structure of *The Open Hand* is formed from a nucleus of archive-based papers, which are interspersed with essays by interpretative critics. In addition,

I have included the personal responses of architects who worked with Le Corbusier—Maxwell Fry and Jane Drew. Their personal experience, combined with specific professional skills, puts them in a unique position to draw interesting observations and conclusions about the summation of Le Corbusier's life work, as expressed at Chandigarh. In this way, through a combination of archive, interpretative, and personal observations, the book seeks to capture an integral sense of Le Corbusier's personality as a thinker, designer, and propagandist. The reassessment is therefore divided into five sections: the intellectual formation of Le Corbusier; *Habitation* and Le Corbusier's Purist position; the urban utopia; the spiritual and technological paradox of Le Corbusier; and finally, Chandigarh.

The Open Hand brings together a wide variety of contributors of different backgrounds, from as far afield as the United States, England, France, Switzerland, New Zealand, and India. By including contributions from this wide cultural horizon, I have aimed at capturing a measure of what Maxwell Fry calls the "gift of sympathy" in dealing with some of the simplicities and complexities of Le Corbusier's career.

I believe that from this book emerges a coherent and consistent view of Le Corbusier's approach to architecture. While Le Corbusier's design process was an intimately personal one and closely linked to his patient search for meaningful symbols, one must not forget that it was conditioned by an idealistic view of the world and nourished by the life energy of the divinity of nature. And if one were asked to describe his design sensibility in a sentence, one could reply that Le Corbusier's approach was inevitably a compound of the emotional and intellectual energy that had its source in the French Romantic tradition. It is this very point that has largely been unappreciated by English-speaking commentators when they have presented their arguments in the past. Indeed, if one examines the ideas that have produced so many tensions in French life today, one cannot fail to realize that these ideas have their roots in the utopian thinking of Jean-Jacques Rousseau, Claude-Henri de Saint-Simon, Charles Fourier, Victor Considérant, and Pierre-Joseph Proudhon. When one examines this sociopolitical yet spiritual background where the sincerity and integrity of the individual were stressed, one can see that Le Corbusier came to terms with problem solving in the spirit of precisely this tradition.

In his sketchbook dated 21 May 1964, Le Corbusier wrote down his thoughts on the design process:

When a task is assigned me, I usually put it aside *in my memory,* which means not to allow myself any sketch for months. The human head is so formed as to possess a certain independence: there is an area where the elements of a problem can be left to work themselves out. They are left thus "to waver," "to simmer," "to ferment." Then one day, with spontaneous subconscious initiative the inspiration comes: you take a pencil, a carbon, some colored pencils (color is the key to the procedure) and you let it flow out onto the paper. The idea comes—as the child comes —it is brought into the world, it is born.[5]

The sincerity of this method of thinking leaves one in no doubt about Le Corbusier's spirit of independence and intellectual lineage. Le Corbusier understood design to be a wholesome activity involving the whole man, both emotional and intellectual. To design in this spirit involved the expression of a full range of problems from functional to symbolic. In fact, the way the functional and symbolic elements are put together was the essential creative concern of Le Corbusier. It demanded a ruthless integrity in expressing the rich and varied life of clients.

And in this matter, the degree of emphasis that Le Corbusier places upon design is where he parts company with most architects. While it is a relatively simple matter to describe the limited concern of the commercial practitioner under headings like profit and economics, land tenure and site ratios, structure and techniques, energy services and materials, it is a somewhat fruitless task to attempt a comprehensive explanation of Le Corbusier from this point of view. Not that Le Corbusier did not have to contend with the everyday realities and contingencies of professional life. He did. Yet the inevitable limitations before all twentieth-century architects were appreciated and exceeded in Le Corbusier's office. Above and beyond these realities, the overriding concern of those who labored at 35 Rue de Sèvres was the struggle to preserve the ideological intentions of Le Corbusier. What was of importance was the *idea* in architecture, and that is perhaps why Le Corbusier used the analogy of birth when talking about his design process.

In attempting to describe the design position of Le Corbusier, one cannot undervalue his sincerity nor his monklike devotion and quest for the expression of a higher consciousness through the medium of symbolic architecture. To acknowledge such a consciousness, this book adopts the symbol of the Open Hand. Le Corbusier's idea of using a duality of imagery, part human and part birdlike, simultaneously linked yet detached in space, was essentially a highly potent symbolic statement of intention. The derivation of this symbol, from the silhouettes of snow-laden Jura boughs to *la main ouverte* designed to be placed above the hot plains of Chandigarh, is a linear progression within the French idealistic and intellectual tradition.

In Volume Five of his *Oeuvre complète,* Le Corbusier describes the birth and development of the Open Hand:

The Open Hand is an idea which was born in Paris, spontaneously, or more exactly, as the result of reflections and spiritual struggles arising from the feelings of anguish and disharmony which separate mankind, and so often create enemies. The first sketch appeared spontaneously—a sort of cockle floating above the horizon, but the stretched fingers showed an open hand like a vast shell. Later, in the following year . . . the idea returned in a different form. It was no longer a shell but a fan, a silhouette. It is the value of the silhouette which developed through the years. Little by little the open hand appeared as a possibility in great architectural compositions.[6]

Thus, in the creation of the Open Hand, Le Corbusier affirmed his belief in a spiritual reality. In his last intellectual testament, written a month before he died in August 1965, he said of the Open Hand, "It was not a political emblem, a politician's creation. It is an architect's creation . . . a symbol of peace and reconciliation. . . ." He concluded his explanation by asserting that the symbol was "open to receive the wealth that the world has created, to distribute it to the peoples of the world" and, therefore, "it ought to be the symbol of our age."[7]

His interest in the Third World helped to confirm his belief in the salvation of contemporary man. In this respect Le Corbusier sought a new idealized order—a renewing spiritual dimension for industrial man. In his search for a symbol to express this consciousness, Le Corbusier went back to one of the oldest gestures in the mythology of the human race. Indeed, the theme extends right back to the cave painters of Pech-Merle (Dordogne) and has remained a major symbol for artists and scientists ever since.

This historical line of imagery was not lost on Le Corbusier. When he came to paint the doors to his pilgrimage chapel on the heights at Ronchamp, he took the theme of the hands to express the spiritual dilemma of twentieth-century man (Fig. 2). He took this strong and unfearing gesture of the human hand to be the symbol of the giving and receiving man.

The red and blue hands were set within a geometrical framework involving a full range of imagery designed to draw attention to man's relationship with nature, with the sky, and with the earth where he works. Therefore, the giving and receiving imagery was interlocked with cogwheels symbolizing this relationship of work. Such an idea was not only central to the concept of life's twisting, tortuous journey as personified in this pilgrimage chapel, it was also a symbolic expression by Le Corbusier of his great human hope for the salvation of contemporary man. But as Alexander Solzhenitsyn warned in his Nobel Speech on Literature:

Figure 2
The south exterior door of the Chapel Notre-Dame-du-Haut at Ronchamp. (Photograph by Russell Walden.)

One artist imagines himself to be the creator of an independent spiritual world, burdens himself with the act of creating and peopling this world, accepts responsibility for it—but he breaks down, because no mortal genius is capable of withstanding such a burden; just as, in a more general sense, man, who has declared himself to be the centre of existence, has been unable to create a balanced spiritual system. And if he is overwhelmed by failure, he lays the blame on the eternal disharmony of the world, on the complexity of the distraught contemporary soul, or on the lack of comprehension of the public.[8]

The predicament described by Solzhenitsyn is precisely that of Le Corbusier. He was a spiritual son of Jean-Jacques Rousseau and a product of late nineteenth-century Romanticism. He found himself stranded as the twentieth century advanced and his vision became increasingly unattainable.

When Le Corbusier's professional reputation has been scrutinized and demythologized for the last time, he will still be a great romantic designer who made mistakes but who left the world richer by the products of his creative soul. The epigram from his *Le Poème de l'angle droit* supports this conclusion:

Pleine main j'ai reçu
pleine main je donne.[9]

The Open Hand symbolizes an essentially human warmth of response and a reciprocity between the creative artist and his public. It can, therefore, be understood as an all-embracing metaphor for Le Corbusier's creative struggle to bring a new degree of harmony and humanity into modern architecture. The task of this book and future reassessments is to decide how far he succeeded.

Russell Walden
Easter 1975

1 Lewis Mumford to Frederic Osborn, 11 August 1967, in *The Letters of Lewis Mumford and Frederic J. Osborn,* Bath, 1971, p. 423.

2 Ibid., p. 334, Osborn to Mumford, 15 February 1963.

3 Ibid., p. 420, Osborn to Mumford, 3 August 1967.

4 See Eduard Sekler's preface to Brian Brace Taylor, *Le Corbusier at Pessac,* Cambridge, Mass., and Paris, 1972.

5 Le Corbusier's unpublished sketchbook, dated 21 May 1964, held in the Archives Fondation Le Corbusier, Paris.

6 Le Corbusier, *Oeuvre complète 1946–52,* Zurich, 1955, p. 159.

7 Willy Boesiger (ed.), *Le Corbusier Last Works*, London, 1970, p. 176.

8 Alexander Solzhenitsyn, *One Word of Truth,* The Nobel Speech on Literature 1970, London, 1972, p. 4.

9 Le Corbusier, *Le Poème de l'angle droit,* Paris, 1955, p. 144.

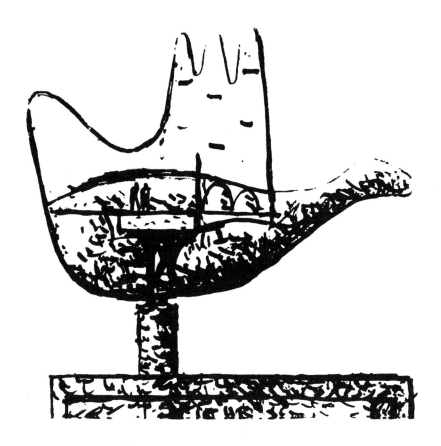

Part One　　　　　　　**The Intellectual Formation of Le Corbusier**

Paul Turner

**Romanticism, Rationalism, and
the Domino System**

The work of Le Corbusier often seems to possess mysteriously elusive, even ineffable qualities. While we can usually describe the essential nature of other architects' works, Le Corbusier's designs elicit from us stronger and less objective reactions, difficult to articulate. Thus, his work has always aroused extremely emotional responses, and any one of his designs can produce varying reactions—for example, some see the Villa Savoye as the very epitome of a cold, passionless machine aesthetic, while others see it as one of the most affective and poetic creations of our age.

This multiplicity is not simply in the observers' eyes but is inherent in the work itself and, more than that, in its underlying theoretical foundation. The architectural thinking of Le Corbusier seems to be structured in a distinctive way that might be called dualistic or dialectical, based on opposing principles or dichotomies that he expresses on many levels in his work and thought. On a physical level, there are contrasts of specific architectural qualities, as in the play of geometric and amorphous forms, which are seen throughout his work. On a theoretical level, in his writings Le Corbusier continually describes the world in terms of paired opposites, such as matter and spirit, active and passive forces, reason and emotion, and so on—as when he explains the use of a painting as the frontispiece to his city planning book *La Ville radieuse* with the statement that "The objective and the subjective are the two poles between which arises the human creation made of matter and spirit."[1]

This dualistic pattern in Le Corbusier's work and thought appears, moreover, to be a manifestation of a basic trait of his personality, a tendency to see everything in terms of a struggle between opposing forces. In his own life, this trait could be seen reflected in his self-image as an isolated, heroic figure, always battling with opponents (an image that is often explained in terms of the many disappointments of his career but that in reality he exhibited even as a young man, long before the nature of his career had justified it).[2] In his architecture, this dualism is expressed in many ways: on a fundamental level, as two opposing conceptions of the nature of architecture; or in dramatic formal terms, as the defiant separation of his buildings from the earth below, suggesting the contrast between the clarity of man's mind and the vagaries of nature (or *la tête et la bête,* to use two of Le Corbusier's favorite terms for this dichotomy). And his image of the Open Hand suggests a similar symbolism: the hand of man, disembodied and isolated from the earth, and often even represented by Le Corbusier as a double image that is not only a hand but also a bird, age-old symbol of the spiritual as opposed to the material world (Fig. 3).

Though it may be futile to seek the ultimate source of the dualism in Le Corbusier's thought, it is worth suggesting that it lies partly in the religious atmosphere in which he was raised. His family (including a devoutly religious aunt who helped raise him) belonged to the strong Calvinist tradition of the area around Geneva, a tradition that emphasized the struggle between spirit and sin more strongly than most Christian churches. Furthermore, there was a tradition, staunchly supported by Le Corbusier himself, linking his family to the Albigensian Catharists of the twelfth and thirteenth centuries in southern France, a sect that had represented the most extreme adherence ever seen in Europe to the radical dualism of the Manichaean heresy, equating spirit with good and matter with evil. Throughout his life, Le Corbusier was fascinated with this Albigensian sect (his library contains a number of books on the subject, which he read and annotated); and whether he truly was descended from the Catharists, he believed he was, and he considered this tradition to be an important part of his heritage.

Specific components of Le Corbusier's thought, however, can often be traced to their sources much more precisely than his general

Figure 3
La main ouverte,
lithograph, 23 August
1963. As in his
architecture, Le
Corbusier's
representations of the
open hand suggest a
dualistic notion of man's
mind in opposition to the
world—or *"la bête et la
tête,"* as he put it.
(Source: Le Corbusier,
Oeuvre lithographique,
Zurich, n.d.)

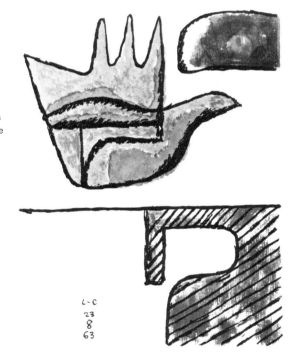

dualism can. A fundamental dichotomy in his thinking involves two views of the essential nature of architecture. One view, which could be called rationalist, is concerned first and foremost with objective, worldly matters—structure, technology, function, other human needs—and is suggested by Le Corbusier's famous definition of a house as a "machine for living." The other conception (implied by another of Le Corbusier's definitions, *"Architecture, pure création de l'esprit"*)[3] could in a general way be called romantic; it sees architecture principally as a spiritual or personal activity—whether as the creation of abstract forms or in a Platonic, idealistic sense, as the embodiment of perfect spiritual ideas that the architect has intuited or discovered. Much of the tension and power in Le Corbusier's architecture derives from the dynamic relationship between these two conceptions, the romantic or idealistic and the rationalist. And their specific sources can be identified quite clearly—corresponding, in fact, to the two major teachers of Le Corbusier in his youth, Charles L'Eplattenier and Auguste Perret.

With the aid of Le Corbusier's early correspondence, sketchbooks, and especially the books that he read and annotated in his youth (which are now in the Fondation Le Corbusier in Paris), it is possible to reconstruct the story of how he encountered these ideas, struggled with them, and then attempted to synthesize them—first achieving this synthesis around 1915 in the Domino System design.

La Chaux-de-Fonds and L'Eplattenier

The basic facts of the youth of Le Corbusier (or Charles-Edouard Jeanneret) in La Chaux-de-Fonds are well known: his apprenticeship at the age of thirteen to learn the profession of watchcase engraving at the local Art School; his decision, encouraged by his drawing teacher Charles L'Eplattenier, to become an architect; his participation in L'Eplattenier's regionalist arts-and-crafts program (including the design and decoration of a house for a local citizen named Fallet); and then his departure, in 1907, on the long series of travels that took him to Italy, France, Germany, Eastern Europe, and the Mediterranean, and back to La Chaux-de-Fonds several times, before he settled permanently in Paris in 1917.

What has remained largely unknown is the aesthetic philosophy to which he was exposed in his early years in La Chaux-de-Fonds. In later recollections, Le Corbusier always recognized L'Eplattenier as the most important influence on his early development, not only as his teacher in drawing and design but also as the man who introduced him to aesthetics and art theory.[4] Yet he never described the specific nature of L'Eplattenier's ideas (except for details such as the fact that he read Ruskin to his students and told them that in designing ornament they ought to start with natural forms but then abstract them to reveal their "vital development").[5] Le Corbusier's library, however, contains several books from this early period that suggest in some detail the aesthetic principles to which he was being exposed.[6] And consistently they represent the view that architecture and art in general are essentially spiritual rather than material activities, and they furthermore suggest that L'Eplattenier was interested in certain esoteric subjects which he considered relevant to art and design.

When Jeanneret was about to leave La Chaux-de-Fonds in 1907, L'Eplattenier gave him a copy of a popular book of the period entitled *Les Grands Initiés,* by Edouard Schuré.[7] The book is a romanticized portrayal of the greatest mystical initiates of the past (listed by Schuré as Rama, Krishna, Hermes, Moses, Orpheus, Pythagoras, Plato, and Jesus); it would seem to be an odd parting gift for an art teacher to give to his favorite student embarking on a career in architecture. Yet it is only one of several similar books that Jeanneret read which glorify the role of the prophet or mystic in human history. And in some of these books (including Friedrich Nietzsche's *Zarathustra* and

Ernest Renan's *Life of Jesus*), Jeanneret's annotations suggest that he had begun to identify with these figures and to think of himself as a kind of prophet, too, in the realm of art and architecture.[8] This discovery is of more than merely psychological interest to us, for it suggests a special conception of the role of the architect—not as someone concerned with solving problems empirically in the world, but rather as someone intuiting universal truths, which he then reveals to the world. Le Corbusier himself was to express this attitude in many ways—for instance, in his descriptions of the Modulor system (which, by the way, are very similar in some respects to Schuré's descriptions of the numerology of Pythagoras).[9]

But another book that Jeanneret read during his adolescent years in La Chaux-de-Fonds has even more obvious architectural implications. This was a little-known work published in 1904, entitled *L'Art de demain,* by a French architect named Henri Provensal.[10] It may have been the first book on aesthetic theory that Jeanneret read, and its ideas seem to have had a profound influence on him. Its general philosophical tone is Platonic, antipositivist, and more specifically in the tradition of nineteenth-century German idealistic philosophers like Hegel and Schelling. Constantly recurring throughout the book is the theme that the major purpose of art is to express the underlying spiritual forces of the universe, to reveal "pure thought," "perfect spirit," "eternal harmony," and so on—many of Provensal's phrases reminding us of those in Le Corbusier's later writings.

When Provensal discusses architecture, he makes an unusual proposal: that the forms best suited to expressing these spiritual ideas are those of the purest geometry, particularly cubic forms—a point that he repeats emphatically, in one place defining architecture as "the harmonious cubic expression of thought."[11] In itself, this advocacy of cubic art is remarkable, since in 1904 *cubism* had not yet been coined as a term in painting. Although there is evidence that Jeanneret had been influenced by some protocubist designs in the decorative arts as early as 1901,[12] it seems to be Provensal who got him thinking seriously about a cubist aesthetic in architecture. And there are more specific indications of his influence on Jeanneret. For example, at one point in his book he suggests that the architect can find inspiration in those few forms in nature which are cubic, such as crystals and crystalline rock formations; we also know that at roughly this time Jeanneret was doing drawings of crystalline rock formations (Fig. 4) in the mountains around La Chaux-de-Fonds; these drawings are almost like studies of the cubic bracket details he included in the Fallet House (Fig. 5), as well as foreshadowing his designs of the 1920s.

Even the language and terminology used by Provensal to describe architecture seem to reappear in Le Corbusier's later writings. In fact, Le Corbusier's famous definition of architecture as *"le jeu savant, correct et magnifique des volumes assemblés sous la lumière"* (found elsewhere in his writings in varying forms, such as *". . . des jeux architecturaux de pleins et de vides"*)[13] is strikingly similar to several of Provensal's own definitions of architecture—such as *"le drame plastique . . . de pleins et de vides, de jeux d'ombres et de lumière."*[14] This is not to suggest that Le Corbusier consciously paraphrased Provensal but rather that this book had made such a deep impression on him in his youth that its concepts and very phrases had entered into his subconscious feelings about architecture.

To define architecture in this abstract way—as pure forms under light—is very typical of Provensal's romantic and idealistic aesthetic and apparently also reflects the training Jeanneret had received from L'Eplattenier. This abstract conception of architecture was to remain an essential component of Le Corbusier's thinking throughout his life. But first it had to undergo a traumatic encounter with an opposing philosophy, in Paris in 1908, which precipitated probably the major intellectual crisis of Jeanneret's youth.

Figure 4
Drawing of rock
formations near La
Chaux-de-Fonds. A
reflection of Henri
Provensal's suggestion
in *L'Art de demain* that
crystalline rock
formations could inspire
the new "cubic"
architecture he was
advocating. (Source: Le
Corbusier, *Le Corbusier,*
Paris, 1960, p. 22.)

Figure 5
Bracket detail of the
Fallet House, La
Chaux-de-Fonds,
1906–1907. In his first
house design, Jeanneret
included this one
tentative expression of
Provensal's cubic
aesthetic. (Source: E.
Chavanne and M. Laville,
"Les premières
constructions de Le
Corbusier," in *Werk,* vol.
50, 1963, p. 483.)

Paris and Auguste Perret

In June 1907, at the age of nineteen, Jeanneret left La Chaux-de-
Fonds, spent several months traveling in Italy, went to Vienna, where
he spent the winter, and then on to Paris, where he was to remain for
more than a year. There he heard that the most exciting things in architecture were done by a man named Auguste Perret, whom he went
to see, and who gave him a job in his office, at that time located on
the ground floor of his reinforced-concrete apartment building on the
Rue Franklin. Perret took Jeanneret on as a kind of apprentice, encouraging him to take courses in technical subjects and architectural
history. But more important, Perret attempted to inculcate him with
the architectural philosophy often called French Rationalism—the tradition whose major exponent in the nineteenth century had been
Viollet-le-Duc, and which Perret himself now exemplified in his researches into the formal potentials of concrete construction.

Several of Jeanneret's annotated books from this period, as well as
his correspondence, reveal the ideas that Perret was presenting to
him. Just as significantly, they reveal that this rationalist philosophy
was totally new to Jeanneret—virtually a revelation—which at first he
embraced with the fervor of a new convert, rejecting what he considered to be L'Eplattenier's overly formalistic thinking. In a long letter
(November 1908) to L'Eplattenier, he implicitly criticizes his former
master for teaching false doctrines, says that he knew nothing before
and that only now has he realized "that architecture is not a matter of
the 'eurythmie' of forms . . ." (a phrase that had recurred in Provensal's book) but is simply the proper use of materials to satisfy specific
needs.[15] And he proudly states that he is now studying subjects like
statics and the strength of materials and implies that he had never before suspected their central importance to architecture.

One of Jeanneret's books from this period gives us a remarkable
view of this program of reeducation. Perret apparently encouraged

him to go directly to Viollet-le-Duc's writings, for he bought an expensive edition of the *Dictionnaire raisonné de l'architecture française du
XIᵉ au XVIᵉ siècle* and inscribed the first volume with this resolution: "I
bought this work on August 1st, 1908, with my first paycheck from Mr.
Perret. I bought it in order to *learn*; because, *knowing*, I shall then be
able to create."[16]

In the text itself, at a passage in which Viollet describes the form of
the Gothic flying buttress as a perfect expression of the structural
problems involved, Jeanneret inserted a note which begins (Fig. 6),
"These lines show how this whole *art lives by its carcass.*" (*Carcass*
was a favorite term of Perret's for the underlying structural form of a
building.) Jeanneret then draws an analogy between this Gothic structural system and reinforced concrete and concludes, "Now, Auguste
Perret has told me, *hold on to the carcass,* and you will have the
Art."[17] That is, if one designs properly from the structure, it is not
necessary to worry about "art"—one of the favorite notions of the
Rationalists.

Jeanneret clearly believed he was adopting the rationalist approach
that Perret represented and that this would be the foundation of his
architectural career, rather than L'Eplattenier's training. Yet in retrospect we can see that this was not quite the case. Jeanneret's enthusiasm for rationalism was in turn to wane, and he was soon to
begin struggling with the two systems of thought. Indeed, even in his
initial excitement over Perret's ideas, Jeanneret reveals a peculiar
ambivalence about them. For example, in his long letter to L'Eplattenier, while proclaiming the primacy of structure and rationalism, he
often shifts to the most romantic descriptions of the architect as an
isolated prophet seeking spiritual answers through intuition and a
turning-away from the world: "[Others] do not know what Art is: the
intense love of one's spiritual 'Self.' I shall find it through retreat and

Figure 6
Jeanneret's annotation in Viollet-le-Duc's *Dictionnaire raisonné,* vol. 1, Paris, 1854, inscribed 1908, p. 66. Jeanneret describes the rationalist lessons he had been receiving from Auguste Perret, such as the principle of concentrating on the structural "carcass" of a building. (Photograph by Paul Turner. Courtesy of Archives Fondation Le Corbusier.)

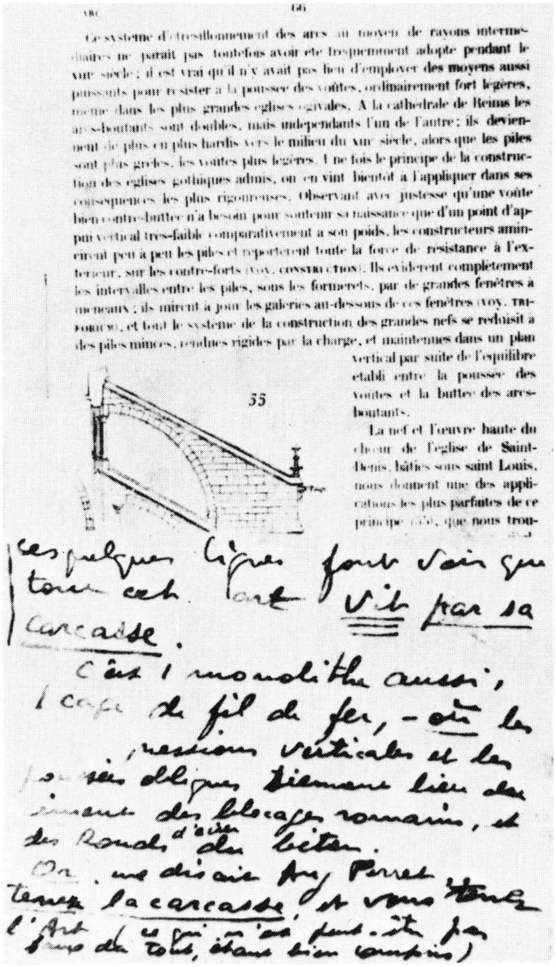
66

Ce système d'étrésillonnement des arcs au moyen de rayons intermédiaires ne parait pas toutefois avoir été fréquemment adopté pendant le XIIIe siècle; il est vrai qu'il n'y avait pas lieu d'employer des moyens aussi puissants pour résister à la poussée des voûtes, ordinairement fort légères, même dans les plus grandes églises ogivales. A la cathédrale de Reims les arcs-boutants sont doubles, mais indépendants l'un de l'autre; ils deviennent de plus en plus hardis vers le milieu du XIIIe siècle, alors que les piles sont plus grêles, les voûtes plus légères. Une fois le principe de la construction des églises gothiques admis, on en vint bientôt à l'appliquer dans ses conséquences les plus rigoureuses. Observant avec justesse qu'une voûte bien contre-buttée n'a besoin pour soutenir sa naissance que d'un point d'appui vertical très-faible comparativement à son poids, les constructeurs amincirent peu à peu les piles et reportèrent toute la force de résistance à l'extérieur, sur les contre-forts (voy. CONSTRUCTION). Ils évidèrent complètement les intervalles entre les piles, sous les formerets, par de grandes fenêtres à meneaux; ils mirent à jour les galeries au-dessous de ces fenêtres (voy. TRIFORIUM), et tout le système de la construction des grandes nefs se réduisit à des piles minces, rendues rigides par la charge, et maintenues dans un plan vertical par suite de l'équilibre établi entre la poussée des voûtes et la butée des arcs-boutants.

55

La nef et l'œuvre haute du chœur de l'église de Saint-Denis, bâties sous saint Louis, nous donnent une des applications les plus parfaites de ce principe (55), que nous trou-

ces quelques lignes font voir que tout cet art vit par sa carcasse.
C'est 1 monolithe aussi, 1 cage de fil de fer, — où les pressions verticales et les poussées obliques tiennent lieu du ciment des blocages romains, et des Rondels d'acier du béton.
On me disait Aug. Perret: tenez la carcasse, et vous tenez l'Art

solitude, the divine 'self' which can be made earthly if one forces it to be. . . . This inner self speaks; it speaks of the profound nature of Being. Art then is born, and springs forth. . . . "

These phrases come right out of Provensal and Schuré and are notions that a true rationalist would have considered irrelevant to (if not incompatible with) the real problems of architecture. Even Jeanneret's inscription in Viollet-le-Duc's *Dictionnaire* reflects this ambivalence. For when he says he is reading it "because, *knowing,* I shall then be able to create," he is expressing much more the initiate's faith that art will spring forth once he has received enlightenment than the rationalist's belief that each specific problem must be approached on its own terms.

Jeanneret was obviously attracted to aspects of both of these philosophies. In the next few years his main energy seems to be spent attempting to resolve them—to create a synthesis that somehow would preserve the integrity of both extremes. But in Paris in 1908, he had not yet found the way to do this. His letters reveal his frustration, and he began a period of vacillation between allegiance to Perret and to L'Eplattenier. Only in this light do his activities of the next several years make sense.

Toward a Synthesis
At the end of 1909, Jeanneret left Paris and returned to La Chaux-de-Fonds. This was a strange move, considering that his letters to L'Eplattenier had praised Paris as the place where he could learn most effectively. Furthermore, after letters that had criticized his former teacher and colleagues, he joined them in a decorative-arts undertaking—called the Ateliers d'art—whose program of activities was stone carving, mosaic, wood carving, repoussé metal work, and so on. This was fully in keeping with L'Eplattenier's arts-and-crafts

background, and to this extent, Jeanneret was setting aside Perret's dedication to modern materials and technology and returning to the handicraft regionalism of L'Eplattenier's classroom.

Even the design that Jeanneret produced at this time for a building to house these Ateliers d'art (Fig. 7), which at first glance might seem to be in the spirit of Perret because it appears to be designed for construction in concrete, is in reality a rejection of Perret's principles, since it shows virtually no consideration of the building's structure or construction (for instance, the second-floor walls are over voids). Instead, it is an extremely formalistic composition of Provensalesque cubes, like a large-scale version of the cubistic bracket ornaments on the Fallet House. In this sense, it represents a way of designing which Jeanneret had criticized, in his letter to L'Eplattenier from Paris, as *"ma conception purement plastique (faite de la recherche* seule *des formes). . . ,"* which he had said characterized his work before he met Perret.

Then, in April 1910, Jeanneret set out on the second phase of his travels, which took him to Germany, Austria, Czechoslovakia, Bulgaria, Turkey, Greece, and Italy. After arriving in Germany, he received a commission from L'Eplattenier and the Art School to study the Werkbund and other design movements in Germany. In this capacity he visited and interviewed many of the important German architects and designers of the time, eventually meeting Peter Behrens in Berlin and joining his firm for a short period. Behrens has the remarkable distinction of having employed the entire trinity of modern architecture—Walter Gropius, Mies van der Rohe, and Le Corbusier— although, contrary to the popular story, the three of them were not in his office at exactly the same time (when Jeanneret arrived in November 1910, Gropius had left already, though Mies was still there).[18] Behrens's position in Germany was somewhat analogous to Perret's in France, since he was among the foremost proponents of a

Figure 7
Design for Ateliers d'art, 1910, compared to the Fallet House bracket detail. Leaving Perret
and returning to La Chaux-de-Fonds and L'Eplattenier, Jeanneret resumed Provensal's
abstract, cubic conception of design. (Source: Le Corbusier, *Oeuvre complète 1910–29*,
p. 22.)

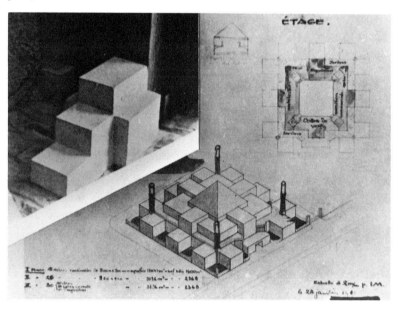

progressive, basically rationalist design process employing modern materials and technology. Thus it has been natural to assume that Behrens's main influence on Jeanneret must have been to strengthen his dedication to this progressive, internationalist vision of modern architecture, leading by an essentially direct route to his work of the 1920s.

So it comes as a considerable surprise to discover that, on the contrary, in Berlin Jeanneret experienced a reaction against Behrens and actually made a written resolution to return to a Swiss regionalist style of architecture. This is revealed in Jeanneret's annotations in a book that he ordered from Geneva in October 1910. This book is not of great interest in itself, but it elicited a powerful response from Jeanneret. Entitled *Les Entretiens de la Villa du Rouet* and written by a Swiss artist named Alexandre Cingria-Vaneyre, it consists of a series of dialogues set in an imaginary villa. Their major theme is that the region known as the *Suisse-Romande* (the French-speaking part of Switzerland) should develop its own regional style of art, which should be based on classical traditions from the Mediterranean rather than on German traditions.[19] It is such a provincial and innocuous proposal that we are amazed to find how strongly and enthusiastically Jeanneret responded to it. He wrote several fervent annotations in the book (each dated separately, some even to the hour of day) attesting to the impact it had on him. In one he wrote: ". . . this book is helping me orient myself. It provokes an investigation, and clear luminous thinking; it unlocks the German vise from me. One year from now, in Rome, I shall re-read it, and with sketches shall establish my Jura, Neuchâtel discipline."[20]

As it happened, Jeanneret was to fulfill this vow perfectly, for he was indeed in Rome, precisely one year later, after having traveled through Eastern Europe to Constantinople and then Greece (his *Voyage d'Orient,* which he later said opened his eyes to the beauty of

Mediterranean forms).[21] Furthermore, his route for this trip roughly followed an itinerary suggested by Cingria, who had lived in Constantinople and compared its topography and beauty to that of the Suisse-Romande. When Jeanneret finally returned to La Chaux-de-Fonds, he designed some houses that, in their simplified classical forms, geometric massing, and some details like color, follow Cingria's suggestions for a Suisse-Romande architecture. Despite all this, it would probably be a mistake to suggest that Cingria's book had a great influence on Jeanneret in the sense of giving him new ideas. Instead, as Jeanneret himself wrote, it "provoked" and aided his own thinking, which must have been ready for a reorientation back to some of the principles represented by L'Eplattenier and his regionalist arts-and-crafts activities.

This unexpected phase in Jeanneret's development helps explain an incident that hitherto has been difficult to understand. Le Corbusier later recalled that while in Constantinople in 1911, he had by chance met Perret, who was there to supervise construction of the French Embassy. Perret urged Jeanneret to return to Paris to work with him on his largest commission, the Champs-Elysées Theater, but Jeanneret declined the offer.[22] This refusal to pursue his career in the progressive environment of Paris can make sense only in the light of his decision to "establish my . . . Neuchâtel discipline" and suggests a return not only to L'Eplattenier's regionalism but also to his aesthetic philosophy. Thus it is not surprising that Jeanneret's diary notes and letters describing his *Voyage d'Orient* reveal an almost exclusive concentration on the abstract, idealistic, and spiritual qualities of architecture—culminating in his experience of the Parthenon, which for the rest of his life was to epitomize the mystical power of architecture to put us directly in touch with the forces of the universe. Le Corbusier's descriptions of the Parthenon often sound as though they could have been written word for word by Provensal, as for instance when he writes in *Vers une architecture* that the Parthenon strikes a chord within us, which produces

... a resonance, a kind of sounding-board, which begins to vibrate. Trace of the indefinable absolute pre-existing in the depths of our being. This sounding-board vibrating within us is our criterion of harmony. It must be that axis on which Man is organized, in accord with nature and probably the universe, that axis of organization which must be the same one on which all phenomena and objects in nature are aligned; this axis leads us to admit a unity of operation in the universe, a unique will at the origin. Even the laws of physics would have come out of this axis. . . .[23]

In late 1911 Jeanneret returned to La Chaux-de-Fonds, where he spent the next five years. Later in his life he seldom referred to specifically this period; yet it was crucial in his development, since this is when he was formulating the methods of designing which were to underlie his work of the 1920s. But it was not an easy formulation for him, and his activities, designs, and notebooks of the period reveal that he was still faced with the conflicts that had plagued him— between L'Eplattenier and Perret, regionalism and internationalism, romanticism and rationalism.

In the first half of this period (roughly up to 1915), Jeanneret's activities seem to be relatively consonant with his Swiss-regionalist resolution. He worked with L'Eplattenier in an experimental Nouvelle Section of the Art School (teaching an elementary course whose assignments emphasized the abstract formal properties of architecture); he cultivated social connections with other artists involved in creating a Suisse-Romande culture (including the novelist Ferdinand Ramuz, the musician Ernest Ansermet, and Cingria himself); and he pursued several commerical design ventures involving the decorative arts, interior design, and the remodeling of houses in the area—besides his own designs for houses.[24]

But then, around 1915, his concerns became more progressive and internationalist and suggest at least a partial reorientation to the attitudes of Perret. His notebooks contain references suggesting increased correspondence with Perret (he had also been visiting Paris occasionally); he did sketches exploring problems of mass housing and urbanism (including the *ville-tours*, which would lead to his city plans of the 1920s, and which he acknowledged had been inspired by Perret); and in his architecture he began to rely almost exclusively on reinforced concrete. The Schwob House of 1916, his major executed design of this period, has a reinforced-concrete structure; and his notebooks refer more and more to problems of concrete construction.

But the Domino System, more than any other design of this period, signals a breakthrough in Jeanneret's search for his own architectural synthesis. Although it might appear at first to embody exclusively the principles of Perret, in reality it represented an ingenious and peculiar combination of aspects of the opposing philosophies Jeanneret had been contending with, and in this sense it was the key he had been looking for.

The Domino System

The design that Jeanneret dubbed the Domino System (probably a pun on the word *domus* and the game of Dominoes, with its connotation of flexible linkage) was conceived, according to his later recollection, in late 1914, partly in response to the widespread destruction of housing in Flanders in the first phase of the war. This dating is likely correct, for in a sketchbook which he kept during 1915 there are several pages of rough sketches and notes relating to this design—though not including any of the more precise drawings that Le Corbusier later published in the *Oeuvre complète.*[25]

At first glance, the Domino design (Fig. 8) seems consummately simple and straightforward: a concrete structural unit consisting of three horizontal slabs, six columns, and a stair connecting the levels. This was to provide two-story housing units, which could be linked or

Figure 8
The Domino System. Visually and conceptually simple, though beset with constructional problems. For Jeanneret it represented a resolution of L'Eplattenier's and Perret's teachings. (Source: *Oeuvre complète 1910–29,* p. 23.)

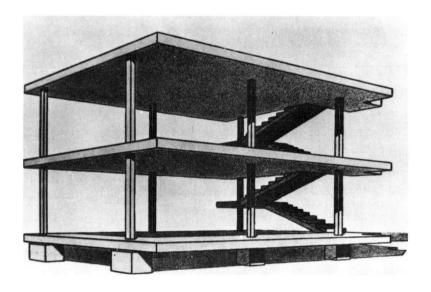

expanded in various ways, as Jeanneret suggested in other drawings and also in a patent that he wrote up in his notebook, which described the design as a "system of constructions able to be arranged according to infinite combinations of plans."[26]

On the surface, this design appears to be concerned largely with structural issues and with the new potentials offered by reinforced-concrete construction. In traditional building methods, the wall tended to be wedded to the structure, but reinforced concrete now allowed the structure to consist simply of thin columns, freeing the wall of any structural function. The French engineer François Hennebique, and then Perret, had been among the first to realize the implications of this method; and in the 1920s Le Corbusier himself was to include this wall-separate-from-function principle among his "Five Points" of architecture (expressing it in *two* of these points, the "*façade libre*" and "*fenêtres en longueur*"). In his notebook patent for the Domino System, Jeanneret refers to this "separation of powers," suggesting its importance in the design—although he seems not yet to have recognized its possibilities fully, since the façades that he actually designed for it have conventionally placed window openings and wall surfaces and thus do not exploit this principle as his later designs were to do.

It is sometimes said that the most distinctive feature of the Domino System is that the columns are set back, away from the edge of the slab. It has even been suggested that this setback was original to Jeanneret—although this is not strictly true, since Perret, for one, had already used it in the interior of his Rue Ponthieu garage of 1905. We can assume that Perret had explained to Jeanneret the structural advantage of this device in reinforced-concrete construction (the short cantilever actually improving the structural properties of a monolithic slab) and that Jeanneret used it in the Domino design for this structural reason, as well as for the fact that it emphasized the "separation of powers" principle. Ironically, however, Jeanneret then proceeded

Figure 9
The Domino System. (Source: *Oeuvre complète 1910–29,* p. 23.)

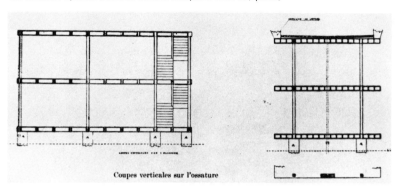

Coupes verticales sur l'ossature

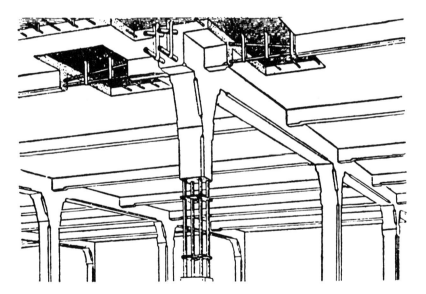

Figure 10
The standard, Hennebique System of reinforced-concrete construction. The opposite of
the Domino design. Though structurally logical, it was unacceptable to Jeanneret from a
formal and conceptual point of view. (Source: Paul Christophe, *Le Béton armé et ses
applications,* Paris and Liege, 1902, p. 106.)

to negate this structural advantage by deciding not to use integral, monolithic slabs in the Domino System (Fig. 9), instead proposing a complex scheme for the slabs (involving the use of hollow blocks, held in place by a special scaffolding, with concrete then poured over them)—a scheme in which the cantilever becomes a hindrance rather than an advantage and which, in fact, would have been very difficult to build. Why did Jeanneret get himself into this predicament? The answer seems to lie at least partly in the *formal* properties he wished to embody in the design.

The one truly distinctive (and unprecedented) characteristic of the Domino System is not structural but formal: its columns and slabs are completely smooth—that is, its columns have none of the splay or brackets, and its slabs have none of the exposed ribs that charac-terized virtually all concrete construction of this period (for example, the commonly used Hennebique System [Fig. 10]). Even in Robert Maillart's Zurich warehouse of 1910, in which the rib beams were eliminated, apparently for the first time, and a flat slab thus achieved, the columns had to be given a broadly extended, "mushroom" splay to provide the necessary rigid connection with the slab. The Domino System, however, with neither rib beams nor column splay would have been difficult if not impossible to construct at this time. Jean-neret seems to have become aware of this problem, perhaps from Perret himself (since he wrote "ask Perret" next to his Domino sketches in his notebook), and this may have been the reason he was looking for a new way to construct the slab—though, as mentioned already, the method he then devised caused even more problems, negating the advantage of the column setback.

All these difficulties suggest that the smooth, simple forms of the slab and the column were the result of a purely formal or aesthetic decision—made in spite of, rather than because of, structural or practical considerations. Jeanneret's own descriptions of the Domino System (both in his notebook patent draft and later in his writings) confirm this by their insistence on the smooth (*lisse*) nature of the parts: *"Système des constructions . . . de béton armé à plancher lisse"*;[27] *". . . il s'agit d'un matériel de chantier spécial qui permet de couler les planchers définitivement lisse."*[28]

This absolute smoothness and simplicity is the one feature of the Domino design which distinguishes it from all earlier reinforced-concrete construction. Jeanneret simply made an uncompromising formal decision to strip the structural elements down to their most generalized forms, a pure slab and a pure column. From a structural or constructional point of view, they may not be simple at all, but visually and conceptually they are, and that was what Jeanneret decided was important. As an image or concept the Domino design embodies, almost Platonically, the Idea of column-and-slab construction in its purest and most general form: the Ideal Column and the Ideal Slab.

This is precisely the method of designing which Provensal had recommended in his book: designing from ideas, and creating pure forms that are general rather than particular, ideal rather than down-to-earth. In this sense, the Domino System represents a rejection of rationalism and a reaffirmation of Provensal's romantic idealism. And yet in a strange way, it seems to have represented for Jeanneret a synthesis of the two methods—since *ostensibly* at least, it dealt with the rationalists' concerns (a structural system, a new material, and to a lesser extent such aspects as mass housing and prefabrication). To Jeanneret, this was the way of resolving, as much as possible, the conflicting philosophies of his training, by taking rationalist objects and transforming them with a romantic or idealistic method. This technique, in one form or another, became from then on a distinguishing characteristic of his work—whether it was a structural system, a housing type, a technological image of some sort, or a whole city that he subjected to this transformation.

After Jeanneret moved permanently to Paris, the theory and designs that he began formulating and then published and built in the 1920s contained elements from many different sources not examined here. But in all of his work, probably the most distinctive quality was embodied in the Domino System: the spiritual transformation of the objects of the modern technological age by their placement within a romantic, poetic, even mystical framework. This was his way of resolving the architectural philosophies encountered in his youth and of remaining true to his two teachers.

1　"L'objectif et le subjectif sont les deux pôles entre les-quelles surgit l'oeuvre humaine faite de matière et d'es-prit." Le Corbusier, *La Ville radieuse,* Boulogne-sur-Seine, 1935, frontispiece caption.

2　For example, in a letter to L'Eplattenier written in 1908 (published in *La Gazette de Lausanne,* 4 September 1965, La Gazette littéraire section, p. 13), he wrote, "Ce n'est pas la quiétude, qu'aujourd'hui j'envisage et me prépare pour l'avenir. Et peut-être moins encore le triomphe de la foule. Mais moi, je vivrai—sincère—et de l'invective je serai heureux."

3　"Architecture, pure création de l'esprit" is the title of the chapter on the Parthenon in Le Corbusier, *Vers une architecture,* Paris, 1923.

4　Maximilien Gauthier, in *Le Corbusier, l'architecture au service de l'homme,* Paris, 1944, p. 19 (a biography based on interviews with Le Corbusier), states that L'Eplattenier's classroom was where Jeanneret "was first introduced to problems in art."

5　Le Corbusier, *L'Art décoratif d'aujourd'hui,* Paris, 1925, p. 198.

6　This subject is treated in greater detail in my article "The Beginnings of Le Corbusier's Education, 1902–07," *The Art Bulletin,* June 1971, pp. 214–224.

7　Edouard Schuré, *Les Grands Initiés,* Paris, 1908 (first published in 1889). L'Eplattenier's inscription reads: *"A mon cher élève Edouard Jeanneret | Souvenir affectueux—|Ch. L'Eplattenier | sept. 07."* The contradiction between this inscription date and the publication date of the book is examined briefly in my *Art Bulletin* article, p. 223. At any rate, other evidence confirms that Jeanneret did receive this book from L'Eplattenier at this time.

8　Friedrich Nietzsche, *Ainsi parlait Zarathoustra,* Paris, 1908; Ernest Renan, *Vie de Jésus,* Paris, n.d. Jeanneret read both books in Paris in 1908 or 1909.

9　Schuré describes Pythagorean numerology as a "scientific" system that unfolds mathematically from simple numbers, each of which contains "a principle, a law, an active force of the universe," and which by addition and multiplication will produce all other numbers. It is interesting that all of Jeanneret's markings and annotations in Schuré's book are found in this chapter on Pythagoras.

10　Henri Provensal, *L'Art de demain,* Paris, 1904. See my *Art Bulletin* article for more information on this book and the question of when Jeanneret read it.

11　This definition is the first sentence of Provensal's chapter on architecture (p. 158).

Notes

12   As seen in his watchcase design of 1901 (see my *Art Bulletin* article, p. 215).

13   Le Corbusier, *Vers une architecture*, p. 57, and *Précisions sur un état présent de l'architecture et de l'urbanisme*, Paris, 1930, p. 136.

14   Provensal, *L'Art de demain*, p. 318.

15   Letter from Jeanneret to L'Eplattenier, 22 and 25 November 1908. Published in *La Gazette de Lausanne*, 4 September 1965, La gazette littéraire section, p. 13.

16   "J'ai acheté cet ouvrage le 1 août 1908, av. l'argent de ma première paye de Mr. Perret. Je l'ai acheté pour *apprendre*, car *sachant* je pourrai alors créer."

17   "Ces quelques lignes font voir que tout cet *art vit par sa carcasse*. C'est un monolithe aussi, une cage de fil de fer,—où les pressions verticales et les poussées obliques tiennent lieu du ciment des blocages romains, et des ronds d'acier du béton. *Or,* me disait Aug Perret, *tenez la carcasse,* et vous tenez l'Art (ce qui n'est peut-être pas faux du tout, étant bien compris)."

18   Jeanneret began working for Behrens on 1 November 1910 (according to a letter he wrote at the time to his friend William Ritter) and stayed there only five months (as he mentions in his 1912 report on the decorative arts movement in Germany, p. 6). Mies was with Behrens from 1908 until 1912, according to the literature on him. Acquaintances of Gropius recall his saying that he had already left Behrens's office by the time Jeanneret arrived; and Gropius himself wrote (in a tribute to Le Corbusier upon his death in 1965), "After the Bauhaus Exhibition in Weimar [that is, 1923], we met for the first time in the Café des Deux Magots in Paris." See *Harvard Newsletter*, vol. 12, no. 1 (November 1965), p. 4, for Gropius's reminiscences on Le Corbusier.

19   Alexandre Cingria-Vaneyre, *Les Entretiens de la Villa du Rouet,* Geneva, 1908.

20   "Pour moi, ce livre vient favorablement aider à mon orientation. Il provoque un examen, les déductions normales, claires, lumineuses; il desserre pour moi l'étau germanique. Dans une année, à Rome, je le relirai, et, par des esquisses, je fonderai ma discipline jurassique, neuchâteloise." Ibid., Jeanneret's copy, p. 383.

21   Le Corbusier's major account of this trip is *Le Voyage d'Orient,* Paris, 1966, composed of diary notes and letters written during the trip itself, with some later additions and recollections.

22   Gauthier, *Le Corbusier,* p. 35.

23 Le Corbusier, *Vers une architecture,* p. 165.

24 The main sources of information on these activities of Jeanneret during this period are his own notebooks and a pamphlet defending the Nouvelle Section of the Art School (entitled "Un Mouvement d'art à La Chaux-de-Fonds . . ."), written by Jeanneret and the others involved, in April 1914.

25 Le Corbusier, *Oeuvre complète 1910–29,* pp. 23–26.

26 "Système des constructions juxtaposables selon d'infinis combinaisons de plans. . . ." This is found in the notebook labeled "A2," which is now in the Fondation Le Corbusier.

27 Ibid.

28 Le Corbusier, *Oeuvre complète 1910–29,* p. 23.

Mary Patricia
May Sekler

**Le Corbusier, Ruskin, the Tree, and the
Open Hand**

In 1907, just before leaving on his first extended trip away from La Chaux-de-Fonds, Le Corbusier—known then as Charles-Edouard Jeanneret—gave to a friend a French edition of John Ruskin's popular book, *Sesame and Lilies.* [1] For those engaged in the intricate process of attempting to order, to understand, and to come to terms with Le Corbusier's vast legacy of visual and written documents, words of admonition—and solace—are found in Ruskin's section "Of Kings' Treasuries," on the treasures to be found in books.

"Do you deserve to enter?" This is the question Ruskin would have us believe is posed to all who wish to pass through the "Elysian gates" to the world of thought contained in the writings of the savants of past generations. He cautions:

> . . . be sure that you go to the author to get at *his* meaning, not to find yours. . . . And be sure also, if the author is worth anything, that you will not get at his meaning all at once,—nay, that at his whole meaning you will not for a long time arrive in any wise. Not that he does not say what he means, and in strong words too; but he cannot say it all, and what is more strange, *will* not, but in a hidden way and in parables, in order that he may be sure you want it. [2]

In his own writings, Le Corbusier described the creations of the artist in somewhat similar terms. "In a complete and successful work," he wrote, "there are hidden masses of implications, a veritable world which reveals itself to those whom it may concern, which means: to those who deserve it." [3]

These ideas are important to keep in mind when dealing with the work of Le Corbusier. Those who search for meaning in his work soon discover that they cannot find it simply by reading his texts in chronological order or reconstructing the chronology of his artistic production. For although there is a great sense of direction in his work and an overall progression from one phase to another, he was in the habit of making frequent allusions to thoughts or images from his earlier work, often using them as a starting point for new variations or developments. For this reason, one can learn a great deal about his total work through the study of one element, but one can learn only a limited amount about that element without studying his total work.

The present essay, which grew from research on Le Corbusier's earliest drawings,[4] attempts to follow from Le Corbusier's youth some of the peregrinations of one recurring element: the tree.

The Tree in Le Corbusier's Early Work at La Chaux-de-Fonds

Arbre, compagnon millénaire de l'homme!
—Le Corbusier[5]

Le Corbusier's awareness of some of the abundant imagery associated with trees began at an early age. He loved the surrounding Neuchâtel Jura and the landscape of the nearby Doubs River, which formed the border toward France. He knew this countryside intimately, having grown up in a family atmosphere where the out-of-doors and Alpinism were among the dominant interests. In addition, his school years coincided with the wave of enthusiasm for natural forms which had characterized the Art Nouveau movement and which still influenced the efforts of one of his teachers, Charles L'Eplattenier, to establish a vocabulary of forms based on Jura motifs. L'Eplattenier's endeavor had its first flowering precisely during Le Corbusier's time at the Ecole d'Art from 1902 to 1906, particularly during 1905 and 1906, the first year of L'Eplattenier's *Cours supérieur d'art et de décoration.*[6]

The training Le Corbusier received at the Ecole d'Art concerned in large measure the analysis of forms from the immediate environment, vegetable in nature, as well as mineral and animal. While all these motifs show up in his early drawings, the tree, without question, occupied a foremost place in his creative work.

Le Corbusier studied the tree from many points of view. Following a method somewhat like that demonstrated in works by Eugène Grasset,[7] he sketched it in its landscape setting, then reduced it to basic elementary shapes, either in whole or in part, to serve as design units to be repeated horizontally and on occasion vertically. In addition, he analyzed growth patterns, investigated the principles of root structure, and studied forms in section as well as elevation and plan. In his drawings, he even considered the tree form for its direct analogies to architectural elements, roots forming the bases of the framing elements of windows, trunks serving as *piloti,* masses of foliage defining the shapes of openings, branch patterns forming mullions and bars. Similarities exist between some of the concepts expressed in Le Corbusier's drawings and those found illustrated or described in other major source books from the nineteenth century.[8]

The tree motif carried over into Le Corbusier's early architectural work at La Chaux-de-Fonds: his designs for façades for Beau-Site (1905), a new structure for the Union Chrétienne de Jeunes Gens;[9] his house for Louis Fallet *fils* (1906–1907), the first of his four houses on the hillside of the Pouillerel overlooking La Chaux-de-Fonds from the northwest; and his collaborative effort with colleagues from the Ecole on the no longer extant music room for Matthey-Doret (1906) and on the interior redecoration of the Chapelle indépendante of Cernier-Fontainemelon in the Val-de-Ruz (1907).

An examination of his use of decorative forms during this early period reveals a general consistency in attitude: motifs from nature—however abstracted—were applied most frequently in their normal position of growth as found in nature, obeying the laws of gravity and the sun. In the music room (Fig. 11), for instance, a pine tree motif was elongated and stylized on the window and door frames; branches, heavy with pendant cones, were worked into the plaster of the upper wall surfaces. The ultimate source of this decorative motif was even made part of the total composition of the room, since one wall (that away from the piano and organ) was dominated

Figure 11
Music room of Matthey-Doret, La Chaux-de-Fonds, 1906. (Photograph courtesy of Pierre M. Wasem.)

by the view through the large window of the living trees outside and by the light which flooded in, giving perpetual life to the plants worked in stained glass. Judging from the typical height of a chair, this window measured almost two meters square, a size unusual for domestic use.

Although Le Corbusier's contribution to the design of this music room ensemble has not been definitively established,[10] surviving drawings give clues to the nature of his involvement. One such drawing (Fig. 12) relates to the woodwork. There is an obvious formal relationship between the finished window and door framing and these studies which combine the tops of branches, pendant cones, and the grouping of four or more implied tree trunks with bark patterns and residual branching.

In Vienna, after his Italian trip with Léon Perrin in the fall of 1907, he designed two houses for sites farther up the hill from the Matthey-Doret house and L'Eplattenier's neighboring home. These were constructed under the supervision of René Chapallaz in 1908, one for Albert Stotzer, the other for Jules Jaquemet. While both houses retained certain motifs relating to the tree, especially for mullions and the barge boards of the Maison Stotzer, they already reflect a new attitude, being far more sparing in the quantity of decorative motifs employed. Le Corbusier's interest in the detailing of the stonework (gained through close observation of Florentine examples) held the upper hand. One of the strongest features is the northwest entrance of the Maison Stotzer (Fig. 13), where the void reads as the motif of a pine tree while the solid reads as a stepped-rock motif—a device used earlier in various ways in the Maison Fallet, where a tree motif had even dominated several elevations.

Even during his subsequent work with the Perrets in Paris, Le Corbusier proposed the application of pine motifs as decoration for no less a location than the ceilings and walls of the loggias of the Perrets'

Figure 12
Le Corbusier drawing of
architectural elements
based on pine tree
motifs, circa 1906. Pencil
on sketchbook paper,
18.4 cm × 11.8 cm.
(Photograph by Patricia
Sekler. Courtesy of
Archives Fondation Le
Corbusier, no. 2006.)

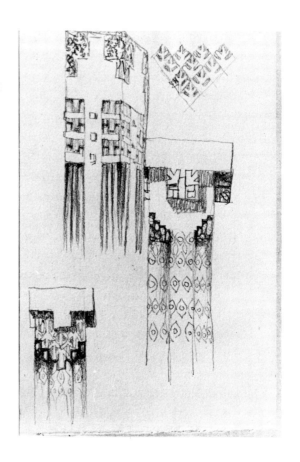

Figure 13
North entrance of Le
Corbusier's Maison
Stotzer, La
Chaux-de-Fonds;
designed 1907–1908,
constructed 1908.
(Photograph by Patricia
Sekler.)

new apartment building at 25 bis Rue Franklin, the building which housed their offices.[11]

During Le Corbusier's absence from La Chaux-de-Fonds in Paris in 1908 and 1909 and later in Germany in 1910 and 1911, tree and plant motifs continued to be important in the designs of his colleagues at home who formed the Ateliers d'art réunis, particularly in their work for the main hall of the Post Office at La Chaux-de-Fonds and for the Crematorium, where trees featured in L'Eplattenier's murals. Soon after this group was officially incorporated on 15 March 1910,[12] Le Corbusier, in a letter to Léon Perrin,[13] suggested designs for their emblem. The pine tree was included, with emphasis on its triangular form, along with a stepped-rock motif and a curved form.[14] The triangle of the pine may even have been relevant in Le Corbusier's proposed structure for artists' studios grouped around a central two-level *Salle du Cours* (the pyramidal roof of this space reads as a triangle in elevation),[15] as it seems to have been in an earlier design for a railway station.

In 1910 and 1911, Le Corbusier's attitude toward the decorative arts and architecture changed radically as the result of his travel, reading, study, and work away from home.[16] This change in attitude reveals itself in his designs. Thus, even though he still produced some of his most handsome ornamental repeat patterns based on pine motifs around the time that he returned from his Orient trip to La Chaux-de-Fonds in November of 1911 (to prepare to take up his teaching post at the Ecole d'Art in L'Eplattenier's Nouvelle Section), his two houses from this period have little applied ornament. But one motif was retained for both houses, that of the pine cone/pine tree. It was used, modestly, as the newel post of the main stair of the house for his parents at La Chaux-de-Fonds (1912) (as it would be later at the Villa Schwob) and was employed in several variations for capitals for *La Forêt*, the Villa Favre-Jacot at Le Locle (1912).

The applied patterns produced by Le Corbusier's students[17] tended toward the drastic reduction of thematic material to simple geometrical shapes, as seen on the bottom of a page from the 1912 *Prospectus* of the Nouvelle Section[18] (Fig. 14). A few of the patterns actually negate the implied three-dimensional form they decorate and would seem to presage Art Deco and Op Art; but triangular pine and stepped-rock motifs can still be recognized as the bases for some of these designs. In their repetition of units both horizontally and vertically and in their avoidance of shadow, the designs achieve a weightless quality not unlike that typical of works of the Wiener Werkstaette.

Although employing different means, Le Corbusier strove for somewhat the same weightless effect in his atectonic detailing of the upper story of the main façade of the Villa Favre-Jacot (Fig. 15). Because of the heavy shadow above it, the lintel over the tripartite entrance seems to have no carrying function. Also, the cone/tree motif serving as a capital for the flanking pilasters seems neither to crown nor to support, since the design unit has been repeated four times, oriented diagonally, as though one were regarding the capital in plan rather than in elevation. In addition, the device of enclosing the major elements of the façade with a continuous straight profile (which is brought downward but never carried upward to the roofline) serves the same purpose of negating load and support. This treatment reveals that Le Corbusier's concept of architecture had indeed changed, and reflects, in its own complexity, the disparate and at times conflicting influences affecting this change.

By 1914, he renounced self-conscious attempts to produce a Swiss or a local architecture and denounced ornament altogether[19]—in principle, if not in practice. As a result, the tree, as a motif for applied decoration, all but disappeared during his remaining years at La Chaux-de-Fonds.[20]

Figure 14
Page from the *"Nouvelle Section" de l'Ecole d'Art. Prospectus* of 1912. The work of Le Corbusier's students is at the bottom.

Figure 15
Detail of the upper story of the main façade of Le Corbusier's Villa Favre-Jacot, Le Locle, 1912–1913. (Photograph by Patricia Sekler.)

But as part of real landscape, the tree took on new importance. Le Corbusier's letterhead of 1912, listing his services as the architect of the Ateliers d'art réunis, included *"architecture de jardins."* Among his schemes involving landscaping was a design for the extensive grounds of the Villa Favre-Jacot. Favre-Jacot also owned one of the oldest farmhouses in the region, the Maison du Diable.[21] Le Corbusier's project for the adaptation of this structure, probably inspired by its partial demolition in March of 1912, called for a far bolder use of plant materials on the roof terrace than his project for artists' studios of 1910. Later, he projected extensive plantings as an integral part of the roofscape of the Villa Schwob (1916) and included double rows and isolated trees in his formal, symmetrical design for the gardens (Fig. 16); a panel with a deciduous tree with the date 1916 was to be the decorative element over the right entrance of the main façade.

Another aspect of Le Corbusier's interest in trees during his La Chaux-de-Fonds years—and one of considerable importance—was that he too followed the lead of the Garden City Movement. He planned for Gustave Arnold Beck in 1914 a *Cité jardin* for a vast tract of land acquired by Beck on 30 April[22] of that year, on ground known as Les Crêtets, across La Chaux-de-Fonds from his early houses. In doing so, he was following in a tradition in which the tree was not only an omnipresent element in physical site planning but was the very symbol in the literature of the movement[23]—stemming from Ruskin and William Morris—of "the good life." In the Beck project, existing *allées* were retained; other trees were planned to border the main central way and to define the semi-circular contour of the land. At the southwest end of the site, space was reserved on an existing knoll for an elevated grove of trees,[24] rather like a symbolic shaded promontory to which one could retire to survey the panorama, or to meditate.

Figure 16
One of Le Corbusier's studies for the Villa Schwob, La Chaux-de-Fonds. Architectural print,
40 cm × 89.5 cm, at bottom right: *"le 14 juillet 1916 Ch E Jt."* (Photograph by Patricia
Sekler. Courtesy of Archives Fondation Le Corbusier.)

From this brief survey, it is evident that the tree as a physical reality and as a stylized motif was very much a part of Le Corbusier's early design vocabulary and that within the time span of his first thirty years (1887–1917), spent largely at La Chaux-de-Fonds, his interest in the tree manifested itself in many different ways. In searching for the meanings which Le Corbusier may have associated with the tree, one must turn to his early formative years and his first concern with this motif.

Ruskin's Teachings on Trees

L'art et la beauté moralisent à leur façon. . . .
—L'Eplattenier[25]

L'Eplattenier's successful attempts to develop with his students a vocabulary of forms based on Jura motifs was not an exercise in empty formalism. The adaptation of motifs had deeper significance for those engaged in the process, over and above its obvious regionalist implications. Some of the meaning attached to the process undoubtedly came from Owen Jones, whose *Grammar of Ornament* was popular in L'Eplattenier's classes not only for its thirty-seven Propositions which set forth principles "in the arrangement of form and colour, in architecture and the decorative arts" but also for its magnificent color plates illustrating the ornament of past ages.

To overcome the eclecticism of the architecture of his day, Jones proposed the comparative study of ornament of the past and of natural plant form as well as the principles which reign in each. In his view, new forms and new ornament developed from such study might eventually lead to a new architecture. While most of his discussion is scientific in tenor, he closed the work on a religious note in speaking of "the Creator." He wrote, " . . . as all His works are offered for our enjoyment, so are they offered for our study. They are there to awaken a natural instinct implanted in us,—a desire to emulate in the works of our hands, the order, the symmetry, the grace, the fitness, which the Creator has sown broadcast over the earth."[26]

John Ruskin also was interested in principles in art and nature, as in *The Elements of Drawing,* but he was just as interested in applying these principles, through analogy, to the behavior of man. In the moralistic writings of Ruskin, one finds many potential sources of inspiration for specific motifs developed by L'Eplattenier's group[27] as well as for the meaning possibly associated with these motifs. Particularly in regard to trees, Ruskin's potential influence was considerable, since unlike Jones he was not content with straightforward description and analysis but interlaced his writings on trees, especially in *Modern Painters,* Volume 5, with references to many other things— even quoting Herodotus and Keats.

Writing at a time when the ill effects of industrialization were rampant, Ruskin lamented the loss of traditional values and likened the acts of a good society to tree growth. "The power of every great people," he wrote, "as of every living tree, depends on its not effacing, but confirming and concluding, the labors of its ancestors." In making such comparisons, Ruskin referred frequently to Biblical sources, seldom bothering to identify a particular passage, such as the famous vision of the Messianic age: "As the days of a tree are the days of my people, and mine elect shall long enjoy the work of their hands. . . ." (Isaiah 65:22).[28]

The Biblical reference and the context in which Ruskin used it seem appropriate to one of the early design tasks Le Corbusier was associated with, the interior redecoration of the Chapelle indépendante at Cernier-Fontainemelon. The work for this chapel—a modest structure set between two villages amid agricultural land in a part of Switzerland famous for its horology—was undertaken just during that period when some of the handcraft aspects of horology in this region were fighting a losing battle for survival, in spite of the efforts of L'Eplattenier and others for their revitalization.

Trees are the dominant motif of the chapel interior (Fig. 17), whose totality was the most complete visual statement made by L'Eplattenier's group before Le Corbusier left La Chaux-de-Fonds in early September 1907. A contemporaneous description reads, in part:

The theme chosen by the student who had conceived the project of the decoration was this: in the middle of a forest all is calm and silent; one does not see the sky except in raising the eyes; all around pine trees form by their branches a tapestry rich in designs and in colors, joined to the earth by columns, the verticals of trunks; lower down the plants, their flowers form the most agreeable carpet. The calm is complete; the attention is involuntarily attracted by the radiance of the sky in which the "Cross" appears resplendent with light.[29]

Upon close inspection, the design reveals that not only is the Cross resplendent with light, with the circular form of the sun behind it, but rays shine forth in all directions, reaching downward to touch the upturned branches of the pine trees.

The forms of the trees of this upper zone of the wall decoration, which is inscribed *"Gloire à Dieu,"* seem to relate to Ruskin's discussion of the four great laws which summarize the principles ascertained in trees:

1. Support from one living root.
2. Radiation, or tendency of force from some one given point, either in the root, or in some stated connexion with it.
3. Liberty of each bough to seek its own livelihood and happiness according to its needs, by irregularities of action both in its play and its work, . . .
4. Imperative requirement of each bough to stop within certain limits, expressive of its kindly friendship and fraternity with the boughs in its neighbourhood; and to work with them according to its power, magnitude, and state of health, to bring out the general perfectness of the great curve, and circumferent stateliness of the whole tree.[30]

Figure 17
Altar wall of the Chapelle indépendante at Cernier-Fontainemelon, 1907. (Photograph courtesy of Pierre M. Wasem.)

Since, for Ruskin, "There is no moral vice, no moral virtue, which has not its *precise* prototype in the art of painting; so that you may at your will illustrate the moral habit by the art, or the art by the moral habit,"[31] there were naturally moral analogies to be drawn from the four laws. He left the reader to draw his own analogies from the first, third, and fourth laws, but took no chances with the second, explaining:

It typically expresses that healthy human actions should spring radiantly (like rays) from some single heart motive; the most beautiful systems of action taking place when this motive lies at the root of the whole life, and the action is clearly seen to proceed from it; while also many beautiful secondary systems of action taking place from motives not so deep or central, but in some beautiful subordinate connexion with the central or life motive.

The other laws, if you think over them, you will find equally significative; and as you draw trees more and more in their various states of health and hardship, you will be every day more struck by the beauty of the types they present of the truths most essential for mankind to know[1]; and you will see what this vegetation of the earth, which is necessary to our life, first, as purifying the air for us and then as food, and just as necessary to our joy in all places of the earth,— what these trees and leaves, I say, are meant to teach us as we contemplate them, and read or hear their lovely language, written or spoken for us, not in frightful black letters, nor in dull sentences, but in fair green and shadowy shapes of waving words, and blossomed brightness of odoriferous wit, and sweet whispers of unintrusive wisdom, and playful morality.[32]

In the footnote "1" of this passage, Ruskin discusses the rays of light from the sun, which come "straight from Him," "the greater Sun," and which, filtered through leaves and striking the ground, still bear "His image."

The pine trees and their branches in the design at the chapel have been regularized in the service of greater decorative power, but their organization certainly reflects what Ruskin prescribed: support from one living root, radiation, liberty in the search for light, and the interrelatedness of the group. Even for those unaware of Ruskin's moral analogies and their social and religious implications, the sense of order achieved by the composition with its assemblage of ordered elements oriented toward "the Light" is very striking. The design in its simplicity and in its directness of iconographic program was well suited to a chapel meant to serve orderly rural Jura communities.

Ruskin had gone to great lengths in *Modern Painters,* Volume 5, to define what the pine tree signified. In his terms, the deciduous tree was the "shield-builder" but the pines were the "wild builders with the sword." Ruskin did not analyze the pine in as much detail as he had its leafy counterpart, leaving that to his reader. But he did make some general statements, for example:

A sword-builder may . . . be generally considered as a shield-builder put under the severest military restraint. . . .
Of the many marked adaptations of nature to the mind of man, it seems one of the most singular, that trees intended especially for the adornment of the wildest mountains should be in broad outline the most formal of trees. . . . The pine, placed nearly always among scenes disordered and desolate, brings into them all possible elements of order and precision. . . . let storm and avalanche do their worst, and let the pine find only a ledge of vertical precipice to cling to, it will nevertheless grow straight. Thrust a rod from its last shoot down the stem;—it shall point to the centre of the earth as long as the tree lives. . . . the pine is trained to need nothing, and to endure everything. It is resolvedly whole, self-contained, desiring nothing but rightness. . . . It may be permitted . . . to these soft lowland trees that they should make themselves gay with show of blossom. . . . We builders with the sword have harder work to do for man, and must do it in close-set troops. . . . we pines must live carelessly amidst the wrath of clouds. . . . we builders with the sword perish boldly; our dying shall be perfect and solemn, as our warring: we give up our lives without reluctance, and for ever.[33]

Ruskin goes on to discuss the main "characters" of the pine: its straightness and rounded perfectness; its magnificent erectness, "Magnificent!—nay, sometimes, almost terrible"; its exquisite fineness, its finished delicacy.[34]

But this for him is not enough. There must be further analogies. He sees the influence of the vegetation of a country on the human character of its residents: " . . . the tremendous unity of the pine absorbs and moulds the life of a race. The pine shadows [pyramidal in form, he notes earlier] rest upon a nation." [35] He concludes by describing the Helvetii as "the foremost standard-bearers among the nations of Europe in the cause of loyalty and life—loyalty in its highest sense, to the laws of God's helpful justice, and of man's faithful and brotherly fortitude." [36]

Once one has read Ruskin on trees, one cannot walk in the woods without being haunted by the imagery of his vivid descriptions and analogies. For someone Swiss-born, and especially for someone from the Neuchâtel Jura where majestic white pines are the dominant features of the landscape, the image of the pine tree would become mingled with prevalent visions of patriotism,[37] with God's justice, with the uprightness of the individual, with an active, building principle— warring for the good of right and brother, with potency, strength, dignity, and resolve. Another look at the decoration of the altar wall at the chapel reveals that the Cross is not isolated in the heavens amid the radiant light but is actually the continuation of the main trunk of the central pines: God and the tree, and by analogy, man, are all inextricably bound in one grand design.

Since this moralizing attitude toward nature and the function of the artist in evidence at the chapel at Cernier-Fontainemelon was such an integral part of Le Corbusier's early training, it is understandable that it would exert an influence on his later development.

Possible Ruskinian Influence during Le Corbusier's Paris Years

If the artist tells, he is betraying himself!
—Le Corbusier[38]

We cannot know what Le Corbusier's vocabulary of forms meant to him. We can, at best, reconstruct contexts, analyze forms, and scrutinize verbal statements in the hope that by doing so we may at least begin to approach the artist's intention.

Since Ruskin put so much emphasis on the pine as the builder with the sword, for example, is there any relation between this notion and a drawing by Le Corbusier[39] that supposedly shows his coat of arms around 1920? The drawing includes, top to bottom, a sword (with red) shown horizontally with the handle at the left, a cloudlike form (with blue) and a star shape (with yellow), with the words, *"La vie est sans pitié."* [40] Is this image, said to be *"les armoiries d'un jeune homme qui n'était nullement pessimiste,"* the sword builder living carelessly amidst the wrath of the clouds or ineffable space, defending "uprightness" or constructing for a high purpose? Is there any connection between what Ruskin wrote on the structure of trees and the statement published in *Après le Cubisme* of 1918 concerning the research of laws of harmony that alludes to *"des axes principaux, comme dans l'arbre les feuilles, les rameaux, les branches, un tronc"?* [41]

While these are isolated examples, many related questions arise concerning Le Corbusier's book *The Radiant City,* [42] the first diagram of which illustrates how to plant a tree. References to trees are scattered throughout. Even on the cover one finds the symbols of this urbanistic concept: an orange-red sun—*soleil,* a blue cloud—*espace,* and a deciduous tree with a double-branched trunk (Ruskin's most perfect tree shape), [43] the base of which also serves as the trunk of a green triangle (the pine) behind—*verdure.* Are there analogies to tree structure, albeit imperfect, in such symbolic notions as façades as the "providers of light" (leaves), partitions considered as "membranes" (secondary branches), floors "carried independently of the façade, by posts" (branches and trunks)? [44] Even the basic materials of city planning were seen to be "sun, sky, trees, steel, cement, in that strict order of importance." "The basic pleasures [*les joies essentielles*]," Le Corbusier wrote, "by which I mean sun, greenery and space, penetrate into the uttermost depths of our physiological and psychological being. They bring us back into harmony with the profound and natural purpose of life."[45] Elsewhere in *The Radiant City* Le Corbusier links psychophysiological needs with "collective participation and the freedom of the individual [*liberté individuelle*]."[46]

Collective participation and the freedom of the individual were basic notions of Ruskin's fourth and third laws ascertained in trees. It seems possible, therefore, that the term *ville radieuse*[47] may be related to Ruskin's second law on "radiation" and his moral analogy "that healthy human actions should spring radiantly (like rays) from some single heart motive." Ruskin's thought that the more one knows trees the more one gains from them "the truths most essential for mankind to know" and his notion that the vegetation of the earth is "necessary to our joy in all places of the earth" are certainly in harmony with Le Corbusier's plea for *"les joies essentielles."*

Indeed, Section 4, "Laws," of Part 3 of *The Radiant City* is very much like a modern-day *Modern Painters* written of course not in defense of a modern-day J. M. W. Turner, but in defense of Le Corbusier's own thought on architectural and urban form.[48]

Le Corbusier's acute awareness of natural events and cosmic phenomena could have found direct inspiration in Ruskin's writings: man in relation to the total environment is the constant theme. By the thirties, the bird's-eye view of the earth possible from an airplane had revealed nature to man in new ways; Le Corbusier expressed these revelations in terms of "character," the same term employed by Ruskin in his discussion of the pine, and elsewhere concerning natural phenomena. "We are confirmed in the belief that character is one of the essential components of the created universe," wrote Le Corbusier. "And that since the order of that universe is so beautiful and the characters that compose it so clear-cut, we too should base our own human creations on the eminent values to be observed in character."[49]

This notion may hark back to his student days at La Chaux-de-Fonds, for on the previous page he speaks of another new way in which technology had permitted man to look at nature. Slow motion studies (photography plus clockwork, he notes) of leaves had revealed their motion, following the sun in the course of a day. "To our insufficiently sagacious eyes," he wrote, "it appeared that the foliage prolonging the movement of the branches, stems, or trunk of a tree or a plant were disposed around it like a symmetrical crown; that the leaves of a tree stood as motionless and quiescent around a tree trunk as the petals around a moon daisy, or the scales around an artichoke." Ruskin had referred to the artichoke[50] by way of comparison in discussing the shape and packing of boughs. Le Corbusier continues his description of the leaves following the sun, "This tiny and pathetic adventure, lived out daily by a tiny little leaf, by the billions of tiny leaves that form part of the complex existence of hedgerows or great forests, always obeying and turning their faces to the great warm star, proclaims the fundamental law of this earth we live on: that the sun is our dictator."[51] The echo of Ruskin seems clear.

To pursue this further, compare texts by Ruskin and Le Corbusier on city life versus country life:

Still if human life be cast among trees at all, the love borne to them is a sure test of its purity. And it is a sorrowful proof of the mistaken ways of the world that the "country," in the simple sense of a place of fields and trees, has hitherto been the source of reproach to its inhabitants, . . . as if it were quite necessary and natural that country-people should be rude, and towns-people gentle. Whereas I believe that the result of each mode of life may, in some stages of the world's progress, be the exact reverse; and that another use of words may be forced upon us by a new aspect of facts, so that we may find ourselves saying: "Such and such a person is very gentle and kind—he is quite rustic; and such and such another person is very rude and illtaught—he is quite urbane. . . .

And indeed I had once purposed, in this work, to show what kind of evidence existed respecting the possible influence of country life on men; it seeming to me, then, likely that here and there a reader would perceive this to be a grave question, more than most which we contend about, political or social, and might care to follow it out with me earnestly.[52]

. . . I am attracted to a natural order of things. . . . in my flight from city living I end up in places where society is in the process of organization. I look for primitive men, not for their barbarity but for their wisdom . . . .

The city? It's already an empty shell. Its product is there all right, polished and superb, clear as crystal. The fruit of culture. But look at the refuse and scum. Look at the misery, the unhappiness and stupidity. People behave like children, negatively and destructively, without meaning to . . . .

I go where order is coming out of the endless dialogue between man and nature, out of the struggle for life, out of the enjoyment of leisure under the open sky, in the passing of the seasons, the song of the sea.

I go where tools are being put to use: the primary tools that are required for the purpose of making existence possible within the limits of the day, the seasons, the years and the generations.[53]

Le Corbusier obviously considered "the possible influence of country life on men" to be a grave question. Whether this has Ruskinian roots can be debated, but his use of visual images in *The Radiant City* suggests a connection. The "harmony" of the pine cone is illustrated, as well as "the stupendous and extraordinary explosion of the bud."[54] The bud shown seems to be a later ink version of a pencil drawing from his student days, dated April 1908.[55] Used isolated as a line drawing (the pencil drawing has several views of the bud, not just one), it has a general resemblance to buds illustrated in Ruskin, such as Figure 6 of *The Elements of Drawing* and Figure 70 of *Modern Painters*, Volume 5. Ruskin uses the latter in "Fellowship," a section on boughs and buds in which he elaborates on ideas similar to those of his four laws concerning trees. It would seem significant that the greenery which formed part of the theme, "The Radiant City, Sun, Space, Green" of Le Corbusier's pavilion design for the Ideal Home exposition in London (plans dating from 1938 to 1939), was not so much a tree as an enlarged branch tip with bursting buds.[56]

Perhaps the most telling statement in *The Radiant City* and that which best sums up Le Corbusier's attitude is his description of a constantly recurring image, that of the unencumbered growth of a plant or tree. He wrote, "It is possible for the works of man to grow and rise in just the same way." He saw man as the product of nature, carrying within him nature's own potential, nature's own forces, her spirit and her essence. "Our fingers and our brains," he goes on, "are capable of creating works that express her harmony, works of perfection and purity."[57] His later casting of the Radiant City symbols in the concrete walls of his *Unités d'habitation,*[58] therefore, would seem to carry with it not only the notions associated with *les joies essentielles* but also the implication of Le Corbusier's personal quest for oneness with nature.

In considering the presence of trees or their parts in Le Corbusier's work during his Paris years, one must take into account the motifs found in one of Le Corbusier's paintings from 1931, the year he supposedly began work on *The Radiant City.* The painting is a grandiloquent visual statement of a woodcutter, the oil *Le Bûcheron* (Fig. 18). In addition to cut trees, tree stumps[59] and the woodman's tool, as well as his knife and daily bread and wine is, at the bottom, a single fallen leaf. At the upper left is the image of the head of a man—the woodman himself? Below the head in large stencil letters, larger than typical for most works from this period (his usual signature being *Le Corbusier* in modest size, somewhere along the bottom) is *LeC* set off by tonal difference from *orbusier 31.*

The work may well be a self-portrait, judging from a later use of the

Figure 18
Le Corbusier's oil painting, *Le Bûcheron,* 1931, illustrated in Le Corbusier, *New World of Space,* p. 56, bottom. The dimensions are given as 38¼" x 57½". (Courtesy of Institute of Contemporary Art, Boston.)

Figure 19
Detail of page from Le Corbusier's *Le Poème de l'angle droit,* Tériade Editeur, Paris, 1955. (Photograph by Patricia Sekler. Courtesy of José Luis Sert.)

Bûcheron motif: Le Corbusier has included it in *Le Poème de l'angle droit* (1955) in section "C. 3. *chair*" on a sheet (Fig. 19), which in word and image (as well as context) has autobiographical implications.[60] This may have no relation to Ruskin—but there could be a very direct one. In his first chapter of *Modern Painters,* Volume 5, after discussing city versus country life, Ruskin continues: "For the present, the movements of the world seem little likely to be influenced by botanical law; or by any other considerations respecting trees, than the probable price of timber." He then describes his method and aim:

I shall limit myself, therefore, to my own simple woodman's work, and try to hew this book into its final shape, with the limited and humble aim that I had in beginning it, namely, to prove how far the idle and peaceable persons, who have hitherto cared about leaves and clouds, have rightly seen, or faithfully reported of them.

If, in forming his own personal mythology, Le Corbusier cast himself in the role of the Ruskin of the twentieth century, doing his own "simple woodman's work," hewing his way through the problems of the new age, seeing to it that leaves and clouds were given their due consideration,[61] then the fallen leaf in *Le Bûcheron* may be related to Ruskin's lessons to be received from the leaf-builders, including:

Let them [dead leaves] not pass, without our understanding their last counsel and example: that we also, careless of monument by the grave,[62] may build it in the world—monument by which men may be taught to remember, not where we died, but where we lived.[63]

These quotations from Ruskin, potential sources for Le Corbusier's complex imagery, illustrate Ruskin's great gift for stimulating the imagination of his readers. He forces one to focus on an object and at the same time suggests its myriad relations to a greater context of accumulated myth and meaning; in the reader's mind, the object gains in amplitude through implied associations. It was this mythopoetic factor that made him such a controversial figure and at once repulsed

and attracted his readers—including Le Corbusier. Le Corbusier's ambivalent reaction is evident in his frequent allusions to Ruskin in *L'Art
décoratif d'aujourd'hui* of 1925.

The single fallen leaves often sketched by Le Corbusier and the
presence of such a single leaf in *Le Bûcheron* remind one of his interest in *"objets à réaction poétique"* which, he says, first occurred in his
work around 1925.[64] This was a period of his life during which he deliberately recalled his youth—in writing the concluding chapter "Con-
fession" for *L'Art décoratif d'aujourd'hui* (most others having appeared earlier in article form in *L'Esprit Nouveau*). Certainly, in considering the *"objets à réaction poétique,"* one must take into account
the use of similar motifs by other artists of the period, particularly
Fernand Léger.[65] Yet Le Corbusier's enrichment in the mid-1920s of
his "man-made" Purist motifs (such as glasses, bottles, books, plates,
and violins) with natural objects (such as bones, shells, flint, stones,
and pine cones) was a phenomenon—whatever its immediate
catalyst—not out of harmony with the preoccupations of his youthful
training at La Chaux-de-Fonds.

We find a similar harmony if not indeed a direct connection with his
youthful training when we consider the probable relation of the tree to
another symbolic image that occurs frequently in Le Corbusier's work:
the hand.

The Tree and the Open Hand

La main révèle donc cette situation ambiguë de l'homme qui est d'être
à la fois supérieur à tous les vivants et inférieur à ce qui fait la vie.
—Jean Brun[66]

An open hand is one of the symbolic forms that plays an important
role in Le Corbusier's late work, [67] associated primarily with the project for the Open Hand at Chandigarh, the new capital city of the Punjab in India. Le Corbusier first proposed it in 1951[68] as a major element

in the composition of the Capitol complex; on 16 November 1954[69] he presented the project to the Cabinet of Ministers; later, in 1958, he proposed it as a crowning feature for the Bhakra Dam.

Le Corbusier wrote about the Open Hand in conjunction with Chandigarh on many occasions. One of the earliest published documents is a sheet dated 22 November 1951 from his *"carnet de route"* on which he discusses a visit with Nehru. Le Corbusier notes that he had been obsessed with the symbol of the open hand since 1948 and wanted to be able to place it at the extremity of the Capitol, before the Himalaya. "One had wanted to involve me in the sterile battle of extremes," he wrote. "I have disowned it.[70] And I have thought that at the moment when the modern world gushes forth in unlimited intellectual and material riches, one had to open the hand to receive and to give."[71] In a letter to Nehru of 26–27 November 1954, he described India's situation as a country that had not had to live through the century of the troubles of the first mechanization. He saw it as awakening, intact, at a time of all possibilities. At the same time, he pointed out that India was not an entirely new country but rather one that had known the highest and most ancient civilizations. He continued:

She possesses an intelligence, an ethic and a conscience.

India could consider precious the conjuncture of raising in the Capitol of Chandigarh actually in construction, in the midst of the palaces sheltering her institutions and her authority, the symbolic and evocative sign of the "open hand":

open to receive the created riches

open to distribute them to her people and to others

The "open hand" will affirm that the second era of the machinist civilization has begun: the era of harmony.[72]

Not only did Le Corbusier use the word *ethic* in describing India; he used the word again in *Modulor 2,* first published in 1955, in writing of his design for the Open Hand. This occurs in a discussion of the development of the project: "Little by little, by stages ever since 1948, this complex work of architecture, sculpture, mechanics, acoustics and ethics had run its course, from the first act of invention to the working drawings."[73]

Why and in what context was the Open Hand to be included? Le Corbusier credits his collaborator, Jane Drew,[74] with having admonished him that he owed it to himself to install in the very heart of the Capitol "the signs by which you have come to express urbanism on the one hand, and on the other, your philosophic thought; these signs deserve to be known, they are the key to the creation of Chandigarh" (my translation). From this came the conception of the great esplanade which joins the Parliament and the High Courts; there the signs were to be erected: among them, the Modulor, the harmonic spiral, the solar day of twenty-four hours, the play of the two solstices, the tower of the four horizons, the Open Hand.[75]

The setting and the form of the Open Hand were described in another letter to Nehru, that of 21 July 1955 from Paris.[76] Le Corbusier wrote that in 1951 he had instituted the notion of *"La Fosse de la Considération"* (the Ditch of Consideration). This was to be forty meters square and five meters deep with two amphitheaters, tribune, and acoustical shell. Here the Open Hand—its enameled, beaten sheet iron form reaching a height of twenty-five meters—was to tower over the debates, debates held not by those with political mandates but by those who would have "the desire and the need to discuss the commonweal."

But the Open Hand had an importance for Le Corbusier far beyond that of its presence at Chandigarh. Earlier in the same letter he referred to it as a *"signe des temps modernes—signe annonciateur des temps nouveaux."* In closing, he stressed its international relevance, asking Nehru to accord to Chandigarh, "city freed from backward traditions and open on tomorrow, this monument at the foot of the Himalaya of an event of immense world-wide bearing." He went on,

"And I am sure that in raising the 'Open Hand' at that place, India will make a gesture which will come to confirm your so decisive intervention at the crucial moment of the machinist evolution and of its menaces" (my translation).

The time at which his first notion of an open hand took form is not clear. He is quoted to have said that it had occupied and preoccupied him for six years: *"Dans la force du signe, j'ai reconnu son droit d'existence. . . ."*[77] On another occasion, he says that it was born in Paris, spontaneously, "or more exactly, in response to preoccupations and inner debates come from the anguishing sentiment of the disharmonies which separate men so often and make enemies of them. . . . A spiritual reaction of 1948 has taken in 1951 an eminent place in the composition of a capital in India."[78] On the other hand, in the same letter to Nehru of 21 July 1955 just quoted, he prefaced his remarks on *"La Fosse de la Considération"* with the statement:

Obsessed by the tragic impasse offered on all sides under the scandalously abusive expression "committing oneself," I took up again a drawing of 1943. One sees there above the horizon an open hand; five women grouped on the earth see it surge. From that moment my design contents itself with the hand all alone. More and more it takes a pure form. I draw it in the course of my voyages. It becomes more and more precise (my translation).

If this date is not a misprint, it would indicate that Le Corbusier considered the Open Hand for Chandigarh to be the outgrowth of an earlier version of an open hand employed as a visual symbol long before the question of Chandigarh arose, indeed, years before India achieved independence.[79] A sgraffito drawing of 1950 (Fig. 20), one of a series thought to date in part from as early as the mid-1940s,[80] fits Le Corbusier's description. A large reclining figure and four others all face in the general direction of an open hand above the horizon line; the position of their bodies echoes the form of the hand.

Le Corbusier's most poetic statement about the open hand—one not necessarily related to Chandigarh—occurs in his *Le Poème de l'angle droit* (1955) in the section "F.3 *offre (la main ouverte)*":

Elle est ouverte puisque	It is open since
tout est présent disponible	all is present available
saisissable	seizable
Ouverte pour recevoir	Open to receive
Ouverte aussi pour que chacun	Open also that each may
y vienne prendre	come there to take
Les eaux ruissellent	Waters stream
le soleil illumine	the sun illumines
Les complexités ont tissé	Complexities have woven
leur trame	their woof
les fluides sont partout.	fluids are everywhere.
Les outils dans la main	Tools in the hand
Les caresses de la main	Caresses of the hand
La vie que l'on goûte par	The life one enjoys by
le pétrissement des mains	the kneading of hands
La vue qui est dans la	Sight that is in
palpation	palpation
Pleine main j'ai reçu	With a full hand I have received
Pleine main je donne.	With a full hand I give.
	(my translation)

Although the implications are extremely personal—the sensuous and the sensual being linked with the spiritual and the symbolic—reciprocal giving and receiving is a basic theme.[81]

Le Corbusier's drawings and paintings had long shown a preoccupation with hands and with gesture.[82] Hands appear singly, in interacting pairs, in groups. Particular attention was paid to hands in one of his last lithographic series, *Entre-deux ou propos toujours reliés,* composed between 1957 and 1964. On Plate 16, an "UBU" is shown to spring forth from the palm of an open hand. His text refers to this action as "the bursting of a bud." But Le Corbusier linked the notion of an open hand and the notion of enfolding plant growth in a much earlier text.[83] It occurs in *Quand les cathédrales étaient blanches,* written in 1936, in a chapter concerning New York, "Aucun arbre dans la ville":

Not a tree in the city! That's the way it is.
The tree, friend of man, symbol of all organic creation; the tree, image of a total construction. A ravishing sight which, although in an impeccable order, appears to our eyes in the most fanciful arabesques; a mathematically measured play of branches geared down each spring with a *new open hand* (my translation and emphasis).[84]

The comparison of tree growth and an open hand can be found still earlier, in Ruskin's *The Elements of Drawing:* ". . . in most trees the ramification of each branch, though not of the tree itself, is more or less flattened, and approximates, in its position, to the look of a hand held out to receive something, or shelter something."[85]

Thus Ruskin's influence may again be relevant, this time as a source for some of the symbolism associated with the Open Hand. In the third and fourth laws governing tree growth quoted earlier from *The Elements of Drawing,* Ruskin emphasized reciprocal action: the boughs reaching forth for their share of nourishment and at the same time respecting a kindly fellowship and fraternity with the boughs of their neighborhood, working with them for the greater good of the whole tree. While other writers may have reinforced or elaborated this basic concept in Le Corbusier's interpretation of it,[86] Ruskin provides the basic notion, clearly and simply stated, with its analogies to the behavior of man directly implied.

Knowingly or unknowingly, Le Corbusier echoed Ruskin's emphasis on fraternity and solidarity in conversations with Costantino and Ruth Nivola sometime during 1951 when he was their guest on Long Island. The Open Hand was featured in Le Corbusier's sand sculptures which Nivola cast. One of Le Corbusier's drawings, done in preparation for the castings, shows the hand on a vertical support with a substantial base (Fig. 21).

Costantino Nivola still has very vivid memories of Le Corbusier's discussions. When asked about the Open Hand he recalled, and his wife Ruth confirmed, having heard these or very similar words:

La main ouverte est un geste plastique chargé de contenu profondément humain.

Un symbole bien approprié à la nouvelle situation d'une terre libérée et indépendante. Un geste qui appelle à la collaboration fraternelle et solidaire tous les hommes et toutes les nations du monde.

Aussi un geste sculptural et plastique capable d'attraper le ciel et d'engager la terre.[87]

Le Corbusier's words take on increased importance if one considers that they date from a time when the form of the Open Hand for Chandigarh was still being developed and refined. The freedom and spontaneity which characterize the drawing were to diminish as Le Corbusier worked through variation after variation reaching toward the final three-dimensional form. Another drawing[88] (which Nivola recalls was probably done as Le Corbusier explained the main characteristics of the site) shows the monument in the landscape near the Governor's Palace with the mountains in the distance; the view is framed, as though one were looking through an arched opening. In later versions of the design, such as one dated "48–51" (Fig. 22), the base has been opened up and itself provides a frame incorporating man and landscape.[89] This idealistic concept had to be abandoned partially in still later versions in order to accommodate the shaft or trunk on which the weight of the hand would be supported.[90] Le Corbusier is quoted to have actually likened the motion of the Open Hand to that of a branch or tree: *"une palme rutilante de couleurs d'émail jaune, rouge, vert et blanc devant la chaîne des montagnes."*[91]

As the central three fingers [92] of the hand gained in importance in these later versions, the hand took on more and more of a birdlike

Figure 20
Sgraffito by Le
Corbusier, 1950.
Plum-brown ink over
verso of commercial
card (Société
d'Entreprises
Industrielles et d'Etudes
. . .), 5″ × 4″. (Collection
of Patricia Sekler.)

Figure 21
Brush and ink drawing of
the Open Hand, by Le
Corbusier, 1951,
13 13/16″ x 10 14/16″.
(Photograph by C. Todd
Stuart. Courtesy of
Costantino Nivola.)

Figure 22
A study for the Open
Hand monument with
open base, by Le
Corbusier, 1951.
Gouache on Ingres
paper, 24 cm x 29 cm.
Bottom right: "L-C 48-51
Chandigarh"; bottom
middle: "Version C 51."
The double date was his
method of indicating
works based on previous
themes. (Photograph
courtesy of Archives
Fondation Le Corbusier,
no. 2346.)

appearance, adding—intentionally or not—still another dimension to the associated imagery.[93]

Nivola, who was familiar with Le Corbusier's working methods from sharing studio space with him in New York, considers the open hand "simply one of his general prophecies created in his perpetual state of intuitive and disinterested creativity." This would agree with Le Corbusier's own contention. In a text dated 7 August 1951 at Cap Martin in which he describes his preoccupation with the theme of an open hand, he refers to it as *"un travail intérieur ininterrompu."* Thus he implies that its sudden manifestations in November 1948 and later can be compared to that phenomenon common in his painting and other work in which old themes were taken up again and given new life.[94]

While Le Corbusier's interest in the image of the hand was by no means an isolated occurrence in the world of art and literature, it is worth noting that the symbol of the open hand became especially important in his *oeuvre* when he was deliberately reviewing his life's work. He had spent much of the summer and fall of 1947 selecting and preparing material for his first major exhibition since the Zurich 1938 show. Called "New World of Space," the exhibition was first shown in Boston, in 1948, the year in which he claims to have had "a spiritual reaction." A hand was important in one of the drawings submitted for this exhibition (Fig. 23); the drawing may even have come about as a result of the reviewing process, since it is dated *"4 oct 47 d'après 1932."* It is inscribed, *"comme si c'était une façade de cathédrale."* In this version, the hand is not upright as it was in earlier related compositions;[95] it has become more squat, with less elegant, stubby fingers, comparable to those of hands designated by Le Corbusier as early versions of the Chandigarh Open Hand.

Le Corbusier also included in this exhibition (which was a general survey of his total *oeuvre*) a large group of drawings from his La Chaux-de-Fonds period. Many concerned trees. If old images indeed inspired new works, then surely, as he handled his La Chaux-de-Fonds drawings, memories associated with them were called forth. Maybe he even recalled his early interest in Ruskin.

Ruskin in Chandigarh? Although never stated in so many words by Le Corbusier—at least not to my knowledge—the Open Hand would have been an appropriate tribute to Ruskin, whose teachings had, after all, played a significant role in the development of modern India, in particular in the programs instituted by Gandhi.[96]

Gandhi, in one of his often repeated acknowledgments of debt to Ruskin,[97] describes a poet as "one who can call forth the good latent in the human breast."[98] Le Corbusier called attention to the poetic intention of his own life's work in writing, just a month before he died: *"Ma recherche a toujours été dirigée vers la poésie qui est dans le coeur de l'homme."*[99]

One readily thinks of Le Corbusier as the poet in conjunction with aspects of the design of the Capitol complex at Chandigarh—but particularly in regard to the monument of the Open Hand. In addition to the intended poetic implications already stated, he gave hints and indications of many others. Foremost among these was the notion that those who would gather in *La Fosse de la Considération* would have nothing visible to them except the sky and the Open Hand rising above them, orienting itself according to the direction of the wind. This, he said, was the *"symbôle de la prise en considération des faits de la réalité quotidienne."*[100] The hand's free rotation—which Le Corbusier actually projected, as in a sketch of 1954 (Fig. 24)—implies the expression of continuous changefulness.[101] Elsewhere, one reads that the hand was to turn on ball bearings like a weathercock, "not to show the incertitude of ideas, but to indicate symbolically the direction of the wind (that is the state of affairs)."[102] The words in parentheses in this English translation in the *Oeuvre complète 1946–52* miss somewhat the meaning of the French version, which reads: *"non pas pour*

Figure 23
One of Le Corbusier's numerous compositions involving a hand, 1947. Pencil, ink, and colored crayons, 26.8 cm x 20.8 cm, on rear of letterhead: "24, Rue Nungesser & Coli (16ᵉ)." This was carried out as a sculpture; illustrated in Petit, *Le Corbusier lui-même,* p. 249, "1964. No. 43. La cathédrale." (Courtesy of Institute of Contemporary Art, Boston.)

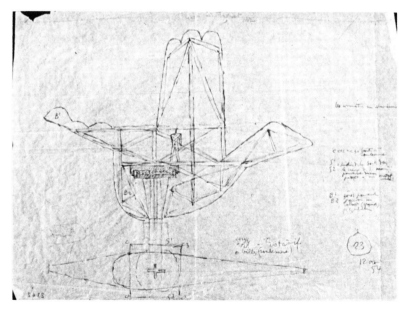

Figure 24
Le Corbusier's design for the armature and turning mechanism of the Open Hand monument, 1954. Ink and ballpoint pen on tracing paper, dated *"12 août 54,"* 29.5 cm x 42 cm. (Photograph courtesy of Archives Fondation Le Corbusier, no. 2342.)

marquer l'incertitude des idées, mais pour indiquer symboliquement la direction du vent (l'état de la contingence)."[103]

If part of the deeper meaning of the Open Hand concerns the notion of a "the state of contingency,"[104] it again accords with Ruskin's ideas on man as presented through analogy to plant growth. For in addition to meaning "quality or state of being contingent, a possible or not unlikely event or condition, an adjunct or accessory," *contingency* has the philosophical meaning of "the fact of existing as an individual human being in time, dependent on others for existence, menaced by death, dependent on oneself for the course and quality of existence."[105] Although one cannot be sure just what Le Corbusier implied by using the word *contingence* (whose many meanings involve a straight line in geometric and a right angle in gnomic constructions), one of his early statements on the Open Hand in regard to Chandigarh does imply uncertainty and interdependence. He wrote, "'La Main Ouverte'—ouverte là-bas aux Indes—à l'illimitée richesse du destin moderne: le machinisme, l'humilité devant l'inconnu de la vie, la fraternité entre hommes, bêtes, et nature. Un peu beaucoup d'optimisme. La vie difficile m'a désigné cette voie."[106]

If Ruskin's writings can be seen to embody some of the philosophic bases for the meaning Le Corbusier associated with the Open Hand, then one may ask if they could have provided some inspiration for the image itself, as far as the gesture and position of the hand are concerned. In continuing the passage in *The Elements of Drawing* in which he likens a branch to the "look of a hand held out to receive something, or shelter something," Ruskin wrote:

If you take a looking-glass, and hold your hand before it slightly hollowed, with the palm upwards, and the fingers open, as if you were going to support the base of some great bowl, larger than you could easily hold; and sketch your hand as you see it in the glass with the points of the fingers towards you; it will materially help you in understanding the way trees generally hold out their hands: . . .[107]

Le Corbusier's sketches of the tip of a pine branch seen from different angles (Fig. 25) would seem to illustrate an awareness of Ruskin's principle. Also, his drawing of the hand with five figures does have the hand (the left one, as seen by the artist as though sketching his own hand) held at eye level in the gesture Ruskin describes (but seen directly, not in a mirror). It is sketched without the arm and wrist, floating in space as a branch flake appears to float.

Le Corbusier gives the date of 1948 to a drawing of a similar hand, published in *Modulor 2*.[108] The same drawing is published elsewhere with a text describing an early version as *"une espèce de coquille flottant au-dessus de l'horizon: mais des doigts écartés montrent une main ouverte comme une vaste conque."*[109]

The shell had had its place in his paintings for many years, as a symbol of mathematical order. By referring to his early design as a shell, he may have been recalling in his own mind the mathematics associated with tree growth and consequently justifying the application of his Modulor to the design of the Open Hand.[110] This would be natural and appropriate.

Unequivocally, it is trees Le Corbusier referred to when recounting the early work which led to the Modulor. In criticizing the proposals of the Association Française de NORmalisation (AFNOR) for the standardization of all objects involved in the construction of buildings, saying that their method seemed arbitrary and poor, he wrote:

Take trees: if I look at their trunks and branches, their leaves and veins, I know that the laws of growth and interchangeability can and should be something subtler and richer. There must be some mathematical link in these things. My dream is to set up, on the building sites which will spring up all over our country one day, a 'grid of proportions', . . .[111]

If one can accept the statements made about the employment of the Modulor for all phases of the design work at Chandigarh, then he indeed realized this dream.[112]

Figure 25
Five views of the tip of a
pine branch with buds,
by Le Corbusier, circa
1906. Pencil on paper,
23.5 cm x 13.2-14 cm.
(Photograph by Patricia
Sekler. Private collection,
La Chaux-de-Fonds.)

But his other dream, that of seeing his favored image—the open hand—rise in Chandigarh, was not fulfilled, in spite of his urging:

This open hand, a sign of peace and of reconciliation, must rise at Chandigarh. This sign which preoccupies me for a number of years in my subconscious should exist to bear witness to harmony . . . . God and the devil—the forces present. The devil is in the way: the world of 1965 is able to put itself at peace. There is still time to choose, let's equip rather than arm.[113] This sign of the open hand to receive the created riches, to distribute [them] to the peoples of the world, should be the sign of our epoch. Before finding myself one day (later on) in the celestial zones among the stars of the "Bon Dieu," I would be happy to see at Chandigarh, before the Himalaya which rises up straight on the horizon, this open hand which marks for "le père Corbu" a deed, a course traversed. You André Malraux, you my collaborators, you my friends, I ask you to help me to realize this sign of the Open Hand in the sky of Chandigarh, city desired by Nehru, disciple of Gandhi.[114]

André Malraux's funeral oration called attention to this unfulfilled wish, quoting Le Corbusier as having said; "I have worked for that which men of today need most: silence and peace, and the principal monument of Chandigarh should have been surmounted by a gigantic 'hand of peace,' upon which the birds of the Himalaya would have come to perch. The 'hand of peace' is not yet in place. . . ."[115]

"Silence and peace" . . . "Hand of peace" . . . These words bring our thought back once more to Le Corbusier's formative years when he first learned to link form and meaning in association with designs such as the decorations of the Chapelle indépendante at Cernier-Fontainemelon where "in the middle of a forest all is calm and silent."

1   John Ruskin, *Sesame et les lys,* translated by Marcel Proust, Paris, 1906. Collection: Bibliothèque de la Ville, La Chaux-de-Fonds. The book was inscribed to André Evard as a token of appreciation for help with stucco work of the Maison Fallet, *"A mon bon compagnon d'études et ami Monsieur A. Evard—modeste merci d'un fameux coup de main. Ch. E. Jeanneret, Août 1907."*

2   John Ruskin, *Sesame and Lilies,* Philadelphia, 1894, pp. 51–52; first published in London, 1865.

3   Le Corbusier, *New World of Space,* New York, 1948, p. 8.

4   From my doctoral dissertation, "The Early Drawings of Charles-Edouard Jeanneret (Le Corbusier) 1902–1908," Harvard University, 1973.

5   Le Corbusier, *Quand les cathédrales étaient blanches,* Paris, 1937, p. 101.

6   Discussed briefly in my essay "Charles L'Eplattenier et Charles-Edouard Jeanneret (Le Corbusier), Le Maître et l'Elève," in *Charles L'Eplattenier 1874–1946,* exposition commémorative organisée à l'occasion du centenaire de la naissance de l'artiste au Musée des Beaux-Arts de La Chaux-de-Fonds du 6 avril au 16 juin 1974, La Chaux-de-Fonds, 1974.

7   For example, Eugène Grasset, *La Plante et ses applications ornementales,* 2 vols., Paris, preface dated April 1896.

8   In particular Owen Jones, *The Grammar of Ornament,* London, (n.d., but the preface to the folio edition is dated 15 December 1856); John Ruskin, *The Elements of Drawing; in Three Letters to Beginners,* London, first edition 1857; and John Ruskin, *Modern Painters,* 5 vols., London, 1843–1860 (the edition quoted here is New York, 1888).

9   For a detailed summary, see my "The Early Drawings," pp. 346–354. Le Corbusier's design emphasized triangular dormers, repeating these patterns in the gables.

10 In the section "La Boîte aux lettres" of the newspaper *L'Impartial,* La Chaux-de-Fonds, 22 September 1965, René Chapallaz claimed for himself the role of architect.

11 Letter from Le Corbusier to L'Eplattenier on *Perret Frères* letterhead dated only *Vendredi soir* [1909?]. Archives Fondation Le Corbusier, Paris.

12 As announced in the newspaper *Feuille d'Avis de La Chaux-de-Fonds,* 17e année, no. 122, 28 May 1910.

13 Letter from Le Corbusier in Munich to Léon Perrin, 28 April 1910, Archives Fondation Le Corbusier, Paris.

14 Such elements are found in local heraldry. Pines on hillocks, for example, are the central motif of the coat of

Notes

arms of the neighboring town of Le Locle. Illustrated as frontispiece in François Faessler, *Histoire de la Ville du Locle,* Le Locle, 1960.

15 Illustrated in Le Corbusier, *Oeuvre complète 1910–29,* 4th ed., p. 22. One drawing is dated 24 January 1910, the other 27 January 1910.

16 Architects whose work particularly influenced this change were Josef Hoffmann, Otto Wagner and his pupils, Auguste and Gustave Perret, Peter Behrens, Hermann Muthesius, Theodor Fischer, Bruno Paul, and Heinrich Tessenow.

17 Student architectural work involved composing structures *"en longueur"* and *"en hauteur."* A few projects seem to be influenced by the work of Otto Wagner's pupil, Emil Hoppe.

18 *Prospectus,* La Chaux-de-Fonds, (n.d.), [1912], p. 16. Le Corbusier did a series of designs of stylized pine trees probably intended for the cover of this publication. The motif on the actual cover is the tip of a pine branch.

19 Le Corbusier, "Le Renouveau dans l'architecture," in *L'Oeuvre,* February 1914, no. 2, p. 35.

20 When it does appear, it is in a new guise, as in Charles Humbert's painted panels of Amor and Psyche in Le Corbusier's library for Madame Raphy Schwob (1916). It has become merely part of the landscape of this classical myth.

21 I made a short presentation of this project at the review session of the Second Modern Architecture Symposium at Columbia University, held 8–10 May 1964. The proceedings of this session were recorded but not published. See Fritz Jung, "Le Corbusier et la 'Maison du Diable,' " in the newspaper *L'Impartial,* La Chaux-de-Fonds, 28 January 1966.

22 According to the document of the transaction, executed by E.-A. Bolle, Notaire, La Chaux-de-Fonds. Beck was a *patron monteur de boîtes.* Courtesy of G. Arnold Beck.

23 See the banner design in Georges Benoît Lévy, *La Cité-Jardin,* vol. 1, Paris, 1911, p. 286. This may be an attempt to render the "tree of life" which "bare twelve *manner of* fruits" and whose leaves *"were* for the healing of the nations," Book of Revelation 22:2.

24 See plan and bird's-eye view in Brian Brace Taylor, *Le Corbusier et Pessac 1914–1928,* vol. 2, Fondation Le Corbusier, Paris, 1972, first plate. The knoll was just southeast of the present Chemin de Solmont.

25 Unpublished notebook, circa 1909, formerly Pierre M. Wasem archive.

26 Owen Jones, *The Grammar of Ornament,* p. 157.

27 Ruskin's discussions of the "earth-veil" in *Modern Painters,* vol. 5, may have inspired Le Corbusier's drawings of sections through the earth's crust—that portion which the Maker made habitable for man. This may well be the motif of his famous watchcase. The Ecole d'Art was awarded a *Diplôme d'honneur* for 108 watchcases sent in 1906 to the International Exposition in Milan. See *Ecole d'Art La Chaux-de-Fonds, Rapport de la Commission* for the years 1905–1906 and 1906–1907. Le Corbusier's watch was among them (as illustrated in a portion of an unidentified periodical, Archives Fondation Le Corbusier, Paris). The watchcase probably dates from 1905–1906 when a special effort was made by the school for the Milan show (this is contrary to Le Corbusier's recollection that it won an award in Turin in 1902). Ruskin's discussion of geological formations in *Modern Painters,* vol. 4, may be relevant to Le Corbusier's many drawings of rock and erosion motifs. Paul Turner has compared these geological motifs to work by Behrens and Obrist in "The Beginnings of Le Corbusier's Education, 1902–07," in *The Art Bulletin,* vol. 53, no. 2, June 1971, p. 215.

28 Ruskin, *Modern Painters,* vol. 5, p. 76.

29 *Ecole d'Art La Chaux-de-Fonds, Rapport de la Commission* 1907–1908, p. 8 (my translation).

30 Ruskin, *The Elements of Drawing,* pp. 288, 289.

31 Ibid., p. 168.

32 Ibid., pp. 289–291.

33 Ruskin, *Modern Painters,* vol. 5, pp. 78–80. Le Corbusier spoke of death as ". . . l'horizontale de la verticale: complémentaire et naturelle." From a letter to André Wogenscky quoted by Pierre Joffroy in "Pourquoi le plus grand architecte du siècle fut-il le plus mal aimé?" in *Paris Match,* no. 857, 11 September 1965, p. 58.

34 For Ruskin the pine seemed firelike when seen silhouetted against the sun (*Modern Painters,* vol. 5, p. 83), "seen in clear flame against the darker sky, and dazzling as the sun itself." This verbal image may have inspired the ceiling decorations of the Crematorium at La Chaux-de-Fonds.

35 Ruskin, *Modern Painters,* vol. 5, p. 84.

36 Ibid., p. 85.

37 A "tree" had a time-honored symbolic meaning in the

region associated with emancipation. It even featured in the concluding verse of a text by Rossel sung at the dedication ceremonies of L'Eplattenier's "Monument de la République." Both Le Corbusier and his brother Albert took part in this celebration at La Chaux-de-Fonds in September 1910. L'Eplattenier's monument commemorated the revolution of 1 March 1848, the history of which is recounted in *La République Neuchâteloise. Publication Commémorative à l'occasion du Cinquantenaire de la Révolution de 1848,* La Chaux-de-Fonds, 1898.

According to Le Corbusier, his family was involved in revolutionary activities: "En 1831, les montagnes se soulèvent; échec; représailles; un de mes arrière grands-pères meurt en prison (côté de ma mère: une Perret). En 1848, la Révolution réussit. Mon grand-père était l'un des chefs." From *Croisade, ou le Crépuscule des Académies,* Paris, 1933, p. 34.

38 Le Corbusier, *Creation Is a Patient Search,* New York, 1960, p. 219. The words quoted are preceded by: "Painting is a bitter struggle, terrifying, pitiless, unseen; a duel between the artist and himself. The struggle goes on inside, hidden on the surface."

39 Inscribed 17 May 1952 and published on the cover of *Aujourd'hui art et architecture,* vol. 9, no. 51 (November 1965); see also inside title page. The same symbols had appeared in Le Corbusier, *Le Poème de l'angle droit,* Paris, 1955, table of contents. The images for his coat of arms may also relate to Assyrian seals sketched in his youth, published in *L'Art décoratif d'aujourd'hui,* Paris, 1959 (first published 1925), p. 123, bottom.

40 Le Corbusier frequently alluded to struggle, using plant growth by way of analogy. In *The Radiant City* (New York, 1967, p. 98), for instance, in speaking of the difficulties faced by the designer in Paris, he refers to the "twenty-year war" waged by a single warrior (oneself) against an "army of past feats" but sees Paris as having precious soil for sinking strong roots, "deep, slow roots that enable us to win the tournament of purity!" An early example is in his letter to L'Eplattenier from Paris of 25 November 1908, quoted in Jean Petit, *Le Corbusier lui-même,* Geneva, 1970, p. 36; his parable of a mature tree (L'Eplattenier) sending out its seed may have had some Biblical inspiration from Jesus' parable of the sower (Matthew 13:5, 6 and Luke 8:4–15).

41 Ozenfant and Jeanneret, *Après le Cubisme,* Paris, 1918,

p. 47. A tree, "... si cet arbre n'est pas un individu exceptionnel," was also suggested as a proper subject for a Purist picture (p. 54).

42 Le Corbusier, *The Radiant City,* New York, 1967. The first French edition, *La Ville radieuse,* was published at Boulogne-sur-Seine in 1935.

43 "... nearly all beautiful trees have a tendency to divide into two or more principal masses, which give a prettier and more complicated symmetry than if one stem ran all the way up the centre." Illustrated, Fig. 41, in Ruskin, *The Elements of Drawing,* p. 278.

44 Le Corbusier, *The Radiant City,* pp. 30–31. In comparing architectural forms with natural forms, Ruskin wrote: "The cylindrical pillar is always beautiful, for God has so moulded the stem of every tree that it is pleasant to the eyes." From *The Seven Lamps of Architecture,* Philadelphia, 1961, p. 101. Le Corbusier compared buildings with trees and considered the American skyscraper to have been built upside down with its roots in the air; see *L'Architecture d'Aujourd'hui,* special Le Corbusier issue, April 1948, p. 22. He is quoted to have said in 1957, upon returning to La Chaux-de-Fonds, "Je me souviens toujours de mes vieux sapins austères: ils m'ont servi lors de mes travaux d'Alger, pour démontrer la naissance d'un gratte-ciel, qui pousse comme un sapin, avec ses racines, ses branches, ses ramifications. . . ." From J. M. Nussbaum, "A bâtons rompus avec Le Corbusier," in *L'Impartial,* part 3 of a 3-part article, 4, 5, and (?) November 1957, p. 7.

45 Le Corbusier, *The Radiant City,* p. 86.

46 Ibid., p. 7.

47 Compare Le Corbusier's noncommittal dialogue on "Why 'radieuse'?" in *Creation Is a Patient Search,* p. 50.

48 When *La Ville radieuse* was reprinted (Paris, 1964), Le Corbusier added an introductory note (p. 3) that the book was drafted between 1931 and 1934. It may be of note that attention was refocused on Ruskin in Paris in 1931 through the publication of *Le Culte du beau dans la cité nouvelle, John Ruskin, poète, artiste, apôtre* (a fourth edition of Jacques Bardoux's *John Ruskin,* Coulommiers, 1900).

49 Le Corbusier, *The Radiant City,* p. 79.

50 Ruskin, *The Elements of Drawing,* p. 281.

51 See Le Corbusier, *Croisade,* p. 24. Compare his discussion of leaf form and circulation in *Une Maison—un palais,* Paris, 1928, p. 78.

52 Ruskin, *Modern Painters,* vol. 5, pp. 4, 5.

53 Le Corbusier, *The Radiant City,* p. 6.

54 Text and images appear in Le Corbusier, *The Radiant City,* pp. 7, 8.

55 Pencil on brown wood-pulp paper, 25 cm x 36 cm. Collection Archives Fondation Le Corbusier, Paris, no. 1965. The left-hand portion had been used by Le Corbusier in *L'Art décoratif d'aujourd'jui,* p. 127.

56 See Le Corbusier, *Oeuvre complète 1938–46,* 4th ed., pp. 13–15.

57 Le Corbusier, *The Radiant City,* p. 184. Compare Maurice Besset, *Who Was Le Corbusier?,* Geneva, 1968, pp. 175, 176 for Le Corbusier's attitude toward trees.

58 At Nantes-Rezé a tree, at Berlin a shrublike tree, and at Firminy a tree. Illustrated in Le Corbusier, *Oeuvre complète 1952–57,* 2nd ed., pp. 181, 194, and in *Le Corbusier Last Works (Oeuvre complète,* vol. 8), New York, 1970, p. 18.

59 Le Corbusier was particularly conscious of felled trees during this period, having designed the house of M. Errazuris in Chile in 1930 which had rough tree trunks for its framing. In *New World of Space,* he includes on the same page with the photo of *Le Bûcheron* two photos of felled trees and a sketch of the interior of the house.

60 According to the advertising flyer for *Le Poème,* issued by Editions Verve, it was written and executed by Le Corbusier between 1948 and 1953. The motif appears later in his *Unité,* Paris, 1965, plate 5, without a text and with three hands replacing the torso.

61 For another manifestation of Le Corbusier's interest in leaves and clouds, compare his discussion on "L'Espace indicible" in *The Modulor,* Cambridge, Mass., 1954, pp. 30, 31. See also his *New World of Space,* pp. 7, 8. Le Corbusier's notion of objects producing resonances may relate to Ruskin's notion, concerning the law of radiation as a principle of composition in pictures, that often the point to which the lines of main curvature are directed is far away out of the picture; see Ruskin, *The Elements of Drawing,* p. 292. Compare Le Corbusier, *New World of Space,* p. 50.

62 Late in life, Le Corbusier likened himself in his sixties to a tree in full flower; see *Entre-deux ou propos toujours reliés,* Geneva, 1968, composed by Le Corbusier between 1957 and 1964. Did he consider himself after death to be a "dead tree"? His simple grave, which he designed for himself and his wife, consists of a concrete

enframement containing a platform with a construction for the inscription adjacent to a round form hollowed out (like the section of a thick tube) and a plot for plants. The tubelike form may simply be intended for flowers; its shape, however, could be interpreted as the stump of a tree whose trunk has been completely severed. His sketch for this, which has a tree placed prominently in the background, appears in Petit, *Le Corbusier lui-même,* p. 145; the grave itself is illustrated in *Aujourd'hui art et architecture,* November 1965, p. 117.

63 Ruskin, *Modern Painters,* vol. 5, pp. 75, 76.

64 Le Corbusier, *New World of Space,* p. 33.

65 The parallelisms between Léger's work and Le Corbusier's are especially strong when one considers specific motifs, as for example studies of pieces of flint. See Chapter 6, "La Fascination de l'objet, 1928–34," in Jean Cassou and Jean Leymarie, *Fernand Léger Dessins et Gouaches,* Paris, 1972. For Léger on trees see p. 115.

66 Jean Brun, *La Main et l'Esprit,* Paris, 1963, p. 17. Brun's far-ranging text is a particularly useful introduction to the subject of the hand. The last item in his extensive bibliography is an exhibition catalogue, *La Main de l'homme. Symbole d'une civilisation à la dimension humaine,* Neuchâtel: Musée d'Ethnographie, 1963; for Le Corbusier's Modulor and the Open Hand, see pp. 54–57.

67 This has been outlined in some detail by Stanislaus von Moos in *Le Corbusier. L'architecte et son mythe,* Paris, 1971, pp. 265–267; see also p. 128 for the Venice hospital project and an open hand.

68 The contract for the Chandigarh work was signed on 19 December 1950, according to a letter from Le Corbusier to Alfred Roth in the latter's *Begegnung mit Pionieren,* Basel and Stuttgart, 1973, p. 109.

69 Petit, *Le Corbusier lui-même,* p. 117.

70 Possibly a reference to the Congrès Mondial des Partisans de la Paix; for the text of Le Corbusier's letter to this group of 17 April 1949 see Petit, *Le Corbusier lui-même,* p. 116.

71 As transcribed in Petit, *Le Corbusier lui-même,* p. 105 (my translation); the actual notebook page is reproduced, with a sketch of the hand and a sketch of Nehru and himself (?) extending their hands, in Le Corbusier, *Oeuvre complète 1946–52,* 2nd ed., p. 156.

72 von Moos, *Le Corbusier,* p. 266 (my translation). For Le Corbusier's (?) English version of part of this text see Lu-

cien Hervé, *Le Corbusier, l'artiste et l'écrivain,* Neuchâtel, 1970, p. 62, Figure 63.

73 Le Corbusier, *Modulor 2,* Cambridge, Mass., 1958, p. 258.

74 Jane Drew supplied the following comments, in a letter to Patricia Sekler of 27 February 1974: "I think (but I can't be 100% sure) that my idea occurred when we went for a walk, which we often used to do together towards Manimagaragh, a village near Chandigarh. I remember telling him that the best way to make everything clear in India was by visual means and I was also worried by the enormous vacant distances he had set his buildings apart (we invented visual town planning sheets). I had the unenviable job of writing Chandigarh Byelaws and discovering how many people were illiterate but understood drawings and symbols."

75 Le Corbusier, *Oeuvre complète 1946–52,* 2nd ed., p. 157.

76 Petit, *Le Corbusier lui-même,* pp. 116–117.

77 Quoted by Jean Petit in *Le Corbusier,* Lausanne, 1970, p. 89. The date of 1954 is given, but no source.

78 Le Corbusier, *Oeuvre complète 1946–52,* 2nd ed., p. 158 (my translation).

79 This was affirmed by Jane Drew. When questioned on when Le Corbusier was first interested in the open hand and on the possible meaning of the drawing mentioned in the quote, she replied: "The open hand was a symbol he was certainly obsessed with before Chandigarh (I don't know what the women in the illustration you refer to symbolised) but women were very important to Corbusier." Letter to Patricia Sekler of 27 February 1974.

80 Le Corbusier sent this as a New Year's greeting to Ingeborg and Paul Lester Wiener. Constantino Nivola indicated that it is typical of a large group done on the backs of commercial cards when artists' materials were scarce because of the war. Conversation of 25 March 1974.

81 Le Corbusier had written of the hand and of giving and receiving in *The Radiant City* (text dated June 1933), p. 15, in the context of the words of St Paul, "It is more blessed to give than to receive" (Acts 20:35).

82 The hand appears in so many guises as to preclude a full accounting here. But one should recall the handlike gloves from circa 1928 onward, the isolated hand with fingers imbedded in a flintlike object, hands as part of the human figure given emphasis extended or combined in various ways, hands indicative of human interaction, hands with interlocking fingers (his symbol for the interdependence of the architect and the engineer). A hand

even appears in a project for a sculpture, 1940 (Le Corbusier, *New World of Space,* p. 115). See von Moos, *Le Corbusier,* pp. 264 ff.

83 von Moos called attention to this in *Le Corbusier,* p. 266.

84 Le Corbusier, *Quand les cathédrales étaient blanches,* p. 101. See also p. 119 for comments on New York "... comme une main ouverte au-dessus des têtes. Une main ouverte qui cherche à pétrir la substance d'aujourd'hui." This may relate to the fact that he thought of the structures as trees.

85 Ruskin, *The Elements of Drawing,* p. 125. In *Modern Painters,* vol. 5, p. 49, Ruskin compares a bough to a hand spread flat on a table or, more specifically, to the fingers separated as if they held a large round ball. In *The Seven Lamps of Architecture,* he describes the common black spruce fir as having "dark, flat, solid tables of leafage, which it holds out on its strong arms, curved slightly over them like shields, and spreading towards the extremity like a hand" (pp. 89, 90).

86 Paul Turner (Ph.D. thesis, "The Education of Le Corbusier," Harvard University, 1971, pp. 56, 59) has noted that Le Corbusier, in rereading in 1961 Nietzsche's *Ainsi parlait Zarathoustra* (Paris, 1908) (which he had inscribed in Paris in 1908 or 1909), added notations in the margins. Next to passages that spoke of Zarathustra "as a Christ-like figure, descending to the level of humanity and voluntarily choosing to sacrifice himself in order to bring men the Truth," Jeanneret wrote, *"la main ouverte."* This would indicate his conception of the symbol as it relates to himself, his own struggle as a superior intellect to extend a generous hand. Turner expresses this as "Le Corbusier's identification with Zarathustra's magnanimous sacrifice to Mankind" and "identification with a Saviour-figure."

87 Text prepared in preparation for discussion with Patricia Sekler on 25 March 1974.

88 Black ink applied with fine pen on paper, 13 $^{13}/_{16}$" × 16¾". Courtesy of Costantino Nivola.

89 The same type of base is found as a variation in one of his studies related to sculpture; illustrated in Le Corbusier, *Oeuvre complète 1938–46,* 4th ed., p. 157.

90 *Le Corbusier Last Works,* p. 67, for example.

91 Petit, *Le Corbusier,* p. 91.

92 The final Open Hand is a right hand—that associated

with divinity (a change from early versions with the left hand).

93 In addition to traditional mythological and religious connotations there is an autobiographical one, since Le Corbusier often used the image of a bird as his signature. Also, the Dove of Peace was an image popular at the time through Picasso's posters for the first and second Congrès Mondial de la Paix, Paris, 1949 and 1950.

94 As quoted by Felix H. Man in *Eight European Artists,* London, 1954, not paginated.

95 The 1932 composition is Salubra colors on paper, pasted on mat of masonite, 67 cm × 49 cm, bottom middle "*L-C,*" bottom right "Peint avec Salubre couleurs 1932 (?)." Archives Fondation Le Corbusier, Paris, no. 35. This composition in turn is related to an oil painting of 1930 known among other titles as "*Ligne* [or *Lignes*] *de la main*" (illustrated in *Peintures—Le Corbusier,* Catalogue no. 1, Mezzanin—Heidi Weber, Zurich, Exposition 2–30 November 1961, no. 8). The lines of the hand, which resemble those associated with chiromancy, were omitted in both the 1932 and 1947 versions in which the hand no longer casts a partial shadow on the horizontal plane but is presented with an almost full shadow or mirror image.

96 For Ruskin's influence in India, especially of his *Unto This Last,* see V. Lakshmi Menon, *Ruskin and Gandhi,* Sarva Seva Sangh Prakashan, 1965. Menon states that Gandhi read Ruskin's work in 1904; Gandhi later translated it into Gujarati, entitling it "Sarvodaya" (the welfare of all) from the first of the three main teachings he found in it, "That the good of the individual is contained in the good of all." See also Chapter 3, "Western Affiliations," in B. N. Ganguli, *Gandhi's Social Philosophy,* Delhi, 1973 (especially pp. 56 ff.); and Chapters 1, 2 (especially the section "Society as an Organism"), and 3 of Elizabeth T. McLaughlin, *Ruskin and Gandhi,* Lewisburg, 1974.

Gandhi was assassinated on 30 January 1948. Did this influence Le Corbusier's "spiritual reaction" in that same year? The Gandhi Bhawan designed by Pierre Jeanneret forms part of Chandigarh's University of the Punjab.

97 Numerous references to Ruskin appear in M. K. Gandhi, *The Collected Works of Mahatma Gandhi,* Delhi (being issued in a continuing series, begun in 1958).

98 From M. K. Gandhi, *An Autobiography or The Story of My Experiments with Truth,* translated from the Gujarati by Mahadev Desai, Ahmedabad, 1958 reprinting, p. 220.

The original was first published in two volumes, 1927 and 1929.

99 Le Corbusier, *Mise au point,* Paris, 1966, p. 22.

100 Le Corbusier, *Oeuvre complète 1946–52,* 2nd ed., p. 10.

101 Ruskin emphasized that nature was in a constant state of flux; the artist had to be aware of this and express it. "Now remember," he wrote, "nothing distinguishes great men from inferior men more than their always, whether in life or in art, *knowing the way things are going." The Elements of Drawing,* p. 121.

102 Le Corbusier, *Oeuvre complète 1946–52,* 2nd ed., p. 159.

103 Ibid., p. 158.

104 Compare the title page of *La Ville radieuse,* 1964 reimpression, for Le Corbusier's use of the word *contingence.*

105 *Webster's New Collegiate Dictionary,* Springfield, 1956, p. 180.

106 Man, *Eight European Artists.*

107 Ruskin, *The Elements of Drawing,* p. 125.

108 Le Corbusier, *Modulor 2,* Figure 148, p. 261, date p. 254.

109 Le Corbusier, *Oeuvre complète 1946–52,* 2nd ed., p. 158.

110 Ibid., p. 160.

111 Le Corbusier, *The Modulor,* pp. 36, 37. The first French edition had appeared in 1948, the same year he published early sketches of pine trees and comment in *L'Architecture d'Aujourd'hui,* special Le Corbusier issue, April 1948, p. 111, and "L'Architecture et l'esprit mathématique" in *Les Grands Courants de la Pensée Mathématique,* edited by F. Le Lionnais; on p. 483 of the latter, he discussed the mathematics of tree growth and age, with reference to his early years at La Chaux-de-Fonds.

112 Le Corbusier, *Oeuvre complète 1946–52,* 2nd ed., pp. 117, 160.

113 Le Corbusier's most direct use of the theme was as *Des Canons, Des Munitions? Merci! Des Logis . . . S.V.P.,* the title of his monograph on the "Pavillon des Temps Nouveaux" at the international exposition "Art et Technique" in Paris, 1937. In *Sesame and Lilies,* in division 48 in the section "Of Kings' Treasuries," Ruskin had written in a similar vein. In criticizing French and English military expenditure, he called for investment in museums, galleries, libraries, gardens, and places of rest rather than in arms and other instruments of terror.

In division 37 he also spoke of the hand in criticizing religious practices common in his day; he called instead for simple compassion toward one's fellow man. "For there is a true church," he wrote, "wherever one hand meets another helpfully, . . ."

114 Le Corbusier, *Mise au point,* pp. 52, 53 (my translation).
115 Petit, *Le Corbusier lui-même,* p. 138 (my translation). The version in *Le Corbusier Last Works,* p. 186, ends the quoted portion after "la paix." The version in André Malraux, *Oraisons funèbres,* Paris, 1971, p. 108 omits the last sentence. According to Norma Evenson, *Chandigarh,* Berkeley and Los Angeles, 1966, p. 86, a mock-up of the Open Hand was constructed on the site in 1955. See Le Corbusier's description of casting an open hand in concrete high on the Secretariat at Chandigarh in Hervé, *Le Corbusier,* p. 56, drawing p. 57.

Maurice Favre

**Le Corbusier in an Unpublished Dossier
and a Little-Known Novel**

The judicial archives reveal that Le Corbusier, when he was known as Charles-Edouard Jeanneret, was involved in some legal proceedings in La Chaux-de-Fonds, before he began a practice in Paris at the beginning of 1917.[1]

One of these lawsuits was against Monsieur A. S.,[2] following the construction of the villa at 167 Rue du Doubs (Fig. 26). The lawsuit caused a stir locally, and some people still remember it.

Half a century later, after the child of La Chaux-de-Fonds has become famous all over the world and has won the hearts of his fellow citizens, who made him an honorary citizen of the town, it is tempting to examine objectively what happened.

From the very first words the dossier makes interesting reading. The documents produced as evidence, such as the letters and the plans, have unfortunately been returned to the parties involved, but the official records give a sufficient idea of their content. The writs were drawn up in a clear and careful style by Maître Alfred Aubert for Charles-Edouard Jeanneret and Maître Eugène Wille for Monsieur A. S., the owner. Those who were called to the bar as witnesses were the friends of the architect or his close collaborators; their testimony was transcribed in a concise style by Judge Eugène Piaget, who went on to become Attorney General. Finally, the two expert witnesses, the architects Eugène Colomb of Neuchâtel and Hans Bernoulli of Basel— after Charles-Edouard Jeanneret had objected to all his local colleagues, because he said his reputation had aroused their jealousy (113)[3]—gave their testimony most conscientiously and it is recorded with an elegance comparable to that of the writs. The reader is presented with an exemplary dossier, drawn up with the same care as if it were to be published. But before coming to the lawsuit, it is worthwhile putting it in its social context.

At the beginning of the century, the advantage that La Chaux-de-Fonds had over other localities in the Jura was largely due to the

Figure 26
View from the garden of the east elevation of the Villa Schwob, La Chaux-de-Fonds, 1916. (Photograph by Russell Walden.)

presence of a Jewish community, which had stimulated the life of the town in a manner all the more remarkable because it was not limited to the economic sphere. Artistic vocations were encouraged, and young artists could hope to find a local audience and clientele. They were most especially welcome in the salon of Monsieur R. S., whose wife had particularly discerning taste and enjoyed meeting talented young people.

A description of this circle figures in the novel of Jean-Paul Zimmermann, *Le Concert sans orchestre* (Editions Victor Attinger, 1937). Four young artists form a friendship and occupy the forefront of the novel. Charles-Edouard Jeanneret can be recognized, under a pseudonym, as well as a painter, a sculptor, and a man of letters, all of them equally gifted. With the exception of the architect, whom the author has made a composer, the other characters practise the same profession in the novel as in real life. The description of the personalities and the account of their adventures are equally true to historical fact, even if some matters are covered up and certain dramatic episodes are invented. The state of mind of the small group is in any case faithfully described. The reader is confronted by a particularly cultivated circle passionately in love with beauty. Each member seeks his inspiration deep within himself, accepting only the example of the great masters and refusing that of the schools.

If we now return to the legal proceedings, we can see that certain characters of the novel reappear predictably during it. Two artists, the painter Charles Humbert and the sculptor Léon Perrin, are in the list of witnesses. Madame R. S. is also there, and during the proceedings she played a role that corresponds well with the impression the novel gives of her influence.

This role is worthy of our attention, because when we analyze it we are taken to the heart of the events.

Charles-Edouard Jeanneret's lawyer stated that the whole matter began when Madame R. S. visited the house which the young architect built for his parents, in 1913, at 30 b Rue de la Montagne (now 12 Chemin de Pouillerel) and which, according to him, had cost "much less than villas which were not so well laid out and not so comfortable" (5/11); Madame R. S., according to the architect's lawyer, had appeared delighted with this house, even exclaiming: "Build one like it for my cousin A."; then she had added that she would urge her cousin to build. The architect had then drawn up plans for a villa on a plot of land which he knew he could acquire, and his drawings, he said, had immediately delighted Monsieur A. S. (3/6).

To begin with, that such facts are recounted in the writs is surprising, for they could hardly influence the outcome of the case. We must therefore suppose that the architect had personal reasons for mentioning them. What could these be?

Charles-Edouard Jeanneret stated that he first came into contact with Monsieur A. S. as early as 1913, when he was asked to redecorate the industrialist's smoking room "in an elegant and comfortable fashion." Monsieur A. S. was then living at 73 Rue Léopold-Robert (1/1). By redecoration, he said, "the two parties understood the wall hangings, the installation of electric lighting, the purchase of furniture, wallpaper, curtains, and light fittings, forming a harmonious whole" (1/2). Monsieur A. S., the architect added, "approved without reservation the sketches of furniture and pastel drawings of the décor which the plaintiff presented to him." We also learn that the definitive bill of quantities, drawn up on 11 June 1914, amounted to 4,837.60 Sw.F. and that the architect's fees were 10 percent—that is, 483.75 Sw.F. (1/3). Because of the war, which made difficult the delivery of furniture ordered from France, the work could not be completed before the end of 1916.

The architect then called several witnesses (91, 96, 107, and 109) to confirm that he had often been "called upon by rich clients in the town to transform their appartments."

This allows us to understand more fully the originality of such work, because we see the architect then asking the witnesses whether it was not true that he used to begin "by demanding the demolition of decorated ceilings, of paintwork encrusted with gold, of imitation marble and imitation wood, the elimination of overornate wooden paneling, so that he could replace these superfluous elements by extreme simplicity." Charles-Edouard Jeanneret further affirmed that he had always aimed for "a simplification of forms, a simplicity in the use of materials, and these were real innovations in that locality." The witness Léon Perrin (96) added that as a rule "M. Jeanneret was not in favor of too many different forms of decoration spread over too wide a surface. He would prefer one rich element on a restrained background surface."

This new way of working was not always appreciated. The architect himself pointed out that it had "at the beginning aroused in workers and contractors alike astonishment and a certain opposition" (91, 96, 107, and 109). Another witness, a masonry contractor, stated more precisely: "It was simple, but all the same it was expensive. I had problems with the client." (96)

Such elements show that in spite of traditions, there prevailed in the local middle class an avant-garde outlook that allowed them to appreciate, even before the First World War, works that were to anticipate the style known as contemporary, which was to become popular only after the Second World War.

They also reveal that in the summer of 1916, Charles-Edouard Jeanneret's clientele, even if they had confidence in his taste, nevertheless seldom entrusted him with important works. When it was a matter not simply of interior decoration, but of building construction, we know from other sources that one of his rivals was preferred, the architect Léon Boillot, who built most of the rich villas of this period and whose name figures in the dossier, with reference to certain criticisms about the villa in question (5/6). Charles-Edouard Jeanneret had in fact attempted to build a large house which could be rented out by a group of people who were to form a limited company, but this had fallen through because of the cost of the construction (5/9).

In this summer of 1916, Jeanneret was not therefore indifferent to the possibility of obtaining Monsieur A. S. as a client. For him it meant an introduction to the circle which was most likely to allow him to fulfill his ambitions, for, as he explained, "the members of the S. family are those who recently have had constructed the largest number of buildings in our region" (113).

Madame R. S.'s recommendation was thus the event that allowed him at last to hope for recognition of his talents and this must be why he attached such importance to it. No doubt not only was his pride flattered, but he also wished to take advantage of this opportunity to build a masterpiece. Did he not call the witnesses whom we have already mentioned to attest that he "wished to make a name for himself with a building in a new style, impeccably designed and that to it he devoted all his care for more than a year"?

For the moment, the architect's luck appeared all the greater as he had found a particularly enthusiastic client. Monsieur A. S. came to a decision as soon as the plans were presented to him (3/6); he made a telephone call there and then to Madame R. S. to say that he was going to take her advice and build (5/11). On 7 August 1916, the two parties fixed the architect's fees at a lump sum of 8,000 Sw.F., having arrived at this figure after a summary evaluation of the cost of the construction, in the region of 110,000 to 115,000 Sw.F. (1/6 and 3/8).

After the event, it is difficult to know the details of this estimate, but it is necessary to try nonetheless to gauge what they were, for this evaluation played a vital role in the lawsuit, the architect having called it "more than summary," while Monsieur A. S. declared he had taken the estimate seriously.

It seems therefore that to proceed a comparison was made with the villa in the Rue de la Montagne, which was to serve as a cost model. This first villa had been valued at 40,300 Sw.F. for the building alone, that is 21.78 Sw.F. per cubic meter, by the experts of the *Etablissement cantonal d'assurance*, in 1913. As the cost of construction had risen by 44 percent (144/3), which would give in 1916 a price of 31.43 Sw. F. per cubic meter for the villa in the Rue de la Montagne, the architect had "thought he was being very far-sighted" (5/11) in allowing 36.71 Sw.F. for Monsieur A. S.'s villa (144/3), that is 76,500 Sw.F. for the building, to which was added 24,500 Sw.F. for the garden (3/6, 144/3). The total of 100,000 Sw.F. thus obtained had subsequently been increased to take into account improvements desired by the client, so that the price of the building alone had been raised to 89,000 Sw.F. (3/6), then to the region of 110,000 to 115,000 Sw.F., as mentioned above.

A safety margin would thus seem to have been assured, but the insurance experts were to declare that serious errors would be incurred in such estimates, based on the price per cubic meter, when the specifications of the two buildings were not identical, even if their design had remained the same. In these experts' opinion, a price of 60 Sw.F. per cubic meter ought to have been allowed from the very start for Monsieur A. S.'s villa (139/3). As a matter of fact, a framework of reinforced concrete replaced the traditional masonry; the central heating was concealed in the walls and floors; the exterior walls were faced in brick—every treatise on the use of reinforced concrete, the architect declared, "points out that a veneer of brick, stone, ceramics, marble, and so on is the characteristic of this method of construction" (5/7); a large bay with windows and two rotundas adorned the ground floor area; at roof level a promenade had been added, with a cornice in reinforced concrete; and finally the garden was laid out on a single level, with two summer houses, a green arbor, a fountain, two garden lamps, a paved walk, a covered sitting area, a private entrance to the south, and a garage at a lower level, below the garden. The insurance experts said that this was an entirely different concept from that "of the modest but picturesque villa in the Rue de la Montagne" (139/18).

In August 1916, however, neither the architect nor his client seem to have been aware of the cost of the venture. They were so unaware in fact, that before drawing up the plans for building approval, which date from September 1916 (76), they agreed at the request of the client to increase the height of the ground floor as well as the radius of the rotundas, to enlarge the main side of the building and the stairwell, and they added the kitchen as an annex on the ground floor. The kitchen had not been forgotten (contrary to the claims of local gossip) but had been provided for in the basement, as was the custom of the period. The increase in volume was 949 cubic meters—that is 46.7 percent. Neither Jeanneret nor Monsieur A. S. thought of drawing up or asking for a new estimate. Monsieur A. S. apparently did expect some overstepping of the estimate but thought this should not involve him in an expenditure greater than 175,000 Sw.F. (3/15).

At this point, then, everything seemed to be going well, and the building went ahead as planned until the alarm was sounded by the contractor Hans Biéri, who announced, toward the end of the work, that the villa would cost "nearer 300,000 Sw.F. than 100,000 Sw.F." (3/4 and 100/1)! Fearful of the consequences, the builder called for a detailed bill of quantities to be drawn up at once, and a collaborator of the architect gave this document to him on 23 January 1917. It came to 303,400 Sw.F. (139/6)! In today's money that is more than 3 million Sw.F., which would be a dreadful shock for somebody who was not expecting to spend more than 1.75 million Sw.F.

Two facts further increased the client's concern. On the one hand, Charles-Edouard Jeanneret had just begun a practice in Paris and could have given the impression that he had lost interest in the project. On the other hand, the client learned through certain tradesmen that the architect had asked for discounts to his own personal profit (3/16 and 17).

Consequently, Monsieur A. S. withdrew overall responsibility for the construction from the architect, retaining him only as aesthetic advisor, and he himself took on the task of dealing with the contractors. He also tried to carry out measures of economy and was helped in this work by M., a collaborator of the architect, whom he ended in engaging on his own account, much to the annoyance of his former employer (1/18).

Finally, the definitive cost of the villa rose to 276,000 Sw.F., including 38,000 Sw.F. for the garden and 8,000 Sw.F. for the architect. As Monsieur A. S. had already paid the architect 5,000 Sw.F. on account, he refused to settle the balance, reproaching him with the inadequacy of the estimates, the absence of any warning as to the consequences of the increase in volume, and various errors in the building's conception, of which the most important was the use of a framework in reinforced concrete, which had occasioned an additional expenditure of 20,000 Sw.F.

The architect was the first to take legal action. On 31 May 1918, he instructed his lawyer to claim on his behalf:

fees agreed for the decoration of the smoking room		483.75 Sw.F.
fees for the villa calculated no longer as a lump sum but according to the real cost of the construction	18,792.10 Sw.F.	
from which is to be deducted the payment on account	5,000.00 Sw.F.	13,792.10 Sw.F.

compensation for having been accused of "actions prejudicial to his reputation"	5,000.00 Sw.F.
total payable	19,275.85 Sw.F.

While acknowledging that he owed the architect fees for the smoking room and the balance of fees agreed as a lump sum, that is 3,483.75 Sw.F., Monsieur A. S. entered a counterclaim for damages of 20,000 Sw.F., so that after compensation he sought in his turn 16,516.25 Sw.F.

The account of the proceedings brings in little that is new. According to the architect, the villa in the Rue du Doubs was to have been conceived in as simple a fashion as that in the Rue de la Montagne (139/17 and 18); thus the summary estimates would not have been exceeded if the client had not required extravagant extensions and improvements. Monsieur A. S., however, had no difficulty in demonstrating that he had requested all the modifications before the drawing up of the plans (3/3), and before that, he had rejected the use of costly materials that the architect was proposing, such as marble trimmings, iron window frames, plateglass windows, wooden paneling, sandstone sheathing, colored paving stones, and so on (98/2). The architect was scarcely more successful when he accused his client of having refused the economies he had proposed after the bill of quantities for 303,400 Sw.F. was drawn up, during the course of construction. These economies, such as the use of concrete for the construction of the interior staircases and for the framework of the bays or the suppression of the ceramic tiles, were not compatible with the character of the construction, as the expert witnesses agreed (144/9). Likewise, Jeanneret failed in his attempt to prove that the rise in the price of materials had been, for the most part, responsible for the estimates being exceeded; most of these rises had in fact been borne by the main contractor (95/1).

For his part, Monsieur A. S. was unsuccessful when he reproached the architect for having used reinforced concrete. The expert witnesses admitted that this method of building was costly by its very nature, and could have occasioned an additional expenditure of 20,000 Sw.F., but, they added, it could not be said "that it was without technical or aesthetic advantages. For a building conceived in such a manner, there was no alternative. If the client had not wanted a reinforced-concrete construction, he would have had quite a different house, and this proposal ought to have been made when the preliminary plans were presented to him" (139/9).

Quite clearly, the overstepping of the estimates, which surprised the architect as much as the client, was due to the inadequacy of the summary estimates that had served as a basis for the agreement between the two parties. What was lacking was an accurate bill of quantities. The expert witnesses emphasized this time and again but yet avoided placing the onus of responsibility on the architect alone. The client, they said, should have understood the approximate nature of the first estimate and realized the expense involved through the increase in volume (144/4).

Thus neither party was successful in his suit. The expert witnesses declared, for example, that in adding a most expensive annex, such as the kitchen, the client ought to have known that the cost would be considerably increased. But they went on to add directly that, with regard to the nature of the materials used and their choice by the owner, the architect had a moral duty to warn his client, and he should have made certain provisions in case he found Monsieur A. S.'s pretensions and choices went beyond what was expected (139/22).

The question of the architect receiving secret discounts from building suppliers also ended inconclusively. The architect complained that his honor had been discredited by public accusations. His friend Auguste Lalive, who was to become headmaster of the high school, testified that he had heard such accusations on the lips of Monsieur A. S. himself. "It was a matter," he stated precisely, "of bills allegedly paid twice and they were talked about in the town" (93/6). For his part, Monsieur A. S. admitted that he had accused the architect of incorrect conduct, but not publicly (1/37). He harbored resentment against him on account of his having "requested the contractors to give him discounts for his own personal profit, without the knowledge of the client" (3/16). Charles-Edouard Jeanneret vehemently denied such conduct, but his lawyer nonetheless asked both witnesses and expert witnesses "whether it was the first time they had ever heard of commissions being received in the building industry, whether it was not common practice (105 and 131) and whether certain architects did not reassign the commission to their clients, whereas others used it to absorb the costs exceeding the bill of quantities" (139/28)!

Witnesses and architects contested whether such a practice was current or not, but certain of them did admit the survival of some bad customs (105, 131, 135). All the witnesses disputed having received commissions. One of them acknowledged that he had granted a reduction of 5 percent, thinking that it was in favor of the client (112). Another admitted that the architect had asked for a personal discount, but added that he had not paid it (104). Finally a third witness, a commercial traveler for the firm of Sulzer and a friend of Monsieur A. S., stated that he had heard the architect say to him that if the business were allocated to that same firm, he would lose a commission of 1,000 Sw.F. (131).

Monsieur A. S. was thus able to substantiate his suspicions but not to justify his accusations, and the architect appears to have withdrawn his claim that his honor was discredited.

Finally the legal proceedings ended on 25 June 1920 in a settlement (147), by which each party agreed to withdraw his suit. In other words, Monsieur A. S. paid the 3,483.75 Sw.F. that he acknowledged owing and dropped his claim for damages, while the architect gave up his claim for the fees calculated against the increase in the cost of the construction as well as his claim for compensation for alleged moral injury.

What are we to make of these legal wrangles? From beginning to end of the proceedings, the architect insisted on the care that he had devoted to the construction. Numerous witnesses testified that he had "himself made, studied, and definitively drawn all the plans, that he had attended to the smallest details of the interior and the exterior, even the specifications, the moldings, the color of the paintwork, the choice of floor tiles, paving stones, etc." (90/5, 92/5, and so on). But the architect on the other hand made a significant admission in a letter that is no longer in the dossier, but from which the expert witnesses quoted: "It is unfortunate that the haste with which circumstances have forced the work to proceed has not left the architect a moment free to make a financial comparison and to submit it to Monsieur S. I sincerely regret this and acknowledge that it would have been proper to do so" (144/6).

It is obvious that the cause of the lawsuit lies in this omission. Charles-Edouard Jeanneret neglected the financial aspect of his commission. He probably did not have an administrative sense equal to his ambitions as architect. He paid dearly for it. On one hand, he lost that part of the fees corresponding to the exceeding of the initial estimate, at a time when, as he stated (but without proof), he had an office to maintain whose general expenses amounted to 2,000 Sw.F. per month (97/6). On the other hand, and this is more serious, he compromised his chances of making a career for himself in the town where he was born. After such legal proceedings, it was of course useless to expect new commissions from members of the S. family or their friends.

But we must not regret this too much. The architect's place was not really in La Chaux-de-Fonds. Even if he had been able to build for Monsieur A. S. the villa whose cost did not exceed what the client was willing to pay, and if the execution of this work had established his name locally, it is difficult to see how far his genius could have flourished in a region that was to be seriously affected by two crises, then a second war. In 1944, the heirs of Monsieur A. S. were to sell for only 80,000 Sw.F. the villa their father had lived in until his death. Shortly afterward, the architect Boillot, the rival whom Charles-Edouard Jeanneret had not succeeded in supplanting, died an unhappy man. Other horizons were needed by the man who was to become Le Corbusier.

Although it lost the genius himself, La Chaux-de-Fonds nevertheless retained some of his works, among them the villa that had caused such a stir because of its cost. It has become an historic monument and is a very fine dwelling, as the expert witnesses previously acknowledged during the legal proceedings, when they paid homage to its layout and to its conception (139/24).The same experts did have certain reservations about the building, maintaining that the construction was not suited to the climate, with regard to the roof, the shape of the cornice molding, the large bay on the south and the rotundas to the east and to the west; but history was to prove them wrong, since flat roofs and large bays are now found as frequently in the Jura as on the Swiss Plateau. The architect's boldness was technically justified.

In regard to aesthetics, the dwelling continues to strike the visitor through its subtle air of distinction, which had delighted Monsieur A. S. and members of his family when the architect presented the plans. The villa draws us into a new realm, where beauty resides no longer in the decoration of surfaces, but in the harmony of spaces (Fig. 27).

It is a building of the Cubist period. Jean-Paul Zimmermann has very astutely caught the spirit of the villa in the description that he

Figure 27
Interior of the living room of the Villa Schwob, looking toward the large bay that opens onto the garden. (Photograph by M. Fernand Perret, La Chaux-de-Fonds.)

gives of it in his novel, and it is worthwhile quoting this by way of conclusion. So as to avoid changing anything in the text, I shall leave the names of the characters as they stand, and this will perhaps inspire the reader to become acquainted with the novel.

The Courvoisier family had just moved into one of the first truly original and unusual houses that Le Corbusier had built, and the musician was receiving his friends in the vast living room: encompassed by glass on three sides, the living room rose to the full height of the building. Yet the first floor bedrooms protruded into this space like false doorways, forming, to the right and to the left of the entrance, two suspended prisms. The vertical planes made a sort of T with the ceiling and were to surprise and amuse momentarily the naive visitor when he was ushered for the first time into this novel dwelling. The glass doors on each side, one of which was open, looked through into a dining room and a smoking room which were both semicircular recesses. A chandelier of frosted glass leaves spread a bright, white, even light, which Ravens was praising, because it illuminated clearly the two or three drawings and paintings on the far wall. The modern furniture, with its metal tubular frames, looked as though it had come from a dentist's surgery. In the end Wild was probably uncertain whether such a house was really lived in, whether people slept and worked there, or whether it offered only a passing, puerile, and refined diversion for people who had a house and home elsewhere, whether in fact it was built only to amuse momentarily overgrown child explorers.[4]

Notes

1 This text first appeared in the *Musée Neuchâtelois*, no. 2, 1974, under the title "Le Corbusier à travers un dossier inédit et un roman peu connu." This translation was prepared for *The Open Hand* by Helen Walden.
2 Monsieur A. S., Monsieur R. S., and Madame R. S. refer to members of the Schwob family of La Chaux-de-Fonds.
3 The figures in parentheses refer to the dossier of the case Charles-Edouard Jeanneret v. A. S., which was heard before the Civil Tribunal of the district of La Chaux-de-Fonds, from 5 July 1918 to 28 June 1920; the first figure indicates the number of the document, according to the official inventory; the second figure, when it appears, refers to the page of the document.
4 Jean-Paul Zimmermann, *Le Concert sans orchestre*, Neuchâtel, 1937, pp. 24-25.

Habitation and Le Corbusier's Purist Position:
Creation, Propaganda, and Defense

Russell Walden

New Light on Le Corbusier's Early Years in Paris: The La Roche-Jeanneret Houses

By the time Charles-Edouard Jeanneret-Gris (Le Corbusier) had arrived in Paris,[1] and settled himself[2] in a garret above the Rue Jacob (Fig. 28), a narrow street of apartments, hotels, and antique shops, the great European war of the masses had reached the last exhausting stage of the Somme offensive.

Jeanneret's departure from La Chaux-de-Fonds was the result of a multiplicity of pressures, a compound of idealism, opportunism, and professional embarrassment.[3] Intermingled with these pressures Jeanneret experienced the psychological necessity to exchange the Rousseauistic atmosphere of the Swiss town of La Chaux-de-Fonds for the manifold stimuli of a great intellectual center. Paris—the symbol and synthesis of French genius, the city of many cultural, political, and economic faces—has never failed to fascinate and draw ambitious young men from the provinces. Like many people before him, Le Corbusier felt the attraction of Paris, and in a letter toward the end of his life he said:

I have the greatest respect for the town of La Chaux-de-Fonds.
I weathered the first storms of my life there (in the sphere of ideas).
I had come to Paris to seek the marvelous atmosphere of this city
where the difficulties are unlimited and fierce; but the battle of Paris is
worth being experienced.[4]

Yet, like the people who came to work there in the novels of Balzac and Flaubert, Paris aroused mixed feelings in Charles-Edouard Jeanneret. On the one hand, living in the Latin Quarter gave him the intellectual atmosphere he needed and provided a base in the years to come from which he could broadcast his ideas, using the nearby publishing houses. On the other hand, the urban phenomenon of Paris stimulated Jeanneret into a permanent love-hate relationship which he described in terms of "a dream that I never again left."[5] Although he loved the vibrance of the Latin Quarter in all its variety and artistic uniqueness, more and more, from the early twenties onward, the general obsolescence and multiple failings of the city as an urban unit

Figure 28
Rue Jacob from rooftop
level, Paris VIe, a scene
Le Corbusier knew
intimately between 1917
and 1933. (Photograph
by Russell Walden.)

became a constant affront to his ideas of what a great city could and should be.

In this conviction Charles-Edouard Jeanneret belongs squarely within the French Romantic tradition, which was animated to some extent by a spirit of protest against the sordidness of the modern age. More specifically, Jeanneret's concern for and dissatisfaction with the urban quality of Paris has certain affinities with the disciplined yet passionate protest in Baudelaire's *Les Fleurs du mal*. Jeanneret's affinity with Baudelaire stems not just from the fact that he was influenced by his writings.[6] Aside from these sympathies, puritanical and passionate elements in the psychological makeup of both men linked them in spiritual kinship to a long line of revolutionary and utopian thinkers reaching back to the eighteenth century. Jean-Jacques Rousseau provided the spiritual dynamic to this line.[7] Without a doubt Rousseau occupies a strategic position in European thought. His influence reached across two hundred years to communicate directly with the twentieth century on many levels—as a philosopher, an artist, and a political theorist concerned with the humanity of man in the modern world. In these respects Rousseau profoundly shaped the vision of Le Corbusier.

One could say that Charles-Edouard Jeanneret was a spiritual son of Rousseau.[8] Although they were born 175 years apart in Switzerland, they had similar formative backgrounds. Both Rousseau and Jeanneret came from families whose ancestors had suffered religious persecution, which had caused them to flee from France and settle in Switzerland. Both were sons of Calvinist fathers who were connected with aspects of watchmaking. Both were initially apprenticed to this industry, and became antiestablishment thinkers without university educations. Both had a genuine understanding and love of nature, and therefore both preserved a certain sense of simplicity. At the same time, both were ambitious, hardworking, and avid for recognition.

Both became voracious readers and writers. Both had been drawn to Paris at the age of thirty and at a time when values and ideas were being questioned and society was in a state of transition.

Twentieth-century sensibilities are largely made up from odds and ends of ideas that have been inherited unconsciously from thinkers whom most people may have encountered only briefly. The mind of any young educated Swiss, born before the end of the last century, would quite certainly hold fragments of the thinking of Rousseau, of the *philosophes*, and of social utopians like Charles Fourier and Victor Considérant, who were their nineteenth-century heirs. Jeanneret, brought up in and around the Swiss Jura, became heir unconsciously to the diffuse Rousseauist tradition that was influential in encouraging a love of nature and a sympathy for egalitarian political theories. This tradition was also fostered by the independent spirit of the peasants of the alpine valleys and by the group of Fourierists living in that area. Such groups were supported intellectually by Victor Considérant, a disciple of Charles Fourier, who exercised influence through the newspapers that he directed, in particular the *Démocratie pacifique* (1843–1850), which was published in the region.[9]

It is difficult to say with authority when Charles-Edouard Jeanneret began to read Rousseau. He appears to have acquired an early edition of *Oeuvres illustrées de Rousseau* before coming to Paris in the spring of 1908.[10] As Paul Turner has already explained, Jeanneret eventually found work with Auguste Perret, who opened his eyes to the practical realities of building in reinforced concrete. This dual influence of Perret and Paris appears to have encouraged Jeanneret to widen his intellectual horizons, and it reinforced the spiritual rhythms he inherited from his native Jura.

This first period in Paris was of great importance to Jeanneret's intellectual development, because, apart from the technological impact of the lessons he learned with Perret, he also came under the influence of some of the more classic works of France's rich intellectual heritage. For example, besides the architectural theorists Viollet-le-Duc[11] and Auguste Choisy,[12] Jeanneret acquired and read Rousseau's *Confessions* and Baudelaire's *Les Fleurs du mal* during the summer of 1909. Probably soon after, he bought Rousseau's *Du Contrat social*.[13] Thus, by the time Jeanneret returned to La Chaux-de-Fonds for the winter of 1909, he was in possession of some critical writing, which made passionate protests against slums, the plight of the poor, the place of the machine in society, the distribution of wealth, the source of political power, and the tragedy of man's spiritual alienation as a result of his technological commitment to an industrial world.

Also, while Jeanneret was working in Perret's office in the Rue Franklin, such matters were professionally debated within the city. The word *urbanisme* was introduced into Parisian planning circles around 1910, suggesting something of the changing intellectual atmosphere of prewar Paris. By the time that Jeanneret started a practice in Paris, *urbanisme* was a word whose professional reality was understood.[14] And one must not forget the collective effect of world war, which ensured a more systematic approach to events that town planning sought to control.

The consequences of this political upheaval on architecture were far-reaching. During the whole of the nineteenth century mass housing was largely ignored by the architectural profession.[15] The destruction of the war signaled the opportunity for change. When the war ended, idealistic architects, some of whom had survived the drama of the trenches, were determined to develop the role of the architect toward a wider realization of social mission. In particular, Walter Gropius, Bruno Paul, Ernst May, Bruno Taut, Tony Garnier, Le Corbusier, Hannes Meyer, and Johannes Oud not only "felt the need for an intellectual change of front,"[16] but they also pioneered, each in his own way, the first postwar working-class housing estates. These experiments forcibly drew attention to a new sense of idealism and provided the vision for mainstream modern architecture.

Thus guided and nourished, the leading modern architects attempted a comprehensive integration with industry. They sought a systematic examination of human needs and, by working in harmony with industry, a full use of modern technology and materials. Within these dimensions, modern architecture was not just another style to be applied with the whitewash render. Modern architecture had a social and technological mission to fulfill. Such idealism was linked directly to the revolutionary social and political thinkers of the French Enlightenment, and provided the driving force that guided mainstream modern architecture in the twenties. Looking back at this period, Catherine Bauer Wurster said:

Instead of the princely patronage which had traditionally sponsored architectural innovations, it was the housing and community planning movement in northern Europe which first opened up major building opportunities to the pioneering theorists of the 1920s.[17]

As modern architectural historians like Wurster and Leslie Martin[18] have detected, the twenties witnessed an important social awakening and a corresponding shift in architectural objectives.

Jeanneret made his professional debut in Paris during January 1917. He first started work as a consultant architect to the Société d'Applications du Béton Armé which was involved in diverse studies relating to national defense.[19] In pondering the question of how a young struggling Swiss architect managed to start a practice in wartime Paris, one must refer to his association with a former Swiss engineer, Max du Bois. Jeanneret noted in his 1915 sketchbook marked "A2" that "if all goes well, Jeanneret sets up in Paris,"[20] and after this he mentioned the name *du Bois*, though gave no clue as to his identity. This early reference to du Bois is all the more significant when one realizes that it was through him that Jeanneret arrived in Paris to open an office, as stated by Max du Bois:

I brought Jeanneret to Paris, by associating with him to set up an architect's office. Since he came from Switzerland, without money, friends or acquaintances, it was my duty as well as in my best interests, in order to get the office started, to introduce him to Swiss society in Paris, where I had numerous friendships.[21]

Apart from the acknowledgment of the bonds of Swiss nationality, the partnership was primarily a business relationship nurtured on patronage drawn from within the Swiss colony in Paris.

Among this group of exiles Max du Bois introduced Jeanneret to engineers, industrialists, and rich bankers, some of whom were eventually to provide the patronage and financial support for launching his engineering, architectural, and publishing ventures.

It was only natural that Jeanneret should avail himself of this opportunity and thus fulfill his ambition to start out in Paris, in spite of the commitments that he had in his hometown at the time. As the Villa Schwob was then in its first stage of construction, Jeanneret's client at La Chaux-de-Fonds, Monsieur Anatole Schwob, preferred that his architect stay and concentrate his sole attention on the building. Yet, Jeanneret left for Paris. Though this departure, inopportunely timed, might appear to suggest that Jeanneret regarded the industrialist's house as relatively unimportant, a letter to Monsieur A. Lavandière in Lausanne proves that this was not so.

In 1916–17 I was called upon to build a villa at La Chaux-de-Fonds for M. Anatole Schwob, conceived on a bold plan which a structure of reinforced concrete permitted. I have always been a strong advocate of reinforced concrete and I brought to the realization of the building in question the fruits of long experience, and I concentrated upon it all my artistic effort and my constructive skills, in the hope of creating a work which would last and which would not simply give just a passing moment of delight.[22]

Jeanneret gained his command of a body of theory and practice in reinforced concrete from the writings of Viollet-le-Duc, Auguste Choisy, and Anatole de Baudot[23] and from the practical systems developed by François Hennebique, which he learned through the teaching of Auguste Perret. His absorption of these ideas is clearly evident in the progression of structural clarity in his work at La Chaux-de-Fonds. By the time Jeanneret designed the Villa Schwob he had absorbed the rudiments of reinforced-concrete construction, though he still had a good deal to learn about the practicalities of this system of building.

Jeanneret's long advocacy of reinforced concrete is further confirmed by correspondence with Tony Garnier of Lyons as early as 1914, when he wrote to him about this very problem of building in reinforced concrete. Garnier's reply, delayed for some seventeen months, gives an interesting commentary on what was animating Jeanneret during this period. After apologizing for the long delay due to pressure of work as *Architecte-en-chef de la ville de Lyon*, Garnier writes:

. . . I wanted to say that your attempt to widen the use of reinforced concrete in buildings appeals to me very much. . . . I have some aerial photographs of my habitations at Saint Rambert, the hospital project and the sports stadium that I am building at the moment.[24]

By December 1915, when Jeanneret received this letter, he was investigating how to market his Domino plans for housing. This mass housing system was to provide accommodation of the highest quality, at a minimum cost, and for the greatest number of people. He had done site plans and technical studies at critical structural situations. His framework system, to be made of standard components, encouraged a rich diversity in the grouping of houses, and inside the dwellings various arrangements would be possible through the use of flexible partitions. As a project intended for postwar housing reconstruction, Jeanneret's initiative was particularly opportune. As Jeanneret was remote from the corridors of political power, however, and as the necessary Loucheur legislation was not passed until 1928, there was no likelihood in 1915 of realizing his scheme. Nevertheless, the Domino project is an interesting exercise in industrialized mass housing, illustrating the potential use of reinforced concrete.

If one considers twentieth-century building to have its roots in contemporary economic and sociopolitical realities, then Jeanneret's first employment as consulting architect to the Société d'Applications du Béton Armé was a major step toward the realization that change in architecture and the environment was only practically possible through the use of modern technology.

During his first year of consultancy he designed a water tower in reinforced concrete, which was built at Podensac (Gironde). He also worked on projects for an arsenal at Toulouse, a hydroelectric plant at L'Isle Jourdain (Vienne), and workers' housing at Saintes (Charente-Maritime) and at St-Nicolas-d'Aliermont, near Dieppe.[25] Under the impact of having to examine new problems where tradition had no influence or aesthetic prejudice, Jeanneret not surprisingly began to feel he was breaking free from the regressive climate that characterized official attitudes to architecture during this period.

Particularly the project for forty-six workers' houses at St-Nicolas-d'Aliermont brought Jeanneret back to where he had left off in his Domino studies. As the project progressed as far as the completion of working drawings, Jeanneret received minimal economic support during the difficult war year of 1917. Yet what was perhaps more important, it brought Jeanneret closer to the critical realities of launching reinforced-concrete schemes in rural France. No doubt this period was professionally frustrating for him. Nevertheless, he learned some important lessons about the difficulties involved in financing projects that broke with normal technical and political procedures. In effect, further thought on the problem led him to consider modulor systems, technically integrated, as a basis for working in mass housing.

Again with the difficulties at St-Nicolas-d'Aliermont in mind, and in order to ensure a continuous supply of building materials in the depressingly difficult climate of war shortages, Jeanneret launched, in October 1917, a brick factory in the Paris suburb of Alfortville. The venture was ill-fated, due to the postwar economic inflation; it was forced to close early in the twenties, leaving Jeanneret to join the growing number of "economic shipwrecks." Suffering from this personal setback, a humiliated Jeanneret declared: "Oh, Bohemian of the Boul' Mich! A Bohemian does not get into that arena of tough competition."[26]

Jeanneret was convinced that the true notion of modern building lay in the use of reinforced concrete, which allowed a new planning freedom. At the same time he was searching for a new approach to contemporary living. In his design for the Villa Schwob he expressed this by a spatial differentiation between the living and sleeping areas. In order to bring harmony to the building as a whole he used the golden mean proportion of regulating lines. In spite of his aesthetic strivings and spatial/technical considerations, however, Jeanneret experienced great anxiety and frustration following the completion of the Villa Schwob, when the dispute with his client, which arose during the construction, formally led to litigation proceedings and he was forced to defend his architectural principles.[27]

Some time after this bitter experience, in a rather revealing letter, Jeanneret spoke of his anxieties and current feelings to his friend and former traveling companion, Léon Perrin.

It is the first time that I have been able to look comfortably at this construction and I confess with much vanity that I am satisfied with it. It is really architecture such as I feel more and more each day. It is true that since that moment I have not done any architecture, except for a few mass-produced houses for the devastated areas, extremely venturesome projects which didn't find their way to realization. Here neither the straight line nor the primary forms are liked yet. It is difficult to shake off the influence of the Ecole. I think that after you return from Rome, there is scarcely nothing but this house, at La Chaux-de-Fonds, which has a right to attract your attention. You see that my vanity is complete; no matter, it's all the same good to know oneself what one is worth.[28]

Such confessions are not uncommon among twentieth-century architects working within the limitations of their age. Jeanneret, who felt himself to be particularly alone in Paris, was forever looking over his shoulder to history to sustain himself and his personal vision in modern architecture.

Paris presented Jeanneret with a particularly difficult challenge. He still had to face the bitter truth that he had been unable to realize his ideas in Paris, and he became increasingly anxious over his failure to obtain commissions, as he revealed in a letter to Madame Schwob: "Many times I have had the opportunity of regretting bitterly that this construction is not situated in the vicinity of Paris where it would be extremely interesting publicity for me."[29]

An atmosphere of gloom pervaded the period, with the casualty lists mounting in the newspapers. It was as though civilization itself was at its nadir and there was little hope left for the living. Yet, perhaps it is just in such dark times that one can begin to look for signs of the birth of a new era. In a newspaper of December 1917, Jeanneret was attracted to such a sign, which argued the case for stronger action in preparation for this new age. Jeanneret not only identified with the most important points, which he marked in green crayon; he also preserved the newspaper clipping. The first two points, marginally lined, are as follows: "Of the two dangers the atrophy or the depravity of the national spirit in idleness is the worse. . . ." and,

It is not a question of knowing whether there exist ten poets, or even just one single poet, from whom we might hope for a great work. It is a question of not allowing the living tradition of French beauty to be broken. . . . It is this treasure which is precious, it is in this that the future generations will derive their resources. Let us not allow it to perish. . . .

Obviously the sense of France's classical tradition in architecture was of primary importance to Jeanneret. Thirdly, this time underlined in green crayon to express Jeanneret's agreement:

If the movement which appears to hesitate between various directions is not encouraged by the approval of an intelligent and enthusiastic public, and if it does not become aware of its purpose thanks to the fraternal collaboration of a scrupulous and enthusiastic criticism . . .[30]

then radical intellectual action must be taken to restore and rescue the situation. Perhaps nothing quite summed up Jeanneret's feelings at the time more poignantly than this article.

Further signs of a new era became apparent from the change in tempo and a greater destructive precision that characterized the final stages of World War I. The importance of physical science and technology was demonstrated clearly when the Germans returned to the Marne battlefields in 1918 with even more ruthlessness, scientific precision, and savagery than before. In a way, the need for precision symbolized the period. Certainly Jeanneret appreciated the importance of engineering precision and sought to express it in his own work.

The first six years that Jeanneret spent in Paris were a period in which he matured. With no building commissions in Paris, he had time to develop the ideas gained during his formative years. Not until 1922 did he have the opportunity of putting his ideas into practice, in building the Ozenfant and Besnos houses.

Through Auguste Perret Jeanneret met Amédée Ozenfant[31] at an *Art et Liberté* group meeting[32] in May 1918. This meeting widened Jeanneret's horizons into Ozenfant's world of painting and journalism. In the summer of the same year, through Max du Bois, who was influential in the Swiss circle in Paris, Jeanneret met the rich young banker Raoul La Roche[33] at the *déjeuner suisse*.[34] Both Amédée Ozenfant and

Raoul La Roche were to become vitally important as Jeanneret's Purist ideas were developing. Jeanneret's meeting with Raoul La Roche led to a lifelong friendship; his creative yet stormy partnership with Ozenfant lasted only until 1925, when it finally broke up over the arrangement of paintings in La Roche's Auteuil gallery.[35]

Meanwhile, however, this partnership had produced two books,[36] two Purist art exhibitions,[37] twenty-eight issues of *L'Esprit Nouveau* (a review of contemporary thought), a studio house for Ozenfant,[38] and a certain renown for both Ozenfant and Jeanneret. Nor should one forget that Le Corbusier of 1925—architect, urbanist, painter, journalist, and propagandist par excellence—overshadowed the somewhat diffident and struggling figure of the Charles-Edouard Jeanneret of 1918. In this transformation the influence of Ozenfant and La Roche cannot be overestimated.

Jeanneret's development as a Purist began in September 1918 under the influence of Amédée Ozenfant when, having returned to Paris from a holiday together at Andernos (near Bordeaux), they shared a studio in which they wrote and painted.[39] Approximately three months later, in fact four days after the armistice was declared, a joint manifesto was published, *Après le Cubisme.* This declaration of a movement called Purism coincided with the first exhibition of paintings and sketches by Ozenfant and Jeanneret, held at Germaine Bongard's boutique at 5 Rue de Penthièvre between December 1918 and January 1919.

The exhibition was indeed timely, for there were then on display around the Place de la Concorde captured German airplanes, tanks, and field and machine guns. For the Purists these articles of war were a prime example of the machine-tooled world, for they manifested the quality of *precision* and were geometrically ordered.

These constant values appealed to Ozenfant and Jeanneret because they symbolized "a system capable of expressing not a mere reflection of one's personal predilections, but a microcosmic synthesis of contemporary history."[40] Thus, in the euphoria of the victory celebrations, Purist proselytism was supported by the belief in objectivity, exactitude, and precision, values that were in full accord with what Jean Cocteau was later to phase as *"le rappel à l'ordre."* The Purist "call to order" heralded the spirit of a new architecture. Jeanneret, having picked up a certain journalistic *joie de vivre* from Ozenfant, confidently announced: "If we pose the question: has the architectural moment of our epoch arrived, the answer is: it has, because since the end of the war period we possess a modern conception of architecture."[41]

Yet, in a more reflective mood ten years later, Ozenfant observed: "Our exhibition was premature. We were clear as to the ideas but less so as to how to make them visually apparent. But we worked on obstinately, painting by day in my studio and discussing at night."[42]

If one looks critically at the so-called revolutionary ideas they were proposing, one finds that their Purist philosophy was based on an absolute quest for harmony of the environment through the discipline of geometry. Such an absolute quest was not uncommon among the writers and artists of the time, for, having done their patriotic duty, they invariably went back to their studios in search of ideals for a new world. Since neither Ozenfant nor Jeanneret had experienced modern warfare at first hand, however, their encounter with and admiration of war machines was a studio-bound psychological reaction to images of precision. Ozenfant, of course, countered with: "It was not a matter of submitting to the period, but of being in it, of working with and for it."[43]

The fact is that neither had the human experience of the war drama and the companionship of the trenches. It is not surprising, therefore, that Purism, although the doctrine of attaining a structured universal harmony, should be essentially an elitist movement. To this criticism

Ozenfant and Jeanneret often made the point that their search for universal harmony was in keeping with the spirit of the modern age.

The intentions of Ozenfant and Jeanneret were very laudable, but their ideas could be realized in only a limited manner. Politically they were beaten from the outset, because, with the war over, the central preoccupation of the French bourgeoisie (which included many artists and writers as well as politicians) was to return as rapidly as possible to their ideals of prewar days. As one writer has put it: "In 1918, bourgeois France had one supreme aim: to return to bourgeois comforts."[44]

If one must look for a real indictment of the values that supported the slaughter of World War I, there is none more bitter than that made by an American poet living in Paris at the time. In these stanzas from "Pour l'élection de son sepulchre" (1920), Ezra Pound tersely weighed the sacrifice of men against the cultural values of civilization, and found the balance questionable.

There died a myriad,
And of the best, among them,
For an old bitch gone in the teeth,
For a botched civilization,

Charm, smiling at the good mouth,
Quick eyes gone under earth's lid,

For two gross of broken statues,
For a few thousand battered books.[45]

Pound's pessimistic description would have been untenable for Jeanneret. It was indeed foreign to the ideals of his native Jura and to his moral philosophy. With visionary courage Jeanneret felt bound to act. So, like the itinerant Don Quixote,[46] he went out into Paris to battle against the suffocating cultural climate of the period.

In a way it was a psychological battle with his time. This is perhaps one explanation why, after Proust won the *Prix Goncourt* in 1919, Jeanneret became one of his reading public.[47] Jeanneret was perhaps attracted to the work of Proust because creatively Proust rediscovered the past actively in the present. The idea of ordering disconnected fragments of his experience and bringing these fragments into a higher reality is a realizable attribute of most creative people. Jeanneret's approach to design was a living embodiment of this idea.

His solution to the problem of providing a bachelor and family living complex illustrates this creative process in architecture. The houses were located at the bottom of a garden in the Square du Docteur Blanche at Auteuil, in the sixteenth *arrondissement* of Paris. In these houses in upper middle-class Auteuil, Le Corbusier brought together the fragments of his vivid imagination in a dramatic Purist synthesis.

This program began indirectly as a result of the influence of the first Purist exhibition on Raoul La Roche (whom Jeanneret had met a few months earlier), for not only did La Roche become interested in the Purist movement, he also decided to start a modern art collection. Raoul La Roche was a wealthy young banker in the Crédit Commercial de France, one of the business class that had ruled France in alliance with various notables since the beginning of the Third Republic. La Roche did not make rash decisions or judgments. Therefore, his decision to start an art collection was important and revealed in him a measure of aesthetic discernment. It was not only fortunate for Ozenfant and Jeanneret that La Roche became interested in Purism, it was even more important for art history. In the words of Franz Meyer:

If in 1920 you gave yourself the brief to build a museum collection of Cubism and Purism out of the important works of Picasso, Braque, Gris, Léger, Lipschitz, Le Corbusier, and Ozenfant you could hardly have chosen in any other way than he [La Roche] did. In 1920 there were no curators and no commissioners who could tell you which pictures should have a place in a museum.[48]

La Roche had an eye for the significant. By 1920 he had acquired the *Flacon, guitare, verre et bouteilles à la table grise* by Ozenfant (Fig. 29), and *Composition à la guitare et à la lanterne* by Jeanneret

Figure 29
Amédée Ozenfant's
Flacon, guitare, verre et bouteilles à la table grise, 1920. (Photograph courtesy of Kunstmuseum, Basel, La Roche bequest.)

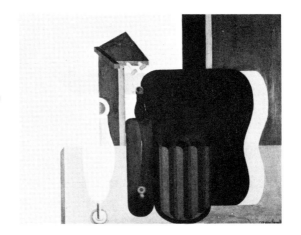

Figure 30
Charles-Edouard Jeanneret's *Composition à la guitare et à la lanterne,* 1920. (Photograph courtesy of Archives Fondation Le Corbusier.)

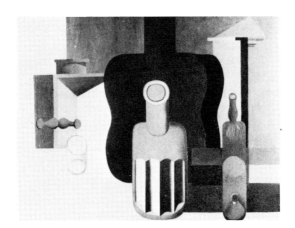

(Fig. 30). La Roche continued to make discerning purchases throughout the twenties. In 1923, he wrote to Jeanneret:

I remind you that the total sum that I have paid to date for the purchase of your paintings, following verbal agreement, amounts to 7,500 francs, in exchange for which you have delivered to me, on account, four paintings and one drawing with which I am delighted.[49]

La Roche's patronage and interest in Purism extended further than his own ambitions as a collector. His personal conviction led him to support the Purists in their broader objectives.

The problem before the Purists was not only the development but the circulation of their ideas. In order to achieve this, Ozenfant and Jeanneret with Paul Dermée outlined the program of a journal (to be called *L'Esprit Nouveau*) in a policy statement dated 28 February 1920. The aims of this international journal were to review contemporary currents in painting, literature, music, architecture, scientific aesthetics, cinema, and sport. Due to the war, such journals were rare in Paris, and *L'Esprit Nouveau* would serve as an open forum for the polarization of contemporary debate.

In this venture Jeanneret had the difficult task of managing the business side of the magazine, as well as contributing toward it intellectually. Under financial pressures it is not surprising that he should turn to his friend Raoul La Roche. In March 1920 Jeanneret wrote:

I enclose for you two documents concerning the editions of *L'Esprit Nouveau,* one program (strictly confidential) and a financial account. I repeat that I attach very great importance to the realization of this business and I would like to thank you now for the interest that you have shown in it, which gives me the most complete confidence in the result which your assistance and that of your friends will bring me.[50]

Following this initiative, La Roche applied for five shares in the Société de *L'Esprit Nouveau.*[51] To ensure his continuing patronage, he received special bound copies of the review, under the title of *Actionnaires de la Société de L'Esprit Nouveau.*[52]

The first edition of *L'Esprit Nouveau* appeared in October 1920, and, apart from four breaks in the monthly sequence, the journal continued in publication until the final issue, Number 28, in January 1925. With the first issue of *L'Esprit Nouveau* Jeanneret took from one of his ancestors the pseudonym of *Le Corbusier,* though his friends continued to call him by his family name of Jeanneret. The whole enterprise marks the transformation of Jeanneret from being a backwoodsman to his Parisian identity as Le Corbusier.

With the successful launching of *L'Esprit Nouveau,* Le Corbusier and Ozenfant were under some obligation to their patron and friend Raoul La Roche. They repaid his encouragement by giving his Purist collection a new momentum, by acting as his bidders for the confiscated Kahnweiler paintings of Picasso, Braque, Léger, and Gris,[53] at the four art auctions held in June and November 1921, July 1922, and May 1923. La Roche had great confidence in their judgment and, in a way, one could say that Ozenfant and Le Corbusier were lucky. The big dealers for various reasons did not seem to be alert to the significance of these painters, besides which there were eight hundred Cubist works from which to choose. So Ozenfant and Le Corbusier were able to acquire their selection cheaply. The real problem, of course, was the selection of what was important, and in this respect Ozenfant and Le Corbusier did a superb job for La Roche. His Cubist collection was unequaled by any other private collector.

Raoul La Roche's interest in this adventure developed into a lifetime pursuit.[54] With such a growing collection, the problem soon arose of housing the paintings; Le Corbusier did not miss his opportunity. "La Roche, when one has a beautiful collection as you have, one must have a house constructed worthy of it." And La Roche replied: "OK, Jeanneret, build me this house."[55]

The first problem to solve was that of finding a suitable site, which was not an easy matter. Several possibilities were examined until Ozenfant, who frequented the sixteenth *arrondissement,*[56] mentioned the recent "Jasmin" subdivision in Auteuil. This area of Paris lies alongside the Bois de Boulogne, and was in the twenties, as it is still today, the spiritual home of the *grande bourgeoisie.*

Le Corbusier responded to the challenge and produced a design in the manner of the studio houses and Citrohan projects that he was to exhibit during the year at the Salon d'Automne of 1922. The interesting feature of this design for La Roche's house[57] was the spatial exploration of the double volume living room through the use of an internal zigzag ramp.

Because of difficulties in securing the site in the Rue du Docteur Blanche at Auteuil, however, this first project did not mature. Le Corbusier was forced to abandon the program as he and Pierre Jeanneret (who had recently joined him from Perret's office) turned to the demanding task of developing the conception of a *ville contemporaine* for three million people on the right bank of the Seine. It was not until this Paris project was finished and exhibited at the 1922 Salon d'Automne that Le Corbusier came to reexamine the Auteuil problem early in 1923.

This Auteuil site, the property of the famous Docteur Blanche, was subdivided in about 1920.[58] Land, street patterns, and ratable values inevitably produce narrow-frontaged, deep, oblong plots, which leave unusable the land in the center of a rectangular development. To solve this problem Le Corbusier planned to take a private roadway off the Rue du Docteur Blanche and form a square at its termination in the center of the development. This area thus became known as the Square du Docteur Blanche (Fig. 31).

There followed a tortuous tale of haggling for building land along the private roadway from March until September 1923 between Le Corbusier, J. M. Esnault, Director of the Banque Immobilière de Paris, and M. Plousey, the architect of the development site, who together controlled the sale of land from this Auteuil subdivision.

Figure 31
Plan of the La Roche-Jeanneret building site at Auteuil, September 1923. (Photograph
courtesy of Archives Fondation Le Corbusier.)

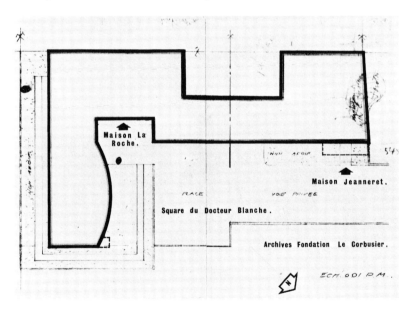

Figure 32
The wedding celebration group at 20 Rue Jacob, showing the Pastor Huguenin and
Amédée Ozenfant holding flowers over the head of the bride and groom, Lotti and Albert
Jeanneret. Le Corbusier is on the right of the group in winged collar. His present to his
brother and sister-in-law was the Purist painting on the wall, entitled *Grande nature morte
des Indépendants*. (Photograph courtesy of Kerstin Rääf.)

In the meantime an event occurred which was to influence the final solution of the Auteuil program. This was the marriage of Le Corbusier's brother Albert Jeanneret[59] to a Swedish student named Lotti Rääf, at the *Mairie* of the sixth *arrondissement* on 26 June 1923.[60] Albert Jeanneret, the teacher and composer, had been living with his younger brother Charles since arriving in Paris in 1919, and he took his bride back to live temporarily at 20 Rue Jacob. Seeing them there after the wedding, enjoying a celebration drink with the Pastor Huguenin, Ozenfant, and Le Corbusier (Fig. 32), one can understand why Lotti Jeanneret later wrote: "We lived together for a year in a small, old-fashioned flat in the Latin Quarter. I longed for more space, air, modern facilities and ordered a house by Le Corbusier."[61]

Le Corbusier now had two clients with whom he was deeply involved, but the land question remained critical. Indeed, if one examines Le Corbusier's letters on the subject of August and September 1923, one senses the mounting tension between Le Corbusier and Messieurs Esnault and Plousey.

Le Corbusier had naturally been seeking plots on the left of the private roadway, as these plots faced in a southerly direction. When he discovered early in August that he definitely could not obtain any land at all on the left, Le Corbusier became concerned. By now he had had to abandon three schemes because of this land question, and, as he wrote to Esnault, "owing to lack of agreement between yourself and M. Plousey, this spring, you made me lose two [other] clients. . . ."[62] On 14 August 1923 Le Corbusier wrote a long letter to architect Plousey expressing his annoyance over "the purchase under dispute": "You will realize the considerable detriment that a change in our agreements would be to me, my clients would be within their rights to find me in the wrong and to be seriously annoyed with me."[63]

With similar sentiments Le Corbusier wrote a fortnight later to

Esnault: "La Roche . . . would not forgive me for having led him up the garden path in this way. . . . I venture to rely on your great kindness to settle without delay this disagreement."[64]

The banker replied briefly on 6 September that as soon as Plousey returned in a few days' time they could meet in order to reach a final agreement; however, as Esnault through illness was absent from the meeting, Le Corbusier felt bound to express his "formal point of view" to Esnault in a letter of 12 September:

In all this business I have never changed as far as my desires are concerned, on the contrary the Banque Immobilière has constantly brought in modifications leading to a real incoherence in its work.

. . . You understand certainly the categorical sense of my letter and you will, in writing, give me the satisfaction that I ask for.[65]

Le Corbusier had become increasingly impatient and anxious, for La Roche had written to Le Corbusier asking him to complete the purchase of two plots of land on his behalf by 30 September. [66] Le Corbusier persevered in his efforts to find a way out of this dilemma. To the architect Plousey his appeals were more subtle:

To reassure you, I let you know that these houses will be constructed without a visible roof, with a single terrace, that they will have an extremely correct and very careful architecture and that they will be an embellishment rather than a disfigurement.[67]

Le Corbusier said nothing controversial. He kept quiet about his intellectual search for a universal harmony. Nor did he mention *les tracés régulateurs* or reinforced concrete. His choice of words was designed to curry favor. And again in a letter of 18 September to Plousey he supported his plea by using the traditional ploy of exhibition propaganda: "Furthermore, the houses which will be constructed around the square are to be exhibited as a large model at the Salon d'Automne where a place is reserved for me at present under the dome."[68]

Thus, in this rather tense situation Le Corbusier was finally able to secure, on 21 September 1923, the remaining three plots of land at the bottom and on the right of the Square du Docteur Blanche.

The agreement was subject to three conditions. First, his clients had to bear the charges for the private roadway and the cost of its construction. Second, Le Corbusier had to observe the *non aedificandi* covenant of 2.50 meters along the back of the La Roche property. And third, the two large trees on these plots had to be preserved, especially the tree at the end of the private roadway.[69]

In effect, this meant that all the available land would be built upon. Le Corbusier would have to lose one more client and for a fourth time revise his plans for two houses on a frontage of thirty meters.[70] He was able to exhibit his now dated model (Fig. 33) in the Salon d'Automne, knowing that at last a real opportunity had arrived for him to realize an imaginative architectural synthesis.

On the program formulation Le Corbusier wrote:

These two houses coupled together to form a single block realize two very different problems: one of the houses shelters a family with children and requires a number of small rooms and all the services needed for the running of a household. The other house is destined for a bachelor, owner of a collection of modern paintings and a man passionately fond of *objets d'art.*[71]

One must not undervalue the influence of the site limitations on the final solution to this program. Besides the limited area of available land to build on, the plots faced the cold north side of the roadway, neighbors were critical, and height restrictions were set. Within this network of constraints Le Corbusier set to work. And yet for Le Corbusier architecture was not just a simple matter of functional analysis. Architecture had to work, of course, but it had to work beautifully and meaningfully, with emotional as well as rational significance.

The instructions of Le Corbusier's clients must not be forgotten. Lotti Jeanneret wanted a family house with light, air, and modern facilities, while La Roche gave Le Corbusier a free hand in working out the design for his house.[72] As the building land available lay at the end of the private roadway, it possible to exploit the idea of living

Figure 33
Model of the La
Roche-Jeanneret houses,
as exhibited in the Salon
d'Automne, 1923. Le
Corbusier's final solution
to the La Roche gallery
was later modified.
(Photograph courtesy of
Archives Fondation Le
Corbusier.)

Figure 34
Lotti and Albert
Jeanneret dining on the
roof deck. (Photograph
courtesy of Kerstin Rääf.)

Figure 35
The Jeanneret living
room. (Photograph
courtesy of Kerstin Rääf.)

in a back garden rather than in a street. Thus family life, like the branches of a tree, gravitated toward the upper part of the house into the sunlight and fresh air. Such a progression, from the enclosed compartmentalized spaces of garages and rooms for maids and caretakers, through bedroom and living room floors, finally culminating in the sunlight and a roof garden, was thoroughly consistent with Le Corbusier's lifelong experiences, which taught him to value the divinity of Nature.

For a psychological reaction to this spatial progression one can do no better than draw attention to the comments of clients. Of the roof garden Lotti Jeanneret said, "It was the best area of all."[73] Three floors up, cosseted by sunshine and trees, the garden roof-deck was ideal for outdoor dining (Fig. 34), for observing nature, for children's games, and for sunbathing. At night, one could imagine oneself oceanbound on the deck of a liner beneath a canopy of stars.

From this roof garden it was only a flight of stairs to the living room below (Fig. 35). About the impact of this room Lotti Jeanneret has said:

The aim was to capture as much as possible of the sun and the free view in the place where one lives the most. The room is 12.5 meters long, which is the width of the house. The first impression is: light, air, gay coloring. . . . The colors in this big room are white, soft pink, light green, clear blue, dark red-brown, burnt umber, and grey. . . . It is a symphony created by an artist, it is a feast for the eye.[74]

Such a solution took advantage of a light-court to overcome the problem of a cold, northerly site. In the north wall of the living room on the second floor, Le Corbusier used square windows, which provided a visual counterpoint to the strip windows of the south wall.

Although the north façade (Fig. 36) does not visually acknowledge the internal division between the two houses, Le Corbusier's niece Kerstin Rääf conceded: "My sister and I find it a plus that the two

Figure 36
North façade of the La Roche-Jeanneret houses nearing completion, late autumn 1924.
(Photograph courtesy of Archives Fondation Le Corbusier.)

houses are built as one. It makes the façade more beautiful. Our house alone would have been small and less interesting."[75]

One should not leave this studied facade without mentioning two interesting examples of Le Corbusier's design intentions. The cantilevered extension on the right side of the Jeanneret house acts as a visual exclamation to halt the eye. Similarly, the small protruding balcony off the La Roche gallery gives visual definition and finality to the other end of the housing complex. This play of one element against another can again be appreciated by comparing the four square windows of the second floor with the adjacent atelier window. Because this atelier window is the main source of light in the north wall, its proportion is greater than its neighboring windows. Thus, Le Corbusier solved both a light and a visual problem by various expressive means, which was distinctive to Le Corbusier's approach to design.

Below this second floor are the long horizontal strip windows interrupted by the regular reinforced concrete structural grid of the columns. Of the effect of these windows on the bedrooms Lotti Jeanneret has said: "All the bedrooms have low and long windows which give a very homely atmosphere."

Commenting upon her husband's bedroom Lotti Jeanneret said:

The room is small but sufficient for a person who only spends his nights there. A couch covered with silver grey velvet, two white chairs, a cupboard for clothes, fastened to the wall. . . . "A cell," said a visitor. "The bedroom of a man with common sense," answered Le Corbusier.

She continued with a description of her own bedroom (Fig. 37):

Further away is my bedroom, a bit more elaborate than the others. Two walls are white, one is burnt umber. Against this wall is a low, large bed covered with velvet in a leopard pattern with white flounces around the sides. Opposite are big cupboards fastened to the wall, stretching from floor to ceiling, painted in light blue, the same as the window sills. . . .[76]

Figure 37
Lotti Jeanneret's
bedroom. (Photograph
courtesy of Kerstin Rääf.)

Figure 38
Temporary lighting in La
Roche's painting gallery,
1925. (Photograph
courtesy of Archives
Fondation Le Corbusier.)

Such simplicity in arrangement and economy of needs and decoration are commonplace today, but one must remember that in 1925 the rich middle class was still thinking in terms of visually complicated and rich interiors on a grand scale. Le Corbusier had clearly begun a reexamination of human needs. He was also deeply committed to the attainment of a visual order, the expression of his conceptual sensibilities.

Le Corbusier treated the Jeanneret house and the domestic portion of the La Roche house in a similar manner. His economy of means and articulation of elements were rigorously controlled to support the conceptual simplicity he sought to express. Overall, the quest for harmony and purity was the ethical and psychological force behind Le Corbusier's work.

There were some technical problems with these houses at Auteuil. The low-pressure hot water boiler in La Roche's house broke down in 1927, 1932, 1934, and again in 1939.[77] After this rather checkered performance Raoul La Roche wrote to Pierre Jeanneret in April 1939:

On the subject of the central heating, I remind you that this would give complete satisfaction, if it were not for the extremely disagreeable noise that it makes and that can be heard throughout almost the entire house. Could not at least a partial solution be found for this question?[78]

Similar technical problems had to be endured by La Roche in relation to electric lighting (Fig. 38). On 18 October 1925 he wrote to Pierre Jeanneret:

I understand perfectly your hesitations about the way you want eventually to provide lighting in my rooms. But until you have found a very good solution, it is essential that at least I see clearly in my house. For more than six months when I come in I am obliged, especially in my painting gallery, to have makeshift lighting. What must the many visitors think about it and what would you have me say to them?[79]

Not the least troublesome was the low thermal insulation inherent to plastered walls consisting of two skins of lightweight cinder blocks, held five centimeters apart, in panels between a post and beam reinforced-concrete framework. As Philipp Speiser, a grand nephew of Raoul La Roche, has written: "The only reason [for La Roche] to leave the house in 1963 was his painful arthritis, which made him unable to live longer in the badly insulated house."[80]

Such specific technical problems, following the traditional procedure of French professional offices, were handled (as indicated in the correspondence) by Pierre Jeanneret, who was Le Corbusier's *chef d'études.* In spite of this arrangement, there can be no doubt but that these problems must have caused Le Corbusier some embarrassment, particularly as he was so fond of using machine-age propaganda.

In the formal solution of the La Roche house and gallery, Le Corbusier tried very hard to realize an architectural synthesis in harmony with the spirit of the modern age.

This second house will be rather like an "architectural promenade." You enter: the architectural spectacle at once is evident, you follow an itinerary and the perspectives develop with great variety. You play with the rush of light which falls on the walls or creates shadows. The bays provide perspectives of the exterior where you find again the architectural unity.[81]

By poising the gallery at first floor level on slab and *piloti* supports Le Corbusier was able to give expression to the plasticity and variety of his formal program (Fig. 39). By emphasizing the unity of curvilinear and rectilinear geometry he could shape the character of his building and exploit the changing light and shade relationships between these idealized forms. In so doing, he realized fully in building form the nature of the Purist language. From his bedroom balcony La Roche could enjoy a daily Purist experience through the spatial exploration of forms in light.

The raised gallery provides a sense of enclosure to the Square du Docteur Blanche and signals the entrance to the La Roche house. The hallway is a spatial experience in itself. From this point onward one is increasingly made aware of the nature of cubic volumes. Visually one is compelled forward from under the entrance balcony into the hallway that opens upward in a burst of light from the large studio window above and behind. This sectional element gives the space—seven and a half meters in height—its effect of light and shade.

Above and to the left an overhanging stair landing dramatically signals the direction of the itinerary (Fig. 40). Rising through this dogleg staircase, one is taken away and then brought back to the central hall space, and on the landing one can pause and observe the play of light on the walls and floor. Such is the intensity of light falling on the Purist volume that Le Corbusier could well have written in 1925 what he wrote thirty-three years later of his pilgrimage chapel at Ronchamp: "The key is light/and light illuminates shapes/and shapes have an emotional power."[82] This principle of light on geometric forms links his early and his late work in direct progression.

Continuing the visual itinerary, one moves forward from the landing to the painting gallery (Fig. 41). Here Le Corbusier's intentions were clear. La Roche's collection specifically from the Parisian school of Cubist and Purist painters gave Le Corbusier, whose own paintings were displayed in the gallery, the unique opportunity to match the significance of this collection in architecture.

Upon entering the painting gallery, one is directed in the spatial progression by the curved wall and ramp (Fig. 42). Le Corbusier relied upon the potency of these poetic elements to indicate the direction of the itinerary wherein one turns back along the length of the gallery as one rises up the ramp along the curving wall to the final destination of the library above.

The poetic elements needed to be highly charged if they were to fulfill their psychological and symbolic functions; in this last idealized gesture Le Corbusier found himself in some difficulty. Visually he re-

Figure 39
Bay view from La
Roche's domestic
balcony toward the
painting gallery. Here Le
Corbusier is expressing
the varied
functional-symbolic
curved and rectilinear
elements, and therefore
the sense of structure is
suppressed. (Photograph
by Russell Walden.)

Figure 40
View from the opposite
side of La Roche's
hallway showing the
first-floor stair landing
and the library above.
(Photograph by Russell
Walden.)

Figure 41
Raoul La Roche seated in his painting gallery among the Cubist paintings of Juan Gris and the sculpture of Jacques Lipchitz. (Photograph courtesy of Thomas Speiser.)

Figure 42
The curved ramp in La Roche's painting gallery. (Photograph by Russell Walden.)

quired a ramp, but the steepness with which it had to rise made it impractical to use, for one cannot really descend the ramp without losing balance or gripping the rail with both hands. Such a problem indicates just how far Le Corbusier was prepared to go to ensure the fulfillment of his philosophical intentions and formal program. In this instance the higher symbolic functions of the program took precedence over more practical considerations.

In preserving the purity of his design concept, Le Corbusier was ruthlessly consistent, fully exposing his idealistic and Rousseauist sympathies. Like all visionaries, Le Corbusier was deeply committed to the preservation of *all* the dimensions of his vision. He could be as interested in details as in the large-scale city plan. In architecture as well as in *urbanisme* Le Corbusier tried to mobilize the idealists in his campaign against the abuses of the established order. Because of his sympathies with the tradition of social thought that stretched back to Rousseau, Le Corbusier was able to fascinate and disturb in a way that few architects in the twentieth century have managed to do.

Le Corbusier sought to bring together spatial, visual, social, and technical elements in his new architecture, and in the Auteuil houses this reintegration was first and most potently demonstrated. On this back-garden site Le Corbusier first crystallized the precise yet dramatic geometrical forms in a Purist spatial synthesis. He "created a building of manifest architectural quality, using the materials of workmen's dwellings."[83] By giving his design intentions precedence over the technical and standardized vocabulary he used, Le Corbusier not only took up a highly individual position but he also exposed his idealistic and philosophical lineage.

Ultimately, however, an architect's work has to be judged by his client, and in this light the final words must be left to Raoul La Roche. I quote *in extenso* his letter of 13 March 1925 to Le Corbusier.

I thank you for the letter which you handed me last night at the moment of the inauguration of my house, 10 Square du Docteur Blanche.

This house gives me great joy and I convey to you my gratitude. You have brought to completion an admirable work which, I am convinced, will mark an epoch in the history of architecture.

Firstly the house contains, at different points of view, innovations which have allowed technical progress but which up until now architects have not thought to use; the success of these innovations will mean that they will be used more and more and the credit is yours for having worked them out.

But what especially moves me are these constant elements which are found in all the great works of architecture, but which one meets so rarely in modern constructions. Your ability to link our epoch to the preceding ones in this way is particularly great. You have "overrun the problem" and made a work of plastic art.

In confiding the construction of my house to you, I knew that you would make a thing of great beauty; my hopes have been more than fulfilled. The relative independence of my life has allowed me to leave you free to work according to your ideas and I can only be well pleased with the result thus obtained.

The price of a work such as this which you have just completed cannot be calculated; if I offer you, as a result, a small supplement in the form of a 5HP Citroën, I shall not feel that I have paid my debt of gratitude toward you. I would rather offer it to you as a souvenir and as a most useful instrument for the work of Paris architects. Will you be so kind as to accept it as such and to let me know what model you prefer.[84]

Surely no client was more pleased with the completion of a modern building.

Finally, I should like to turn to what Le Corbusier thought of the La Roche-Jeanneret houses. It is fortunate that a record was made of an interview with him two months before his death in August 1965. When asked which of his works he regarded as essential and was fondest of, Le Corbusier cited as his first example, "La Maison La Roche. It was a crisis, and it was also an open door . . . a point of departure."[85] It is quite clear from this admission, made as his life was drawing to a close, that Le Corbusier considered the La Roche-Jeanneret houses an important landmark in his career.

Thus, with the completion of these Auteuil houses by March 1925,[86] Le Corbusier's formative development was complete. The Auteuil houses can be regarded as epitomizing his intellectual and spiritual position following World War I. Le Corbusier could now eagerly look forward to giving his next shock to the sensibilities of the architects of Paris. With the 1925 Paris Exposition des Arts Décoratifs just around the corner, and his Pavillon de L'Esprit Nouveau in his mind's eye, Le Corbusier could look down upon Paris from his attic window above the Rue Jacob, and in the spirit of Rastignac, the hero of Balzac's *Le Père Goriot,* he could defiantly exclaim, *"A nous deux maintenant!"*

1 I have taken the date of Jeanneret's arrival in Paris during World War I from the evidence supplied by his Swiss
passport, which was officially stamped by the Prefecture
of Police, Paris, on 29 October 1916. This document gave
Jeanneret a residence permit and stated that his occupation was architect. I am grateful to Brian Brace Taylor for
drawing my attention to Jeanneret's passport, held in
the Archives Fondation Le Corbusier, Paris (hereafter
AFLC).

Jeanneret's passport records the first shift in his professional activities to Paris, though because the Villa
Schwob was under construction he seems to have
commuted between La Chaux-de-Fonds and Paris. This
was definitely brought to a halt with Jeanneret's dismissal as job architect for the Villa late in January 1917. See
Maurice Favre, "Le Corbusier à travers un dossier inédit
et un roman peu connu," in the *Musée Neuchâtelois,* no.
2, 1974, p. 54.

All the French documents supporting this paper have
been translated by my wife, Helen Walden. The German
documents have been translated by Igor Kolodotschko,
and the Swedish article written by Lotti Jeanneret was
translated for me by her daughter Kerstin Rääf, niece of
Le Corbusier.

2 In a letter from Paris to William Ritter of La Chaux-de-
Fonds, dated 26 January 1917 (Archives Bibliothèque
Nationale, Berne), Jeanneret stated that he had moved
into an apartment at 20 Rue Jacob, Paris VIᵉ. The letter
also referred to his provisional installation in an office at
13 Rue de Belzunce, Paris Xᵉ. This office was adjacent to
that of the Société d'Applications du Béton Armé, which
was based at 11 Rue de Belzunce. He used this office
until 1 October 1917, when he moved to 29 bis Rue d'As-
torg, Paris VIIIᵉ.

3 "Embarrassment" denotes Jeanneret's professional dilemma with reference to the cost of the Villa Schwob. On
23 January 1917, a bill of quantities revealed that the
Villa Schwob would cost approximately 100,000 Sw.F.
more than Jeanneret or his client had anticipated. See
Maurice Favre, "Le Corbusier à travers un dossier inédit
et un roman peu connu," pp. 53–55.

4 Le Corbusier, letter from Paris to Monsieur Louis Secretan at La Chaux-de-Fonds, 12 July 1961, sent 27 July
1961. Archives Bibliothèque de La Chaux-de-Fonds, ref.
Af 15.

5 Le Corbusier, *La Ville radieuse,* Boulogne-sur-Seine,
1935. English edition: *The Radiant City,* London, 1967,
p. 12.

Notes

6 Paul Turner, *Catalogue de la bibliothèque de Le Cor-*

busier avant 1930, Fondation Le Corbusier, Paris, 1970, p. 3. Le Corbusier owned Baudelaire's *Les Fleurs du mal* (acquired 1909), his *Modernité et surnaturalisme,* Paris, 1924, and his *La Peinture romantique,* Paris, 1924.

7 Ronald Grimsley, *The Philosophy of Rousseau,* Oxford University Press, 1973.

8 Russell Walden, provisionally entitled "Le Corbusier, Ideals and Realities," Ph.D. dissertation, University of Birmingham.

9 Pierre Hirsch, *attaché de recherches,* Bibliothèque de La Chaux-de-Fonds, in a letter to Russell Walden, 8 November 1973.

10 Turner, *Catalogue,* p. 11. Le Corbusier's copy of the illustrated work of Rousseau was printed in 1851.

11 Ibid., p. 12. Le Corbusier bought the ten volumes of Viollet-le-Duc's *Dictionnaire raisonné de l'architecture française du XIᵉ au XVIᵉ siècle,* Paris, 1854, with his first paycheck from Auguste Perret in August 1908.

12 Ibid., p. 5. Le Corbusier acquired the two volumes of Auguste Choisy's *Histoire de l'architecture* in 1913.

13 Ibid., p. 11.

14 Françoise Choay, *L'Urbanisme: utopies et realités, une anthologie,* Paris, 1965.

15 John Tarn, *Five Per Cent Philanthropy,* Cambridge University Press, 1973, p. 16.

16 Walter Gropius, *The New Architecture and the Bauhaus* (German edition published in 1918), English edition, London, 1935. Paperback edition, 1955, p. 48.

17 Catherine Bauer Wurster, "The Social Front of Modern Architecture in the 1930s," in *Journal of the Society of Architectural Historians,* Yale University Press, March 1965, vol. 24, no. 1, p. 48.

18 Leslie Martin and Lionel March, *Urban Space and Structures,* Cambridge University Press, 1972, pp. 28–54.

19 Jeanneret's dealings with the Société d'Applications du Béton Armé can be verified by correspondence dating from 7 April 1917 to 3 January 1919, AFLC.

20 C. E. Jeanneret, Sketchbook "A2," 1915, AFLC. I am grateful to Silvia Sutton of Boston, Mass., for drawing my attention to this point.

21 Max du Bois, letter from Antibes to Russell Walden, 20 February 1974.

22 C. E. Jeanneret, letter from Paris to Monsieur A. Lavandière, D.P.L.G., in Lausanne, 20 April 1919, AFLC.

23 Turner, *Catalogue,* p. 3. Le Corbusier's copy of Anatole

de Baudot's *L'Architecture: le passé, le présent* was a
1916 edition printed in Paris.

24 Tony Garnier, letter from Saint-Rambert, Rhône, to C. E.
    Jeanneret at La Chaux-de-Fonds, 13 December 1915,
    AFLC.

25 Brian Brace Taylor, *Le Corbusier et Pessac,* Fondation Le
    Corbusier, Paris, 1972, pp. 3–4.

26 Le Corbusier, *L'Art décoratif d'aujourd'hui,* Paris, 1925.
    New edition, Paris, 1966, p. 217.

27 For an explanation of the legal proceedings of the Villa
    Schwob see Maurice Favre, "Le Corbusier à travers un
    dossier inédit et un roman peu connu," pp. 49–59; the
    translation of it appears in this book.

28 C. E. Jeanneret, letter from Paris to Léon Perrin, sculptor,
    at La Chaux-de-Fonds, 12 June 1920, AFLC.

29 C. E. Jeanneret, letter from Paris to Madame Anatole
    Schwob at La Chaux-de-Fonds, 9 October 1920, AFLC.

30 Charles Morice, "Nécessité présente du travail intellec-
    tuel," in the Paris newspaper *L'Homme libre,* 20 De-
    cember 1917, p. 1, AFLC.

31 Amédée Ozenfant was born in 1886 at Saint-Quentin,
    Picardy. Son of a building contractor, he studied ar-
    chitecture at the Ecole des Beaux-Arts and painting at
    the Académie de la Palette, Paris. He founded a patriotic
    journal *L'Elan* in 1915. He was cofounder of Purism and
    L'Esprit Nouveau. Ozenfant's *Mémoires 1886–1962,*
    edited by Katia Granoff, were published posthumously in
    Paris in 1968.

32 Maximilien Gauthier, *Le Corbusier ou l'architecture au
    service de l'homme,* Paris, 1944, p. 40.

33 Raoul Albert La Roche was born 3 February 1889 at
    Basel. Son of a banker, he was educated in Basel, and at
    the Ecole de Commerce of Neuchâtel. He underwent
    training in banking in Basel and Paris, with short periods
    in Berlin and London. He settled in Paris in 1911. Later he
    became head of the foreign section of the Crédit Com-
    mercial de France. He was also President of the Swiss
    Society in Paris. He was a collector of French modern art,
    a client and lifelong friend of Le Corbusier. La Roche
    died two months before Le Corbusier in June 1965. See
    Basler Nachrichten, 17 June 1965, no. 250, for his
    obituary.

34 See *Raoul La Roche (1889–1965),* a commemorative
    brochure by the Fondation Le Corbusier, 23 October
    1970, p. 2.

35 C. E. Jeanneret, letter to Ozenfant, 16 April 1925, AFLC, Dossier Villa La Roche, ref. 506.

36 Ozenfant and Jeanneret, *Après le Cubisme,* Paris, 1918, and *La Peinture moderne,* Paris, 1925.

37 The first Purist art exhibition was held between December 1918 and January 1919 at Germaine Bongard's boutique, later renamed Galerie Thomas. The second took place from 22 January to 5 February 1921 at the Galerie Druet, 20 Rue Royale. See *L'Esprit Nouveau,* no. 7, pp. 807–832.

38 The plans for Amédée Ozenfant's house at 53 Avenue Reille, Paris XIVᵉ, were done in 1922; the construction was completed in 1923.

39 Amédée Ozenfant, *Mémoires 1886–1962,* Paris, 1968, p. 102.

40 Le Corbusier, *Oeuvre complète 1910–29,* 1964 edition, p. 11.

41 Ozenfant and Jeanneret, *Après le Cubisme,* preface.

42 Ozenfant, *Foundations of Modern Art* (French edition 1928), New York, 1952, p. 326.

43 Ozenfant, *Mémoires 1886–1962,* p. 105.

44 Herbert Tint, *France Since 1918,* London, 1970, p. 9.

45 Ezra Pound, *Selected Poems 1908–1959,* London, 1975, p. 101.

46 Pierre Emery, letter from Geneva to Russell Walden, 7 February 1974. "Par contre, il me semble que personne n'a parlé de la portée de l'oeuvre de Cervantès sur L.C. Il disait faire de *Don Quichotte* son livre de chevet. En 1946, ma femme et moi avons relié, en peau poilue de vieille chèvre (c'est lui qui l'avait demandé ainsi) l'édition de jeunesse du *Don Quichotte,* annotée par lui, à laquelle il tenait par-dessus tout et qui était dans un état lamentable."

47 Turner, *Catalogue,* p. 10. In 1919 Jeanneret purchased *Du Côté de chez Swann* (1913) and *A l'Ombre des jeunes filles en fleurs* (1918), the first two books of Marcel Proust's *A la Recherche du temps perdu.*

48 Franz Meyer, "Die Schenkungen Raoul La Roche an das Kunstmuseum," Separatabzug aus dem Jahresbericht 1963 der Offentlichen Kunstsammlung Basel, p. 47.

49 Raoul La Roche, letter to C. E. Jeanneret, 4 November 1923, AFLC. From the sketches of paintings in this letter that La Roche had purchased it is possible to account for the following: *Livre, pipe et verre,* 1918, pencil sketch, 46 x 55 cm.; *Nature morte à la pile d'assiettes et au livre,*

1920, 81 × 100 cm.; *Composition à la guitare et à la lan-terne*, 1920, 81 × 100 cm.; *Nature morte claire*, 1922, 114 × 146 cm.; and *Bouteille de vin rouge*, 1922, 60 × 73 cm.

50 C. E. Jeanneret, letter to La Roche, 22 March 1920, AFLC.

51 The shares were set at 1,000 francs each, but La Roche made four payments of 1,250 francs for his five shares. The first payment was acknowledged by Jeanneret on June 1920 and the second on 13 September 1920, AFLC.

52 La Roche's volumes of *L'Esprit Nouveau* are now in the Kunstmuseum in Basel.

53 Ozenfant, *Mémoires 1886–1962*, p. 117. Daniel-Henry Kahnweiler's Cubist collection of eight hundred paintings and drawings, dated between 1907 and 1914, was confiscated by the French government at the outbreak of war in 1914, because of Kahnweiler's German nationality.

54 Most of Raoul La Roche's art collection was bequeathed to the Kunstmuseum in Basel. A small number of paintings were also given to the Musée d'Art Moderne in Paris and to the Musée des Beaux-Arts in Lyons.

55 Comment recalled by Raoul La Roche in a letter to C. E. Jeanneret, 24 May 1926, AFLC, Dossier Villa La Roche, ref. 506 bis.

56 Ozenfant, *Mémoires 1886–1962*, p. 48.

57 Le Corbusier, *Oeuvre complète 1910–29,* 1964 edition, p. 58. The first sketch design for a villa at the entrance to the Square du Docteur Blanche at Auteuil has been described by the editor, Willy Boesiger, as the "Premier projet de la maison double (La Roche et Albert Jeanneret)." Until Albert Jeanneret married Lotti Rääf in June 1923, such a project was not financially possible for him; therefore, this first project must have been for La Roche himself.

It is interesting to compare this sketch design with the brief given to Jeanneret for Amédée Ozenfant's house at 53 Avenue Reille, Paris XIVᵉ, built 1922–1923. See Ozenfant, *Mémoires 1886–1962*, p. 126.

58 Pierre Emery, letter to Russell Walden, 7 February 1974.

59 Albert Jeanneret (1886–1973) studied the violin at the Royal Conservatory in Berlin and later taught the violin at the Institut de Ribaupierre at Vevey in Switzerland. He was a follower of Emile Jaques-Dalcroze, the master of rhythmic composition. In 1919 Le Corbusier had him come to Paris where he first taught at the Schola Can-

torum, before opening his own school, the French School of Rhythm and Body Education. He wrote twenty-five symphonies for "sound elements." He also founded an orchestra for children whom he enthusiastically introduced to his experiences in sound.

At the beginning of the Second World War Albert Jeanneret returned to Switzerland and settled in the house at Vevey that Le Corbusier had built for his parents.

He composed the "Symphony of Exchanges" for the National Exhibition of 1964 and in 1970 he received the *Prix de la Fondation "Pro Arte"* at Berne.

For his obituary, see *Feuille d'Avis de Vevey*, no. 96, 26 April 1973, p. 14.

60 Lotti Rääf (1887–1973), Swedish journalist, was born in Halmstd, Sweden. After an unhappy first marriage she went to Paris in 1922, where she studied French at the University and started as a pupil of Albert Jeanneret at his Jaques-Dalcroze School of Rhythm in the Rue de Stockholm. They were married in June 1923, and lived at 10 Square du Docteur Blanche at Auteuil, with Lotti Rääf's two daughters, Brita and Kerstin Rääf, from the winter of 1924 until 1938.

This information is from Kerstin Rääf in a letter to Russell Walden, 16 December 1973.

61 Lotti Jeanneret, "Mitt hus i Paris av Le Corbusier," in the Swedish journal *Svenska hem och trädgårdstidningen*, no. 3, 1958, pp. 49–52. This article was sent to me by Kerstin Rääf.

62 C. E. Jeanneret, letter to J. M. Esnault, 29 August 1923, AFLC.

63 C. E. Jeanneret, letter to M. Plousey, 14 August 1923, AFLC, Dossier Villa La Roche, ref. 101.

64 C. E. Jeanneret, letter to J. M. Esnault, 29 August 1923.

65 C. E. Jeanneret, letter to J. M. Esnault, 12 September 1923, AFLC.

66 Raoul La Roche, letter to C. E. Jeanneret, 6 August 1923, AFLC, Dossier Villa La Roche, ref. 0.

67 C. E. Jeanneret, letter to M. Plousey, 14 August 1923, AFLC.

68 C. E. Jeanneret, letter to M. Plousey, 18 September 1923, AFLC, Dossier Villa La Roche, ref. 102.

69 M. Plousey, letter to C. E. Jeanneret, 21 September 1923, AFLC, Dossier Maison Jeanneret-Rääf, ref. 84.

70 C. E. Jeanneret, letter to M. Plousey, 24 October 1923, AFLC, Dossier Maison Jeanneret-Rääf, ref. 89.

71 Le Corbusier, *Oeuvre complète 1910–29,* 1964 edition, p. 60.

72 Raoul La Roche, letter to C. E. Jeanneret, 4 January 1924, AFLC, Dossier Villa La Roche, ref. A and B.

73 Lotti Jeanneret, "Mitt hus i Paris av Le Corbusier," p. 52.

74 Ibid.

75 Kerstin Rääf in a letter to Russell Walden, 22 January 1974.

76 Lotti Jeanneret, "Mitt hus i Paris av Le Corbusier," p. 51.

77 Raoul La Roche, letters to Pierre Jeanneret, AFLC, Dossier Villa La Roche, 27 December 1927, ref. 364; 13 April 1934, ref. 372; 3 January 1939, ref. 391.

78 Raoul La Roche, letter to Pierre Jeanneret, 3 April 1939, AFLC, Dossier Villa La Roche, ref. 72.

79 Raoul La Roche, letter to Pierre Jeanneret, 18 October 1925, AFLC, Dossier Villa.La Roche, ref. 235.

80 Philipp Speiser, letter to Russell Walden, 8 March 1974.

81 Le Corbusier, *Oeuvre complète 1910–29*, 1964 edition, p. 60.

82 Le Corbusier, *The Chapel at Ronchamp*, London, 1957, p. 27.

83 Le Corbusier, *My Work*, London, 1960, p. 68.

84 Raoul La Roche, letter to Charles-Edouard and Pierre Jeanneret, 13 March 1925, AFLC, Dossier Villa La Roche, ref. 13 bis.

85 This interview with Le Corbusier on a record entitled "L'Architecture contemporaine" was produced by Réalisations Sonores Hugues Desalle, Paris. The record bears the date of his death, 27 August 1965.

86 Refer to AFLC, Dossier Villa La Roche, ref. A and B, 4 January 1924—construction commenced; ref. 13 bis, 13 March 1925—construction completed and inauguration. AFLC, Dossier Maison Jeanneret-Rääf, ref. 90, 25 October 1923—construction commenced; ref. 156, 20 February 1925—construction completed.

Brian Brace Taylor

Le Corbusier at Pessac:
Professional and Client Responsibilities

The ultimate basis for judging an architect's worth is the built work rather than the unachieved projects, but the quality of its realization is rarely in the architect's hands alone. In France, the architect of the recent past earned his living from the fees obtained during construction. Since these fees were generally calculated on a rather low percentage of the total costs, it is not surprising that many architects traditionally found other means for augmenting their financial share in a given venture, quite frequently by obtaining a commission from contractors whom they were at liberty to select. Le Corbusier was vehemently outspoken in his condemnation of such practices in France. Nevertheless, these two aspects, direct control over the execution of architectural work and the payment of fees, regularly created delicate situations and occasionally caused bitter arguments between Le Corbusier and his clients.

The history of the achievement of more than sixty housing units at Lège and Pessac (Fig. 43) warrants elucidation in this regard, in part for its typically personal dimensions and also in order to dispel certain misconceptions (sometimes cultivated by Le Corbusier himself) about the role of the local authorities in the Pessac affair.

Utilization of the cement-gun equipment for the construction of dwellings at Lège (Fig. 44) depended upon the calculations of a M. Poncet, the head of Henri Frugès's department of buildings and overseer of the construction site itself. Toward the end of 1924, two months after building at Lège had begun, the foundations of part of the bachelors' dormitory collapsed, and not long after that the upper floors of some of the individual dwellings were found to be defective. The inhabitants were evacuated while repairs were made. In the meantime, Poncet had begun surveying and preparing the site at Pessac, under Frugès's orders. By 1 April 1925, work had advanced on the concrete skeletal structure of houses in a block (Fig. 45) and those in a Z-formation.

Figure 43
General view of the
Quartier Moderne Frugès
at Pessac. (Courtesy of
Archives Fondation Le
Corbusier.)

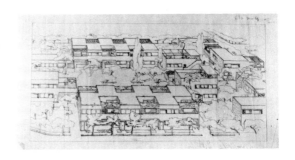

Figure 44
Demonstration of the
cement-gun "gunite"
technique for creating
wall panels. Exposition
des Arts Décoratifs,
Paris, 1925.

Figure 45
The construction site at Pessac, houses 49 to 54, 1925. (Courtesy of Archives Fondation Le Corbusier.)

Poncet's dangerous incompetence both at Lège and at Pessac, compounded by both his and his crew's inexperience in the use of the cement gun, finally induced Le Corbusier to seek his immediate dismissal before construction proceeded any further. He proposed replacing him by M. Summer, who was the Parisian engineer at that moment constructing the Pavillon de l'Esprit Nouveau (also financed in part by Frugès) for Le Corbusier in Paris. Because this would cost more, Frugès was understandably reluctant to comply with the request for a complete change of personnel—Summer was to send his own workmen from Paris to Bordeaux. He agreed to engage Summer for a short period of time—eight months—during which his men would train a local crew in the techniques of concrete construction with the cement gun. As a result Poncet visited the Le Corbusier-Jeanneret *atelier* in Paris, at the architects' request, to discuss the new arrangement. Experiencing the kind of local labor difficulties encountered by most Paris-based firms even today, the Bordelais engineer declared that only he could make the present crew of guniters work and that if Summer and his men arrived on the scene, he and his men would leave the operation altogether.

In the end, he and the others stayed on the site for a period of time after the Italian workers of Summer arrived, but the use of the cement gun was drastically curtailed, and a more conventional system of construction was adopted by the new contractor.[1]

The choice of the cement gun for house construction was a costly and mismanaged venture. A mixture extremely rich in cement content was required, while at the same time it was nearly impossible to obtain a wall of uniform, optimal thickness. Sprayed cement was ill-suited for the creation of thin panels for hollow-wall construction;[2] when this became apparent, Le Corbusier experimented with a kind of pressed-straw insulating material called Solomite, which could be cut into panels of any size, set into the structural frame of a building, and coated with gunite. The Pavillon de l'Esprit Nouveau was built in this way, but the experience seemed not altogether positive, and when Summer took charge of Pessac in June 1925, common concrete block infill was employed instead of gunite panels for the walls. The cement gun served after that for facing the curved wall of the room for wine storage, for garden walls, and for similar minor tasks. The anticipated assets of speed and durability of construction that the cement gun seemed to possess were nullified by an inability to control the efficient and economical use of material.

To this difficulty with the cement gun must be added the more general dilemma that the architects confronted, that of obtaining prefabricated items such as doors, window frames, and traditional solid window blinds (volets), drains, and so on.

In the first place, the correspondence between architect and client demonstrates quite clearly that design barely kept ahead of execution at Pessac; details were often neglected and Frugès was perpetually asking for last-minute directions. Second, manufacturers had to be found who would mass produce, for instance, the window frames of steel, wood, and glass with the peculiar profiles specified by the architects, and as rapidly as possible.[3] Instead of attempting to utilize to the maximum the products already on the market (and preferably at Bordeaux rather than Paris), the designers sought to stimulate the production of prefabricated (as opposed to handmade) elements, while at the same time they were seeking to minimize the cost of the finished houses. The incompatibility of these two objectives raised the construction costs at Pessac immensely.

Finally, the site planning had been improperly executed according to accepted standards (Fig. 46). Faulty surveying and siting of the houses on the terrain, as well as the complete neglect of the capacity of the roads to serve the future dwellings, were partly the responsibility of Poncet, the engineer in charge, and partly that of the architects.

The waste of the client's time, effort, and money in rectifying these errors could have been avoided through more preliminary studies. As it happened, the design of a particular house type was often barely ahead of actual construction, which may explain why the house's integration into an overall system of utilities and drainage was neglected until afterward (Fig. 47). Some houses (duplex "skyscraper" types) had to be eliminated altogether when it was discovered that the foundations would extend on to the existing road, but this was of lesser gravity in terms of the success of the endeavor than the ultimate realization by client and architects that the constructed houses would not be accepted by the authorities. The reason? Neither the existing laws regulating the provision of public services for new developments nor acceptable standards of engineering for these services had been respected.

Contrary to later accounts given by Le Corbusier of what happened at Pessac, the administrative entanglements that blocked the provision of water—and hence the immediate sale of the completed houses—occurred because first, the existing laws that defined procedures for obtaining official sanction to build a housing development had not been adhered to at the outset, and second, the engineering of roads, drainage, and utility installations was nonexistent or poorly done. The houses had, in fact, come into being before a complete file had been deposited at the town hall and a building permit duly obtained.

In the first instance, it seems that neither Frugès nor his architects bothered to become fully informed on the regulations then in force throughout France concerning new expansion in cities. According to the "Law of 14 March 1919, supplemented by the Law of 19 July 1924 concerning the plans for extension and arrangement of cities," a plan must be submitted specifying all characteristics of the road network to be constructed and a program describing all hygienic facilities, includ-

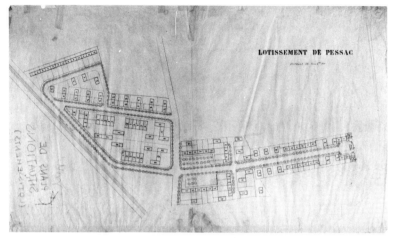

Figure 46
Site plan for the original project of 130 dwellings near Pessac, 1924. Only the sector between the road and the railway was executed. (Courtesy of Archives Fondation Le Corbusier.)

Figure 47
The construction site of the Quartier Moderne Frugès in 1925, with the promotional signboard that was "later removed at the request of the local authority." Note the conventional cement block infill that replaced the gunite panels. (Courtesy of Archives Fondation Le Corbusier.)

ing the distribution of drinking water. The law required that a pro-
moter deposit these plans and specifications for the development with
the municipality for approval before any kind of advertising could be
undertaken. Proper installations for the supply and drainage of water
were to be executed at the developer's expense. Le Corbusier, Frugès,
and even the mayor's assistant at Pessac, who issued a provisional
building permit in October 1924,[4] seem to have been negligent in
seeing that their actions conformed strictly to the legal constraints
then in force. When the Prefect of the Department inquired of the
mayor in March 1926 whether a permit had been issued for the
Quartier Moderne Frugès, the reply was at first (and correctly) ''no,''
and then a rather equivocal followup explanation of ''only in principle,'' since Frugès had failed to complete the necessary documents as
requested. Subsequently, for many months Frugès attempted to obtain an authorization to sell his houses and regain some of his large
capital investment, while the municipality waited for him to rectify the
deficiencies so the development could be approved according to the
legislation.

Official attention was first drawn to the neighborhood when the
communal and cantonal road surveyors submitted a report in September 1925 on current road conditions. The nearly nonexistent street
and drainage system—the builders had been employing the drains of
the nearby railway line—became public knowledge. Frugès urged his
architects, with little apparent success, to study and to send him new
plans and sections for all utility installations. The sanitation engineer
for the city of Bordeaux visited the site and advised that all installations should follow the public right of way rather than cross the gardens between the two blocks of houses, as the architects had
suggested; in this way problems of riparian rights and accessibility for
repairs could be simplified. As an indication that local opinion was in
some measure favorable toward the Quartier Moderne Frugès, the

client reported that M. Hugon, the engineer for the city of Bordeaux, visited the site to offer his counsel, claiming to have read books by Le Corbusier and to be enthusiastic about the principles behind their enterprise. In an attempt to comply with the regulations, Frugès delegated an engineer from his sugar refinery, René Vrinat, to draw up the necessary specifications and plans of streets, which were submitted in April 1926.[5]

In attempts to extricate his client from a difficult situation at Pessac, Le Corbusier became an advocate of the rightness of their cause among higher authorities in the bureaucratic structure in Paris. His overtures to government officials on behalf of Frugès, particularly to the Minister of Public Works at the time, Anatole de Monzie,[6] were completely apolitical; it was administrative maneuvering through personal contacts in the central government, first to obtain a special exemption from a 15 percent tax on the assessed value of the Quartier Moderne Frugès, and then, at the time of the official inauguration of the development, to obtain a less strict application of the Law of 19 July 1924.[7] The case in point is typical of Le Corbusier's tendency to gravitate toward sources of power, financial, political, or simply bureaucratic, in order to realize his projects.

The Prefect of the Department issued a decree of approval in November 1926 authorizing the sale of houses in the Quartier on condition that Frugès construct the streets, installations, and drainage at his own expense; this was all that the municipal authorities were demanding. He was given until I January 1928 to complete the work. In February 1927 Frugès obtained an estimate of 100,000 francs from the Société Lyonnaise des Eaux, a private water company that had the sole distribution franchise for water and electricity to the town of Pessac. Finding this cost for installation much too high, he sought other solutions, such as drilling a well and constructing a watertower. But nothing could be done until the streets of the Quartier were approved as part of the Commune's street system, which occurred only in October 1927. The price and guarantees asked by the Société Lyonnaise were still too high for Frugès. The dwellings remained vacant and without water for another full year. The municipal council of Pessac was apparently to appoint a commission of inquiry in November 1928 to sample public opinion concerning the Quartier Moderne Frugès and to file a report as to whether people in the town felt favorably disposed toward the empty development. In the meantime, Le Corbusier had arranged for Louis Loucheur, the new Minister of Labor, to visit the Quartier and to explain to the populace the possible ways by which the sale of the dwellings might be facilitated by the recently passed housing legislation that carried his name.

A financial appraisal of the Pessac endeavor is crucial to an assessment of the economic character and social impact of what was finally achieved. Questions of cost—never a minor consideration for the person who pays to build or simply to purchase a house—also shed light on the personal aspirations and beliefs of those who collaborated at Pessac. Within a broader framework, the social consequences of this effort to build minimum-standard, low-cost workers' dwellings can be evaluated according to the economic criteria of a free market.

On the level of personal and professional behavior in the venture at Pessac, the calculation (and payment) of the architects' fees became a psychological as well as an economic issue.[8] Le Corbusier had persuaded his client to invest in machinery for a system of construction not yet tested by himself, while offering at the same time to reduce his fees to one-half of the official rate, which was then 6 percent of the construction cost. The anticipated costs in 1924 for building one of Le Corbusier's house types at Lège came to an exceptionally low sum of 10,000 francs. After the important visit of the architects to Bordeaux during the construction of the Maison du Tonkin (the first trial house, July 1924) (Fig. 48), Le Corbusier sought to confirm by letter that his

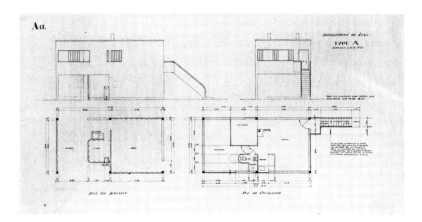

Figure 48
Plan and photograph of
the experimental
modulor house-type
Maison du Tonkin in
Bordeaux. (Courtesy of
Archives Fondation Le
Corbusier.)

fees would be based upon 3 percent of the construction costs, which, for the newly projected 135 houses at Pessac, would amount to 3 percent of 1,350,000 francs. When Frugès replied that his understanding had been a fixed sum of 350 francs per dwelling, Le Corbusier admitted having suggested this figure as a base by which one could move toward a more "modern and equitable" means for remunerating the architect. He proposed a system of rewarding the architect's personal ingenuity in discovering inexpensive solutions by paying him 10 percent of the client's profit when the dwellings were sold. The architect explained that the current system of a direct percentage of the building costs hardly encouraged members of the profession to search for economical designs.

Frugès, recently confronted with a costly outlay for the new machines and cautious about just how inexpensive the constructions would turn out to be, countered Le Corbusier's percentage proposal with the following formula: he would pay the architect at a fixed rate per cubic meter of each dwelling constructed according to his plans. In addition he suggested that the site planning, roads, utilities and services, and so on should be calculated according to a rate per square meter. The client, always anxious to establish a fixed rather than a sliding scale by which to calculate the architects' fees, found the design of houses by modular units a convenient (and rather novel) means of determining Le Corbusier's remuneration. Once this was established, Frugès indicated he would be willing to discuss a percentage on top of the fixed base. He seems to have had his way, for notes of an agreement (reached in a personal meeting on 5 February 1925) indicate that 100 francs per module measuring five meters by five meters by three meters was the payment adopted.

One year later, Le Corbusier once more raised the issue of fees, as houses at Pessac were nearing completion. Among other things he outlined the extent to which prevailing economic conditions had affected the enterprise. (It should be remembered that the cement gun had long since been abandoned in favor of more conventional techniques and that Frugès was then engaged in trying to repair the gross deficiencies of site planning.) Le Corbusier pointed out that, according to the 1925 agreement, his fees would amount to only 31,000 francs for the total of 310 half modules constructed at Bordeaux, Lège, and Pessac. Having previously agreed to reduce his fees by one-half, and then in a second instance to a fixed sum per module, the architect now attempted to raise his own present financial bond by means of various arguments. He noted that a simple draftsman, earning 1,000 francs a month during the preceding two years in which 112 plans were sent to Frugès, would have cost 24,000 francs; supposing the architects' contribution to be at least equal to that amount, the fees could be considered to be 48,000 francs. Then reverting to his original proposal of 3 percent of the total construction costs, Le Corbusier noted that the average cost per house for the fifty-three houses then under construction was 30,000 francs, yielding 47,700 francs in architects' fees. This sum, when divided by the number of modules, as Frugès wished (there were 272 at Pessac), showed an average cost of 175 francs per module, or an increase of 75 percent over the rate agreed upon in 1925. Le Corbusier maintained that, in the light of the considerable monetary instability of the period (the franc had fluctuated between 65 and 132 per pound sterling during the fiscal year 1924 to 1925) and the rising cost of living, a revision of his fees was desirable. In short, he was feeling the strain of engaging his staff over many months on work at Pessac for a fixed sum, when costs were rising across the board: "All our effort is directed towards this goal: to make savings for you . . . to get the maximum with a minimum; to establish standards is an overwhelming, exhausting problem. It's necessary to reconsider repeatedly the dimensions."[9]

He concluded by proposing to Frugès a rate of 175 francs per module and 200 francs per house for site planning, or, 3 percent of the total cost of construction. Frugès agreed that the project itself and the role of the architects had become more complicated than previously anticipated and that their fees should be modified; nonetheless, he declared himself on the verge of stopping all construction completely until some of the houses could be sold.

This discussion is, on the one hand, quite typical of the financial burdens of an entire project that a *private* client is compelled to shoulder alone even when he considers his efforts to be in the public interest, and on the other hand, it demonstrates the perennial difficulties that the architect encounters in placing a monetary value on his contribution—and then obtaining his remuneration. Celebrated architects with clients devoted to their cause are obviously no exception.

Although construction costs in France did not rise more than 2 percent from November 1923 to November 1925, the cost of dwellings in the Quartier Moderne Frugès increased by three or four times the original price envisaged in order to attract a working-class population. Part of this rise at Pessac was the result of adopting more elaborate house types—units comprising five and six modules (bays) instead of only two or three. The Type A of two full bays constructed in Bordeaux cost 12,000 francs in 1924, or 6,000 francs per module. When the houses in the Quartier Moderne Frugès were completed, the average construction cost was 40,000 francs, the price per module ranging from 7,000 to 15,000 francs. These figures, supplied by Frugès, included only materials and labor, *not* the land, site preparation, paying off of material, interest on capital, and general costs and fees. Six months later, in March 1927, Frugès sent a breakdown of the total costs for each house type: the least expensive were those in a block (nos. 49–54) (Fig. 49), valued at 51,300 francs; the individual pavilions (nos. 14 and 37) had cost 72,000 and 74,500 francs respectively. These prices did not include the average of 2,000 francs per dwelling that the water company demanded. By way of contrast, one finds minimum-standard Ribot Law dwellings costing 30,000 to 35,000 francs during the same period. As a result, Le Corbusier's dwellings were quite out of the market for which they were originally intended.

To what factors can one ascribe this failure to remain within the price range of working-class housing? The disparity between their intentions—"to achieve the maximum with the minimum"—and the final product resides in both the nature of the house types themselves, which would not be considered minimal, and in the actual processes of production, in Paris, Bordeaux, and elsewhere. The choice of the cement gun turned out to be a poor one, as did the choice of the first supervising engineer. The savings obtained by changing to more con-ventional techniques and materials were not sufficient to counterbal-ance the costs arising from, first, Le Corbusier's insistence upon a contractor and laborers from Paris to execute his designs, second, the primitive and hasty attempts to obtain prefabricated building ele-ments from industries not yet equipped to offer these at a reasonable price, and third, the repair, tardy execution, and private maintenance of roads and utility systems. The dishonesty or occasional bankruptcy of local contractors precipitated delays and higher costs, as did the architects' inattention and slowness in providing the necessary plans sufficiently in advance of actual construction. Time and cost would have been minimized with an efficient, "taylorized" system of plan-ning or industrialization of the construction site, neither of which existed.

Publicity to attract buyers for the houses was prohibited by law until the development was approved by the municipality.[10] Before this ap-proval was given, the Mayor of Pessac suggested on one occasion to Frugès that the French Ministry of War might be interested in purchas-ing the houses in order to offer free lodging to underpaid army officers and their families. Well before the streets of the Quartier were ever incorporated into the communal system as required, Frugès engaged in 1926 a Paris-based real estate firm, Bernheim, at Le Corbusier's insistence, to promote the sale of houses (which were still without water) on the open market. At the time there was hopeful expectation that the administrative difficulties would be settled rather quickly. Le Corbusier sought and obtained from the German planner Werner Hegemann copies of brochures containing the by-laws of different garden city associations, including Hampstead Garden Suburb in England, Washington Highlands in Milwaukee, Wisconsin, and others in Berlin, all of which he forwarded to Frugès as model *cahiers de charges*.

The Quartier Moderne Frugès gained the attention of several professionals—in 1926 the Dane, Steen Eiler Rasmussen, visited, and, according to Frugès, "a German whose name I don't know" came (we know today this was Walter Gropius), Robertson and Yerbury were there in 1927. Visitors had "first moments of customary stupefaction on seeing Pessac for the first time, then passed successively through periods of curiosity, attraction, and finally enthusiasm." But in spite of this notoriety, the sales agent was unable to proceed with publicity on a local or regional basis until September 1927.

A number of criticisms came from the general public to the sales office on the site, once advertising began; Frugès transmitted these to the architects; however, no sales and only two leases were concluded during the first year. Principal criticisms by visitors of the interior planning of the houses included the disconcerting necessity of entering many of the houses through the kitchen or service areas (Fig. 50) ("this annoys their little bourgeois pride," observed Frugès); the absence of vestibules; the smallness of the kitchens and the storerooms; the absence of cupboards; and the narrowness of the staircases when

Brian Brace Taylor   178

Figure 49
The attached houses in a block, numbers 49–54, were the least expensive at the Quartier
Moderne Frugès. (Courtesy of Archives Fondation Le Corbusier.)

Figure 50
The floor plans of the
attached houses in a
block, numbers 49–54, at
the Quartier Moderne
Frugès. (Courtesy of
Archives Fondation Le
Corbusier.)

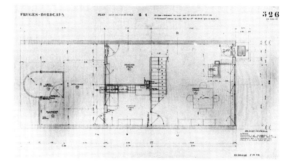

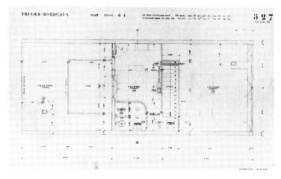

it came to moving furniture. House number 14 (Fig. 51), with living quarters on a single level and shelter or *atelier* below, was the most popular with the public, most certainly because it had a large garden and was detached from other dwellings.

As Frugès pointed out to his architects for future reference, the amount of habitable space was extremely limited in relation to the construction cost for this type. The dimensions of the communal room and the bedrooms seemed satisfactory to nearly everyone, which was a significant reaction giving reasonable validity to Le Corbusier's choice of dimensions, after many years of research and experimentation. Finally, concerning the form of the houses, Frugès reported this from his conversations:

Contrary to what one might think, the architectural form only intervenes negatively for a small percentage of people. However, another important element in the lack of sales is that, given the distance from Bordeaux, people would like to be alone in the middle of their garden and I think it will be difficult to sell the villas which touch one another.[11]

It seems, in fact, that the high prices of the dwellings and the lack of an assured water supply were the chief obstacles to their sale.

The passage of the Loucheur Law in 1928 opened a new possibility for populating the neighborhood, for Frugès to extricate himself financially, and even for building on Sectors A and B as originally envisaged, but with a new developer. According to Le Corbusier, the law would permit Frugès to set up a low-cost housing corporation, exempt from a number of taxes, and to which the state would guarantee the mortgage of eventual buyers.[12] Persons taking advantage of this law would purchase the property outright but not the house itself, being required to pay only annually on the mortgage. Le Corbusier was at the time in personal contact with Loucheur and arranged for him to visit Bordeaux and the Quartier Moderne Frugès at the beginning of

Figure 51
The individual detached house, number 14, was the most expensive at the Quartier
Moderne Frugès. (Courtesy of Archives Fondation le Corbusier.)

1929, at which time the architect himself would give a lecture, sponsored by a national reform group, the *Redressement français,* to explain and promote his model.

Notwithstanding this concerted effort, the houses remained without inhabitants for many months; understandably, some of the first to come were members of the bourgeoisie from Bordeaux, looking for a second, country house.[13] The Loucheur Law did eventually aid some low-income families to move into the Quartier, although they did not actually become owners of the houses nor did they maintain them in good repair. The incentive of personal possession was missing, and the condition of the dwellings, that had stood unused for several years, was hardly encouraging.

1   This sequence of events, which proved critical to completion of the project, is significant for two reasons: first, the inability of the architects to control the quality of execution, and second, the magnitude of the endeavor as a whole. Le Corbusier and Pierre Jeanneret had visited Clermont-Ferrand, where the Michelin company, already possessor of a vast industrial apparatus, had undertaken the building of housing on an industrialized basis for their workers. The company was able to assure qualified technical supervision and the necessary labor force on the scale required for the operation to be a real test of industrialized processes. Frugès was not able to undertake an operation on a similar scale at Pessac, nor were the architects capable of assuming direction of the building site while residing in Paris.

2   The Ingersoll-Rand company, which marketed the cement gun in France, had publicized the utility of the method for house construction in regions susceptible to earthquakes such as southern California. The sprayed cement process was also widely used in mining operations to coat the walls of tunnels.

3   The window frame fabricated by Decourt and Company was already found to be defective one year after construction. A letter from Frugès (22 January 1927) explained that moisture entered around the windows because of poor drainage from the window sill Le Corbusier had designed, and the cement joining the metal frames to the concrete structural frame acted as a sponge.

4   The Mayor of Pessac, Cordier, in a letter to Henri Frugès, 28 October 1924, Municipal Archives, Pessac.

5   Henri Frugès, letter to Le Corbusier and Pierre Jeanneret, 26 January 1926, Archives Fondation Le Corbusier (hereafter AFLC)."The streets are laid out and to have pavements, straight roads, etc. completely transforms the ensemble. . . .''

6   Anatole de Monzie was the ex-husband of one of the clients for the Villa Stein-de Monzie in Garches, 1926.

7   Not *all* of the maneuvering at the time of the inauguration was without political overtones: "The Mayor of Pessac has made known his great regret that he could not be with us on the 13th [the day of the dedication ceremonies]. . . . Furthermore, given the persons which we shall have with us, I see difficulty in inviting the Mayor of Bordeaux. He will find himself in direct contact with some of his most ardent political enemies and I ask myself, moreover, if in inviting him, we will not be running up against a refusal, and this is what we wish to avoid.''

Notes

Frugès, letter to Le Corbusier and Pierre Jeanneret, 31 May 1926, AFLC.

8 The confrontation between Le Corbusier and Henri Frugès over the question of fees (and publicity for the two parties concerned) is immensely interesting psychologically—often amusing, but it cannot be treated in detail here. In summary, first, Frugès claims credit for discovering Le Corbusier in 1923, an architect without reputation, resources, and so on, and launching him on his architectural career. Second, Le Corbusier sends back newspaper clippings dating from 1922 to prove that he was already celebrated, and adds that, furthermore, the publicity surrounding the Quartier Moderne Frugès is going to profit Frugès's sugar business more than anything else. Third, Frugès replies that the publicity is all bad because of the failure to obtain the authorization to sell the houses, due to the architects' negligence. The two men were each overburdened by their different affairs at this moment; Frugès was to suffer a nervous breakdown in 1929 and be compelled to give up his professional life in France for a life of farming in Tunisia. Le Corbusier's letter of 4 October 1926, however, gives a moving account of how he viewed his struggle as an artist and individual; and the truly high esteem in which Le Corbusier held Frugès is best seen in a letter of 10 February 1931, reproduced in the French edition of my catalogue *Le Corbusier et Pessac, 1914–28,* Paris, 1972.

9 Le Corbusier, letter to Frugès, 19 February 1926, AFLC.

10 Frugès was ordered to take down the signs he had posted for publicity reasons.

11 Frugès, letter to Le Corbusier and Pierre Jeanneret, 28 October 1928, AFLC.

12 Le Corbusier, letter to Frugès, 29 November 1928, AFLC. Nonetheless, Le Corbusier strongly recommended to Frugès not to make contact directly with the Minister, since it would be extremely dangerous for Frugès if his own financial troubles, caused by the Quartier Moderne Frugès, were known to Loucheur; the latter could be accused of having saved someone, thereby creating a scandal. Only the *positive* aspects of Frugès's efforts to achieve the model housing should be known.

13 A number of the earliest tenants of the Quartier formed a kind of association (*syndicat*), and in a letter from their spokesman to Le Corbusier we gain an insight into prevailing popular attitudes toward the newly acquired houses. The description of the transformations already

Brian Brace Taylor   184

accomplished, or envisaged, underline the fact that people considered the houses to be unfinished, in the sense of awaiting personalization.

Knowing the great interest which you have in the Quartier Moderne de Monteuil (Frugès) in Pessac, I think that you would be happy to learn that the purchasers of Frugès's houses are following your conceptions. Some of them have made real wonders of interior and exterior decoration.

Two types on the Avenue Frugès in particular are remarkable: one of them has its entire base and the interior of the court in pale blue with a large frieze representing branches and flowers of wistaria, and the upper carries the name "Villa Gae." The second house with façade opposite the one mentioned above is painted in buttercup yellow with trim in white-silver . . . it is also very cute.

My neighbors, owners like myself of a "skyscraper," ask me to advise them in their exterior decoration of the façades. I would very much like to give them a model but not my own advice because I am not competent.

I would appreciate it if you would be so kind as to give me a small model of a decoration for the façade of the "skyscraper" as we are presently inspired only by our individual tastes, and furthermore the Quartier would be truly beautiful.

Gabriel, letter to Le Corbusier, 21 May 1931, AFLC.

Charles Jencks

**Le Corbusier on the Tightrope of
Functionalism**

By the late twenties, Le Corbusier had pushed himself into a difficult position. Like Mies van der Rohe, Walter Gropius, and Bruno Taut, he had seen his early functionalist position outflanked on the left: by the upcoming technocrats, by communist designers such as Hannes Meyer, by materialists, and by the creative youth. All these people could be called the "Young Turks" because they were about to over-throw (or so they hoped) the immediate generation before them—Le Corbusier and the "pioneers of modern architecture"—in short, the "Old Turks." Furthermore, a functionalist style was now in existence whose very banality, yet closeness to Purism, threatened Le Corbusier's message, if not existence (Figs. 52, 53). Houses were now built like "soap boxes"[1] and the Germans, Czechs, Poles, and Russians were throwing up thousands of "inhuman" *existenzminimum*, that is minimum houses that were, according to Le Corbusier, like "cages" or "prisons."[2]

The difficulty was that several years earlier he had proclaimed slogans which led directly to this reductive functionalism. "The vacuum period of architecture," "man is a geometric animal," "a city built for speed is built for success" and so forth. Any number of such catchwords could be adduced to show that Le Corbusier was himself, in part, a reductive functionalist. So he felt a double problem. How could he extract himself from a previous position without entirely reversing fields? The document where he wrestles with this dilemma is "Défense de l'architecture" (1929), a not altogether edifying document even if it is passionate, persuasive, and in its own way quite beautiful. Before I attempt a paraphrase, I will rehearse Le Corbusier's arguments concerning functionalism, because around this broad notion crystalized many of his cherished values.

Figure 52
Pessac, the four-storied "skyscrapers," as Le Corbusier called them, were also known negatively as "the sugar cubes," because the patron who commissioned them made his millions from sugar. The area was also seen as a Sultan's district, a harem, and less gloriously as a Moroccan settlement. Very *Sachlich,* these buildings could be seen the way Le Corbusier characterized the *Existenzminimum.* (Photograph by F. Yerbury, 1925. Courtesy of Architectural Association.)

Figure 53
Interior of Raoul La Roche's bedroom, La Roche-Jeanneret houses, Auteuil, 1925. (Photograph courtesy of Architectural Association.)

Reductive Functionalism

In justifying his kind of Purist architecture, he touched on most of the ways functionalism had been considered up to that time—first, reductive functionalism, the idea (starting with Socrates but proclaimed by the communist designers in Russia and Germany) that utility leads to beauty. Those supporting *Sachlichkeit*, the dry and objective, would do away with "beauty" and simply say "utility is enough," or "utility and social concerns are so important that they render aesthetics and questions of the spirit irrelevant." Hans Schmidt and Mart Stam, who edited *ABC—Beitrage Zum Bauen (Contributions toward Building)*, published a characteristic polemic called "ABC Demands the Dictatorship of the Machine."[3] This editorial of 1928 typically sets the machine and industrial economy in opposition to "morality and aesthetics" and to Le Corbusier's notion of an ideal aesthetic and spiritual language based on geometry. Soon thereafter, in typical dialectical manner, Le Corbusier grasps the terms of his adversaries' arguments and demands the "dictatorship of plans." If nothing else this answer is more humanistic than the initial formulation because it implies leadership by experts and values rather than impersonal necessity.

In any case, the major reductive argument was put forward by Hannes Meyer when he took over the Bauhaus in 1928. It is this polemic, accompanied by the attack of the Czech Teige on the Mundaneum, which Le Corbusier sought to refute in his 1929 "Defense of Architecture." Meyer places *building* (democratically not capitalized) in opposition to *Architecture.*

building
all the things in this world are a product of the formula: (function times economy).
all these things are, therefore, not works of art: all art is composition and, hence, is unsuited to achieve goals.
all life is function and is therefore unartistic.
the idea of the "composition of a harbour" is hilarious!

but how is a town plan designed? or a plan of a dwelling? composition or function? art or life????
building is a biological process, building is not an aesthetic process. [4]

Extreme and polarized as this argument is, Le Corbusier had himself used similar terms previously.

Architecture is stifled by custom.
The "Styles" are a lie. . . .
Machinery contains in itself the factor of economy, which makes for selection.
The house is a machine for living in. . . .
Standards are a matter of logic, analysis and minute study: they are based on a problem which has been well "stated." . . .
Industry, overwhelming us like a flood which rolls on towards its destined end, has furnished us with new tools adapted to this new epoch, animated by the new spirit.
Economic law unavoidably governs our acts and our thoughts. [5]

These quotes, taken from *Towards a New Architecture* (1923), show that Le Corbusier was using reductive arguments when it suited him, the very ones that his Marxist adversaries used. (He was later to add *biology* and *life* to his arsenal, perhaps in response to Meyer.)

His reductive functionalism could be summarized in the following way: the designer must state the problem to be solved, if he is to create standards, or prototype designs meant for mass production. He must design from the inside plan and section to the outside skin and volume of the building. Form is organic in the sense that it stems from function, even if it is not determined by function.

A good designer, like Auguste Choisy, will show the section on the elevation and use materials in a straightforward way according to their inherent logic. (At this point Le Corbusier most obviously slips, unconsciously, into convention, custom, "style" and hence "lie," since Choisy's method of design and drawing was as arbitrary as any other. Science itself cannot escape convention, a point Le Corbusier did not recognize.

A good culture will throw away the outdated tool, the old technologies, and be true to the "spirit of the age"—that curious demiurge which is half technical progress and half cultural sensibility. Useless consumer goods, decorative objects such as paperweights in the shape of snarling, bronze lions, should be thrown out in favor of useful, *sachlich* objects like rubber boots and camping equipment (Figs. 54, 55). Then the economy of conspicuous consumption and waste will be redirected to more humane goals.

Spiritual Functionalism

Le Corbusier always went beyond these reductive positions, as is well known, in a kind of dualistic argument.[6] As soon as he said that architecture must spring from prosaic requirements, he would state that it must go beyond these. Indeed his attitude toward the prosaic was that of the Cubists and Surrealists, a very ambiguous position, which tried to make a "heroism of everyday life," or at least something beautiful and striking out of banal objects and functions. From the poetry of mundane objects to the celebration of crass objects, the urinal, is a small step that Duchamp and Le Corbusier made along with so many other artists (Fig. 56). It can lead to a sophisticated taste, an inverted snobbery, and, much against the wishes of Madame Le Corbusier, a bidet placed right next to the bed (which she covered with a tea cosy).

This love of the prosaic was, however, overlaid with something approaching classical, architectural taste.

The purpose of construction is TO MAKE THINGS HOLD TOGETHER; of architecture TO MOVE US. . . .
Architecture, pure creation of the mind.
Profile and contour are the touchstone of the Architect.
Here he reveals himself as artist or mere engineer. . . .
Geometry is the language of man. . . .[7]

Here, in condensed form, we see in which ways Architecture was

Figure 54
"Useless consumer goods." Le Corbusier's caption: "Waste! I am not outraged because such things are bought. But I am deeply distressed to see Authority remaining indifferent in the face of such sacrilege: the time lost in manufacturing these tomfooleries! A healthy, aware, strong nation ought to say: enough!" (Source: Le Corbusier, *The Radiant City*, p. 94.)

Figure 55
"Useful consumer goods." Le Corbusier's caption: "Proof that a healthy turn of mind could lead us towards a general renewal of our material and spiritual economic systems. Try to work out the consequences: such an attitude could be far-reaching and pull us out of the hole we are in." (Source: Le Corbusier *The Radiant City*, p. 95.) The emphasis on a nation's health, guided by some Authority, which is left unclear, characterizes Le Corbusier's classical notion of culture. *Authority* meant, perhaps, three different things: a modern Colbert, "The Minister of Public Works," or "The Regulator."

more than building, form than function. It was a plastic phenomenon that engaged the spirit because of visual matters, particularly those which had been composed according to right angles and regulating lines. In other words, Le Corbusier's idea of the spiritual and social values in architecture is *perilously close to being reductive toward aesthetic concerns*. He did reiterate that one should create "the spirit of living in mass-production houses"[8] and therefore did bring up the important notion of ideology and way of life, but he never could generalize these notions to include much beyond his own particular ideology and life style. Like so many architects of his generation, he thought his way of life was both universal and, paradoxically, unacceptable to the masses. The way he came to this contradictory conclusion was through the idea of a universal, geometric language and the notion of the *Zeitgeist*.

He looked at periods of history, mostly the classical epochs, and found their hidden geometric order, which only the enlightened few could see. Thus, by 1925, he could propound the unlikely proposition that "culture is an orthogonal state of mind"[9] and that periods which lacked a right-angled brain were uncivilized.[10] The leading architect was then, like the Marxist prophet, to act as the midwife of history and ease the birth pangs of the inevitable, tending now, because of industrialization, toward geometric forms.[11] In short, a civilized, square-headed babe had been conceived, so the perspicacious architect should claim paternity. No wonder, when the French Communist Party asked Le Corbusier to join them, "I told them it was they who ought to join me."[12] His *Zeitgeist* was just as voluntaristic as theirs; in both cases one received moral credit for marching with the inevitable course of history.

Thus in yet another crucial sense Le Corbusier was like the Marxists he was counterattacking. While their specific, spiritual goals differed (geometry versus equality), they would spring from and be driven by

Figure 56
Bathroom, Villa Savoye, 1928–1931, opens off a bedroom and makes a Purist still-life from prosaic objects—the bathtub, wash basin, bidet, radiator, toilet, and light fixture—all unified by tiles and white paint. (Photograph by Charles Jencks.)

Figure 57
A Woman Lying with Curtains, 1930. Strong, bold curves of plump women fascinated Le Corbusier at this time. (Photograph courtesy of Heidi Weber.)

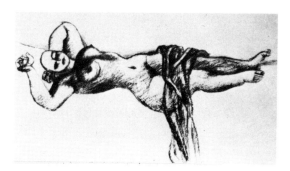

a material base (industry versus class struggle), which was deter-
ministic (or, of course, "almost so," "in the last analysis"). The am-
biguity on this last point was always present in Le Corbusier's writing.
An article he wrote for Americans in 1929, attacking Beaux-Arts ideology, was entitled "Architecture, the Expression of the Materials and
Methods of Our Times."[13] This reiterates his basic point of several
years earlier: "I have said that the technical consideration comes first
before everything and is its condition, that it carries within it unavoid-
able plastic consequences, and that it leads sometimes to radical
aesthetic transformations."[14]

But, as always, there is a basic counterstatement emphasizing freedom of the creative will above this technical determinism. Insofar as
there is a resolution of this dualism, it comes when natural evolution
and enlightened states of mind happily intersect: "A system of
thought is imbued with life only when there exists a balance between
the results of evolution and the spiritual direction of its progress."[15]

When does this occur? When "geometry is supreme. Precision is
everywhere. The right angle prevails. . . ." Unfortunately then, this po-
tentially fruitful dualism is cut short as both goals evolve toward the
superior right angle. Is it any surprise that Le Corbusier the artist
started introducing curvilinear forms into his painting (Fig. 57) at the
very point Le Corbusier the architect told him this was inferior? The
dialectical relationship between necessity and consciousness was asserting itself in action at the very time it was being denied in theory.

A final point should be made about the way Le Corbusier extends
functionalism, because it still causes confusion today. Reyner
Banham, a neofunctionalist, ends *Theory and Design in the First
Machine Age* with a curious misunderstanding. He contends that
technology and industry lead toward "an unhaltable trend to constantly accelerating change" and that architects such as Le Corbusier
tried to stop this process by enforcing certain norms or perfected

standards. This is probably true enough, but then the reason for this is carefully overlooked.

Whether or not the enforcement of norms and types by such a conscious manoeuvre would be good for the human race, is a problem that does not concern the present study. Nor was it a question that was entertained by theorists and designers of the First Machine Age.[16]

But this is not true of the main protagonists of the twenties. It is hard to read Gropius, Le Corbusier, or even Mies without coming across some emphasis on human values set against technical evolution. "Défense de l'architecture" is a case in point. The arguments vary from moment to moment—"harmony, perfection, community," and so on—but there is always a goal in mind, independent of technology. Nonetheless, functionalism is still such an emotionally charged concept that otherwise scrupulous critics and architects seem to lose their customary detachment when discussing it and characterize the adversary in most uncharitable terms.

A Speculative Soliloquy

Le Corbusier is not above this in his 1929 "Défense." In a footnote introduction to its republication in 1933, he sets the warlike tone, the metaphorical terms in which the battle will be fought:

Through its enormous production, Germany occupied the architectural field. The foundation of CIAM at la Sarraz in 1928 had been the occasion of a violent conflict: the Germans attacked many houses which were called "modern." I carried on a combat in which what was at stake was a coherent line of conduct, a line which could lead the congress to useful tasks. Our road was blocked by the catch phrase "poets, utopians. . . ."[17]

The rest of the introduction builds up the militaristic rhetoric—"clap of thunder, *volte-face*, treason?"—until the reader is somewhat ready to surrender to Le Corbusier's sweet reasonableness: "I have persisted in this single declaration: 'I am an architect and urbanist.' Such is my profession of faith. The word is in the plans. The plan is dictator: the technique of modern times and the lyricism of the eternal human heart." In fact the bellicose tone should warn us that the "enemy" will be treated as such and that, as in war, arguments will be used to win a position already determined beforehand, not to lead off in a new, or unknown, direction.

In summarizing this article I will use a method of speculative soliloquy, a dramatic paraphrase, which is not exactly fair to Le Corbusier's intentions, but which has the virtue of being able to introduce an imaginary self-doubt. There is no accepted scholarly convention for probing possible motives and revealing what is called iconology, the hidden symbols and symptoms of an artist or era. The virtue of speculative soliloquy is that it uses the conventions of drama to raise points which could not otherwise be raised as forcefully and allows them to be criticized as well. Thus the aside (placed italicized here in parentheses) comments like the actor's conscience, or *alter ego*, on his explicit speech (the actual statements from the article are in quotation marks, the rest is paraphrase). The soliloquy thus becomes a new text parallel to the original, one that perhaps Le Corbusier might have whispered to his wife in bed, were he of that disposition. No doubt this parallel text is no substitute for the original and should not be read as if it were what Le Corbusier wrote: it is more what he did not completely mean to write, but rather betrayed. The parallel text:

"My Dear Teige,"
Your *Neue Sachlichkeit* substitutes "construction" for "architecture" and "life" for "art" and tries to be objective—just as I did in 1921. But whereas when I do it that's all right, because I go beyond "objectivity" and "zero," when you do it that's mere fashion, and you remain at zero.

(Well, of course it's more complex than this because you are a poet in spite of your supposed objectivity. I'm a clever person and can

second-guess your objective line—it's really fashion and poetry, both denied because of Marxist dogma. Pity.)

"With you, it (your *Sachlichkeit*) is a case of being a dilettante of a new romanticism. *(That will put Teige in his place.)* With the other materialists, Hannes Meyer and his gang, "it is a police measure" to coerce the masses. *(What about my own police tactics? "Economic law unavoidably governs our acts." Am I guilty of this? Yes.)*

"If you adopt the attitude of a leader of the people, perhaps you have reason to accept these measures of martial law." *(There, that perhaps acknowledges my strong-arm tactics and the fact that I too lead the masses.)* "I intend to remain in my state of anarchy (with respect to your police measures) and to pursue from day to day the passionate search for harmony." *(Harmony? I've never valued domestic peace or tranquillity. It's the harmony of the Parthenon that I love, something really quite terrifying, a gesture of perfection thrown at a hostile universe. People won't want my sort of harmony, it's too heroic, austere, and cosmic. Well then, I'll give them the harmony of explicit organization and order. The geometry, my dictator, will keep their lives in order. Now I'll throw a little semantic paradox at those functionalists.)*

"I will tell you now, without further delay, that in my opinion, the aesthetic is a fundamental human function." *(It's on a par with prosaic, physiological functions. But there is a grave problem with functionalizing things of the spirit such as aesthetics—it makes them utilitarian, turns them into commodities, gives them an exchange value, makes them—gasp!—expendable! Good God, this trick of logic has actually lost me the whole argument, I hope no one notices!)*

"And I will add that it (the aesthetic) surpasses, in strength and in the way in which it guides our lives, all those benefits which are brought by progress." *(There, I'm having it both ways, just in*

Charles Jencks 198

time!) "Man is a brain and a heart, reason and passion." *(Having set up this dualistic paradox, I'll now be brilliant and solve it with . . . unity!)* The reasoned search for solutions leads to competition, which leads to perfection; and perfection is an aesthetic notion, as mathematicians know. Q.E.D. Functionalism pursued passionately equals beauty. *(There's trouble, I'm almost* Sachlich, *I must attack Hannes Meyer.)*

"Architecture is a phenomenon of creation, resulting from an ordering process. Whoever says 'to order' says 'to compose.' " *(Now on to attack the technical progressivists—a Reyner Banham to come.)* Man remains the same in spite of technical evolution and new tools, because he has the same spiritual needs. Peasants have this universal passion, this sentiment, just as you functionalists have need of "spiritual nourishment." *(There! Human values transcend technology! Just to make sure there's no misunderstanding, I'll underline the point with my own work.)*

"A machine for living . . . I immediately pose this question—'for living how?' And I pose nothing but the question of quality. I am not able to find it resolved except in 'composition.' " *(Good God! What an admission on my part! To me a way of life, the spirit of man, the social wishes and daily life can . . . almost . . . be reduced to composition, geometry. If only there were a believable social and political philosophy, then I could go beyond visual matters, organizational problems. Alas.)*

Architecture is a plastic event, forms seen in light, forms generated by plan and section. The way in which objects are "architectured" is what counts, and this is done visually by proportion. Obviously you functionalists must agree with me, because you really can't believe a mere collection of useful objects makes the good house. Otherwise you'd have to believe the best house would belong to a millionaire. *(So much for those Marxists, they're hoist by their own materialist petard. The argument is getting rather dirty,* n'est-ce pas? *Well, that's war. They treat me this way, making my arguments appear ridiculous by taking them to absurd conclusions. An eye for an eye.)*

Now for your doctrine, which is of course old and academic, that the "useful is beautiful." This is absurd, as the following story will show.

A German functionalist in my office was stuffing papers into a beautiful wire mesh basket, until all of a sudden it collapsed into an ungeometric shape.

"That's hideous," said Roth.

"Excuse me," I replied, "this basket now contains much more than it did before; it is much more useful, so according to your principles it must be more beautiful. . . . (Thus I showed) the function *beauty* is independent of the function *utility*; they are two separate things. What is displeasing to the mind is waste; for wastefulness is ugly; it is because of this that utility is pleasing to us. But the useful is not the beautiful." *(There, I've clinched the argument, except for the social problem. I'll go halfway with them, socialization plus "captains of industry," a mixed economy. That's a mixture, like beauty and utility, two things which I hope don't mix me up—as they've done in the past.)*

We must give the masses what they really need—"a theme for the socialization of the present epoch. But should we implicate architecture in this matter completely and totally? No!" *(I'm an architect, no one's going to make a politician of me.)* Besides, look at me, I've led a life of hardship without material comforts—but I've enjoyed it. Why? Because of my overwhelming creativity. *(My penance. Oh how I wish there were a viable political philosophy. Mies, Gropius, the other idealists, we're all trapped in the sterile polarization between communists and fascists.)* Utilitarian objects are "ephemeral," spiritual ones are "permanent."

Now for my Mundaneum project, which sparked off the attacks on me as a bourgeois formalist because it resembled the form of an ancient pyramid (Fig. 58). Well, listen, you functionalists, I discovered architectural laws deriving from techniques and, in 1925, excluded decoration and formalism from my Pavillon de L'Esprit Nouveau. I transgressed academic rules and "it cost me dearly." *(I'm Sachlich too, I'm no toady of the ruling taste, the bourgeoisie! They call me bourgeois . . . what nerve! I may work for the captains of industry, but I try to revolutionize their taste, never follow it. Stupid, irrelevant Marxists— they never try to reach the real audience, whereas I write manifestoes to the . . . bankers, telling them they are producing the new beauty. My manifestoes reach everybody—thirteen printings of Vers in four years. . . .)* Look here, on the League of Nations project, on the design of the façades I "spent precisely three hours!" And these façades were technically determined by the plans and sections. And in Prague I proposed the title "Techniques are themselves the foundation of Lyricism." And . . . *(Methinks I doth protest too much. I'm almost saying form follows function. I've almost capitulated to the enemy!)*

Well, the Mundaneum is a "sacrarium" dedicated to ideas and great men, geniuses who have "overturned the world." You see it is ideas, idealism, not material things which rule the world and "come to the rescue of the masses." *(The ideas, ideology of Marxism, not dialectical materialism.)*

"You say: 'The need poses the programme: the factory, the station; no longer churches, palaces, country houses. At this moment nothing succeeds in architecture except what is dictated by social and economic need.' I have never thought or written anything else," and last year I refused to build a church. *(Now I'm really in deep water. There are all my villas for the rich, Ronchamp to come and, besides, bourgeois society is still very much with us. Therefore churches, palaces, and country houses will go on being commissioned. But I don't want to face this ugly truth, I'll be a social utopian and design*

Figure 58
The Mundaneum, world museum, 1929, in the shape of a spiral pyramid, classifies all
cultural growth in a linear manner. This scheme later gave way to the museum of
unlimited growth, which was all on the same level. (Source: *Oeuvre complète 1910–29,*
p. 193.)

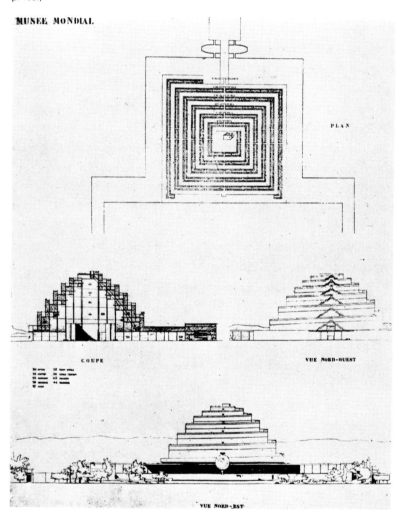

the ville radieuse *as if we had a new ecomonic order. In any case, what the devil is a "social and economic need"? How possibly can we determine this objectively, beyond all time and cultural history? I will invent my fiction, the universal man, who looks, acts, and feels, I am pleased to say, rather like me.)*

The Mundaneum is a "BUILDING OF INTERNATIONAL ASSOCIA-TIONS," and it responds to world needs and crises. What could be more reasonable and "*Sachlich* . . . technical, sociological, and economic, and not at all academic"?

The pyramidal form, which you attack, was determined by function and the World City, of which it is a part, by axes of view and regulating lines. The regulating lines, which you find abominable, are cruel verifiers and therefore very *sachlich*—which is why I'm attacked by both bohemians and engineers. *(Here go the bullets flying over my head, from opposite directions, proving, doesn't it, that I occupy the true center, midway between reason and passion.)* Cubic forms are not academic; "on the contrary, they are accepted as being the expression of Contemporary Architecture." *(Could it be that some day in the future, contemporary architecture will itself become conventional and academic? I hope not—that would mean my approach was not universal???)*

"But if a precise and indisputable function demands that the accommodation should be arranged on a spiral axis, should I refuse to accept the architectural consequences of this function on the grounds that it is only the cube that is contemporary?" *(Oh dear, form follows function again. Not only that, but a single form is determined by function. I am a reductive functionalist who believes, in spite of my above disclaimers, in a materialist universe demanding specific outcomes. There's no choice, spirit, aesthetics involved. Alas, how confused I am. I oscillate back and forth between materialism and idealism like a yo-yo. Maybe there's a fault in reality, maybe philosophers will never be able to solve this perennial problem. Help! I'm desperate, I'll try an absurdity, with an utterly straight face.)*

"I simply remark that the dictionary of architecture has always been limited to the forms of Euclidean geometry, and that the cube, the sphere, the cylinder, the pyramid, and the cone are the only architectural words in our possession" (Fig. 59). *(Can I really get away with this? What about my own Art Nouveau past and the architectural words I tried to evolve from nature? (Fig. 60) Luckily few people know this past . . . but can they forget the Gothic, Baroque, Rococo, Expressionism, the organic? I'd better be frank about my love affair with geometry. It is personal, a matter of choice, not universal after all.)*

"Nature penetrates our heroic and geometric gesture. You know that I love this attitude: to be able, in one's own house, to reign supreme within a magisterial geometry; to rest one's eyes, out there, on the charm of nature, in which we have imperishable roots." *(Yes, I remember as a small boy in La Chaux-de-Fonds the beauty of nature and geometry juxtaposed. It formed and changed me; architecture can . . . shape man!)*

"Listen, Teige, let us speak seriously. I believe that this man (experiencing my Mundaneum) will be transformed: he will be relieved, during his ascent, of all the petty preoccupations of his daily life, he will have stopped worrying about his digestion or the crease in his trousers. . . . Teige, you are a poet. . . ." *(The poets are the unacknowledged legislators of mankind, and the force of my poetry and love for geometry can change people's lives. This is my final idealism, which unifies all the polarities, because now spiritual consciousness and material function are inextricably linked in a kind of architectural determinism. But, can architecture really shape man??? It certainly changed me.)*

At the end of this confessional paraphrase, it is only right that Le Cor-

Figure 59
"Euclidean geometry" at Chandigarh, 1956, in the General Assembly and High Courts
(background). The perfect solids are here distorted and smashed into each other to give
more emphasis to each architectural "word." (Photograph by Romi Koshla.)

Figure 60
Elevations of the Fallet House, La Chaux-de-Fonds, 1905. (Photograph by Charles Jencks.)

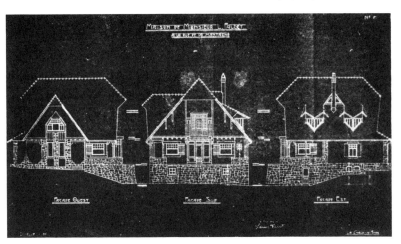

busier has the final word, especially since it mediates extremes and puts the author in the place he finds most congenial, the center of a raging storm: "I know that in the present notes, my words will be used against me, put into inverted commas, by the academics here, by the *avant-garde* there."

Ways of life

There is no need to criticize detailed points in conclusion, since the parenthetical self-doubt, which I have invented, acts in this way. Rather, I should like to draw some general conclusions about Le Corbusier's position, which he shared with other architects of his age, the "pioneers" of the modern movement.[18]

On a positive level, functionalism served to deepen these architects' social and technical commitment. No matter how naive subsequent detractors such as Jane Jacobs and Buckminster Fuller may find it, the new concern for these requirements was deeper than that of the previous Beaux-Arts architects. But more important than this was the seriousness and symbolic depth to which this commitment led. No matter what we may think in retrospect of the wisdom of their particular functionalism, I think we have to admit that it gave them a credibility and purpose, perceivable in their buildings, which other architects lacked. This symbolic potency is, as the architects knew, the *sine qua non* to any great art; to do justice to their building we must continually remember that they intended to produce great, symbolic art. This entails, inevitably, a kind of *curtailed* functionalism. These architects were really only interested in social tasks and technology in so far as they could be encapsulated formally and given seminal expression. They never followed functions too far, with the legitimate fear that they would be led out of architecture into sociology, politics, or engineering, while they saw their role as that of the cultural demiurge or prophet. Of course one can criticize this role and the way civilization turns leaders into prophets, but it is precisely on this level and not on the strictly technical or social level that appropriate criticism should be made. As for the content of their curtailed functionalism it was often bad sociology, hopeless politics, and leaking, flat roofs.

On a negative level, I think it fair to say that the debate on functionalism was disastrously *simplistic,* as is too much architectural polemic. The argument was carried on with the acrimony of warfare, with Hannes Meyer launching his salvo as he took control of the Bauhaus, and Le Corbusier, like Trotsky in the Civil War, shooting off his reply from a train crossing Russia. Hence the epithets and carica-tures, the systematic misunderstanding, and childish arguments that confused reductive functionalism with the spiritual, social, and aesthe-tic tasks that might generate form. To Le Corbusier's credit, he an-swered Meyer's oversimplification with a more developed dualism, but not a great deal of credit is due since this position is the norm of classical architects and can be found stated by Viollet-le-Duc, Choisy, Antonio Gaudi, as well as most academics.

In any case, the pioneers and especially Le Corbusier never came to terms with the cultural nature of functions, the way they are always seen through a specific historical *code* and are never transparent, ob-vious, or universal (in the sense of being identical across cultures). The way the pioneers talk about functions implies a certainty, preci-sion, and singularity—as if all chairs should be a certain distance off the floor, made from steel tube, and so forth—but even with so de-terministic a thing as a ramjet engine, there are, apparently, 25,344 different conceivable possibilities.[19]

The attempt to produce a single *homme type* with his universal needs should be seen as an unstated desire to increase productive efficiency and the repressed wish to lead civilization in a single direc-tion, the dream of a prophet, not a sophisticated functionalist. Functions, in so far as they can be specified, fit loosely, change, and can be realized only if people understand the codes on which they are based. Nor were the pioneers aware of the *arbitrary* nature of the architectural sign, the way form and function are, in most cases, united by convention, feedback, and usage. Nor were they aware of the *plurality* of signs, or the most important sign—that of a "way of life" (except fleetingly, as in the above polemic where it is quickly reduced to "composition").

When one analyses what Le Corbusier meant by social and spiritual life it often becomes, ultimately, visual expression as an analogue of civilized life (Parthenon = Periclean Age and Greek Democracy; Gothic cathedrals = medieval communes; and so on). And while this view may serve as a convenient shorthand and be acceptable on TV, for example, as in Kenneth Clark's account of Civilization,[20] it is too crude for the design of cities. Most cities of the world have institutionalized styles of life—high, formal, bureaucratic, and informal—which make nonsense of anything so inclusive as a single style or *Zeitgeist.* In Chinese culture as much as Western, this stylistic pluralism has undergone incessant internal borrowing and transformation quite at odds with, say, social and economic transformation, so there is no *direct* way to read off the spiritual health of an epoch from the life of forms. Even if there are some connections, they remain historically specific both to place and art form; they do not have anything important to do with "culture [as] an orthogonal state of mind." We are still in a period when prophets of architecture wish to convince us of comparable ennobling thoughts, when the politics of architecture and art are still conducted as stampedes toward the inevitable, and the *Crisis in Architecture* has to be read with *The Decline of the West,* while we rush gleefully over the cliff into future devolution.

To criticize Le Corbusier in this way may sound unfair, for how could he, any more than the other pioneers who were committed to the *Zeitgeist,* have a notion of these views, of semiotics, *avant la lettre?* He was working with bad theory, and anyone can be unfortunate enough to be born at the wrong time. He should not bear personal responsibility for questionable ideas that were widely held at the time. True. And yet he, more than the others, publicized these universalist and determinist notions; he built architecture to celebrate them and believed in them strongly, which meant he was often the most intolerant of local customs, traditions, and all the social usage he had no use for (those he would condemn with "the styles are a lie").

To probe the question of personal responsibility and apportion praise and blame inevitably leads me, no matter how amateur my skill at psychoanalysis, to the imputation of motives—stated or repressed. I think the above soliloquy makes it clear that Le Corbusier repressed his own reductive functionalism while adopting the very terms and underlying mentality of those he was attacking. For my part, he gave too much to his opponents when he functionalized aesthetics and introduced such ideas as the "dictatorship of plans." This is nearly utilitarianism; the only way to avoid it would have been to insist on the ultimate validity of certain goals, irrespective of their function. Le Corbusier did this when he insisted on beauty independent of utility. But, and this represents another repression, he could not face the basic issue he raised, the "quality of life," because this would have led him directly to politics, ideology, and social reality.

Once there he would have had to confront the "churches, palaces, country houses," or at the very least the continuation of bourgeois functions which he, along with the Marxists, wished into oblivion. It is one thing for him to be a social utopian, but quite another for him to believe this utopia had arrived. How else can we interpret his agreement with the Marxists: "At this moment nothing succeeds in architecture except what is dictated by social and economic need"? Presumably he had mass housing in mind, something neither the masses nor the leaders in 1929 were actually prepared to build on the scale he envisaged.

His buildings are ideal models for a possible future social and ethical order. In this sense they are positively dialectical, but at the same time they imply a leap of history over several stages. They do not use enough of the existing architectural codes to persuade and reeducate the people who will (mis)use them. They are best inhabited by the elite and other architects who may have a partial grasp of his codes. This is how I understand his continual remarks predicting the failures of his buildings. "The right state of mind doesn't exist"; "We must create the mass-production spirit . . . the spirit of living in mass-production houses."[21] Indeed, but ". . . the one person who won't want to live in them *is the worker!* He has not been educated, he is not ready to live in such apartments. . . . We have an immense programme of social education before us."[22] The implication in this, however well-intentioned, is still coercive, the "police measures" of teaching the masses what is good for them, as conceived by an elite.

In *Précisions,* Le Corbusier illustrated this idea of elitism with "The Cultural Pyramid" (Fig. 61).

The workers, whom I have often admired for their clairvoyant mind, have been horrified by my houses: They called them "boxes." And for the moment we build "cheap houses" under the Loucheur Law, combining several frameworks, only for the aristocrats and intellectuals. One cannot burn the stages of history: you see the pyramid by which I express the hierarchic phenomenon of society; one cannot change it in spite of all the revolutions. The base of the pyramid, the good people, is, for the moment, suffocated by the most characteristic romanticisms; its notion of quality is established on the forms of luxury of generations before 1900. It is for them that we still make enormous sideboards in the Henri II Style and cupboards with huge mirrors. The mastodons of old cannot even enter through the doors of our houses. There we have a cell in human scale which still awaits the right inhabitants.[23]

This quote is notable for its confusion and suppression: "the good

Figure 61
"The Cultural Pyramid," drawing from Le Corbusier's *Précisions,* Paris, 1930, p. 96.

people" are not actually drawn into the diagram, Le Corbusier could not bring himself to being this explicit about elitism. He mentions twice that "for the moment" these good people are not ready for his housing, but then implies they never will be, because the pyramid never changes "in spite of all the revolutions."

Of course, Le Corbusier would never agree with the view which I have extracted from his work and if confronted with it would immediately insist on creative freedom. After all, he said when confronted with the changes made in his Pessac housing, "Life is right, the architect wrong," suggesting a reversal of the values I have imputed to him. And any number of counter instances could be added. His dualism, it is true, mediates the view which I have built up, but it does not essentially alter it for the workers who have to live in his buildings. Perhaps, had he lived in a different age, he would have come up with a definition of architecture more in keeping with his momentary insights on life—"architecture is the masterly, correct, and magnificent play of meanings seen through social conventions." One thing is certain—he never stopped moving and absorbing new ideas.

1 Le Corbusier, "If I Had to Teach You Architecture," in *Royal Architectural Institute of Canada,* February 1943, p. 17. (Reprinted from *Focus,* London.)

2 Le Corbusier, *La Ville radieuse,* Boulogne-sur-Seine, 1935, translated into English as *The Radiant City,* New York, 1967, p. 53.

3 *ABC—Beitrage Zum Bauen,* vol. 2, no. 4, Basel; the quote is translated in Ulrich Conrads, *Programmes and Manifestoes on 20th-century Architecture,* London, 1970, p. 115.

4 Quoted at the beginning of Le Corbusier's "Défense de l'architecture," and is reproduced in more extensive form in Conrads, *Programmes,* p. 117.

5 Le Corbusier, *Towards a New Architecture,* London edition, 1946, pp. 82, 100, 122, 210.

6 For dualism see, for instance, my "Charles Jeanneret-Le Corbusier," in *Modern Movements in Architecture,* London, 1973, pp. 141–165.

7 Le Corbusier, *Towards a New Architecture,* pp. 23, 186, 68.

8 Ibid., p. 210.

9 Le Corbusier, *The City of Tomorrow,* London, 1971 edition, p. 43. This was originally published as *Urbanisme,* Paris, 1925.

10 See Le Corbusier, *The City of Tomorrow,* p. 43. Barbarism versus Culture—Le Corbusier's sketch shows Notre Dame made by the barbaric Goths versus a wing of the Louvre made by the classicist Perrault. "One is a symbol of perfection, the other of effort only. One enchants us, the other startles us. . . . I do not speak disparagingly of the Cathedral. It merely occurred at its right date. . . ." The tautology of the last sentence shows to what amazing idiocy one could be led by the *Zeitgeist.*

11 Le Corbusier, *The City of Tomorrow,* 1929 edition, pp. 33–53.

12 Quoted from Geoffrey Hellman profile, "From Within to Without," in *The New Yorker* Magazine, 26 April, 3 May 1947.

13 Le Corbusier, "Architecture, the Expression of the Materials and Methods of Our Times," *The Architectural Record,* August 1929, pp. 123–128.

14 This quote is from a 1926 article translated in Reyner Banham, *Theory and Design in the First Machine Age,* London, 1960, p. 258.

15 Le Corbusier, "Architecture," p. 125.

16 Banham, *Theory and Design in the First Machine Age,* p. 329.

17 "Défense de l'architecture" originally appeared in *Stavba,* a Czech journal, in 1929 and was republished in *L'Architecture d'Aujourd'hui,* no. 10, 1933. All the quota-

Notes

tions are taken from a translation that Alan Colquhoun
prepared for me. I am grateful for his aid on this paper,
but for the opinions expressed here he is in no way responsible.

18 See for instance Nikolaus Pevsner, *Pioneers of the
    Modern Movement (from William Morris to Walter
    Gropius),* London, 1936.
19 "Forecasting the Future," *Science Journal,* London, Oc-
    tober 1967.
20 The documentary series based on Kenneth Clark, *Civili-
    sation. A Personal View,* London, 1969.
21 Le Corbusier, *Towards a New Architecture,* 1929 edition,
    p. 211.
22 Le Corbusier, *The Radiant City,* p. 146.
23 Le Corbusier, *Précisions,* Paris, 1960 edition, pp. 95, 97.

Part Three

**The Urban Utopia:
Le Corbusier's Ideas, Plans, and Politics**

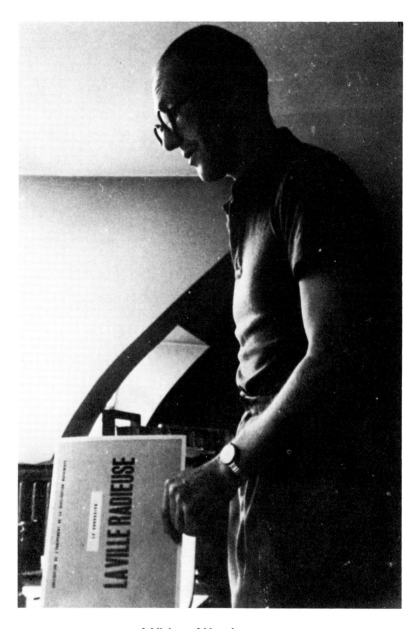

Anthony Sutcliffe

**A Vision of Utopia:
Optimistic Foundations of Le Corbusier's**
Doctrine d'urbanisme

The key to city planning is a man, who may be brutalized by the disorganization of the urban phenomenon, but who may be showered with well-being if care is taken to cater for specifically human needs.[1]

Studies that investigate details of Le Corbusier's work or brief periods in his development are essential to supersede the broad generalizations which until recently have often passed as informed comment, but there is a certain incongruity in thus approaching a man whose ecstatic vision and frequently intuitive thinking rid him of all fear of the broad generalization in his ceaseless quest for absolute truth.

Nowhere is this breadth of view more apparent than in his system of urban and regional planning, which he began as early as the 1920s to describe as a "doctrine" based on a number of "certainties" derived from observation.[2] At the very least, this system constituted a universal program of environmental improvement; at most, it was a formula for world social reform.

Clearly, the choice of any conscious reform program rests on certain assumptions about the nature of the world and the process of change. In Le Corbusier's case, his very distinctive world view does much to account for the individuality of his specific planning proposals. First of all, however, some outline of his doctrine must be provided.

Le Corbusier published his first major study of town planning in 1925, at the age of thirty-eight.[3] It related principally to his plans for an idealized city, the Contemporary City for Three Million Inhabitants, which he had exhibited in 1922 and which had established his reputation as an architect-planner. At this early stage he was concerned almost exclusively with the problems and opportunities of Paris—the large, capital city which he had directly experienced since his permanent settlement in 1917. In the years to come the scope of his planning precepts broadened considerably, but they already exhibited that potent combination of four major modes of planning, which gave his ideas their universal, comprehensive quality.

The first mode, aesthetics, sprang from his ambition to create physical environments that would be visually and emotionally satisfying through the application of the principles of harmony and balance. This motivation had emerged from his early training in art and architecture, and he had been aware of it a least since his early twenties.[4]

The second mode, habitation, originated in his interest in mass housing from the early part of World War I, when he had soon recognized that it was not enough to design merely comfortable homes, but that access, surroundings, amenities, and location were also crucial to the creation of a satisfactory living environment.[5]

A third mode, efficiency, stemmed from his recognition that a better urban environment depended on the economic prosperity of cities. This aspect of his thinking did not emerge fully until the early 1920s, but from then on he devoted much attention to transport, industrial location, design of commercial areas, and other aspects of urban efficiency.[6]

The fourth mode, social reform, was the most enigmatic but also the most important, since it underpinned the other three and provided a major inspiration for Le Corbusier's ceaseless propagandizing. It was founded on his confidence that the reform of the physical environment would be a major, if not *the* major contribution to the creation of an ideal society that would provide all the prerequisites of complete happiness and fulfillment. The origins of this conviction are difficult to establish in time, but it certainly informed Le Corbusier's reactions to the Ema charterhouse in 1907 and 1911:

So here I was again at the Ema charterhouse [in 1911]. I did some sketches this time, and I understood things better too. . . . My first impression of the charterhouse was one of harmony, but not until later did the essential, profound lesson of the place sink in on me—that here the equation which it was the task of human wit to solve, the reconciliation of "individual" on the one hand and "collectivity" on the other, lay resolved. But in the very solution of this problem another equally decisive lesson was to be learned: that to solve a large proportion of human problems you need locations and accommodation. And that means architecture and town planning. The Ema charterhouse was a location, and the accommodation was there, arranged in the finest architectural biology. The Ema charterhouse is an organism. The term *organism* had been born in my mind.[7]

Although these four modes had considerable scope for further development, Le Corbusier's practical approach to planning in the mid-1920s was based on a total acceptance of the big city as the home of the greatest technical efficiency, and as the provider of substantial social and cultural benefits to its residents. To resolve the apparent contradiction between the needs of this hive of activity and the maintenance of a pleasant living environment, he put forward the novel solution that has become his most important single contribution to twentieth-century planning practice—to increase the height of both commercial and residential buildings so that they could occupy only a small fraction of the ground without reducing overall densities.

Like most of Le Corbusier's planning proposals, this procedure had more than purely utilitarian value. At the very least it assured adequate space for recreation while maintaining sufficient densities to support an active community life; on a more spiritual level it constituted both a reintegration of nature with the city and a full acceptance of the potential of modern technology. The huge increment of space also allowed him to provide express roads, totally segregated from pedestrians, to permit full freedom of movement for motor traffic, which he saw as a prerequisite of economic success. At the same time, high densities would increase land values, thus attracting the investment needed to carry out the development.

Although Le Corbusier vigorously defended his 1925 program into the late 1920s, he admitted later that certain difficulties still needed to be resolved.[8] The product of his rethinking was the Radiant City, another idealized form, which appeared first as an exhibit in 1930 and was explained and justified a few years later by a second major book, *La Ville radieuse.* The Radiant City marked a further step toward the great metropolis as the ideal form of human habitation. Residential densities were increased to a maximum of 1000 persons per hectare from about three hundred persons per hectare in the Contemporary City,[9] and a linear plan was adopted to allow unhindered growth of the built-up area. These arrangements, combined with a more efficient road network and an integrated underground railway, allowed Le Corbusier to dispense with the so-called garden cities beyond a rigid green belt to which the vast majority of the Contemporary City's residents had been relegated. He was obviously delighted with this solution, which not only allowed him to renew his condemnation of existing low-density suburbs, but provided him with sufficient population densities to prevent his huge areas of open land from becoming "dead spaces." He also maintained that this living arrangement was perfectly suited to the needs of "machine-age man" and was based on a careful definition of his functions.[10] Yet, ironically enough, the year of the Radiant City marked the first step in Le Corbusier's partial reaction against the great city.

The development of the Radiant City began with Le Corbusier's acceptance in 1930 of an invitation to design a farm and cooperative center for a peasant organization in the Sarthe. Typically, Le Corbusier chose to set this problem in a broader context, that of the reorganization of the rural environment. He viewed this reform in terms of extending the benefits of planned urban life to the countryside, a process that, as he soon recognized, would blur the distinction between town and country.

At about the same time, Le Corbusier began to have doubts about the desirability of really large cities. His first misgivings seem to have occurred in 1929 during his gloomy stay in Buenos Aires, and he began to be depressed by the ceaseless struggle between individuals, which he regarded as a feature of Parisian life.[11] The mass urban unemployment of the great depression probably reinforced this mood and led him to the conclusion that the relative social attraction of the big cities had inflated their populations far above the level of economic efficiency, producing mass poverty among the unskilled and unqualified elements.

As early as February 1931, he was suggesting that Paris's population figure of three million, which he had used as a yardstick in the 1920s, was too large, and by 1934 he was advocating one million as the city's optimum population.[12] This implied a major redistribution of population, which was to be permitted by the new system of regional planning that Le Corbusier developed between the early 1930s and the mid-1940s and that he set out in a further major book in 1944—*The Three Human Establishments.*[13]

Under this new arrangement, a substantial (but unspecified) proportion of the population would remain on the land in planned agricultural communities and "radiant farms" with adequate social and cultural facilities. Manufacturing would be carried on, not in special quarters of the big city as it had in both the Contemporary City and the Radiant City, but in "linear industrial cities" stretched along major long-distance communications routes, grouping both factories and high-density workers' housing. Only a minority would live in the business and administrative centers located at the focal points of the communications routes, which Le Corbusier now categorized as "concentric cities of exchange," but these towns would gain in efficiency by being allowed to concentrate on tertiary activities. To offset the possible disadvantages of dispersal, he placed strong emphasis on efficient regional and interregional communications.

Having thus derived what amounted to a system of world planning, Le Corbusier scarcely modified its essentials between the end of the Second World War and his death. He continued, however, to perfect detailed aspects of his theory. The most important of these developments were his formulas for a hierarchy of urban roads (*la règle des sept voies*) and for the planning of urban sectors, both of which date from about 1948. Clearly, these had a greater relevance to large cities than to the other two units in Le Corbusier's overall scheme.

Most of his detailed postwar planning schemes (as at Bogota and Berlin) also dealt with big towns, a consequence of the requests made to him and the competitions he joined. His rejection of his earlier ultra-urbanism was reflected in these schemes in lower densities (though still with multistory blocks), less dominating buildings, even greater emphasis on open space, and a growing priority accorded to conservation. Generally he became much more flexible; in working on a large hospital in Venice at the very end of his life, he may even have been on the threshold of a totally new urban form based on low buildings.

On the other hand, he continued to authorize reprintings of his early books on planning without modification or qualification, and he certainly never disowned his older ideas.[14] As he had neither the time nor the inclination to write more didactic works on planning after the late 1940s, his doctrine lost some of its earlier clarity, but his statements suggested that "the three human establishments" remained his basic objective.

His planning system was both comprehensive and internally consistent. These qualities allowed him to rebuff criticisms of its details with ease, not to say contempt, and he frequently expressed surprise and impatience when it failed to convince. Even that nagging criticism which any program of radical reform will attract—that it is too ambitious to have any chance of being carried out—could be rejected on the grounds that the Corbusian system was simply a more efficient reordering of current arrangements and could therefore be introduced without any serious disturbance of existing economic and political interests.

Anthony Sutcliffe 222

But are the assumptions on which the system was based equally in-vulnerable? No, they were not; indeed, an essentially *optimistic* view of the world inclined Le Corbusier to a *utopian* program of social re-form and obscured both the limitations and dangers of that program and the obstacles to its adoption.[15]

Many investigations of Le Corbusier's ideas have vied with one another in identifying artists and thinkers who influenced him. Valu-able though these studies are, I suspect that his fundamental ap-proach to the world and its problems was formed in early childhood, mainly through the influence of God-fearing and nature-loving par-ents. Self-education would then have confirmed this belief system rather than disturbed it, for wide though Le Corbusier's reading un-doubtedly was, I suspect that he used it as a source of support for his own thinking, much of which was on his own admission intuitive.[16] Consequently, his basic assumptions did not substantially alter during his career.

Absolutely fundamental to Le Corbusier's belief system was his op-timistic view of the natural world. He saw it as an ordered, harmoni-ous environment, idyllic and benign. Certainly it included death and a measure of competition, but Kenneth Frampton has surely gone too far in emphasizing its *dialectical* character.[17] Le Corbusier made clear time and time again that balance and harmony were the keynotes of his natural world: "Yes, in everything nature shows us a picture of flexibility, precision, and unquestionable reality in its combinations of harmonious developments. Serene perfection throughout. Plants, animals, trees, landscapes, seas, plains or mountains. Even the perfect harmony of natural disasters, earthquakes, etc."[18]

Le Corbusier also emphasized that man, though qualified by his in-tellectual capacities and inherent ambition to master the natural world,[19] was very much a product of it, capable of sharing its rhythm and likely to lose equilibrium if he ignored it (Fig. 62): "Man is a prod-

Figure 62
The dwelling in the landscape. This cross-section of the Corbusian city stresses the combination of personal privacy with community and harmony with nature. (Source: Le Corbusier, *The Four Routes*, p. 65.)

Figure 63
Trees as a medium between massive buildings and men. Le Corbusier's caption contended that trees, being on a "human" scale, would prevent his towers from dwarfing passersby. His sketch, however, suggests that both buildings *and* trees will dominate—a rare example of Le Corbusier's pencil being less convincing than his pen. (Source: Le Corbusier, *The Radiant City*, p. 221.)

uct of nature. He has been created according to the laws of nature. If he is sufficiently aware of those laws, if he obeys them and harmonizes his life with the perpetual flux of nature, then he will obtain (for himself) a conscious sensation of harmony that will be beneficial to him."[20]

Le Corbusier believed that the achievement of harmony and order constituted the ultimate human happiness: "The highest delight of the human spirit is to perceive order, and the greatest human satisfaction is the feeling of sharing or participating in that order."[21] Certainly, this satisfaction was to be achieved by activity—his natural world offered no lotus-eating existence to man[22]—but it was activity directed toward spiritual ideals rather than simple material accumulation (Fig. 63): "Architecture and music are the distinctive manifestations of human dignity. In them man affirms, 'I exist, I am a mathematician, a geometrician, and I am religious. That is to say that I believe in some gigantic ideal which dominates me, but which I can reach. . . .' "[23]

He often expressed his abhorrence of crude materialism as an aberration that diverted man from happiness: "Contemporary society has, to its own misfortune, given itself up to the endless manufacture of objects of varying degrees of stupidity, which only clog up our lives—senseless production of sterile consumer goods."[24]

Apart from the occasional reference to human weaknesses, Le Corbusier said very little to qualify this picture of man as a sober, rational, hard-working, and intensely spiritual creature, inspired by the noblest of motives. When writing of man's *natural* inclinations, he never referred to such conflict-creating forces as greed, jealousy, or lust. Thus he was able to believe in a natural form of human society based on cooperation, in which relationships between individuals and between groups were governed by an implicit social contract.[25] Wealth and status were not equally distributed—indeed, Le Corbusier was a firm believer in meritocratic elites—but in such a society they were not a cause of conflict, for material well-being was merely the basis for the greater joys of family life, social intercourse, and physical recreation, all of which contributed to an overall harmony with nature. The Marxist concepts of class and class-conflict were totally alien to him. In short, Le Corbusier believed in an earthly paradise as man's natural state, and in this respect he was quite clearly utopian.

Still, it was evident to Le Corbusier that this vision of an earthly paradise did not correspond to the contemporary world in which he lived. How was the discrepancy to be explained? All utopian thinkers have to face this problem, but Le Corbusier's solution was distinctive. It was based on his idiosyncratic identification of industrialization (*machinisme*) as an independent force in human development. Briefly stated, Le Corbusier believed that a happy and harmonious world[26] had been distorted by the corrupting influence of the industrialization that had been suddenly and brutally imposed on it in the nineteenth century. In particular, industrialization had alienated man from nature and so deprived him of that essential element in his happiness, participation in an ordered, blissful universe:

A machine civilization established itself, slyly and secretly, under the carpet, where we could not see it clearly. It plunged us and held us in a life which is now in question. Symptoms are now appearing of breakdowns in people's health, and of economic, social, and religious changes, etc.[27]

The effect of inventions has been to shatter the ancestral statute. Everything has been broken, torn asunder. Social life is different. The life of the individual is threatened.[28]

By emphasizing that industrialization had been a *totally* disruptive force, Le Corbusier was able to argue that it had produced all the defects of contemporary society and even of individuals. In effect, he diagnosed in society a pathological condition that allowed him to maintain his belief in the natural goodness of man. This point can be illustrated by some of his judgments on India when he was working on Chandigarh, notably: "India is a country which has not yet been molested by *machinisme* and inhumane theories. India seems to me to be supremely humane."[29]

The idea of industrialization causing a pathological condition was most clearly developed in Le Corbusier's descriptions of the unreformed industrial city. This, the location of most of the antisocial phenomena which Le Corbusier blamed on industrialization, was frequently described as "sick." He probably found it easier to apply this image to cities than to society as a whole because of an established practice among French geographers and sociologists of viewing cities as biological entities.[30] This precedent no doubt helped to confirm his own independent interest in biology[31] and encouraged him to use biological analogies in explaining social phenomena. At least as early as 1923, he was referring to "the sickness of great cities,"[32] and he eventually developed a wide range of medical metaphors. He often spoke of "the cancer of Paris,"[33] and he would sometimes combine more than one biological process to grotesque effect: "City centers are fatally ill, while their outskirts are being gnawed away as if by vermin."[34]

Le Corbusier most frequently applied the image of sickness to features of the urban physical structure—slums, low-density suburbs, clogged business districts, and so on. But he also believed that the behavior of individual citizens was distorted, with the influence of the physical environment, itself unbalanced, producing disequilibrium in its residents:

The tentacled cities were born; Paris, London, New York, Rio de Janeiro, Buenos Aires. The countryside was emptied. Here was a double catastrophe. A menacing loss of equilibrium. In these tentacled cities life is madness. Men move seated about their cities, in trams and underground railways, in cars and suburban trains, living a disordered and demoralizing existence. It is a new slavery. The wars were but explosive crises of revolt.[35]

The city? It is the aggregate of these local disasters [breakup of the family unit under the impact of urban employment patterns]. It is the sum of these disappropriated parts. It is equivocal. Sadness weighs it down.[36]

Even the Darwinian idea of a law of survival, which Le Corbusier certainly entertained, was usually portrayed as a product of the unbalanced growth of cities:

Paris is pitiless; there, a battle is fought with no quarter asked or given. It is a venue for championship fights or gladiatorial contests. We face up to one another and kill one another. Paris is paved with corpses. Paris is a congress of cannibals, which fixes the dogma of the moment. Paris is a selector.[37]

It is only recently that the available material means at our disposal have made it possible for a wealth of ambition to be tapped and directed into the centres of our great cities. . . . The law of survival operates perpetually and with a recurring and brutal force. . . . And these great cities challenge one another, for the mad urge for supremacy is the very law of evolution itself to which we are subjected.[38]

Le Corbusier blamed all divergences from his ideal of the happy man and the idyllic society on the sudden impact of industrialization, which had upset the lives of individuals mainly by creating an unbalanced environment.

To identify industrialization as a disruptive force in society was by no means uncommon in nineteenth- and early twentieth-century thought. But what distinguished Le Corbusier from thinkers such as William Morris was that his philosophy prevented him from any suspicions that industrialization might be *intrinsically* harmful to human happiness. On the contrary, as the product of a combination of man's intelligence and endeavor and of the properties of the physical world, technical progress could not itself be anything but good.

Le Corbusier's solution to this contradiction was the fulcrum of his whole system. He achieved it by using two interrelated concepts. The first was the idea of technical progress as an independent variable in human history, meaning that inventions are not dependent on general social or economic development, but are the product of chance or the operations of individual genius. In other words, technical advance is seen as an independent process with its own internal system of causation, which determines the speed at which it proceeds.[39] This interpretation allowed him to apply the second concept, that of "culture lag," first developed by Thorstein Veblen, according to which human individuals and institutions take some time to adapt to independently proceeding technical change. Thus Le Corbusier could maintain that in an industrialized world machines set the pace, with humanity in a permanent state of inadaptation to their demands: "The machine is so capital an event in human history that it is permissible to assign it a role as conditioner of the human personality . . .";[40] ". . . the machine is a reality entirely independent of human desires or wills. . . ."[41]

Thus Le Corbusier had the answer to his enigma. The way to restore that blissful state which industrialization had destroyed was not to reverse the process, as William Morris had wanted, but to accept it fully in terms of behavior, attitudes, and the ordering of the environment. Once man took the plunge, he would find that the infinite resources of a machine civilization would allow him to reestablish that essential intimate contact with nature.

As far as man's productive activities were concerned, Le Corbusier seems to have believed that this acceptance of the machine was not difficult to achieve. Man had merely to follow wholeheartedly the example already set by technology and the organization of production associated with machines. Le Corbusier made no secret of his idealized view of machinery, which, since its operations were governed by natural laws, could even be regarded as a natural form. He frequently referred to machines as "biological" or "organic": "Modern techniques have revealed the way to other things. New things mutually coordinated by a biology which is whole, unique."[42] More than once, he even expressed a conviction that efficiently designed machinery could run in total silence.[43] His admiration extended to the organization of whole factories; in 1932, for instance, he claimed that factories were the only elements in the urban environment that obeyed natural laws.[44] Consequently, Le Corbusier could believe that technical and economic efficiency were natural virtues, and that their achievement would of itself create harmony with nature. This argument emerged strongly in a statement of the new editorial policy of *L'Esprit Nouveau* in 1923, and echoes of it are to be found in many of Le Corbusier's later writings:

. . . we have shown that the machine is a product which obeys natural laws more faithfully than did the products of the artisan. The machine is, above all, a measure of our new social being, the symbol of the overriding law which governs our civilization, *the law of Economy*. Today we can clearly formulate a new ideal, an ideal which already shines through every aspect of contemporary activity—efficiency: in the interest of Economy, our civilization's single guide toward Purity. Economy, Purity, the guiding light of the new spirit.[45]

This implicit confidence in the happiness of industrial man while at work allowed Le Corbusier to define the problem of adaptation to a machine society almost exclusively in terms of the environment experienced by the individual outside the workplace. As it was essentially the environment of the unreformed industrial city that had thrown man into a state of unbalance, it was necessary merely to provide the right environment in order to restore his equilibrium and, in consequence, to guarantee him complete fulfillment and happiness. The principal features of this environment were a healthy and comfortable dwelling to allow a natural and wholesome family life, the grouping of dwellings and the provision of facilities to permit an active community spirit, and extensive green surroundings to reestablish the link with nature. It was these requirements which the *unité d'habitation* was developed to satisfy:

By bringing together a natural social grouping, a community, in one harmonious unit, it [the *unité d'habitation*] puts forward the "vertical garden-city" solution, to replace the "horizontal garden-city" which has dominated the last century and caused the "denaturalization" of the urban phenomenon which has let loose on the world the evils, the catastrophe, of an urban planning which has no relation to its [true] objectives. These objectives are to order the social phenomenon (in this case, to co-ordinate the basic acts of daily life; that is, to live, and to know how to live). This is a universal problem.[46]

And "natural conditions" (*conditions de nature*) will be reintroduced into the lives of the men, women and children of the machine civilization.[47]

Here then was the cure for the sickness of cities, and henceforth both the environment and society would return to equilibrium and health. Cities, under the new dispensation, would be organized biologically and therefore naturally: "All architectural products, all city neighbourhoods or cities ought to be *organisms.* This word immediately conveys a notion of character, of balance, of harmony, of symmetry."[48]

This is all very well, the reader may now be saying, but could Le Corbusier *really* have believed that a reform of the environment *alone* could produce an ideal world? Did he not concentrate on planning and architecture because he was qualified in those fields, leaving it to others to advocate the necessary political, economic, and social reforms? The following advice to the Congrès International d'Architecture Moderne (CIAM) of 1930 has often been quoted as indicating Le Corbusier's recognition of the limited role of the reform of the physical environment in the creation of a better society:

Contemporary architecture and especially city planning are direct results of the social situation; this goes without saying. By means of personal inquiries let's keep up to date with the present evolution but, I beg of you, let's not get into politics or sociology here, in the midst of our Congress. They are too endlessly complex phenomena; economics are closely linked to them. We are not competent to discuss these intricate questions here. I repeat: here we should remain architects and city planners and on this professional basis we should make known, to those whose duty they are, the possibilities afforded by modern techniques and the need for a new kind of architecture and city planning.[49]

What is most striking about this statement is how untypical it is of Le Corbusier, who rarely hesitated to pronounce on "these endlessly complex phenomena" and who founded much of his architectural and planning doctrine on assumptions made in these areas. *The Radiant City* itself, in which this modest statement was reprinted, contains numerous assertions of Le Corbusier's strong belief in environmental determinism, notably: "Miraculous architectural age! Everything is architecture! Architecture is the creation of order!"[50] More sober, but still assigning a promotional role to environmental planning in world reform, is the following statement from *The City of Tomorrow*:

A form of planning which preoccupied itself with our happiness or our misery and which attempted to create happiness and expel misery would be a noble service in this age of confusion. Such a preoccupation, creating its appropriate science, would imply an important evolution in the social system. It would denounce on the one hand the harsh and futile individualistic rush for egotistical gratification, by which our great cities have been created. It would show, on the other hand, that at the critical moment an automatic recovery had taken place; that feelings of solidarity, pity and the desire for good had inspired a powerful will towards a clear, constructive and creative end.[51]

In 1930, the year of his modest CIAM statement, he also wrote that the world's cities

. . . could become not the reliquaries of a beauty which was revolutionary in its own time, but irresistible forces stimulating collective enthusiasm, collective action, and general joy and pride, and in consequence individual happiness everywhere. All that would be needed is an authority, a man (though he would need a certain lyric sensibility) to set the machine in motion, to issue a law, a set of regulations, a doctrine—and then the modern world would begin to emerge from behind its labor-blackened face and hands, and would beam around, powerful, happy, believing. . . ."[52]

In 1946, he came even closer to isolating the physical environment as the key determinant of human happiness: "Habitation is life, knowing how to live! How to use the blessings of God: the sun and the spirit that He has given to men to enable them to achieve the joy of living on earth and to find again the Lost Paradise."[53] In 1960, he continued to reiterate this ideal and his role in it: "My duty, my research, is to try to remove today's man from misery and disaster, and to set him in happiness, daily joy, and harmony. For this it will be necessary in particular to re-establish, or to establish, harmony between man and his environment."[54]

Even if the reader has accepted the argument this far, his reaction may still be: so what? That Le Corbusier overestimated the benefits of his planning system does not necessarily devalue the system itself; however, optimism might have detracted from Le Corbusier's planning system in three important ways. First, it might have blinded him to practical difficulties or well-founded opposition to his system and so increased the odds against its acceptance. Second, his confidence in the operations of the business world and the directive power of governments might have encouraged him to advocate planning solutions that could be applied by others to achieve personal gain or mean economies rather than the welfare of the community. Third, and most serious of all, Le Corbusier's apparently limited awareness of the nonenvironmental causes of social problems and of the possible drawbacks of modern technology might have allowed him to incorporate in his system elements that could actually detract from the quality of the environment and even accentuate the problems of society.

Perhaps the first question to ask is why Le Corbusier's planning system did not gain the general acceptance that he was convinced it deserved (Fig. 64). He himself blamed the atrophied minds and outdated attitudes of the human products of the unreformed industrial world. But unless one shares Le Corbusier's distinctive view of the world, one has to explain the failure in terms of the program's unattractive input-output ratio. In other words, Le Corbusier's planning system

Figure 64
Sketches for a worldwide urban system. On the left, a section of a linear industrial city, including an experimental low-density residential area of small houses. On the right, a glimpse of linear urbanization along the major arteries of economic activity. (Source: Le Corbusier, *Oeuvre complète 1938–46,* p. 75.)

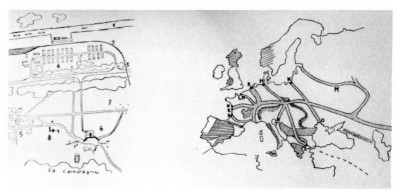

would have been seen as too expensive and too disruptive of existing interests to be justified by the results anticipated. In effect, Le Corbusier failed to win general acceptance for his basic claims. That his system was the path to an earthly paradise was, of course, accepted by few, and this skepticism increased the relevance of the cost factor in any decision to apply his ideas.

Here again, Le Corbusier's optimism did not correspond with the reality seen by those who did not share his assumptions. He always maintained that all the works carried out in his system would pay for themselves, owing to a big increase in the value of developed land, as a result of high densities. This improvement value should have overcome all opposition by landowners and doubts on the part of the political authorities, and it should have attracted the necessary investment.

But Le Corbusier apparently never realized that higher densities at a given point mean lower densities and therefore lower values elsewhere. As many landowners stood to lose as those who stood to gain, while the collectivity gained nothing. Land nationalization might have provided a firmer foundation for Le Corbusier's planning system, but realizing that it would either place a heavy compensation burden on the community or forfeit the support of landowners and private capital, he was always careful never to advocate it. Instead, he proposed "land mobilization," a form of cooperation between public and private interests limited to development land.[55] This solution conformed to his ideal of a community of interests, but in practical terms it fell between two stools, convincing neither the private nor the public sector.

If the redevelopment of land on Corbusian lines could not alone produce a capital gain equal to the investment made, it was still possible to argue that the greater efficiency of the reformed environment would produce a bigger return on all capital, whether publicly or privately invested. As it happens, Le Corbusier, who had only a rudimentary knowledge of economics, rarely made much of this argument, but it was certainly implicit in much of what he wrote. But like the land-owners, business and industry looked on Le Corbusier's proposals with a quizzical eye. Any benefits for them would be long-term, while in the immediate future they would have to acquiesce in a radical re-location of employment. In particular, Le Corbusier convinced himself that locations along the major transport routes were the most eco-nomically efficient for manufacturing industry, as well as the most so-cially desirable, but firms' actual locational decisions rarely conformed to this theory. Of course, industry could be directed into new areas by political decision, but here again the support of an influential interest would be lost.

If landowners and industrialists could at best be ambivalent, the middle and upper classes had good reasons to be totally opposed to Le Corbusier's planning. In 1922, the Contemporary City had been very crudely divided into what could be regarded as middle-class and working-class areas, but Le Corbusier was clearly not very interested in the distinction. In fact, he stated later that ever since the beginning of his researches into city planning in 1914, he had never been con-cerned with rich or poor, but solely with man.[56] By the time of the Radiant City he had moved to a completely egalitarian arrangement, based on the assumption that housing demands, in terms of both ac-commodation and location, were not related to income; the all-embracing community would overcome social distinctions: "I had created the prototype of a *classless city*, a city of men busy with work and leisure in surroundings that made these possible."[57]

This residential mixing remained a feature of his system thereafter, and was incorporated into the theory of the *unité d'habitation*. Le Cor-busier probably based the idea on the traditional mixing of social classes in Parisian apartment houses, but even there social segrega-tion had been emerging since the nineteenth century. To design whole cities on this basis was totally unrealistic in societies where great disparities of wealth existed. It is significant that in the only city planning scheme which he was allowed to realize (Chandigarh), Le Corbusier had to accept the residential segregation of different social groups. More significant still, this segregation raised serious problems, owing to the varying demands placed on open space and social equipment within the standardized sectors.

Le Corbusier's system might well have worked in a socialist society without great disparities of wealth and a deliberate political effort to minimize social distinctions, but, as we have seen, he did not recognize the need for so radical a measure of political and social reform. This whole dilemma is illustrated by Le Corbusier's tentative efforts to promote his planning in the Soviet Union in the late 1920s. It was pure irony that while Le Corbusier clung to his cherished ideal of the liberty of the individual (which the application of his planning system would effectively have restricted), the Soviets remained distrustful of this utopian who had no awareness of the class dimension, even though his planning was tailor-made for egalitarian societies.[58] Meanwhile, Le Corbusier wasted his time appealing to fascist political forces and governments that were sufficiently authoritarian to apply his system but lacked the necessary egalitarianism.

Because the most influential forces in capitalist society were the enemies of Le Corbusier's planning rather than its natural supporters, such elements of his planning as *were* put into effect were almost always devalued and distorted. His advocacy of skyscraper commercial buildings helped to sweep away building height restrictions in London, Paris, and other cities; but most of the resulting towers produced only profits for developers, not an improvement in the environment, because the concomitants of high building in his system, such as more open space, were usually ignored. In the same way, his call for tall blocks of flats as the modal housing type helped harassed local authorities to justify high-density slum redevelopment schemes that almost always lacked the amenities and social mixing which Le Corbusier considered essential. His ideas were used when they could help make private profits or save public funds and avoid political problems, but they rarely contributed to social reform or even environmental improvement.

Of course it was not Le Corbusier's fault that his ideas were abused, nor was he the only modern movement architect to advocate tall buildings and high densities. But in making them part of a planning mode which his extraordinary artistry undoubtedly made visually exciting and stimulating, he did more than most of his contemporaries to help gain acceptance for elements of his system which, however, selfish interests applied totally out of context. Moreover, Le Corbusier was so eager for recognition that instead of emphasizing that it was necessary to apply the whole of his system or nothing at all, he usually welcomed these caricatures as a step in the right direction.

Although Le Corbusier's doctrine was more appropriate to the socialist societies of recent decades than to capitalist ones, its technical content is not therefore beyond criticism. It was more suited to socialism because such societies possess the social controls to make it work, but in practice those controls may well be regarded as an intolerable intrusion into private lives. Without such controls, a Corbusian environment may well be associated with a new range of social problems. These problems would stem from his overoptimistic view of human motivations and behavior and his consequent overestimate of the influence of environmental determinism and uncritical acceptance of technical innovations. If worst came to worst, the result could easily be an inhuman environment, the opposite of Le Corbusier's hopes.

The most dangerous of his assumptions was his belief in the strength of man's communal instincts, which led him to maximize communal space and facilities, to reduce private space to a bare minimum, and to raise residential densities. This arrangement could well be associated with the desired result; however, if the residents proved less communally minded than Le Corbusier's stereotype, the environment could be a disaster. The fate of the Pruitt-Igoe development at St. Louis showed what could happen when faith in the essential goodness of man proved unfounded. At least in this respect Le Corbusier may be said to have aimed high on the basis of his confidence in people, which indicates a strong respect for humanity.

But his equally strong and uncritical respect for technology led him into less pleasant paths. Even had he recognized that technical advance is more the product of investment choices than the operation of human genius, his respect for entrepreneurial capitalism would have kept him from all criticism. But as it was, he often argued that man had a *duty* to apply innovations. Part of his case for high building was founded on this argument, though fortunately in residential building he stopped at about twelve stories and restricted his advocacy of height-for-height's-sake to commercial buildings.

More serious was his uncritical acceptance of the motor car. As a product of modern technology there could be nothing wrong with the car; that it appeared to be noisy, dirty, and abusive of space in existing cities had therefore to be the fault of the cities themselves. In particular, he argued, it was only the channeling effect of the traditional street that magnified noise and concentrated fumes, which otherwise would be imperceptible. The answer was to adapt the environment to machine-age demands, in this case by abolishing the street. Toward the end of his life, the generous provision of urban expressways was producing serious pollution and diffused noise up to considerable heights over wide areas, but it was too late for him to reconsider his position.

As the product of an honest, fearless, and independent mind, Le

Corbusier's environmental planning system was inspired by the noblest of motives, and it is above criticism. But Le Corbusier himself was clearly embittered by what he seems to have recognized as its double failure; on the one hand, it had been unable to secure the universal application that it required to display its full benefits, while on the other it had come to be blamed for some of the excesses of the modern urban environment, with its tower blocks, expressways, and parking lots seemingly caricaturing the Corbusian ideal. He blamed this failure on the stupidity and inertia of those in authority and on the ignorance of the masses. On occasion, perhaps, when reflecting on the rejection of his good and reasonable ideas, Le Corbusier may even have begun to doubt his fundamental faith in the virtue of the human race. But if such doubts ever entered his mind, he must have quickly dismissed them, for in apprehending the principal reason for its failure, Le Corbusier would have destroyed the very foundation on which his whole doctrine rested.

1 Le Corbusier, quoted in Jean Petit, *Le Corbusier lui-même,* Geneva, 1970, p. 56. I have made this and subsequent translations from the French.

2 Le Corbusier, *Précisions sur un état présent de l'architecture et de l'urbanisme*, Paris, new edition, 1960, p. 152. ("Ces certitudes font une doctrine. Une doctrine d'urbanisme.") For a detailed study of the content and application of the doctrine, see Norma Evenson, *Le Corbusier: The Machine and the Grand Design*, London, (n.d.) [c. 1970].

3 Le Corbusier, *Urbanisme*, Paris, 1925. Quotations in this article are taken from *The City of Tomorrow*, the English translation published in London in 1947.

4 Le Corbusier, *The City of Tomorrow*, p. xxiv, suggests that his recognition of this aspect of planning can be dated to about 1910, though he made other remarks that suggest that it occurred even earlier.

5 Ibid., pp. 71–72, and *The Radiant City* (English translation, London, 1967, of *La Ville radieuse*, Boulogne-sur-Seine, 1935), p. 146.

6 The first clear expression of this preoccupation is Le Corbusier's article, "La grande ville," in *L'Esprit Nouveau*, no. 23, May 1924, pp. 183–198.

7 Petit, *Le Corbusier lui-même*, p. 44.

8 Le Corbusier, *Radiant City*, pp. 106–108, 168.

9 Ibid., p. 38; *Oeuvre complète 1910–29*, p. 38.

10 Le Corbusier, *Radiant City,* pp. 106–108.

11 Le Corbusier, *Précisions*, p. 18.

12 Le Corbusier, *Radiant City*, pp. 110, 197.

13 Le Corbusier, *Les Trois Etablissements humains*, Paris, 1946.

14 See for example the pride Le Corbusier took in the reprinting, in 1960, of his South American lectures of 1929, without a word being altered, in *Précisions*, p. viii.

15 Some utopian aspects of Le Corbusier's thinking have already been pointed out, notably by Françoise Choay in *Le Corbusier*, London, 1960, and "L'histoire et la méthode en urbanisme," *Annales E.S.C.*, vol. 25, no. 4, July-August 1970, p. 1147.

16 See for example Le Corbusier's statement that the scale of the Contemporary City was partly the product of "an overwhelmingly powerful intuition," in *Radiant City,* p. 105.

17 Kenneth Frampton, "The city of dialectic," in *Architectural Design,* vol. 39, no. 10, October 1969, pp. 541–546.

18 Petit, *Le Corbusier lui-même*, p. 82.

19 Le Corbusier, *City of Tomorrow*, pp. 5–6.

20 Le Corbusier, *Radiant City*, p. 83.

21 Amédée Ozenfant and Charles-Edouard Jeanneret, "Le

Notes

Purisme," in *L'Esprit Nouveau*, no. 4, January 1921, p. 386.

22 Le Corbusier, *City of Tomorrow*, pp. 5-6.

23 Le Corbusier, *Précisions,* p. 12.

24 Speech to the Congrès International d'Architecture Moderne (CIAM), 1933, quoted in Petit, *Le Corbusier lui-même*, p. 181.

25 Le Corbusier, *City of Tomorrow*, p. 130.

26 See Le Corbusier's ecstatic description of medieval society in the early pages of *When the Cathedrals Were White*, English translation, London, 1947, of *Quand les cathédrales étaient blanches*, Paris, 1937.

27 Le Corbusier, *Précisions,* preface to the 1960 edition, p. vi.

28 Le Corbusier, *Radiant City*, p. 18.

29 Petit, *Le Corbusier lui-même*, p. 111.

30 See F. Bédarida, "The growth of urban history in France," in *The Study of Urban History*, edited by H. J. Dyos, London, 1968, pp. 58, 61.

31 See Pierre Winter's tribute to Le Corbusier's qualities as a biologist in *Oeuvre complète 1934-38,* pp. 14-15.

32 In a speech to the Strasbourg town planning congress, quoted in *L'Esprit Nouveau*, no. 23, May 1924, p. 192.

33 See unidentified newspaper feature, 27 September 1928, in cuttings file no. 21, Archives Fondation Le Corbusier.

34 Le Corbusier, in *L'Esprit Nouveau*, no. 23, May 1924, p. 192.

35 Le Corbusier, *Concerning Town Planning*, London, 1947, p. 46; translation of *Propos d'urbanisme*, Paris, 1946.

36 Le Corbusier, *Précisions*, p. 28.

37 Ibid., p. 18. But for a later statement suggesting that Le Corbusier saw "the spirit of competition" as a natural human motivation, see pp. vi-vii.

38 Le Corbusier, *City of Tomorrow*, pp. 86-87.

39 This and other concepts of technical change are discussed in Jacob Schmookler, *Invention and Economic Growth*, Harvard University Press, 1966.

40 Le Corbusier, *Vers une architecture*, Paris, 1923, quoted in F. Choay, *L'Urbanisme: utopies et réalités,* Paris, 1965, p. 236.

41 Le Corbusier, *Radiant City*, pp. 195-196. For the diffusion of Veblen's ideas in France in the 1920s, see Georges Friedmann, "Veblen: un précurseur," *Annales E.S.C.*, vol. 26, no. 3, September-October 1971, pp. 977-981.

42 Le Corbusier, *Radiant City*, p. 29.

43 Ibid., p. 125, carries an example—his assertion that motor cars in his cities will run silently.

44 Ibid., p. 8.

45 Le Corbusier, *L'Esprit Nouveau*, no. 18, November 1923, editorial foreword.

46 Petit, *Le Corbusier lui-même*, p. 99.

47 Le Corbusier, *Oeuvre complète 1952–57,* p. 174.

48 Le Corbusier, *Radiant City*, p. 147. For a later reference to biological planning, see *Manière de penser l'urbanisme*, Boulogne-sur-Seine, (n.d.) [1945], p. 50.

49 Le Corbusier, *Radiant City*, p. 37.

50 Ibid., p. 197.

51 Le Corbusier, *City of Tomorrow,* p. 59.

52 Le Corbusier, *Précisions*, p. 18.

53 Le Corbusier, *When the Cathedrals Were White*, p. xviii.

54 Le Corbusier, *Précisions*, p. v.

55 Ibid., pp. 180 –187.

56 Le Corbusier, *Radiant City*, p. 146.

57 Ibid., p. 13.

58 Ibid., p. 46, S. Gorny's report on Le Corbusier's "Answer to Moscow."

Robert Fishman

From the Radiant City to Vichy:
Le Corbusier's Plans and Politics, 1928–1942

In his politics as in his architecture, Le Corbusier defies generalizations. He escapes like Houdini from even the most entangling categories. In the 1920s he seemed the embodiment of the conservative technocrat, the elitist who tried to place his genius at the service of banks and international corporations. Percival and Paul Goodman, in their book *Communitas* (1947), denounce him as a spokesman for finance capitalism whose urban theories serve to reinforce the class structure.[1] Yet, almost twenty years before *Communitas* was published, Le Corbusier had himself broken with capitalism and declared himself a revolutionary syndicalist. Throughout the thirties he was an influential and tireless spokesman for this doctrine, an indigenous French socialism that called for the trade unions (*syndicats*) to take over the means of production while the workers elect from their midst a new managerial elite.

Le Corbusier's conversion to syndicalism was no doubt comforting to those who wished to identify modern architecture with leftist politics; nonetheless, it still fails to define the "real" Le Corbusier. His activist period of the thirties was also characterized by his growing fascination with authoritarian, quasi-fascist groups at the fringes of French political life. After the fall of France in 1940, this fasincation became commitment. He announced his allegiance to the reactionary regime of Marshal Pétain and sought to join the government himself. He spent eighteen fruitless, farcical months as a minor official at Vichy, the regime's capital, convinced that he was destined to become the aged Marshal's adviser and the great dictator of French architecture.

One might be tempted to conclude from this rapid summary of Le Corbusier's affiliations and vacillations that his genius did not manifest itself in his politics. If we understand politics in a narrow sense, this is surely true. His *engagement* had all the shortcomings we associate with "the intellectual in politics." He was sometimes opportunistic, sometimes utopian, sometimes both at once. As a leader, he could be spiteful, uncooperative, as sensitive to his own prerogatives as he was insensitive to the rights of others. Indeed, for a lifelong proponent of organization, Le Corbusier was singularly incapable of working within one.

Yet, if his activism had its miseries, it also had its quixotic grandeur. Even at Vichy he never lost his dedication to his own complex vision of a harmonious future. For him, politics existed only to provide the authority for the great works of environmental reconstruction that he believed could end social strife and inaugurate a new era. Political power was necessary to carry out this transformation, but, to enter the new world, power had to be guided by imagination. The true founder of the new era would be the planner: the man who combined technical expertise with social vision. His designs would not only symbolize social harmony, they would create that harmony by bringing the citizens together into a community and directing their relationships into cooperative channels. In the transformed environment the order that was always a potential in industrial society would become real; the conflicts that divided society would disappear; politics itself would wither away. Urban design would thus become the real constitution of the new society, the "manifestation in daily life of a wise social order" (Fig. 65).[2]

Le Corbusier's activism, therefore, always had a double aspect. First, it expressed itself theoretically in his plans for ideal cities. These were never blueprints for building; rather, they were ideal types of the new industrial society that he believed was possible. They enabled Le Corbusier to show in graphic terms the relationship between the transformations in the environment he was proposing and the transformed social order that the environment would support. In his ideal cities Le Corbusier's innovations in architecture and urban design appear in what he believed was their true context: as integral parts of a new civilization.

Second, his activism expressed itself in his attempts—desperate attempts, by the time of Vichy—to find the authority that would begin to carry out his plans. Of course, such an authority would necessarily belong to the old civilization, and even during his technocratic phase of the twenties he was careful to distinguish between the ethos of the great works he was planning and that of the capitalists he hoped would undertake them. Although his first ideal city, the Contemporary City for Three Million Inhabitants (1922), was put forward at the height of his infatuation with big business, he pointed out specifically that the Contemporary City was not capitalist or communist. "On my plan I wrote *Administrative Services, Public Services.* That will suffice."[3] This distinction did not prevent him from turning both to capitalists and then to communists for aid, but it does provide a convenient starting point for the consideration of Le Corbusier's social thought.

Le Corbusier's ideas began and ended with the concept that industrial society had an inherent form, an objective order derived from the nature of man and the nature of machines, an ideal structure, which—if realized—would bring prosperity, harmony, and joy. Capitalism or socialism might under different circumstances be better equipped to reach this ideal, but both must submit to the requirements of industrial society or risk chaos. For Le Corbusier, any industrial society must be centrally controlled, hierarchically organized, administered from above, with the most qualified people in the most responsible position. He believed that the industrial era would be an age of triumphant rationality, and, as Max Weber had already observed, the rule of reason in Western society means the dominance of bureaucracy. Le Corbusier did not shrink from this conclusion: he embraced it. His ideal city is above all a City of Administration. "From its offices come the commands that put the world in order."[4]

In the Contemporary City the towers of administration occupy the place of honor at the center. These skyscrapers are "the brain of the city, the brain of the whole country. They embody the work of elaboration and command on which all activities depend."[5] This administrative center is the true capital of the country, the headquarters of headquarters. It is also the natural home of the elite, the directors of the great bureaucracies. Le Corbusier emphasized that the elite includes the administrators of the intellect as well as of industry. He listed the leading occupants of the central towers as "captains of business, of industry, of finance, of politics, masters of science, of pedagogy, of thought, the spokesmen of the heart, the artists, poets, musicians."[6]

These leaders would bring order and beauty to industrial society through beneficent acts of administration. The whole Contemporary City is structured to serve their needs. The administrative center is designed to provide the conditions for efficient coordination. "Everything is concentrated there: the tools that conquer space and time—telephones, telegraphs, radios; the banks, trading houses, the organs of decision for the factories: finance, technology, commerce."[7] Around the towers are the luxurious apartment houses for the elite. Elaborate communal services, which Le Corbusier compared to those on a luxury liner, free the leaders from the mundane tasks of housekeeping and offer the opportunities for leisure and meditation that the elite need in order to carry out their burdensome tasks. The subordinate bureaucrats and workers, whose needs Le Corbusier considered less pressing, live in more modest satellite cities at the outskirts.

The structure of the Contemporary City thus reflects the hierarchy that Le Corbusier believed was necessary in any industrial society. Although, as we shall see, he was later to modify his narrow elitism, he never lost the conviction that modern life requires centralized administration. In putting forward this interpretation, Le Corbusier believed he was speaking as an objective "technician"; in fact, he was aligning himself with one of France's most venerable political traditions, one which dates from the writings of the nineteenth-century utopian socialist Henri de Saint-Simon (1760–1825).

Saint-Simon was one of those utopians who turned out to be far more realistic than his more hardheaded contemporaries. Writing in the turbulent Napoleonic and Restoration periods, he argued that society was evolving a new order based on the organization of industry. The future, he predicted, belonged to large-scale enterprises in which men would "henceforth do consciously, and with better directed and more useful effort, what they have hitherto done unconsciously, slowly, indecisively and too ineffectively."[8] These enterprises would impose a hierarchy of authority on all workers and bring an elite of proven ability and knowledge into the commanding positions, an elite which, he claimed, was already taking the most important decisions into its hands: the exploitation of natural resources, the development of industry, and the administration of production and distribution.

Saint-Simon looked forward to the time when the men he called *industriels,* the elite of managers, scientists, and artists, would, in their capacities as heads of the great organizations of production and learning, take over the functions of government. The repressive functions of the state would wither away. In Saint-Simon's famous formula, the "administration of goods" would replace "the government of men."[9] Inequality would remain, but would no longer lead to social strife. The workers would have jobs and prosperity; they would feel themselves to be part of a great collective enterprise headed by their natural leaders, the *industriels.* In the twentieth century Saint-Simon's ideas were invoked both by businessmen and socialists. The neo-Saint-Simonians, a group with which Le Corbusier had important ties, called for an elite of technically trained managers to rationalize production; this alone would end social disorder by satisfying working-class demands for higher wages and better living conditions. On the Left,

Lenin and his followers invoked Saint-Simon's industrial hierarchy as the proper model for a communist economy after the capitalists had been expropriated and an elite of communist *industriels* put in their place.[10]

Whether as conservative or revolutionary, Le Corbusier retained his allegiance to the Saint-Simonian vision. He never doubted that society would eventually take the form he outlined in his ideal city. The only question was which group would finally give the order to build and thus prove itself to be "worthy of the machine age." The Plan Voisin for Paris (1925) assumed that the heads of the large corporations would take on this role. Acting only as businessmen, they would buy up a large tract in the center of Paris, knock down the existing structures, and erect in their place eighteen skyscrapers. This would not only be a profitable enterprise (Le Corbusier carefully concocted a set of imaginary figures to prove this), it would also provide an international headquarters for *industriels* who headed the largest corporations and controlled the world economy (Fig. 66).

Le Corbusier's gradual realization that the capitalist magnates were unwilling and unable to carry out the Plan Voisin did not affect his confidence in the Plan; it destroyed his faith in capitalism. The Plan, he believed, defined the steps that any society must take to fulfill the promise of the machine age. If private enterprise was not equal to the task, then it must be replaced by a system capable of great works. Otherwise, "the life-blood of the new era will be squandered by obsolete, cruel, and inhuman organizations."[11]

In 1928 Le Corbusier published a pamphlet, *Towards the Paris of the Machine Era,* in which he first put forward the radical themes that would preoccupy him in the thirties. The pamphlet was published, ironically enough, under the auspices of the *Redressement français,* an organization headed by the president of France's largest utility, dedicated to the revitalization of France through the efforts of an "industrial elite of intelligence, talent, and character." Le Corbusier called for land mobilization; he wanted the government to purchase all the land within a given tract at its assessed value and to deliver the tract to builders who would undertake projects like the Plan Voisin.

The main interest in this pamphlet lies not in the proposal itself, which was perfectly consistent with the technocratic concerns of the *Redressement français,* but in the supporting arguments. First, Le Corbusier emphasized that the growing industrialization had already profoundly disturbed the traditional bases of society and made gradual responses impossible. "[We must] put ourselves in accord with a situation that has been revolutionized. If this accord is not reached quickly, the sickness that already threatens society will disorganize social life and produce these evils: confusion, incoherence, chaos, all leading to mental disarray and panic—the revolution."[12] Neither capitalism nor parliamentary democracy had the power to forestall this revolution of panic. Capitalism was inherently chaotic, while parliamentary politics could not solve problems; it "devoured energy."

What was needed, Le Corbusier argued, was an Authority outside the "established disorder" to assert the common good. In this pamphlet he put forward the first of many such hoped-for authority figures—the "Minister of Public Works." This Minister would not be responsible to Parliament; he would stand above politics. He would be a modern Colbert, "at home in his own times, with a discernment infinitely precise, a man who does not bow before the present or the past. Seeking to build on a firm basis, he works out the *future.* The scope of his vision will be the greatness of his country."[13] The new Minister would have control over land mobilization; he would have the power to oversee projects from beginning to end, to override all opposition, and to ensure the triumph of order (Fig. 67).

Le Corbusier closed his pamphlet with four sentences that could

Figure 65
Architecture reconciles
individual liberty with
collective power.
(Source: Le Corbusier,
*Quand les cathédrales
étaient blanches,* Paris,
1937, p. 169.)

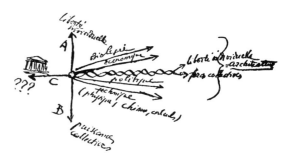

Figure 66
A City of Administration:
The Plan Voisin for Paris,
1925, with eighteen
skyscrapers and a
superhighway for the
Right Bank opposite the
Ile de La Cité. (Source:
Le Corbusier, *La Ville
radieuse,*
Boulogne-sur-Seine,
1935, p. 207.)

Figure 67
Construction begins by
decree. Le Corbusier's
drawing in 1929 of the
decree he hoped the
President of the French
Republic would issue,
ordering land
mobilization and the Plan
Voisin. The order never
came. (Source: Le
Corbusier, *Précisions,*
Paris, 1930, p. 183.)

serve as the theme of his activist period:

A machine age is born.
We still act under the authority of a premechanical age.
This leadership destroys all our initiatives.
We must create the leadership of a machine age.[14]

When he wrote these words, Le Corbusier still hoped that the old system would revitalize itself. This, however, was more a pious wish than
a reasoned conclusion; it did not survive very long after the stock
market crash in the United States. In an article published in 1931, he
placed this caption under a photograph of Wall Street: "All is paradox,
disorder; the liberty of each destroys the liberty of all. Indiscipline."[15]
The floodtide of disorder following the Depression activated Le Corbusier's worst fears of social chaos. He still recoiled at revolution, but
he was even more afraid that capitalism and parliamentary democracy
were allowing society to drift toward a catastrophe. Le Corbusier became a revolutionary out of fear of something worse.

At the same time, he fervently hoped that the crisis could be turned
into an opportunity to create a new leadership and a new social structure which would have the strength to begin the era of great works. In
the late twenties he investigated and then adopted the doctrine he believed would guide the society of the future: syndicalism. This complex (some might say confused) ideology combined several elements
that were especially attractive to intellectuals at that time. It claimed to
transcend the distinctions between Right and Left and to provide a
doctrine that could unite the nation; it was revolutionary in tone without adhering to the Marxist theory of class struggle and dictatorship
of the proletariat; it denounced the capitalist power structure but
promised to put in its place an even more elaborate hierarchy of
merit. Le Corbusier was attracted to syndicalism in part because it was
undefined. Through his commission to design an office building in
Moscow, the Centrosoyus, he had seen a unified ideology at work.
Although he was attracted by the communists' vigor in industrializing

their country, he knew he could never be part of someone else's orthodoxy. The disparate elements of syndicalism were the raw materials out of which he created his own synthesis. He shaped the doctrine to fit the requirements of urban planning; syndicalist ideas inspired him to alter fundamentally the form of his ideal city.

The major conflict in syndicalist thought—and the one that became the center of Le Corbusier's concerns—was between authority and participation. Syndicalism began in the 1880s and 1890s as the quasianarchist ideology of the trade union movement. After the revolution, each *syndicat* would run its own factory; each member would participate equally, and there would be a minimum of organization. The syndicalist leaders were hostile to the state, and they were especially hostile to all attempts to subordinate the trade unions to a parliamentary party. Their concept of revolution was a mass rising—the General Strike.

If syndicalism originated as a participatory movement of the extreme Left, it was soon modified by authoritarian elements of the extreme Right. The agent of this modification was Georges Sorel, the movement's first intellectual advocate. Sorel sought support from all who hated the bourgeoisie, even the anticapitalist reactionaries of the *Action française* who dreamed of the revival of the medieval guilds under the auspices of a resurrected monarchy. Some young disciples of Sorel sought out their counterparts in the *Action française* to see if some fusion of syndicalism with reaction could be found. This group, the *Cercle Proudhon,* met regularly before the First World War. Its members shared the belief that the era of individualism was ending, and a new age based on authority was about to begin. Laissez-faire capitalism and parliamentary democracy, the two great individualistic institutions, would both disappear. In place of capitalism there would rise a hierarchy of *syndicats* organized like the medieval guilds. These would control production, prices, and wages in their trades. They would also replace the parliaments. Men voted only as members of their trade. A council of Masters drawn from each trade would govern the country.[16]

This plan had one special merit: it could mean anything. It could be the basis for anarchy or dictatorship; it was either the victory of the proletariat or the final end of the workers' movement. For a postwar generation that distrusted all the old ideologies, its ambiguities were its attraction. Syndicalism was a radical doctrine for workers who had lost faith in the proletariat, sons of the bourgeoisie who hated the middle class, and all who knew only that the parliamentary system must go. Seen from any perspective, syndicalism seemed to promise a new order. We shall see what use Le Corbusier made of the doctrine.

He was first introduced to it by a friend, the physician Pierre Winter. Both men were physical fitness enthusiasts who played basketball together each week during the twenties. Winter was also an enthusiast for the authoritarian wing of the syndicalist movement and a follower of the self-proclaimed "French Mussolini," Georges Valois. In 1925, Valois had founded his own party, the *Faisceau,* which called for the abdication of parliament, a "national dictatorship above parties and classes, under the command of a Leader," and the formation of syndicalist assemblies.[17] Winter was active in the party and occasionally expounded Le Corbusier's town planning theories in Valois's daily newspaper. In 1926, he concluded an article on the Plan Voisin with his own commentary: "Only a strong program of urbanism—the program of a fascist government—is capable of adapting the modern city to the needs of all."[18]

Le Corbusier was still attached to capitalism and to technocracy in 1926. By the late twenties, however, he was more receptive; through Winter he met some of the leading syndicalist intellectuals. At that time the *Faisceau* no longer existed. Valois had grown disillusioned with Mussolini, and the syndicalists were now anxious to disassociate themselves from what they considered to be Italian fascism's compromises with capitalism. Instead of one party, syndicalism was now expounded in many little reviews, each claiming to be the nucleus of a movement. In 1930 Philippe Lamour, a young lawyer and former associate of Valois, proposed to Le Corbusier that they found their own review, devoted equally to syndicalist politics and to the arts. The first issue of *Plans* appeared in January 1931.

To his careers as architect, painter, and theorist Le Corbusier added one more: editor and spokesman for syndicalism. He abandoned the Purist dream of a smoothly functioning capitalist elite and entered into the rough world of political activism. This new vocation, however, was not a rush to the barricades. He was reluctant even to call himself a revolutionary. "Nothing is more dangerous," he observed in 1932, "than the revolutionary with beak and claws, the negator, the destroyer, the scoffer."[19] His concept of his own role was to imagine "a complete system, coherent, just, and indisputable." Such a system would be "nothing more or less than a revolutionary event."[20] His contribution took the form of an ideal city for a syndicalist society: the Radiant City.

The Radiant City is at once a plan for urban reconstruction, a prescription for economic planning, and a call for political revolution. For Le Corbusier, the three aims are inseparable. Only a syndicalist revolution could begin the rebuilding of the cities, but only in the cities of the future could the syndicalist dilemma of authority and participation be resolved. The Radiant City is Le Corbusier's design for an environment in which both elements of the doctrine could find intense and appropriate expression. His method, as always, is not compromise but synthesis. He first separates a hierarchical sphere of production and administration from a participatory sphere of leisure and family life, giving to each its own well-defined realm where its values are supreme. The two realms, juxtaposed, form the Radiant City. Harmony is in the structure of the whole city and in the complete life of its citizens.

In the Radiant City the world of industry is the world of planning and top-down control. Le Corbusier hoped that syndicalism would finally create the natural order inherent in large-scale organization. He tried to define this order in his "pyramid of natural hierarchies," his version of the syndicalist program. The bottom of this pyramid is the individual *syndicat*: the group of workers, white collar employees, and engineers who run their own factories. The workers participate according to their own specialized knowledge; in addition, they choose their "natural leaders" as foremen and manager (Fig. 68).

The *syndicat* gives the workers the feeling of real participation in their work that they lacked under capitalism. But this participation does not extend beyond the *syndicat.* Le Corbusier was confident that everyone was "capable of judging the facts of his trade"; he was also extremely dubious of the average man's ability to look beyond his immediate experience. Indeed, his principal critique of parliamentary democracy was that it constantly required the man in the street to judge the most difficult questions of policy. The result was chaos, demagogy, or both. In Le Corbusier's scheme, once the average man has chosen his natural leader he has no further say in policy. The larger questions are the responsibility of those higher up in the natural hierarchy.

The plant managers form the first rank of leaders, and the regional council of plant managers represents the first step in the hierarchy. Each level corresponds to a level of administrative responsibility. The manager runs his factory; the regional leaders administer the plants in their region. The regional council sends its most able members to a national council, which is responsible for the overall control of the trade. The leader of this council meets with his fellow leaders to coordinate the production of the entire country. They allot the capital needed for each region and set the goals for production.

This hierarchy of administration has replaced the state. As Saint-Simon had urged, a man's power corresponds exactly to his responsibilities in the structure of production. Seen from this perspective, Le Corbusier's syndicalist hierarchy represents not the rejection of his technocratic concerns of the twenties but their culmination. The "pyramid of natural hierarchies" extends the bureaucratic organization he had extolled in the large corporation from the individual firm to the economy as a whole. No longer would the order and planning of isolated businesses be negated by the chaos of laissez-faire. Nor would such factors as the profit-motive or class conflict be allowed to disturb the efficient allocation of manpower and resources. In a syndicalist society, technocratic rationalism would have a firm base, for everyone shares a common concern that the economy be administered as efficiently as possible.

Confronting a world threatened by depression, chaos, and collapse, Le Corbusier concluded that administration must become conscious and total. Society needed above all Authority and a Plan. He was fascinated by the dream of a single Plan that would regulate the economy for an entire nation. This Plan would be the score for the industrial symphony, a "rational and lyric monument" to man's capacity to organize. Created by a corps of experts free from outside pressure, the Plan's complex provisions would cover every aspect of production, distribution, and construction. This Plan would be more than a collection of statistics and instructions; it would be the supreme social work of art. It would bring to consciousness the complicated and yet satisfying harmonies of an orderly productive world; it would express the unity that underlies the division of labor in society; it would sum up the full range of exchange and cooperation that is necessary to an advanced economy. For Le Corbusier, the Plan would embody human solidarity in the face of the hostile forces of nature.

The major aim of the Plan would be to marshal the resources to reconstruct the cities, and, above all, to build mass housing. Le Corbusier believed that the real test of any industrial society was its capacity to house its citizens well. The workers, who had suffered the hardships of the factory system, would comprehend its benefits only when the factories began turning out magnificent machine-age dwellings for them to occupy. They would then see the connection between their labors and the new civilization they were helping to create. The "essential joys" of the machine age would become part of their daily life.

Le Corbusier's conception of housing in the Radiant City represents a significant departure from his earlier Contemporary City plans. In the Contemporary City, housing exactly mirrors the hierarchical structure of society: the elite live luxuriously in the center and the workers live modestly at the outskirts. In the Radiant City, however, all citizens live in the high-rise apartments at the center. This residential area is wholly egalitarian. There are no good or bad neighborhoods; apartments are not assigned on the basis of the worker's position in the hierarchy but according to the size of his family and their needs. Everyone has equal and ready access to social services and to recreational facilities. "If the city were to become a human city," Le Corbusier pointed out, "it would be a city without classes."[21]

The Radiant City is thus divided into two cities: the hierarchical, totally administered world of production and the egalitarian, participatory world of leisure. The split corresponds to the division within Le Corbusier's concerns during his syndicalist period. He was anxious that society be put in order, that the natural elites be permitted to organize the world, but his activist concerns had made him more sensitive to the problems of those on the bottom of the hierarchy who spent their working lives taking orders. When, for example, he visited the United States in 1935, he found much to admire in the luxury apartment houses that lined Central Park and Lake Shore Drive, but he added, "My own thinking is directed toward the crowds in the subway who come home at night to dismal dwellings. The millions of beings sacrificed to a life without hope, without rest—without sky, sun, or greenery."[22]

For Le Corbusier, however, the solution was not to abandon mass production or large-scale organization. Rather, it was to intensify industrialization and administration and then to use the materials provided by disciplined labor to create a realm of freedom and individual fulfillment: the residential community. The problems of work are thus solved in leisure and family life. Out of the products of mass production the planner fashions a world of play, and this world restores to the worker his creative independence.

In the Radiant City, therefore, the egalitarian residential community is not the contradiction of the hierarchical industrial order but its completion. "Modern organization," Le Corbusier wrote, "must, by the rational arrangement of the collectivity, redeem, *liberate the individual.*"[23] Both the residential and the administrative realms are planned, but planning in the latter is designed to weld the work force into a tight organization, whereas planning in the residential community exists to widen the individual's choices for self-fulfillment.

The major institutions of the residential sphere are the great apartment blocks, which Le Corbusier called *unités d'habitation.* They are the successors of the luxury apartment houses of the Contemporary City with important modifications. First, Le Corbusier wished to get away from both the concept of luxury dwellings, in which the conspicuous consumption of space becomes a sign of status, and the concept of *Existenzminimum,* the design of public housing based on the absolute hygienic minimums. He believed that housing could be made to the "human scale," right in its proportions for everyone, neither cramped nor wasteful. The size of the apartment would vary

with the size of the family that occupied it. No one would need anything larger nor get anything smaller. In designing these apartments
Le Corbusier remarked, "I thought neither of rich nor of poor but of
man" (Fig. 69).[24]

The family apartment is the real center of the residential community, the embodiment of privacy and equality within an organized
world. This privacy, however, would not lead to isolation, for each
apartment is part of a great communal structure, the *unité*. Having
provided a refuge for the individual and his family from the rest of the
world, Le Corbusier then set out to design the facilities that would
permit individuals to join each other in freedom and cooperation.
Each *unité* would have a cooperative food store and laundry; each
would have its own day-care center, nursery school, and primary
school. There would also be a health-care center adjacent to the building. These essential services would be the primary forces linking the
residents with each other and creating a community. In addition to the
essential services, the *unités* had facilities that permitted the residents
to share what Le Corbusier called "the essential joys." There were
meeting rooms, youth clubs, hobby centers, and an indoor gym-
nasium. On the roofs of the buildings he proposed to put tennis
courts, swimming pools, and sand beaches for sunbathing. Since the
buildings covered only 15 percent of the land, the open space surrounding them would be devoted to playing fields, gardens, and
parks.

The juxtaposition of this realm of freedom with the industrial realm
of organization represents Le Corbusier's resolution of the syndicalist
dilemma of participation and authority. Both are supreme within their
proper spheres; both comprise the Radiant City. The juxtaposition
also represents Le Corbusier's own attempt to sum up his basic values. In the clearest statement of his aims Le Corbusier put forward his
belief that

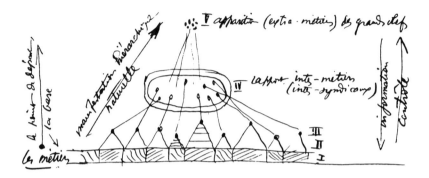

Figure 68
The Pyramid of Natural Hierarchies. Each trade or profession (I) elects its natural leaders
(II). The heads of each trade (III) meet in an intertrade council (IV), which regulates the
economic life of the nation. Assisted by a secretariat of experts (V), the intertrade council
draws up the Plan. (Source: Le Corbusier, *La Ville radieuse,* p. 192.)

Figure 69
The residential district of the Radiant City. From the plan for Antwerp, 1933. (Source: Le
Corbusier, *La Ville radieuse,* p. 284.)

Life flows between two poles, each capable of attaining the sublime. One of these poles represents what man does alone: the exceptional, the moving, the holy act of individual creation. The other represents what men undertake when organized in groups, cities or nations: those forces, those great movements of the collectivity.
Here, individual grandeur, the scope of genius.
There, administration, order, direction, leadership, civic action.[25]

Man at work creates a world which is truly human. But this world, once created, is a world of freedom where man lives in accord with his fellow man and in harmony with nature. The triumph of the realm of administration means that it no longer need engross man's whole life. The triumph of administration is the liberation of man from its clutches, the liberation of man to live another life of individual creativity with his family. The *ville radieuse* is thus a city of leisure as well as order, a city of meditation as well as production. Le Corbusier's two paths to the sublime meet at the Radiant City (Fig. 70).

The text of *La Ville radieuse* (1935), Le Corbusier's most complete exposition of his syndicalist ideal city, begins with the assertion, "These studies rest on an inalienable, unquestionable truth that is fundamental to all plans for social organization: individual liberty."[26] The book, however, is dedicated to Authority. Le Corbusier refused to recognize the contradiction. The Radiant City expressed his faith that society was moving toward an order which would be at once more authoritarian and more libertarian. Even in the realm of practice he insisted that the Authority to whom he dedicated *La Ville radieuse*—the all-powerful syndicalist Authority that would finally decide to build the Radiant City—would rest on mass participation and enthusiasm. Whatever the merits of his theoretical synthesis, his hopes for syndicalism as a mass movement were disappointed. As the Depression deepened and support for syndicalism remained low, Le Corbusier became more and more fascinated by the idea of a leader and a small elite that would seize power and enforce order. In his quest for the

Figure 70
Ground plan of the
Radiant City. The place
of honor at the center (A)
belongs to housing.
Other features include
(B) hotels and
embassies; (C) business
center; (D) factories; (E)
and (F) satellite cities, for
example, the seat of
government, a center for
social studies. (Source:
Le Corbusier, *La Ville
radieuse,* p. 141.)

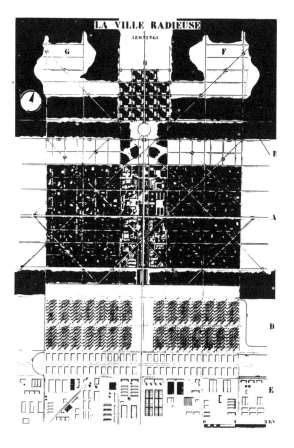

new collective society he often forgot his own "unquestionable truth" of individual liberty and put all his faith in authority.

In part, Le Corbusier's authoritarianism represented his response to trends that were already present in syndicalism. Syndicalism regarded parliamentary democracy as an outmoded relic of the liberal era. The inability of the Western democracies to combat the Depression was taken as proof that a pluralistic society could never cope with the demands of the modern age. Even liberals believed that some form of collectivism was inevitable. Intellectuals of all parties were fascinated by the idea of a charismatic Leader whose unquestioned personal authority would suppress the devisive interest-politics of the parliaments and unite the masses behind a positive program. Robert Aron, the editor of the influential syndicalist journal *L'Ordre nouveau,* remarked, "Russia has found her Stalin, Italy her *Duce,* Germany her *Fuehrer.* When will France find her *Chef?*"[27] The syndicalists, who prided themselves on having "gone beyond the shibboleths of Right and Left," looked with tolerance and even approval on the successes of both communist and fascist parties. These successes confirmed that the liberal era was at an end. Le Corbusier included a photo of a mass rally in Venice in *La Ville radieuse* and put this caption underneath: "Little by little the world approaches its destiny. In Moscow, in Berlin, in Rome, and in the United States, the masses gather around a strong idea."[28] This strong idea was the respect for authority—any authority that seemed capable of building the new age. "France needs a Father," Le Corbusier proclaimed. "It doesn't matter who. It could be one man, two men, any number."[29]

Le Corbusier's growing interest in authoritarianism must be seen in the context of a revulsion from liberal democracy so widespread in the thirties that it was almost the spirit of that troubled age. Nonetheless, this interest also reflected his own problems and preoccupations. His whole conception of planning predisposed him to authoritarian methods. For Le Corbusier, rebuilding the cities was too important to be left to the citizens. A machine-age city could never emerge from discussion, individual action, and compromise: that was the path to chaos. The harmonious city must first be planned by experts who understand the science of urbanism. They work out their plans in total freedom from partisan pressures and special interests; once their plans are formulated, they must be implemented without opposition. Planning, he declared, is a "synchronic" phenomenon; it requires the simultaneous coordination of all facets of construction, and this coordination requires overall control.[30]

Le Corbusier thought of politicians as, at best, the people who provide the power that enables the planners to do their work. In this conception it is the planner who is the real leader of society; the politician is merely the technician who carries out predetermined designs.

The Radiant City is on paper. When a technical work is drawn up (figures and proofs), *it exists.* Only spectators, gapers, impotents need the certainty that comes from execution. The Radiant City that will dissipate out anguish, which will succeed the reigning darkness—it exists on paper. We await a "Yes" from an Authority that will come and will prevail.[31]

This authority, however, must be absolute within its sphere. If individuals or private groups were allowed to modify the plan to suit themselves, the planners' solutions would be mangled in execution. Le Corbusier's concept of a rational, technically objective plan drawn up by experts thus implies the existence of an absolute authority to carry it out. Only unobstructed power could realize a work of harmony and truth.

Le Corbusier's quest for authority in the thirties reflects finally his deeply ambivalent attitude toward industrialization. His social thought and his architecture rested on the faith that industrial society had the inherent capacity for a genuine and joyous order, but behind that faith there was the fear that a perverted, uncontrolled industrialization could destroy civilization. As a young man at La Chaux-de-Fonds he had seen ugly, mass-produced timepieces from Germany virtually wipe out the watchmakers' crafts. The lesson was not forgotten. In the thirties he expressed it in his theory of the two stages of industrialization.[32] In the First Machine Age (1830 to 1930), the machine oppressed man. It was an Age of Greed, of ugliness, conflict, and oppression. The Second Machine Age about to dawn would be an Age of Harmony where the machine's potential for liberation would be realized. The Depression was the Time of Troubles that separated the two ages, but for humanity to reach the Second Machine Age there must be Authority to lead it.[33] In the *Redressement français* pamphlet of the twenties, Le Corbusier's fears of anarchy were answered by his hopes for a Minister of Public Works to take charge. In the Age of the Dictators this figure would take other forms.

In 1932, Le Corbusier broke with Philippe Lamour and *Plans* and became a member of the Central Committee for Regionalist and Syndicalist Action and an editor of its journal, *Prélude*. The best known member of the committee—which was more impressive in name than in fact—was Hubert Lagardelle, a protégé of Sorel and the Grand Old Man of French syndicalism. Lagardelle had close ties with the left wing of Italian fascism, those followers of Mussolini who still held to the young Mussolini's revolutionary syndicalist pronouncements long after the *Duce* himself had abandoned them. *Prélude,* whose editors included Lagardelle and Pierre Winter, was cautiously profascist. Fascism was "worthy to be studied very closely," even though "the financial ties which ensnare the fascist government prevent it from attempting to resolve the problem of capitalism."[34]

Le Corbusier at first had little respect for fascism. In a 1933 article in *Prélude* he attacked both "Mussolini modern" architecture and the regime itself. "Rome imitating Rome: a foolish redundancy."[35] In 1934, however, Mussolini began to encourage progressive architecture. Le

Corbusier was invited to go to Italy and was enthusiastically received; his view of fascism changed immediately. In Filippo Tomaso Marinetti's profascist *Stile futuristica* he wrote: "The present spectacle of Italy, the state of her spiritual powers, announces the imminent dawn of the modern spirit. Her shining purity and force illumine the paths which had been obscured by the cowardly and the profiteers."[36] As the language clearly indicates, Le Corbusier was hoping that Mussolini would be the Authority who would decree the Radiant City. But the "imminent dawn" refused to shine. Mussolini lost interest in modern architecture, and Le Corbusier returned to France empty-handed.

This foreign adventure only emphasized the difficulties of building a syndicalist movement at home. The raw materials were there; the bankruptcy of the parliamentary system was evident, the trade unions had made syndicalist ideas widely familiar among the working class, and the "little journals" such as *Plans* and *Prélude* had spread syndicalism among the intellectuals. Le Corbusier plunged into the work, spending almost every evening writing, editing, or at meetings. His associates at the Central Committee were men like Norbert Bezard, a peasant turned syndicalist activist who persuaded Le Corbusier to design a "radiant farm"; François de Pierrefeu, an engineer and fervent advocate of the Radiant City; and Father Bordachar, a priest sympathetic to syndicalism who was a leader in Catholic veterans organizations. With these modest associates he shared his surprisingly elitist hopes for revolution. "It may entail the most violent struggles," he confided, "but the conflict will never exceed its proper limits and spread outside the official decision-making groups."[37]

These groups, however, were not to be won over by the Central Committee. The most damaging blow to syndicalism came, ironically, from the left-wing parties that united to form the Popular Front in 1935. The Popular Front refocused attention on electoral politics, and its victory in 1936 made Parliament once again the center of attention.

The syndicalists, who claimed that electoral politics was a snare and a delusion, now seemed increasingly irrelevant. *Prélude* was forced to suspend publication in late 1935.

It was in this context of disappointed hopes that Le Corbusier put forward his most revealing vision of political life in a syndicalist society: the National Center of Collective Festivals for 100,000 People.[38] This Center took the form of a huge sports stadium, which, in the syndicalist era Le Corbusier still wished for, would also serve as a "civic tool for the modern age." It would be the site of the great political rallies of the future. The huge arc of concrete on which the spectators sit is focused on a speaker's platform behind the playing field. There the leader would inspire his people, speaking directly to all and receiving approval directly from all.

Yet Le Corbusier did not intend the spectators to be passive. Even in his most authoritarian stage he believed that a true revolution must create a collective consciousness, a spontaneous sense of participation and union. This great transformation cannot be imposed from above. It arises from the individual's feeling of belonging to a world reborn. The collective consciousness is the highest achievement of the new order. The conclusion of every rally, therefore, would be a parade of the masses. The spectators would stream down and occupy the field. They would become the actors in their own pageant. Men and women in work clothes carrying their tools would group themselves spontaneously into columns. There would be marching, perhaps dancing.[39]

What is the relationship between the leader on the platform and the masses on the field? How can a regime of authority create a feeling of participation? Le Corbusier could never say. He knew only that both must be present in his ideal city. They were two elements in a synthesis he could never define. In his many drawings and plans for the National Center, the great stadium is always empty (Fig. 71).

Figure 71
The National Center of Collective Festivals for 100,000 People. (Source: Le Corbusier, *Oeuvre complète 1934–38,* p. 93.)

Le Corbusier's career as an activist might well have ended in 1935. Although he continued "with obstinacy and tenderness . . . to *make Plans,*"[40] he was increasingly aware that the threat of war was making his plans irrelevant. After the First World War Le Corbusier had suggested that the heavy war industries be retooled for making houses. The "era of great works," the alternative to the era of great wars, never took place. Now the factories were retooling, but to make new munitions. In 1938, he published a book titled *Cannons? Bombs? No thanks. Housing please!!* His request was not followed. When the war broke out, he received his first major commission from the French government: to build a munitions factory.

The fall of France in June 1940 created the unexpected conditions that led to the bitterly ironic culmination of his activist period. The factory was still uncompleted when the armistice was signed. There was no work or food for him in Paris; he and his wife left for the small town of Ozon, in the south of France. There he attempted to evaluate the new regime of Marshal Pétain. As an opponent of parliamentary democracy, Le Corbusier had no regrets for the fall of the Third Republic. The Vichy regime, moreover, seemed to promise the authority that Le Corbusier and his fellow syndicalists had been advocating in the thirties. In *La Ville radieuse* he had quoted with approval Pétain's statement that "the leader must have three qualities: imagination, will, and technical knowledge . . . and in that order."[41] In 1940, Le Corbusier permitted himself to hope that the aged general himself might become the Leader who would implement his plans.

From his remote place of refuge he set out to gain a position with the new regime. He discovered that he knew Marcel Peyrouton, the Minister of the Interior. Peyrouton had been Governor General in Algiers when Le Corbusier had presented his plans for that city; in 1934, Peyrouton had presided at the public lecture at which Le Corbusier had expounded his theories. Through Peyrouton he obtained the position he sought. With his old mentor Auguste Perret he would be Commissioner for the rebuilding of devastated areas.

In January 1941, he arrived at Vichy. "I enter into the tumult," he wrote to Father Bordachar, "after six months of doing nothing and equipped with twenty years of hopes."[42] Thus began eighteen months of fruitless attempts to persuade Authority. It was not his finest hour. There is something both comic and frightening in the spectacle of the greatest architect of his time currying favor with the decaying notables of the past; presenting plans for social harmony to the ministers of repression; begging—in vain—for an interview with Pétain; intriguing to keep the tiny hotel room that the regime had allotted him.

One is tempted to explain the episode as an artist's total misapprehension of the politicians he was dealing with. Le Corbusier, however, understood very well at least one aspect of Vichy and wholly approved of it. A powerful faction of the regime wished to use the Marshal's autocratic power to control and rationalize French industry, to organize the trades into self-regulating corporations and to institute planning from above. In this group were many of Le Corbusier's syndicalist associates, including Hubert Lagardelle, as well as many of the *Redressement français* technocrats he had known in the twenties.

The technocrats were enthusiastic supporters of the idea of national planning, an idea that was also of vital interest to Le Corbusier. François Lehideux, a nephew of Louis Renault, had been chosen to formulate a Directive Plan for National Equipment, which would govern the allocation of the nation's capital investments. Le Corbusier was pleased to discover that he knew the man who had been put in charge of construction for the Plan, Robert Latournerie, a leading jurist and member of the *Conseil d'Etat.* He asked Latournerie to make him a consultant. At the same time he found another powerful backer within the regime, Henri du Moulin de la Barthète, a member of the elite Inspectorate of Finance who was serving as Chief of the Marshal's Civil

Cabinet. (He had been introduced to du Moulin through a mutual friend, the playwright Jean Giraudoux.)[43]

His efforts bore fruit. On 27 May 1941, Pétain signed a decree creating a Study Commission for Questions Relating to Housing and Building. The Commission was charged with advising Lehideux and with "proposing any measures necessary to begin and to put into effect a national policy" for building. The Commission could embark upon "all inquiries or missions which it judges useful, in France, in the Empire or in foreign countries." The members of this Commission were Le Corbusier and two of his associates, François de Pierrefeu and André Boll.[44]

Le Corbusier believed that Authority was about to act, and, more importantly, to act on his plans. He immediately set out to make his concept of architecture and city planning the official one for France. Through his position as adviser to the Directive Plan he would have a decisive voice in the Corporation of Architects that Vichy had already created. This Corporation was part of the regime's attempt to organize each profession into a self-regulating guild. Le Corbusier proposed that a new elite be created within the Corporation of Architects: the Master Builders. These men would be the town planners and industrial designers of France. They would head large offices of architects and engineers that would undertake mass housing and urban reconstruction. They would have the power to override local building codes and to overrule opposition from local authorities.

The principal task of the Master Builders would be to carry out the instructions of the Directive Plan. A corps of experts in Vichy would define the basic methods of construction for the whole country; they would set up factories in which the components of buildings could be prefabricated; and they would allocate these and other materials to the Master Builders for use in the projects they would specify.[45]

At the head of the whole structure of authority would be an official

Le Corbusier called the Regulator (*Ordonnateur*). He was the last and most grandiose of the modern Colberts that Le Corbusier devised. The Regulator was both an architect and an administrator, and he was supremely powerful in both fields. He was the natural leader of the Master Builders; by example and by command his doctrine of construction would become theirs. He formulated the national plan for building and thus had responsibility for the structure of the whole country. He could zone the nation, reserving some areas for cities, others for agriculture, others for wilderness. He determined the equilibrium between industry and agriculture. If the Regulator believed that the growth of a city threatened its surrounding agricultural region, he could stop that growth or even reverse it. His control over the location of industries gave him a decisive voice in the distribution of population. If a region seemed overconcentrated he could forbid new factories and homes there and assign construction to less crowded areas. The Regulator had supreme power over the environment. The Chief of State must secure his approval before any legislation affecting the environment can be approved. Aided by a staff of experts, the Regulator "serenely, lucidly puts the world in order."[46] Le Corbusier never named his nominee for so august a post. "For many years," Le Corbusier remarked in 1929, "I have been haunted by the ghost of Colbert."[47] By 1941, it was apparent that the specter that had been pursuing him was always his own shadow.

The Regulator was a hope for the future. Le Corbusier also wished to begin building immediately a series of "exemplary works" that would reveal the grandeur of his conceptions and demonstrate his power within the regime. His attention was focused first on Algiers. He had executed three remarkable plans for that city during the thirties. They had won him a place on the Algiers Planning Commission, where he was ignored.

Shortly after his arrival in Vichy he received a letter from a friend in

Algiers, Pierre-Auguste Emery, informing him that the Planning Commission there was about to approve a rival plan.[48] Le Corbusier believed he had the influence to impose his will and make Algiers an "exemplary" city, "guiding the future of architecture in metropolitan France and in the rest of Europe."

In June 1941, he flew to Algiers to present his own plan (Fig. 72). Although he delivered public lectures to arouse "collective enthusiasm," his relations with the local authorities were distant and hostile. His real aim was always to persuade the Vichy regime to "delegate to Le Corbusier the mandate to give orders."[49] As he explained to Marshal Maxime Weygand, then Vichy's representative in North Africa, "In the present administrative state, only the highest authorities of the country can permit the necessary innovations, create the useful precedents, authorize the ignoring of old regulations, permit the Plan to enter into life."[50] With support from du Moulin he called upon Weygand to suspend the local commission and give control over planning to Le Corbusier and his associates.

By an order from above the local plan must be interrupted and its continuance forbidden. This gesture of authority will have a decisive effect on Algerian opinion, showing that the government of Marshal Pétain has taken into consideration the most pressing problems of urbanism and that from now on it intends to impose a new orientation.[51]

The spring of 1941 marked the high point of Le Corbusier's power or, rather, his illusions of power. Despite the decree signed by Pétain, his Study Commission was only one of a score of bodies, each seeking to impose its own views on a Directive Plan, which was never implemented.

The Vichy of the technocrats was not the only Vichy. Of equal influence with the Marshal were the more traditional authoritarians who argued that industry and cities had been the cause of France's downfall. Although Le Corbusier believed he was on the verge of power, he was in fact a minor member of an embattled faction. He never understood—or refused to understand—his real position. The phantasmagoric atmosphere of Vichy, the absence of real power combined with the illusion of omnipotence, had encouraged his wildest speculations.

He was soon awakened from his dreams of Regulators and exemplary works. Lehideux, the Plan's Director, grew annoyed at Le Corbusier's pretensions. On 14 July 1941—Bastille Day was not celebrated at Vichy—the Study Commisison received the message that "The Minister does not envisage cooperating with Le Corbusier in any way."[52]

This notice was the "decree of death," as Le Corbusier put it, for the Study Commission. Nonetheless, continued support from du Moulin and the general confusion permitted the Commission to maintain a posthumous existence. Le Corbusier convinced himself that all his problems would be solved if Pétain gave his personal blessing to the Algiers plan. As he wrote to du Moulin, "You must be there to realize what the name of the Marshal means in Algiers and the least of the opinions he voices."[53] All his efforts were directed to securing an interview with Pétain. "I'm down on my hands and knees doing everything to get results," he wrote to Emery. "But, my dear friends, it's really *tough* to preach in the desert and make others act!!!"[54]

The interview was never granted. The most he obtained was a letter from Pétain's personal secretary, Bernard Ménétrel, acknowledging that *On the Four Routes,* a book which Le Corbusier published in 1941 and sent to the Marshal, contained "many suggestions for the regeneration of urban life, often happy ones."[55]

Writing to Emery in January 1942, he remarked that he found only "mediocrity, hostility, cliques" at Vichy. "Is this a reason for surrender? Never."[56] From his tiny hotel room he plotted a spring offensive. He prepared a complete Directive Plan for Algiers, his last and most ambitious plan. It covered seventy-five years of urban development and was to be kept secret throughout that time to prevent speculation (and, one suspects, opposition). He was concerned initially with the creation of a new business center organized around a skyscraper. This center, he hoped, would make Algiers the point of contact between Western Europe and Africa. He emphasized that the plan represented the twentieth-century equivalent of the spirit that had conquered Algeria in the nineteenth century. To the leaders of Algiers he declared, "I give you my help; the least you can think of it is that it represents the result of courage, tenacity, and an unshakeable confidence in the possibilities of our time" (Fig. 73). [57]

This, it seems, was insufficient. In April 1942, Le Corbusier went to Algiers to make a final effort to get his way. He applied directly to the Governor General of Algeria, A. R. Chatel, to create a Committee for the Study of Housing and Urbanism for Algeria. This committee was to be advisory, but his real aim was to turn it into a superagency that would have power over all the local bodies. [58] The new plan soon provoked even more opposition than the old. The municipal officials were hostile to modern architecture and unwilling to risk the capital investment that Le Corbusier's plan required. They objected in particular to Le Corbusier's proposal for preserving the Casbah untouched. The municipality wished to demolish a large section of it as slums and replace it with housing for Europeans.

If Le Corbusier had been in Vichy working through his remaining friends in power, he might have saved the situation. Unfortunately, he was in Algiers, the worst position for him, for he lost no time in antagonizing his enemies and exasperating his friends. The *coup de grâce* was delivered when a conservative Algiers newspaper reprinted an old attack by Alexandre de Senger that identified Le Corbusier as "The Trojan Horse of Bolshevism." [59] The mayor of Algiers denounced him to the Prefect as a communist and (according to Le Corbusier) demanded his arrest. [60] He returned to Vichy on 22 May, and two

Figure 72

Le Corbusier's concept of Algiers as the point of exchange between Europe and Africa and the meeting place of European and Islamic cultures. (Source: Le Corbusier *Oeuvre complète 1938–46,* p. 44.)

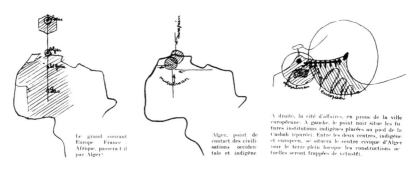

Le grand courant
Europe France
Afrique, passera-t-il
par Alger?

Alger, point de
contact des civili-
sations occiden-
tale et indigène

A droite, la cité d'affaires, en proue de la ville
européenne. A gauche, le point noir situe les fu-
tures institutions indigènes placées au pied de la
Casbah (épurée). Entre les deux centres, indigène
et européen, se situera le centre civique d'Alger
(sur le terre-plein lorsque les constructions ac-
tuelles seront frappées de vétusté).

Figure 73

Le Corbusier's final plan for Algiers, the Directive Plan of 1942. On the left is the European center for business, government, and transportation; on the right, the Casbah and the Moslem center. (Source: Le Corbusier, *Oeuvre complète 1938–46,* p. 45.)

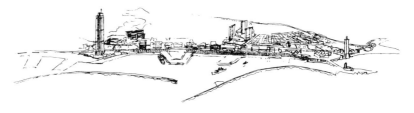

weeks later the Algiers City Council voted definitively and unanimously to reject his plans.[61] The authorities in Vichy were unwilling to reverse the decision. Le Corbusier conceded defeat and left Vichy for Paris on 1 July 1942. *"Adieux, merdeux Vichy!"* was his parting judgment.[62]

Le Corbusier was deeply disappointed by his Vichy experience, but never deeply troubled. One more regime had proved its unworthiness by rejecting him and his plans; that was his final judgment of Vichy. What seems worst about this episode in his life is that he never acknowledged the link between his plans and the authoritarian nature of the regime. Even while at Vichy he was fond of calling himself a technician without politics who dealt objectively with problems of technology and design.

There is a certain truth in this assertion. He never modified his plans to suit the tastes of his superiors. The designs he attempted to force on Algiers in the name of the Marshal were among his most joyous conceptions of the potentials for modern life. It was precisely this self-absorption in the plan that was his integrity—but also his failure. He had reduced politics to a simple yes or no to the plan, and he was willing to support any regime that said yes. In his anxiety to build, he failed to distinguish between coercive and noncoercive authority, exploitive and nonexploitive hierarchies. In his concern for the administrative state he had lost touch with the just state.

Le Corbusier never apologized for his role at Vichy, but his social thought was irrevocably changed by it. He had gone to Vichy filled with the hope that the end of the Time of Troubles was imminent. In 1937, he had published *When the Cathedrals Were White*, a book whose title expressed his faith that the modern age was about to enter a great age of synthesis comparable to the burst of medieval creativity that built the cathedrals. Our age was as young and as promising as the early Middle Ages. "I feel young as well," he added. "Before I die I hope to participate in great transformations."[63]

After Vichy he no longer wished for a great wave of enthusiasm and authority to sweep Europe; the prospect scared him. He realized that the great transformation he had longed for would have to occur slowly—if at all. "The dreams of my twenties," he predicted in 1947, "will be realized in three hundred years."[64]

In the postwar years his constant adage became, "The river flows between two banks. There is no truth in the extremes."[65] This moderation was perhaps admirable in itself, but it meant the end of his search for the ideal city—for where could the Radiant City be found if not at the extremes? Moderation might build a *Unité* in Marseilles or even a capital in Chandigarh, but it could never erect a Radiant City. The plans of the thirties could not be separated from the hopes for radical social change that inspired them. They embodied Le Corbusier's conviction that a triumphant syndicalist revolution would create the political conditions for his architectural synthesis of liberty and authority. They reflected his belief that an all-powerful leader would resolve to put an end to the era of conflict and compromise by carrying out his plan. When these fervent hopes were disappointed, Le Corbusier's attitude toward collective action changed from uncritical anticipation to an equally uncritical mistrust. Although he never repudiated the Radiant City, he turned away from any political movement that might have brought his dream closer to realization. References to Colbert in his writing ceased; he compared himself instead to Don Quixote. The Radiant City survived only as Friedrich Engels's definition of utopia: an isolated individual's doomed attempt to impose his idea on history.

1 Percival and Paul Goodman, *Communitas*, Chicago, 1947; 2nd ed., revised, New York, 1960, pp. 42–49.
2 Le Corbusier, *Des canons, des munitions? Merci! Des logis . . . s.v.p.,* Paris, 1937, p. 71.
3 Le Corbusier, *Urbanisme*, Paris, 1925, p. 283.
4 Ibid., p. 177.
5 Ibid.
6 Ibid., p. 93
7 Ibid., p. 177.
8 Sixth Letter of Henri de Saint-Simon to an American, 1817, in *Social Organization and Other Writings*, edited by Felix Markham, New York, 1953, p. 69.
9 See Frank Manuel, *The New World of Saint-Simon*, Cambridge, Mass., 1956, pp. 305–321.
10 For the neo-Saint-Simonians, see the statement of an organization to which Le Corbusier had affiliations, *Le Redressement français: organisation et réformes*, Paris, 1927. For Lenin, see V. I. Lenin, *State and Revolution* (Moscow, 1917), in the English translation: *Selected Works*, Moscow and New York, 1935, vol. 2.
11 *Vers le Paris de l'époque machiniste*, supplement to the bulletin of the *Redressement français*, 15 February 1928, p. 12.
12 Ibid., p. 1.
13 Ibid., p. 13.
14 Ibid.
15 Le Corbusier, *La Ville radieuse*, Boulogne-sur-Seine, 1935, p. 129.
16 Eugen Weber, *Action française*, Stanford, California, 1962, pp. 204–240.
17 These aims can be found in Georges Valois's daily newspaper, *Le Nouveau Siècle*.
18 Pierre Winter, "La ville moderne," in *Le Nouveau Siècle*, 16 May 1926, p. 4.
19 Le Corbusier, *Plans*, new series, vol. 2, no. 5, 1 July 1932, p. 8.
20 Le Corbusier, *La Ville radieuse*, p. 181.
21 Le Corbusier, *Le Lyrisme des temps nouveaux et l'urbanisme*, Paris, 1939, p. 15.
22 Le Corbusier, *Quand les cathédrales étaient blanches*, Paris, 1937, p. 216.
23 Le Corbusier, *Précisions sur un état présent de l'architecture et de l'urbanisme*, Paris, 1930, p. 217.
24 Le Corbusier, *La Ville radieuse*, p. 107.
25 Le Corbusier, *Précisions*, p. 217.
26 Le Corbusier, *La Ville radieuse*, p. 45.
27 Robert Aron, *L'Ordre nouveau*, vol. 2, no. 3.
28 Le Corbusier, *La Ville radieuse*, p. 92.
29 Le Corbusier, "Programme pour une grande industrie,"

Notes

in *Plans*, vol. 1, no. 3, p. 6.

30 Le Corbusier, "Réflexions à propos de la Loi Loucheur," in *La Revue des vivants*, vol. 2, no. 8, August 1928, p. 240.

31 Le Corbusier, *La Ville radieuse*, p. 92.

32 Ibid., introductory sections.

33 Ibid.

34 Le Corbusier, *Prélude*, no. 2, 15 February 1933, p. 1.

35 Ibid.

36 Le Corbusier, in *Stile futuristica*, vol. 1, no. 2, August 1934, p. 13.

37 Le Corbusier, *La Ville radieuse*, caption to the Pyramid of Natural Hierarchies.

38 Le Corbusier, *Des canons*, p. 98.

39 For Le Corbusier's concept of spontaneous theatre, see "Théâtre spontané," in *La Revue théâtrale*, vol. 5, no. 12, Spring 1950, pp. 17–22.

40 Le Corbusier, *Des canons*, p. 54.

41 Le Corbusier, *La Ville radieuse*, p. 78.

42 Letter of Le Corbusier to B. Bordachar, quoted in B. Bordachar, "Le Corbusier à Betharran. Témoignage d'un prêtre qui fut son ami," in *Les Rameaux de Notre Dame*, Betharran, B.-P., no. 67, August, November 1965, p. 170.

43 See Henri du Moulin's memoirs, *Années des illusions*, Geneva, 1946.

44 "Décret du 27 mai portant création d'une commission d'étude pour les questions relatives à l'habitation et la construction immobilière," in *Journal officiel*, vol. 73, no. 148, 29 May 1941, p. 2241.

45 François de Pierrefeu and Le Corbusier, *La Maison des hommes*, Paris, 1941, pp. 30–38.

46 Le Corbusier, *Poésie sur Alger*, Paris, 1950, p. 32. This work was written 1941–1942.

47 Le Corbusier, *Précisions*, p. 187.

48 Pierre-Auguste Emery to Le Corbusier, Algiers, 25 January 1941, Archives Fondation Le Corbusier, Paris (hereafter AFLC), Algiers dossier no. 120.

49 Le Corbusier, "Note à l'intention de M. Dumoulin [sic] de la Barthète," 27 July 1941, AFLC, Algiers dossier no. 53.

50 Le Corbusier to Maxime Weygand, Vichy, 30 June 1941, AFLC, Algiers dossier no. 29.

51 "Note relative au Plan directeur d'Alger," 12 June 1941, AFLC, Algiers dossier no. 30.

52 Bordachar, "Le Corbusier à Betharran," p. 174.

53 Le Corbusier to du Moulin, Vichy, 20 June 1941, AFLC, Algiers dossier no. 138.

54 Le Corbusier to Emery (manuscript letter), 26 January 1942, AFLC, Algiers dossier no. 4.

55 Bernard Ménétrel to Le Corbusier, 1 April 1942, AFLC, Algiers dossier no. 435.

56 Le Corbusier to Emery (manuscript letter), 26 January 1942, AFLC, Algiers dossier no. 4.

57 "Note relative au Plan directeur d'Alger," 12 June 1941, AFLC, Algiers dossier no. 30.

58 Ibid.

59 Le Corbusier had carefully preserved a score of the offending articles in his files.

60 Le Corbusier, *Poésie sur Alger*, p. 47.

61 Bordachar, "Le Corbusier à Betharran," p. 176.

62 Ibid.

63 Le Corbusier, *Quand les cathédrales étaient blanches*, p. 48.

64 Jean Petit, *Le Corbusier lui-même*, Geneva, 1970, p. 132.

65 Le Corbusier, "Message de sympathie au congrès mondial des intellectuels pour la paix [Wroclaw, Poland, 1949]," mimeographed flyer dated 17 April 1949, AFLC, dossier "Documents sur la paix," no. 106.

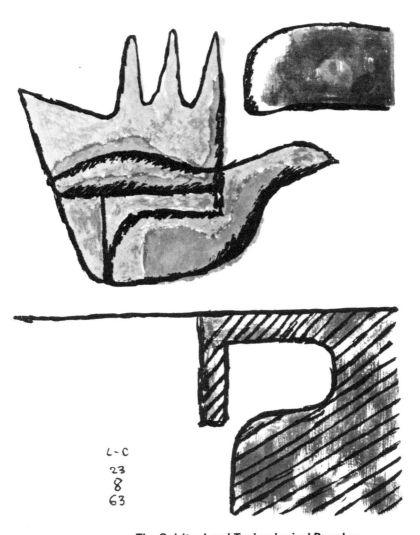

L-C
23
8
63

**The Spiritual and Technological Paradox
of Le Corbusier**

Part Four

Martin Purdy   **Le Corbusier and the Theological Program**

One of the ideas that has greatly influenced the development of architecture in this century is that of the building program. In simple
terms, this can be defined as the statement which lists the requirements of a particular project and the rational manner by which those
requirements are met. Less prosaically, the idea encompasses the
total understanding of the architectural problem: an understanding
that extends the architect's role from that of mere coordinator to one
of creative catalyst.

"The modern school holds to the programme as the source of
unity," writes John Summerson. "The concept of the building must
arise from within the programme; the programme itself must be the
architect's medium, just as much as the materials with which he
builds."[1] The task of the architect in this process is to absorb himself
fully, yet dispassionately, with all the issues that constitute the program, and then produce, in formal and spatial terms, an architectural
synthesis that will enable the client more fully to carry out the tasks
for which the building is designed.

So natural is this approach of the modern movement, so obvious its
ultimate consequences, "that although the outward forms of the New
Architecture differ fundamentally in an organic sense from those of
the old, they are not the personal whims of a handful of architects
avid for innovation at all costs, but simply the inevitable logical product of the intellectual, social and technical conditions of our age."[2]
This method of working lay at the heart of the Bauhaus teaching, and
has helped produce much socially inspired architecture of recent
years.

Applying these directives to the specific problem of church building,
a serious architect would expect to acquaint himself with the liturgical
and other functions that make up the theological program. He need
not have personal faith in those functions, but his professional concern for the impact of architecture upon society should lead him to a

natural interest in the likely relationship of the Church, its buildings, and the social milieu, and the hope that his architecture could foster that activity. Indeed, an appreciation of the Liturgical Movement, that endeavor to reintegrate Christian life and worship, which has been described by one scholar, David Edwards, as "an understanding of the Church as drama in which all who take part review their faith in the Lordship of Christ,"[3] enabled such architects as Rudolf Schwarz (1897–1961) to create new, if rather stark, architectural forms for the Church. These, and buildings by architects of like interest, have their focus in the gathered nature of the assembly.

Schwarz's own architectural theories and writings on church design are very similar to the general propaganda put about by so many of the pioneer modern architects. Much of this had sprung from the pen of Le Corbusier, whose *Vers une architecture* is a gospel of program theory. Yet it is one of the eternal fascinations of that master that he so often failed to follow in practice what he had preached in his writings. Certainly by the time he came to produce the church buildings during the latter part of his life, the paradox is revealed most fully. The pilgrimage chapel of Notre-Dame-du-Haut at Ronchamp, the monastic college of La Tourette, and the parish church at Firminy Vert are profoundly serious and heartfelt works, but they do not seem to seek their justification within an orthodox theological program.

Le Corbusier did not ignore contemporary liturgical understanding; in fact he went to some pains to satisfy it, but he was never really concerned with stimulating that understanding, nor with giving it a new emphasis by his architecture. Despite the apparent modernity of his churches, they do not significantly advance the theory of ecclesiastical building, a situation in direct contrast with his work on urbanism and housing, where he sought to shape a better social order through physical ideas. More nearly, Le Corbusier's church buildings seem to represent the architect's own struggle to come to terms with the spiritual insights that occupied him throughout his life: the reconciliation of mankind within a natural order and the resolution of the apparent conflict between individual freedom and the collective society.

These insights are worthy of a place in any sacred philosophy, but they are not specifically or wholly Christian ones, and, as such, are somewhat tenuous ideas on which to construct church buildings. "I am not a churchgoer myself, but one thing I do know is that every man has the religious consciousness of belonging to a greater mankind, to a greater or lesser degree, but in the end he is part of it. Into my work I bring so much effusion and intense inner life that it becomes something almost religious."[4] This rather romantic understanding pervades much of Le Corbusier's musings on the sacred, but it is no substitute for a sound theological approach. It may explain why the churches he designed, so exciting in many ways, fail to stand the test of theological analysis.

In common with other utopian planners, Le Corbusier had no place for institutionalized religion within his ideal society. He did, however, stress the importance of spiritual values. "A new truth can only emerge from the technical and spiritual revolution of modern times," he wrote in the part of *La Ville radieuse* that describes the Radiant Village.[5] "The spiritual would incite in the peasant family an urge to become a thinking entity in the heart of modern society. An entity that will think with the special and precious quality found only in people who are in permanent contact with nature." Le Corbusier here reveals his faith in nature, but the church building has no part to play. The symbol of the technical revolution in the Radiant Village was to be the grain silo: the spiritual was to manifest itself in a community center, a building with educational as well as social pretensions.

"The laws of nature exist. It is useless to ignore them. . . . The laws of nature are always there to urge us on towards the creation of human laws that will in their turn be prodigiously simple and yet prodigiously effective."[6] He follows this comment with:

mankind, endowed by heaven with three precise and totally different characteristics, . . . reason, . . . the nature of our earthly destiny, . . . and passion. . . . There exists a universe already immense and marvellous enough, that is made up of all we can see or perceive, and to that universe we have given the name *nature*. . . . All man has to go on are the laws of nature. He must just understand the spirit of them, then apply them to his own environment in order to create out of the cosmos something *human*. In other words, a genuine new creation for his own use.[7]

Le Corbusier endowed nature with religious significance and, as he claimed himself that architecture contains an essence of the religious experience, it follows that nature should have an important influence upon his specifically spiritual works. It is not without importance that these particular commissions came to him late in his career, when, with his reputation established, he was free largely to dictate the terms on which he worked. Clients wanted a Le Corbusier building, and the architect was relatively free to explore his own preoccupations. Some argument developed early in the work on Ronchamp, which was resolved by the diocesan authorities claiming responsibility for liturgical matters and leaving artistic matters to the architect's judgment. Canon Lucien Ledeur, who carried much of the administrative responsibility for the project for the Besançon archdiocese, later described their conversations with Le Corbusier: "We know why we approached you, we didn't ask you specifically to do this or that, but we did say to you that we needed a chapel which must respond to certain conditions. For the rest, we know who you are, we have chosen you, now try to put something forward to us."[8] The need for a fundamental appraisal of the program, in this case the highly complex one of the place of pilgrimage within the demythologized society of the second half of the twentieth century, seems never to have been considered.

In the postwar years, Le Corbusier turned away from the Purist symbols of crisp technology that he had employed in his earlier period and expressed himself in a more earthy idiom. The problems of access for plant and materials may have affected the construction at Ronchamp, but that at La Tourette bears a brutal crudity that cannot simply be excused as economic necessity. In the second chapter of *Manière de penser l'urbanisme* Le Corbusier claims that there should be no conflict between spiritual and technical ideals.[9] In his overtly religious works, the man-made image of imperfection appears to be the conscious choice of expression.

The church buildings of Le Corbusier remain highly personal investigations, late in life, of the fundamental questions that fascinated him throughout his career. He undertook the work only if the conditions were right, and the importance of the actual setting was paramount. In June 1961, a few months after the triumphant completion of La Tourette, he received a letter from Louis Secretan, the pastor in his birthplace of La Chaux-de-Fonds, asking him to build a church in that town. Le Corbusier replied:

I have received your letter of 20 June 1961 asking whether I would build a church at La Chaux-de-Fonds.

I built the Chapelle de Ronchamp (a chapel of pilgrimage) and the Couvent de la Tourette (the inner life of meditation and religious activity) because the program (ritual, human scale, space, and silence, etc.) was favorable, as also were the landscape conditions exceptional. I am not a builder of churches. I am continually obliged to decline the offers made to me. . . .

I cannot envisage myself inserting a church into the context that you have evoked in my mind through your photographs. Forgive me for giving you a negative response. Had you said to me, "Will you create a place open all the year, situated on the hilltops in the calm and the dignity, in the nobleness of the beautiful Jura site?", the problem could have been considered. It was a problem of psychic nature and, for me, of decisive value.

With my deepest regrets and my best wishes.[10]

This letter would seem to demonstrate Le Corbusier's own lack of interest in the task of church building, as a means of extending Christian understanding. It gives weight to the claim that the architect used the commissions he did accept to explore natural and spiritual values that were more real for him. "People were at times surprised to see me participating in a sacred art. I am not a pagan. Ronchamp is a response to the desire that one occasionally has to extend beyond oneself, and to seek contact with the unknown."[11]

Notre-Dame-du-Haut, Ronchamp

Of all Le Corbusier's religious works, those built, or those which remain as ideas, the chapel at Ronchamp is both the most well known and the most mysterious. The plea to rebuild the war-shattered shrine to Our Lady on its hilltop setting above the Saône Valley came in 1950, when Le Corbusier had barely recovered from the rude rebuttal of his project for the sanctuary at Sainte Baume. He was finally persuaded by a combination of personal requests, perhaps the most influential being that made by Father Pierre Marie Alain Couturier, the Dominican priest who had such a marked influence on his liturgical understanding. Father Couturier, who died in 1954 at the age of 56, had been trained as an artist particularly interested in stained glass, before joining the Order of Preachers. In 1937, he became codirector of the magazine *L'Art Sacré*, which had been founded two years previously.

Couturier considered that a revival of Christian art and architecture would occur if the most talented artists of the day were employed, irrespective of their personal beliefs. He had been a friend of Le Corbusier's for some years and was to support him over both Ronchamp and La Tourette. Elsewhere he was instrumental in bringing together a whole series of artists, among them Pierre Bonnard, Marc Chagall, Fernand Léger, Henri Matisse, and Georges Rouault, to adorn the

Church of Notre-Dame-de-Toute-Grâce in Assy, and he also supported the commission of Matisse to decorate the Chapel at Vence.

Couturier's policy was perhaps the antithesis of the more liberal understanding of the program theory. Excellence and artistic sincerity were to come not only before faith and piety, but also before what might be described as liturgical empathy. Unfortunately, he lived to see neither Ronchamp nor La Tourette, but both buildings stand as apt memorials to his philosophy.

The site at Ronchamp has been a holy place since pre-Christian times, and Le Corbusier's building has a strong affinity with so many other hilltop shrines, not least of which is the Acropolis at Athens, which had such a profound affect upon his thinking.[12] Marcel Maulini, a local resident, wrote to the architect about the site in March 1951, pointing out that the setting had been a place of sun worship. "Your chapel will soon become part of the ancient solar system of Rond-Champ,"[13] he observed, and his letter contains a sketch of the double-natured Dionysius.

So well known is this chapel now (it has already passed into the world of popular art, adorning travel posters and postage stamps) that its impact upon the architectural world of the 1950s is difficult to recall. It is even more difficult to procure a reason for its form. Shortly before the dedication in the summer of 1955, Alfred Canet, who had acted as secretary for the local building committee, wrote to Le Corbusier, saying that a small booklet was to be prepared for the opening, explaining the story of the building. He asked the architect for a statement, but the reply was evasive, referring Canet instead to the explanation in the fifth volume of *Oeuvre complète*. "I have no more complete explanation to give, since the chapel will be before the very eyes of those who buy the booklet. That is better than the most eloquent speech."[14]

Figure 74
The southeast corner of
the Chapel of
Notre-Dame-du-Haut,
Ronchamp, 1950–1955.
(Photograph by Martin
Purdy.)

The text about Ronchamp in Volume Five of *Oeuvre complète* is virtually the same as Le Corbusier had used for the press release in May 1953. It briefly relates the history of the chapel and the importance of "the acoustics of landscape" to the germination of the design (Fig. 74). The original idea for the construction is described, but perhaps the most telling remark states: "It was agreeable for once to become absorbed in a disinterested problem without any real practical programme, the reward being the effect of architectural forms and the spirit of architecture in the construction of a vessel of intense concentration and meditation. The researches of Le Corbusier have led him to the perception of an 'acoustic component in the domain of form.' "[15]

But neither this nor the subsequent publications[16] really explain this mystifying building. Le Corbusier's answer to Canet could be excused as the reaction of any architect at the end of a long and difficult project, when the real anxieties of successful completion loom so large. It also shows that he himself considered an experience of the building infinitely more worthwhile than a written apologia, and perhaps he felt that so personal a creative statement defies justification.

Other commentators have had similar difficulty in tracing the origin of the ideas behind the architecture of Notre-Dame-du-Haut. A. M. Cocagnac, writing on the chapel at Ronchamp,[17] tells how, after absorbing and sketching the impact of the site, Le Corbusier let the impression gestate for a few weeks. Then one day, he took a piece of charcoal, a drawing medium he did not usually favor, but one that enabled him to work quickly, and he sketched the idea.

René Bolle-Reddat, the present chaplain, ventures the explanation of creative inspiration as "a phenomenon which had always surprised the human race and caused the downfall of the clinical and logically minded,"[18] but he does believe that some key may be found in *Le Voyage d'Orient*, especially in the chapter describing the visit to

Athos. This passage is a wonderfully evocative description of the remote monastic promontory, and it vividly conveys Le Corbusier's appreciation of sculptured architectural forms amid wide and beautiful
landscape. Le Corbusier's writings on the cultic significance of Athos
are, however, tinged with the somewhat fey romanticism he often
seemed to employ when describing the sacred. It is not perhaps unfair
to suggest that Ronchamp suffers from similar sentimentality.

Stanislaus von Moos offers a more down-to-earth view.[19] He re-
minds us of the teaching based on the study of natural phenomena—
trees, shells, roots, and so on—which Le Corbusier received from
L'Eplattenier. In his early days at La Chaux-de-Fonds, the young Jeanneret had expressed the desire to build a temple to nature in the Jura
hills, and this notion would certainly tally with Le Corbusier's vision of
spiritual matters, a natural religion beyond the sounds of conventional
theology.

Charles Jencks considers that the forms of Ronchamp have their
root in Le Corbusier's painting, and that the building contains many
examples of "consistent irony." "Le Corbusier's faith in the established Church and dogma seem quite tenuous, as if it would be
strengthened by being denied."[20] Many have claimed that the building
represents a departure from rationalism, and a refutation of the architect's early beliefs. It seems to have shocked James Stirling, who
wrote within a year of the dedication:

It may be considered that the Ronchamp Chapel being a "pure expression of poetry" and the symbol of an ancient ritual, should not
therefore be criticized by the rationale of the modern movement. Remember however that it is a product of Europe's greatest architect. It
is important to consider whether the building should influence the
course of modern architecture . . . , and certainly the forms which
have developed from the rationale of the limited ideology of the
modern movement are being mannerized and changed in a conscious
imperfectionism.[21]

The shapes may seem perverse, the ideas an apparent departure from mainstream modern architecture, but Le Corbusier's classical vocabulary of curved and rectilinear forms (first given clear expression in the La Roche-Jeanneret houses at Auteuil) is merely continued in Ronchamp's sweeping, yet developed curvilinear expression.

All these theories would seem to suggest that attempts to explain and define the reasons for the building obscure rather than clarify them. Ecclesiologically, Ronchamp makes no attempt to give new architectural understanding to the setting for pilgrimage: it is simply the response of a complex visual artist to Canon Ledeur's challenge, and each individual must now make his own response to that answer.

Le Corbusier had intended the visual acoustics of the landscape and building to be echoed audibly. Nowadays, tasteful melody issues occasionally from loudspeakers set among the trees, but this is a rather watered-down realization of the architect's idea. A detached bell tower was planned to emit electronic music to the assembled congregation and the far horizons. Early in 1954, Le Corbusier even wrote to Edgar Varèse in New York, requesting a composition for the inauguration ceremony.[22]

It is interesting to speculate how the whole understanding of the design might have been influenced if it had been backed by atonal music. Notre-Dame-du-Haut appears to have its cultural tradition rooted in the ideas that inspired the late Romantic compositions of Mahler and the philosophy of Nietzsche, yet Le Corbusier was, perhaps, seeking a less contained expression.

The chapel at Ronchamp may defy analysis, and may contain contradictions, but as a place of pilgrimage for the spiritually and architecturally devout it is still a popular success. There can be little doubt that Le Corbusier's response to the somewhat abstract notion of sacred architecture, within and yet against landscape, is a triumph. The white shape sits against the sky, the building itself a backdrop to the occasional outdoor services, attended by many thousands of wor-

Figure 75
The northeast corner of
the Chapel of
Notre-Dame-du-Haut,
Ronchamp. (Photograph
by Martin Purdy.)

Figure 76
The interior of the
Chapel of
Notre-Dame-du-Haut,
Ronchamp, looking
toward the sanctuary
and devotional statue.
(Photograph by Russell
Walden.)

shipers. The concave east wall defines the open-air sanctuary, the roof soaring out to encompass not only the pilgrims on the hilltop but the infinite landscape (Fig. 75). Inside, the building is much less successful and, strangely, less mysterious in reality than in photographs (Fig. 76).

The reason for this probably relates to Le Corbusier's own instinctive understanding of the problem. The interplay of built form with a gathering of humanity in nature completely absorbed and fascinated him, but the requirements of the pilgrimage church were of less interest. "I have not experienced the miracle of faith, but I have often known the miracle of inexpressible space, the apotheosis of plastic emotion."[23]

Le Corbusier's handling of space and volume in tangible and symbolic terms has been one of his greatest contributions to architecture; externally the chapel at Ronchamp captures this magical essence, but the inside is spatially disappointing. So vacuous is the interior that it raises the suspicion that Le Corbusier was more concerned with the sculptured nature of the enclosing surfaces than with the volume they surround. "The key is light,"[24] wrote the architect, but the dynamic quality of the south wall kills the subtlety of the floating, crab-shell inspired roof. Only when the sun is low in the sky does the interior take on an ethereal quality, and even then the glare around the statue of the Virgin—the spiritual focus of the building—is somewhat disconcerting. The idea that this image should be related both to worshipers inside and without is a brilliant one and fully expresses Le Corbusier's sophisticated understanding of spatial relationships. But its implementation fails to convince in fact, as it does in notion.

The architect raised certain questions about the elements of the building in December 1950, and in June of the following year he met with Canon Ledeur and the local *curé* to discuss the finer details of the program. Despite these meetings, the liturgical arrangement appears arbitrary, and the different elements do not seem to have been given significant architectural "place" within the total volume. The position of the two public entrances, and the rather leftover space to the west of them; the precise number of side chapels; the seats and their situation within the building; indeed, the interplay of nave and sanctuary; all these crucial parts seem to have been considered artistically rather than ecclesiologically.

Some two years after completion, Le Corbusier had the free-standing cross moved from its original position immediately behind the high altar to its present place on the diagonal, coordinating the sanctuary with the devotional statue. Aesthetically this is a distinct improvement, but the need to make the change is somewhat strange. The project architect, André Maisonnier, had written to Canon Ledeur to verify the position of the cross some six months before completion.[25] All this perhaps reveals that the conflicting needs of Catholic liturgy, pilgrimage space, and the architect's more primitive spiritual vision were never fully resolved.

Le Corbusier sacrificed the seeming fashion of both architectural and theological logic to achieve the result he sought. For the student of architecture, trained to think in a linear manner, Notre-Dame-du-Haut is disturbing, as the puritanical straitjacket of modern rationalism is apparently thrown to the winds. The south wall is not massively load bearing; it is a framed structure. The hovering effect of the roof above the southeast buttress is only maintained by recessing the top of the pier, so that it does not appear to touch the horizontal plane. The so-carefully composed elements of the main entrance, enameled doors, concrete panel, roof and curving chapel wall are only controlled from the outside. Within, the ceiling is seen to carry beyond the glazed slot that marks the external cantilever of the curving soffit.

For the present-day student of theology, encouraged to believe in the social realities of everyday religion, Ronchamp is something of an anachronism—perhaps the last of the self-consciously designed "holy places." Yet for some it seems to touch the very nature of existence in a way that disturbed the radical theologian from his contact with a more immanent God. Is this a valid feeling of the numinous, or mere *Kitsch*? Here again we encounter the paradox of Le Corbusier, who took the whole building most seriously.

Two months after the dedication of June 1955, he went to Cap Martin for a holiday. From there he wrote letters to Alfred Canet, the *curé*, and Marcellin Carraud, a lawyer from Vesoul and a prominent member of the building committee. These letters are more than the common courtesy of an architect writing to his client, and that to the chaplain tells how worthwhile the efforts to realize the project had been:

After being away for two months I greet you and ask if you are pleased. It seems that after all this great effort by a lot of people things have succeeded.

You are making a stand, resisting a great many assaults and replying to a great many questions. You must have been worried at times. Nevertheless you have been one of the courageous people in the adventure. I wanted to say thank you to you, for *Notre-Dame-du-Haut* is placed on one of the sites sympathetic to my effort and without our agreement and that of the Committee this rash enterprise could have come up against an obstacle.[26]

Sainte-Marie-de-la-Tourette

If the chapel at Ronchamp represents Le Corbusier's belief in the divinity of nature, the monastic college of Sainte-Marie-de-la-Tourette is his resolution of the individual versus collective dilemma (Fig. 77). Building began on the beautiful site above Eveux-sur-L'Arbresle within a year of the completion of Ronchamp, but the idea for the design had been established a few weeks before Couturier's death, toward the end of 1953. A letter from Couturier to the architect in July of that year said: "I know, in advance, that in its poverty, it will be one of the purest and most important works of our time, and I hope that you also will be pleased with it."[27]

La Tourette, even more than Ronchamp, owes its inspiration to Couturier, and his early letters to the architect are full of encouragement and advice. He suggested that Le Corbusier should visit the Cistercian monastery of Le Thoronet in Provence (and, as Wolfgang Braunfels has pointed out,[28] La Tourette bears more than a superficial resemblance to that medieval building). "[Le Thoronet] has the real spirit that a monastery should have, no matter in what period it is built, as man devoted to silence, to recollection and meditation, in a community life does not change very much with the passing of time."[29] Basically this statement of Couturier's remains true to this day, but subtle yet radical expressions of the monastic life have recently called for a very different architecture.[30]

Ronchamp may not have attempted to redefine the architecture of Christian pilgrimage; even less does La Tourette show the way toward a new understanding of monasticism. It is perhaps unfair to criticize the building for a situation that was not apparent twenty years ago, but such have been the changes in the Religious Life that for all its brilliance as a work of formal architecture, La Tourette is now somewhat outdated. André Belaud, who administered the project for the Dominicans, has himself said, "We would not build a similar place today."[31] But there is still immense admiration for Le Corbusier from among the community. Perhaps La Tourette failed as a monastic college because it kept too rigidly to the traditional program suggested by Couturier; judged simply as architecture of its time, however, it still has much to communicate.

The monastic ideal first impressed itself upon Le Corbusier during his European tours from 1907 to 1911. The celebrated visit to the Charterhouse of Ema in Tuscany is considered to have had a profound effect upon Le Corbusier's architecture and planning theories.[32] After

Couturier's death, *L'Art Sacré* planned to publish some of his reminiscences. Among these were extracts of his conversation with Le Corbusier, and P. R. Regamey, writing for the journal, asked for verifica-
tion of the ideas discussed concerning the visit to Ema. Le Corbusier
explained that his understanding of humane architecture (*"faite pour
le bonheur de l'homme"*), which had been aroused there, really concerned the resolution of the individual versus collective problem:
". . . which is the key to sociability. Respect for individual freedom,
benefit to the common good, true harmony constantly focusing itself
amid ever-changing circumstances."[33]

The commission for La Tourette gave Le Corbusier the opportunity
to express this understanding in the building type that first presented
the idea to him; yet he seems to have accepted the project because it
was concerned with housing a community, rather than simply encas-
ing a cultic act.

He visited the site early in May 1953, and wrote immediately to
Couturier that "the idea is already in my head."[34] But he did not want
to commit himself to paper until he had had more time to think about
the problems and discuss them with his clients. Toward the end of
that year, he discussed his ideas with Couturier, then a dying man. On
I January 1954, the priest wrote: "I have written to Father Belaud to let
him know of our conversations: he came last Wednesday and is entirely in agreement with what was said about the general disposition."[35] These ideas remained the essence of the realized project.

During the slow design work (building did not start on site until the
summer of 1956) economies had to be made, and the cost was cut by
about 50 percent. But Le Corbusier would not allow the essential elements of the idea to be compromised. A few months before construction began, he wrote to his chief assistants about proposed savings: "I
have made total revisions with all the reductions that the project will
allow. I am not able to indulge in any other savings, and I will not

Figure 77
Sainte-Marie-de-la-
Tourette, 1956–1959,
from the south.
(Photograph by Martin
Purdy.)

Figure 78
Sainte-Marie-de-la-Tourette from the west. (Photograph by Martin Purdy.)

sanction any other changes. Excuse my lack of modesty, but I love this scheme: I think it is a good work and I want to see it built as it is."[36]

The building remains, therefore, much as the original concept discussed by Le Corbusier and Couturier. There is no doubt that financial cuts, which had to be made, have seriously affected the quality of the structure. The construction is poor, and the mechanical services are inadequate; the building should have been double-glazed, and the heating and hot water installations are only partially complete. The poverty of which Couturier spoke has been achieved in fact, but perhaps not in idea; Sainte-Marie-de-la-Tourette is a grand, maybe even grandiose building. Its strength, however, lies in the conviction with which the idea has been carried out. The different elements (community rooms, teaching areas, living quarters, and worship spaces) combine in a most comprehensive composition. The apparent dilemma of the individual among the collective is resolved. The building is intricate, yet simple, completely unified both physically and symbolically. The utter self-confidence of the intellectual statement makes La Tourette a masterpiece, a brilliant expression of the order of authority that so obsessed Le Corbusier. The paradoxes that make it an unsatisfactory monastery now are those of this particular master architect, even of the Church today.

Landscape is again the touchline of the idea. From a horizontal roof line, whose backdrop is the wooded slopes of the rolling Rhône countryside, the tight, formal composition marches down the grassy slope (Fig. 78). The church erupts from the soil, the rest scarcely touches the ground. As Anton Henze says:

The building is open to the forces of the landscape but as a man-made structure it stands aloof from the fields and forests of nature. The overall aspect of La Tourette stands in contrast from nature, emphasizing the frontiers which separate the sacred precincts from the world. In its detail Le Corbusier abandoned the conception of the claustrum

Figure 79
The internal courtyards of Sainte-Marie-de-la-Tourette. (Photograph by Martin Purdy.)

but in general terms he restated his own basic ideas about the closed precinct.[37]

This divorce from the world, yet desire to save it, is the eternal dilemma of monasticism, and is a particulary searching question for the Religious at this time. The Dominicans of La Tourette seem to have inflicted this problem upon themselves: the Order of Preachers is an urban foundation, and yet Furneaux Jordan justifies the rural setting of La Tourette on the basis of its collegiate function—the countryside offers seclusion to the students before they face the rigors of the world.[38]

The difficulty is compounded at La Tourette. The building is developed around a courtyard plan: the church occupies the northern side, the communal accommodation with the cells is elevated on the other three sides. The central enclosed space is a continuation of the falling landscape, which flows virtually uninterrupted through the columned structure. In some senses, this is a subtle way of introducing the world of nature to the world of spiritual and scholarly asceticism, but in reality it is a strange experience. The monastery sits templelike within its country setting: with its hollow form, it defines a private open space, but fails to make proper use of it (Fig. 79). The rectilinear courtyard is divided into four unequal parts by the cruciform cloister, a further example of a clever idea, yet one only superficially related to the monastic ideal. The continuous form of the traditional cloister admitted endless perambulation, a far more apt symbol of monastic existence than can be gleaned from the cross-shaped routes at La Tourette, which are mere circulation passages. If *cloister* has no significance for twentieth-century monasticism, it seems somewhat perverse to give the form so much importance.

These conflicts of form and understanding can be found throughout the building, and can be explained perhaps by the aspirations of architect and client to produce "high art" with limited resources and in a manner increasingly at odds with changing theological understanding.

The main church with its crypt chapels is a magnificent space, so much more controlled than the interior at Ronchamp. The traditional plan of the monastery church has been adopted, and this must have helped to give the place coherence. It is an awe-inspiring volume in which to keep silence, but acoustically it is a disaster. A faceted treatment to the walls, which would have helped remedy this, was omitted for economic reasons, and the architect considered its omission would spoil a space that he claimed had an admirable acoustic.[39]

As an architectural statement La Tourette has had a profound influence upon subsequent buildings. Robert Venturi, while acknowledging the Mediterranean vernacular of La Tourette, traces examples that follow a similar form: Boston City Hall, the Art and Architecture building at Yale, the Agronomy building at Cornell, and the Neiman-Marcus store in Houston.[40] To these might be added the British Embassy in Rome and the Birmingham Central Library. In 1965, the monastery was classified as an historic monument, which should guarantee its permanence.

But as a lasting response to the problem of twentieth-century monasticism, it has already proved a failure. The monastic college was a victim of the student unrest that swept through France in 1968, and the building, while still occupied by the Dominicans, is now serving as a theological study center. It is some measure of the structure's success that it can adopt this role without undue physical change or embarrassment and that the architecture can stand for itself, devoid of its original function. But the building as it is now used must be very different from Couturier's original understanding. Following the liberal influence of the Second Vatican Council (1962–1965), the outward formality of religious discipline has largely disappeared, and the architecture is no longer a framework for strictly regulated activity. The inherent truths of the Religious Life remain, but in a different, more relaxed guise. La Tourette remains as an interesting architectural statement by dint of its aesthetic quality. Like seaside rock, it carries its message right through, and for this integrity it will always be worthy of respect.

St. Pierre at Firminy Vert

The physical distance between the rural retreat of La Tourette and the industrial town of Firminy is not great, but the demands of a monastic college are very different from those of a parish church in a mining community. Firminy lies at the head of the industrial belt that sprawls from the Rhône through St. Etienne. Only the beauty of the undulating countryside provides relief from the pervading atmosphere of a worn-out environment. It seems a strange place to find a new suburb, Firminy Vert, with buildings designed by some of the best architects in France—until it is known that Eugène Claudius-Petit, Minister of Reconstruction after the Second World War and champion of Le Corbusier for the original *Unité d'habitation* at Marseilles, was mayor of the town from 1953 to 1971.

In 1960, Claudius-Petit asked Le Corbusier to assist in the layout of the new suburb and to design himself a group of civic buildings: Youth Club (now the Maison de la Culture), stadium, swimming pool, and church. The following summer, Le Corbusier wrote to A. M. Cocagnac, then director of *L'Art Sacré,* "about a Church I am designing for Claudius-Petit at Firminy. He forced my hand, but I accepted because the geographic and typographic conditions were favorable. I have a plan and I would like to discuss it with you . . . to see if you approve of the liturgical arrangement."[41]

The idea for this design dates from a sketch drawn by Le Corbusier for a church in the 1920s; *"venue un beau jour = venue 'un beau jour,'* " he scribbled on the drawing, and he does not seem to have considered it necessary to revise his thoughts. The project for St. Pierre at Firminy suffered many setbacks, reductions, and cancellations. "They have circumcised me,"[42] the architect is reported to have exclaimed, but despite these problems the germ of the idea has not been sacrificed (Fig. 80). After the architect's death, his supporters have kept the project alive, and an agency was set up specifically to promote the enterprise. A start was finally made on site in the autumn of 1973 (Fig. 81).

Le Corbusier's sketch of the building[43] shows it as a thumb punctuating the landscape, and this importance of the church to the urban design of Firminy Vert was one of the arguments used by Le Corbusier's followers for the retention of the scheme. The setting of Firminy Vert is a northward facing bowl, far more hilly than Le Corbusier's drawing suggests. The funnel-shaped profile of St. Pierre will rise from its sunken site, above the lip of the stadium. It is in close proximity to housing—some of it in multistory form—and the recently completed swimming baths (architect André Wogenscky). But from nowhere can it be seen in isolation, and the form suggests that it should be so considered, despite the claim that the design should be understood in relation to the rest of the town. The main body of the church, in a shape reminiscent of the main hall of the Legislative Assembly at Chandigarh, grows from a two-level base of vestries and ancillary accommodation. The congregation enter the church by an external ramp, and the seating rises again in a floating, segmental tier from the sanctuary level. It will be a dramatic interior, in which the introduction of natural light has again been sensitively considered. Even if the exterior promises to have less impact than the idea demanded, the inside should provide a thrilling experience. But it is just this excitement which casts doubt upon the validity of the design.

Figure 80
The 1964 model of St.
Pierre, Firminy Vert.
(Photograph by Martin
Purdy.)

Figure 81
St. Pierre at Firminy Vert
under construction,
March 1974. (Photograph
by Martin Purdy.)

Le Corbusier and the Theological Program   311

For the last two decades, there has been increasing concern about the form and content of ecclesiastical architecture, and the representatives of almost all Christian denominations are now seeking to portray themselves in the role of servants rather than masters. It would seem that the ecclesiastical authorities for Firminy have had grave doubts about the suitability of the design of St. Pierre, and only the supporters of Le Corbusier's architecture have managed to get work started with money raised by themselves.

The early architects of the Liturgical Movement were almost wholly concerned with creating an internal space where the cult could be performed in reverent participation. The design of St. Pierre, with its pedigree going back to the 1920s, would seem to suit this requirement well, but with a number of important omissions that an architect more concerned with the theological program would not have made. The multilevel congregational space of the Le Corbusier church was partially employed to relieve the impression of emptiness when only a few worshipers are gathered together. Tiered seating is more suitable for theatrical appreciation than involved worship and fails to acknowledge the subtle relationship between celebrant and congregation. Many successful churches before and after World War II show little concern with external appearance; the basis for their design is internal relationships rather than the setting of form within landscape.

Last and most important, ecclesiastical architecture has developed rapidly. Its concern now is not simply for the creation of space for cultic acts, but the fuller realization of the place of the church in society. This has resulted in a wider understanding, which goes beyond mere change in ecclesiological fashion. Sacred and secular are viewed not as opposite poles, but as elements within the same spectrum. Buildings designed for this realization have sought to break down the barriers that the preceding centuries had set up between the church and the world; they are more human in concept, providing for a greater variety of activities.

Much of this has happened since the final form of St. Pierre was agreed in 1964, but it is against this that the completed building will have to be judged. St. Pierre at Firminy Vert promises to be the most exciting parish church built this century; theologically it could prove to be the most irrelevant.

All this can be understood largely by Le Corbusier's attitude toward the design. Claudius-Petit forced his hand to accept the commission, and the architect satisfied the liturgical understanding then prevalent. But for Le Corbusier the important ingredient was the building as an object, and it is on this subject that the contemporary saga of the scheme for a church in Bologna is most revealing.[44]

The revival of interest in liturgical art and architecture in Italy was due largely to the inspiration of Giacomo Lercaro, Cardinal Archbishop of Bologna. A conference on the subject was held in that city in September 1955, and drew attention and good wishes from a number of well-known architects and scholars, including Le Corbusier.[45] Following this, Cardinal Lercaro set up the quarterly magazine *Chiesa e Quartiere* and began the Centro di Studio e Informazione per Architettura Sacra. The sixteenth edition of *Chiesa e Quartiere,* published in December 1960, was devoted to La Tourette, and Le Corbusier was very pleased with the praise bestowed upon him by the magazine.

The Church at Bologna
Bologna at this time was a rapidly expanding city, and Cardinal Lercaro wanted the new churches to be built by the very best architects. The directors of the Centro di Studio asked Cocagnac of *L'Art Sacré* to approach Le Corbusier about one of these projects, but Le Corbusier remained cool about the offer.

A year later (February 1963) Le Corbusier visited Florence to inaugurate an exhibition of his work at the Palazzo Strozzi. While in Italy, he received a personal letter from Cardinal Lercaro asking him to work in Bologna: ". . . it would be for me and my diocese a truly precious gift if you would design one of your churches."[46] Le Corbusier wrote almost immediately: "You ask me to become involved with the problem of your churches. Alas, I haven't a moment. I am, like the last of mankind, subject to a twenty-four-hour day, and the annual calendar."[47] But he did offer the ray of hope that he might change his mind: "Don't despair, if you really want something. A popular song says 'A day will come.' Be confident like the youth who sings this lyric with other things in mind." It was a strange letter perhaps to write to an eminent Cardinal Archbishop, but in fact for some reason it was never sent. It is reported, however, that Le Corbusier remarked of this request to Cocagnac: "Why does one have to wait until one is old and useless before being asked to do all the interesting things?"[48]

The apparent lack of commitment and casual attitude of Le Corbusier does not appear to have deterred the Italians, and various documents about three alternative sites were sent to his studio. A sketch appears in Jean Petit's *Le Corbusier lui-même* for a church in Bologna,[49] but there is little other evidence that he thought greatly about this scheme.

The Italians were ever-optimistic, and a delegation from the Centro di Studio visited the office in the Rue de Sèvres on 25 February 1965 with Capellades of *L'Art Sacré*. During this visit Le Corbusier explained his project for St. Pierre at Firminy, and expressed the difficulties that were besetting the scheme, which at that time seemed unlikely to be built. The offer then came from the Italians that Le Corbusier should build his original Firminy design in Bologna. At the end of the following month, the architect wrote to Cardinal Lercaro: "I have had a visit from two young envoys, sent to ask on your behalf if I would be willing to construct in Bologna the church which I designed for Firminy. The plans are finished and, if you think it useful, we would be grateful if you would send photographs of the chosen site, a survey plan with levels. . . ." (Fig. 82)[50]

Work continued at a great pace on the design during the summer, and after Le Corbusier's death, Cardinal Lercaro declared that the promise to build the church in Bologna would be maintained. José Oubrerie who had worked closely with Le Corbusier on the Firminy scheme (and is now in charge of that project) visited Bologna. He rejected the original site selected in the district of Beverara and found a more suitable one.

The problems caused by the settling of Le Corbusier's estate compelled Maurice Besset, who directed the committee looking after the dead architect's practice, to write almost immediately to Cardinal Lercaro. Besset reported that it would not be possible to go ahead with the Bologna project until all legal matters had been resolved. This decision could only be taken by the Administrative Council of La Fondation Le Corbusier, then not properly constituted, and the rights of the design were still held by the Parochial Association in Firminy.

Since 1965, Cardinal Lercaro has resigned from his position in Bologna (1968), the Centro di Studio has disbanded, and work has begun on site at Firminy.

These dealings with the enthusiastic group from Bologna, who were greatly impressed with his work in general and with the scheme for the parish church in particular, is so typical of Le Corbusier's attitude toward his church commissions. By this time he was an old man. A postscript in the letter he failed to send to Cardinal Lercaro stated, "I forgot to tell you that my doctor has given me orders to cut down on work. I am seventy-five years old, three-quarters of a century."[51] Throughout his career he had always been unwilling to compromise

Figure 82
Plan and section for a church project at Bologna, 1963. (Photograph courtesy of Glauco Gresleri.)

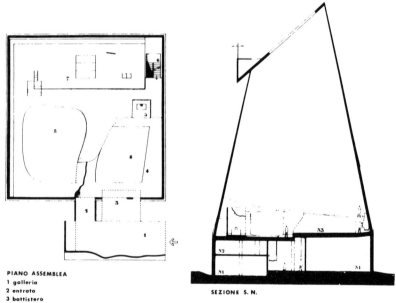

PIANO ASSEMBLEA
1 galleria
2 entrata
3 battistero
4 capp. feriale
5 altare SS
6 scala della sagrestia
7 presbiterio e mensa
8 assemblea

SEZIONE S. N.

the essential idea of his architectural vision; with the church projects, and especially during the last years of his life, he was perhaps more concerned with the actual realization of that vision than with the ultimate relevance of its meaning. For Firminy, he had been content to work up a thirty-year-old sketch for the design of St. Pierre; at Bologna he finally did not even suggest this. Instead of thinking out the particular program required for a suburb in the expanding Italian city, he was quite prepared to transpose another solution, and look for, even modify, a site on which to place it!

Architecture is a "pure creation of the spirit,"[52] he had written in *Vers une architecture*, and no one would deny the spiritual content of Ronchamp, La Tourette, or the Firminy/Bologna churches. But in the same book he had to remind us that "Architecture is governed by standards. Standards are a matter of logic, analysis and precise study. Standards are based on a problem which has been well stated. . . . We must first of all aim at the setting up of standards in order to face problems of perfection."[53]

The church buildings of Le Corbusier fail theologically because he was neither willing nor perhaps able to set the ecclesiological standards that might have allowed him to approach a perfect solution. Yet because Le Corbusier remains so absolute an artist, some commentators would claim that his churches do set new pinnacles of excellence. Of Ronchamp, Kidder Smith doubts "if a finer church has been built since Filippo Brunelleschi's 1446 Pazzi Chapel. . . . It is the greatest building of our time."[54] Anton Henze describes La Tourette as "a new physical type of Christian monastery."[55] No doubt St. Pierre at Firminy will be heralded by many as the ultimate type of twentieth-century parish church.

Adulation of this sort actually obscures the real lessons that Le Corbusier's church buildings have to teach, and invites others, less gifted, to use the superficial images the architect created without appreciating their real strengths and weaknesses.

The tragedy of Le Corbusier's church buildings is the tragedy of an opportunity lost. No other architect of his generation was better equipped to give ecclesiastical architecture a new creative impulse. Le Corbusier's concern for humane and spiritual values and his utter rejection of the pompous and sham are qualities the church so urgently needs to express through its buildings. He proudly told Edgar Varèse that he had been described, before the Archbishop of Besançon, as "truly a Christian, but a Christian of 5000 years before Christ."[56]

Yet the church failed to harness his talent, and he failed to project for them his own interests toward a new understanding of church architecture. Instead of leading a new renaissance of religious architecture, he was content to develop and expound his own limited theories of the sacred.

The resulting works may have little to teach the student of ecclesiastical architecture who is primarily interested in the relevance of the church to society, but while part of the creative process is still concerned with the bringing together of forms in light, Le Corbusier's buildings will always demand attention.

1   John Summerson, introductory essay in Trevor Dannatt's *Modern Architecture in Britain*, London, 1959, p. 11.

2   Walter Gropius, *The New Architecture and the Bauhaus* (English translation), London, 1935. The quote is from the 1965 edition, p. 20.

3   David Edwards, *Religion and Change*, London, 1969, p. 287.

4   Jean Petit, *Le Corbusier lui-même*, Geneva, 1970, p. 183, translated by Helen Walden.

5   Le Corbusier, *La Ville radieuse*, Boulogne-sur-Seine, 1935. English translation: *The Radiant City,* 1964 edition, p. 323.

6   Ibid., p. 76.

7   Ibid., pp. 82–83.

8   Reported from conference held at La Tourette, quoted in *L'Art Sacré*, Paris, September–October 1966, p. 19.

9   Le Corbusier, *Manière de penser l'urbanisme*, Paris, 1946, chapter 2.

10 Le Corbusier, letter to Louis Secretan, July 1961, researched in the archives of the Bibliothèque de La Chaux-de-Fonds by Russell and Helen Walden, translated by Helen Walden.

11 Petit, *Le Corbusier lui-même,* p. 128.

12 Le Corbusier's fascination for the Athens Acropolis is apparent throughout *Towards a New Architecture*, London, 1927 (translation of *Vers une architecture*, Paris, 1923). The architect refers to it in the Preface to *The Chapel at Ronchamp*, London, 1957, p. 6. Colin Rowe develops the influence in his criticism of La Tourette, in *Architectural Review*, June 1961, pp. 400–410.

13 Marcel Maulini, letter to Le Corbusier, 5 March 1951, Archives Fondation Le Corbusier (hereafter AFLC).

14 Le Corbusier, letter to Alfred Canet, 5 May 1955, AFLC.

15 Le Corbusier, *Oeuvre complète 1946–52*, Zurich, 1953, p. 88.

16 Le Corbusier, *Chapel at Ronchamp,* and Jean Petit, *Le Livre de Ronchamp,* Paris, 1961, both further describe and illustrate this building.

17 M. A. Couturier, M. R. Capellades, L. B. Rayssiguier, and A. M. Cocagnac, *Les Chapelles du Rosaire à Vence par Matisse et de Notre-Dame-du-Haut à Ronchamp par Le Corbusier*, Paris, 1955, pp. 97–106.

18 René Bolle-Reddat, letter to Martin Purdy, 7 November 1973.

19 Stanislaus von Moos, *Le Corbusier. L'architecte et son mythe*, Paris, 1971, p. 242.

20 Charles Jencks, *Modern Movements in Architecture*, London, 1973, p. 155.

Notes

21 James Stirling, "Le Corbusier's Chapel and the Crisis of Rationalism," in *Architectural Review*, March 1956, p. 161.

22 Le Corbusier, letter to Edgar Varèse in New York, 21 January 1954, AFLC.

23 Le Corbusier, *Le Modulor*, Boulogne-sur-Seine, 1948. English translation: *The Modulor*, London, 1954, p. 32.

24 Le Corbusier, *Chapel at Ronchamp*, p. 27.

25 André Maisonnier, letter to Lucien Ledeur, 11 January 1955, AFLC.

26 Le Corbusier, letter to the *curé* of Ronchamp, 24 August 1955, AFLC.

27 M. A. Couturier, letter to Le Corbusier, 28 July 1953, reproduced in Jean Petit, *Un Couvent de Le Corbusier*, Paris, 1961, p. 23. (English translation in separate booklet obtainable from La Tourette.)

28 Wolfgang Braunfels, *Monasteries of Western Europe* (English translation), London, 1972, p. 230, records how the pavilion at Le Thoronet has a form and position similar to the Oratory at La Tourette.

29 Petit, *Un Couvent de Le Corbusier,* p. 22.

30 For a longer exposition of this, see my "Monastic Contrasts: Ste. Marie de la Tourette and St. André, Ottignies," in *Research Bulletin 1974,* edited by J. G. Davies, Institute for the Study of Worship and Religious Architecture, University of Birmingham.

31 André Belaud, discussion with me and with students from the Birmingham School of Architecture, 26 March 1974.

32 Françoise Choay in her book, *Le Corbusier*, London, 1960, claims "the collective individual twosome . . . guides all his architecture and town planning," p. 29, footnote 28.

33 Le Corbusier, letter to P. R. Regamey, April 1954, AFLC.

34 Le Corbusier, letter to Couturier, 11 May 1953, AFLC.

35 Couturier, letter to Le Corbusier, 7 January 1954, AFLC.

36 Le Corbusier, memo to André Wogenscky, 21 March 1956, AFLC.

37 Anton Henze, *La Tourette* (English edition), London, 1966, p. 17.

38 Robert Furneaux Jordan, *Le Corbusier*, London, 1972; see pp. 146–147 in Chapter 6: "Building for Christ."

39 Talk given by Le Corbusier to the Dominican Community, in Petit, *Un Couvent de Le Corbusier*, p. 29.

40 Robert Venturi, Denise Scott Brown, and Steven Izenour, *Learning from Las Vegas*, M.I.T. Press, 1972, p. 96.

Martin Purdy   320

41 Le Corbusier, letter to Cocagnac, 10 July 1961, AFLC.

42 Le Corbusier, *Towards a New Architecture*, 1972 edition, p. 23.

43 Sketch dated 19 September 1963. Illustrated in Le Corbusier, *Oeuvre complète 1957–65*, p. 137.

44 I am indebted to Glauco Gresleri for much of the information about the efforts to encourage Le Corbusier to build in Bologna. Glauco Gresleri (with his brother Giuliano and Giorgio Trebbi) was a leading figure in the Centro di Studio. A memo from that office by Trebbi, *Storia della Chiesa di Le Corbusier per Bologna*, 10 March 1966, related the chain of events. I am indebted to Leo Davies, Librarian of the Art and Design Centre, City of Birmingham Polytechnic, for helping with the Italian translation.

45 Cardinal Giacomo Lercaro's address to the conference has been printed in English under the title "The Christian Church," in *Documents for Sacred Architecture*, 1957, booklet published by Liturgical Press, Collegeville, Minnesota.

46 Giacomo Lercaro, letter to Le Corbusier, 16 February 1963, AFLC.

47 Le Corbusier, letter written, but not sent, to Lercaro, 21 February 1963, AFLC.

48 Trebbi, *Storia della Chiesa di Le Corbusier per Bologna*.

49 Petit, *Le Corbusier lui-même*, p. 137.

50 Le Corbusier, letter to Lercaro, 30 March 1965, AFLC.

51 Le Corbusier, letter to Lercaro, 21 February 1963, AFLC.

52 Le Corbusier, *Towards a New Architecture*, 1972 edition, p. 23.

53 Ibid., pp. 135–136.

54 G. E. Kidder Smith, *The New Architecture of Europe* (English edition), London, 1962, p. 92.

55 Henze, *La Tourette*, p. 17.

56 Le Corbusier, letter to Varèse, 21 January 1954, AFLC.

John Winter   **Le Corbusier's Technological Dilemma**

Le Corbusier exhibited his paintings widely but kept quiet about his early experiences as a brick manufacturer, so he cannot complain if the world has seen him as an "art" architect and largely ignored his attitude to construction and building technology. But this ignorance has let to a serious omission from the documentation of the man's work, an undervaluing of his real, if patchy, achievements as a constructor, and a lack of appreciation of the technical determinants of his work.

From his years with Auguste Perret and Peter Behrens, Le Corbusier emerged as an admirer of the new technology of building. In 1908 he was fascinated by the glass and steel house in the Rue Réaumur and could see through its post-Art Nouveau styling to admire its building technique. His Villa Schwob is probably the first house ever built with a reinforced-concrete frame, and among its array of technical inventions are cavity walls housing services, double glazing with heating between the panes, and planted roof terraces.

In written work he becomes much more demanding: *Vers une architecture* is a hymn to the machine, whose products are to be compared to Doric capitals; his contributions to *L'Esprit Nouveau* emphasize the advantages of the machine for making buildings. So, in the first third of this century, when the building industry was still based on handicraft skills, Le Corbusier's machine-image buildings such as the Pavillon Suisse acted as a rallying point. "Thin and precise" became a modern movement canon.

In the late 1930s, Le Corbusier's friends Eugène Beaudouin, Marcel Lods, and Jean Prouvé built Buc Airport and Clichy Market Hall, the first buildings designed right through as machine-made products. Machine-age building had arrived. And what was Le Corbusier doing at this time? He was designing houses in rough masonry and heavy timbers. In the decade following the war, Le Corbusier positively gloried in primitive construction, while the rest of the Western world slowly mechanized its building industry in accordance with Le Corbusier's ideas of the twenties.

In the 1960s, a reaction arose against "curtain wallism" and the glibness of so much of the metal and glass of the previous decade, and Le Corbusier's primitive technology was copied round the world. The world had swung his way. But Le Corbusier turned again, and his last European projects were sophisticated metal and glass objects.

There is of course an element of logic in Le Corbusier's changes of approach; he is developing as a designer and learning from the shortcomings of the buildings he has completed. But there is also an element of cussedness, of reacting against the view held by the rest of the world, so that he could fulfill his lonely heroic role, or, as Charles Jencks would say, his tragic role.[1]

Vers une architecture: The Stand Is Taken

Vers une architecture was published in 1923 when Le Corbusier's mature practice was just beginning. With this book he takes a stand that gives precise direction to his work for the next ten years and less precise direction for the rest of his life. It is not only polemic; it is also image. Here are the ocean liners whose superstructure becomes the Maison Lipchitz and whose companionways become the stairs of the Pavillon de L'Esprit Nouveau; here is the factory façade that is refined into the Pavillon Suisse; here are sketches of the Acropolis that lead us to Chandigarh. Throughout the machine aesthetic, the stand is clear.

Industry, overwhelming us like a flood which rolls on toward its destined ends, has furnished us with new tools adapted to this new epoch, animated by the new spirit. . . .
Industry on the grand scale must occupy itself with building and establish the elements of the house on a mass-production basis. We must create the mass-production spirit.

The spirit of constructing mass-production houses.
The spirit of living in mass-production houses.
The spirit of conceiving mass-production houses.

If we eliminate from our hearts and minds all dead concepts in regard to the house and look at the question from a critical and objective point of view, we shall arrive at the "House-machine," the mass-production house, healthy (and morally so too) and beautiful in the same way that the working tools and instruments which accompany our existence are beautiful.[2]

Every modern man has the mechanical sense. The feeling for mechanics exists and is justified by our daily activities. This feeling in regard to machinery is one of respect, gratitude and esteem.[3]

Delage. Front-wheel Brake. This precision, this cleanness in execution go further back than our reborn mechanical sense. Phidias felt in this way: the entablature of the Parthenon is a witness. So did the Egyptians when they polished the pyramids.[4]

And again of the Parthenon: "All this plastic machinery is realized in marble with the vigour that we have learned to apply in the machine. The impression is of naked polished steel."[5]

So the Parthenon is like a highly polished machine-made object, and architecture is a love affair with the machine, the adding of poetry to the engineer's aesthetic.

But what explains the uncaptioned inclusion of Walter Gropius's Faguswerke among the anonymous engineer's factories? Perhaps he was scoring a point off the Berlin Functionalists, by implying that they had the engineer's aesthetic without the added poetry.

Period 1: The Machine Aesthetic

The decade following the publication of *Vers une architecture* is the period when Le Corbusier remained true to the machine aesthetic stance of his book. This period can be divided into two phases. The first is the time of the white cubes of Volume One of *Oeuvre complète*; the second covers the large glossy buildings of Volume Two. In 1929 Volume One is firmly closed, for after completing the design for the Villa Savoye at Poissy, he never again used white painted rendering or designed a hard-edged house. Volume Two chronicles the next five years and includes all the big impeccable glassy buildings and a couple of little houses that show the first stirrings of Le Corbusier the primitive.

During the period recorded in Volume One, the feel of the machine-made was more image than reality. The Le Corbusier houses of the twenties are, generally speaking, as hand-made as other buildings of the time; the walls are not even of reinforced concrete, as the elevations might imply, for construction generally is a reinforced-concrete frame with block infill, all stuccoed and painted to try to give it the precision both of machine products and of Cubist paintings. The machine admired in *Vers une architecture* was shiny and metallic, but it was not practical to make houses like motor cars in the twenties, so Le Corbusier's houses of the time can almost be regarded as traditional buildings decorated to look machine-made. Almost. But not quite. The Maison Domino is a machine-age image too, and in terms of displaying the clear, regular, reinforced-concrete frame, the houses are much more successful—at Pessac the frame extends to define outside spaces, at Carthage it stands clear outside the skin on all sides, and in almost all of the houses the columns are kept clear of wall lines to display the frame.

The 1927 double house at the Weissenhof, Stuttgart, is supported on steel columns, perhaps because Germany is a steel-building country, perhaps because the office had now expanded and employed Swiss assistants who were outside the Paris reinforced-concrete tradition. The adjoining single house is a *maison type* following the Citrohan image, and hence it has a complete reinforced-concrete frame. The double house has columns made of steel channels placed toe to toe, with large holes cut through the webs below floor levels to allow *in situ* reinforced-concrete beams to pass through; these beams carry floor and roof slabs of reinforced concrete poured over boxes of reed matting, which gives lightness, insulation, and a key for plaster. Walls are of hollow pumice blocks with rods inserted in the hollows, which are then filled with concrete—an unnecessarily strong wall, one might think, to form a panel within a reinforced-concrete frame. Window lintels are suspended from the frame on steel hangers. On the ground floor the steel columns are exposed and painted, but on the upper floors they are plastered over in international style, and one is left with the impression that Le Corbusier was not anxious, at that time, to explore the possibility of steel.

The year of 1929 saw the last of Le Corbusier's designs in the white stucco box tradition and the first of his designs where the machine aesthetic was not surface-applied—in the precise metalwork, the luminous ceiling, and the square shiny furniture of the Salon d'Automne exhibition (Fig. 83). This exhibition shows a mastery of industrial design across a whole range of skills.

In the Maisons Loucheur, designed at the same time, concern for the industrialized product is again apparent. The steel structure is clearly expressed, not just for the ground floor columns as at the Weissenhof, but for the complete frame, with aggressively exposed steel beams, stairs, and landings. These houses indicate another tendency foreshadowing Le Corbusier's future buildings—the rough stone wall "executed by the local mason."[6]

The Maisons Loucheur were never built, but the study of steelwork leads to the important period covered in Volume Two, the five great steel and glass buildings constructed around 1930. These buildings, plus the competition entries of the same time, turned an office that had designed "one-off" houses in the Paris suburbs into a major international practice. None of these large buildings have the magic of the Villa at Garches or of the Maison Savoye at Poissy, but technically they tackle many new problems and solve quite a few of them.

Figure 83
The sleeping area in the Salon d'Automne apartment, 1929. Machine-made, hard-edged, synthetic materials were used to imply a new world of luxury. (Source: Le Corbusier, *Oeuvre complète 1929–34,* p. 46.)

The Centrosoyus at Moscow

This office building was constructed for a client who "wished that this building should express the latest resources of modern technology,"[7] so it has a steel and glass curtain wall erected from the top down. Mechanical ventilation was designed, to give comfort to the occupants in such a glassy building, but, "unfortunately, the Russian authorities did not agree to the application of the principle of *'respiration exacte,'* "[8] so it was built with opening windows and radiators, adequate in winter but too hot in summer. The answer, Le Corbusier stated later, would have been to add *brise-soleil*.

Immeuble Clarté at Geneva

This block of forty-nine flats was built with Edmond Wanner as client, builder, and adviser, and the architects absorbed a great deal of technical know-how from this man. Although it is not such an exciting building as some of the others, it is probably the most technically suave, with a delicious staircase that allows light to filter down through eight floors of glass treads. Reinforced-concrete piles support a steel frame with all joints electrically welded (surely one of the first anywhere) and frames for the double-glazed windows are welded to the frame. It was never intended to have mechanical ventilation, so blinds and balconies are provided to protect the glass area from the summer sun.

Pavillon Suisse, Paris

This student hostel stands on strongly modeled *piloti* that foreshadow their successors at Marseilles. Above first floor slab level all is *construction à sec* with steel frame and precast concrete or glass skin. Partitions between rooms contain quilts and lead sheets for sound insulation. Le Corbusier was already facing up to the problems created by using lightweight construction for large buildings, but his beautifully detailed *"pan de verre en façade sud"* (Fig. 84) does not show equal understanding of the problem of solar heat gain. That had to

Figure 84
The Pavillon Suisse, Cité Universitaire, Paris, 1930–1932, has its main elevation facing
open ground to the south and was built entirely of glass. (Photograph by John Winter.)

Figure 85
Detail of the Pavillon
Suisse showing the
external venetian blinds
added after World War II.
(Photograph by Russell
Walden.)

wait another five years until he had invented the *brise-soleil* to cope
with it. In the Pavillon Suisse itself the occupants managed for thirty
years until the owners of the building provided external venetian
blinds—a form of *brise-soleil* (Fig. 85).

Cité de Refuge, Paris

This hostel for the Salvation Army should have been the machine-age
miracle. An awkward site was turned into a dazzling series of spaces;
the curtain wall was elegantly detailed with air at a controlled temperature designed to pass between the skins. "It is the first entirely her-
metically sealed dwelling structure, comprising in particular a
thousand square meters of glass with no openings."[9] There are
shortcomings to the theory of the *mur neutralisant* method of maintaining internal temperature by passing heated or cooled air between
two skins of glass, for radiant heat could pass through and cause
overheating in summer; but the real disasters at the Cité de Refuge
were not in theory but in practice, for neither the inner glass skin nor
the cooling system were installed, while the skin was sealed tight.

The building opened late in 1933 (Fig. 86) and seemed comfortable
enough. But when the summer sun of 1934 beat down on the glass
façade, the discomfort became very real. When wartime damage, neglect, and the action of rust on the window frames caused glass to
break, the owners patched the windows with solid panels and concrete blocks (Fig. 87). Then in the early fifties opening windows were
provided for ventilation, spandrels were used to reduce the glass area,
and *brise-soleil* were added to cut down the sun's heat (Fig. 88).

24 Rue Nungesser-et-Coli, Paris

This block of thirteen flats is a modest version of the Immeuble Clarté.
Reinforced-concrete floors span on to load-bearing stone party walls
and five intermediate concrete columns; all is clad in steel and glass,
with lots of glass brick. Le Corbusier and his wife Yvonne moved into
a penthouse maisonette with bathrooms and terraces like an ocean

Figure 86
The Cité de Refuge,
Paris, 1929–1933, was
built with a sealed
façade, but without the
inner skin and cooling
system originally
intended. (Source: Le
Corbusier, *Oeuvre
complète 1929–34,* p. 99.)

Figure 87
During World War II the
damaged skin of the Cité
de Refuge was patched
up with anything that
would reduce the glass
area. (Photograph by
John Winter.)

Figure 88
The main façade of the
Cité de Refuge was
reconstructed in the
early 1950s with
brise-soleil. (Photograph
by Russell Walden.)

liner; over the years they softened it and continued to change it through Le Corbusier's subsequent development as an architect, so the open hard-edged interior finally became the enclosed chunky-wood apartment of 1953.

With the completion of these five buildings within three years, the Le Corbusier-Pierre Jeanneret office had become the most influential architectural practice in the world. They had given architecture a direction: thin and light, technically sophisticated and glossy. The demands of *Vers une architecture* for an architecture as satisfying as a Delage had been met. With his direction established, Le Corbusier could be expected to extend his practice and refine his designs. He chose to do just the reverse.

Period 2. The Fascination of Peasant Technology

By 1930, the Villa at Vaucresson was eight years old and the white cube buildings were weathering poorly. Anyone who asked Le Corbusier in later life for directions to visit one of these early houses was firmly told that it had been demolished, such was his embarrassment about its condition.

It was in the year 1930 that Le Corbusier was asked to design a house for M. Errazuris in Chile (which, in fact, was never executed). Here he could claim that the remoteness of the site necessitated primitive materials, and he designed an interior of logs and rough masonry. "The rusticity of the materials is in no way a hindrance to the manifestation of a clear plan and a modern aesthetic."[10] So technique and aesthetic can be separated; this is not what *Vers une architecture* had said nor indeed what he was writing at the time, for within a few months of designing the Chile house he wrote, "The new calculation and the steel and concrete construction on which it is based bring in place of antiquated methods of construction new solutions which set aside radically the planning and style of the past."[11] But to return to the Chile house, was that rusticity really necessitated by the location? Parts of the walling were to be stuccoed like his French houses. If he could have steel handrailing and big sheets of glass, he could presumably have had a flat roof and a smooth interior as well. The importance of this design is that it enabled Le Corbusier to indulge his new fascination for primitive materials in a site that gave him a chance to do so without seeming disloyal to the principles of *Vers une architecture*.

The rough stone ground-floor walls of the gardener's house at Poissy could be justified as being a continuation of an existing boundary wall, while the rough stone and logs of the Chile house were explained by the remoteness of the site.

But with the house for Madame de Mandrot at Le Pradet, designed after the Chile house but before the Villa Savoye at Poissy was finished, Le Corbusier felt sufficiently confident of his newfound love of rough materials to give them to the Convenor of the first Congrès International d'Architecture Moderne (CIAM). The roof is flat, and the floors, columns, even bookcases are of precisely made reinforced concrete. In spite of this, the house shows a total shift in mood from Poissy; instead of the *prisme pur* held above the Virgilian landscape, a wandering plan provides an outriding pavilion that gives a relaxed feel and stone garden walls and stair that tie the house down tightly to the land.

Two other houses of rustic charm continue the line of development initiated at Le Pradet. These two houses have great finesse and delight but what a comedown! The man who built five of the most marvelous buildings of the modern movement between 1930 and 1934 built just two little houses in the next decade. Le Corbusier was indeed in the wilderness. Reaction, fascism, and lack of clients for modern buildings have all been blamed, but these forces did not stop Jean Prouvé or Beaudouin and Lods from developing modern architecture and building technology during the thirties.

Somehow, however much he fought against it, a period of retrenchment was necessary to Le Corbusier after his great successes of the early thirties. The split with Charlotte Perriand and Pierre Jeanneret in 1940 and his period of ill health and idleness during the war were time for reflection, for gaining the confidence to reject some of the arguments of *Vers une architecture*.

During this unhappy phase in Le Corbusier's career his attitude to building technology veers from one extreme to the other. Writings are almost always in favor of high technology, with apologies or at least reasons given for rustic buildings. The 1940 *Maisons montées à sec* was the last joint Le Corbusier-Pierre Jeanneret design; carried out in association with Jean Prouvé, it has chunky Le Corbusier forms made with elegant Prouvé steelwork. A few weeks later and Le Corbusier is on his own designing *Murondins*, self-build adobe houses with grass-covered roofs for refugee populations without access to industry; a few more months and he is back with Prouvé and a sophisticated metal structure for schools for the same refugees. But when the designs for this last project were completed, metal technology ceases to occupy an important place in Le Corbusier's work for a long time.

Le Corbusier's abortive trip to North Africa in 1942 resulted in the designs for the Peyrissac house, his most extreme excursion into the realm of peasant technology. In the description of the house in Volume Four it is written: "At this period of the occupation, people only spoke about folk-lore and did their best to copy ancient buildings."[12] Hence at this moment the Vichy viewpoint is not so far removed from Le Corbusier's statement about the Peyrissac house that "in building in a modern way, we have discovered a harmony between the countryside, the climate, and tradition!"[13] One may wonder where the "modern" is, but the Peyrissac house is certainly a lovely play with traditional Arab building forms. The written description has the usual apology that "there were no specialized craftsmen, and materials were almost unobtainable."[14] But it is difficult to believe that, at this moment of his life, Le Corbusier was anything but relieved to be forced to produce a peasant work.

After the disasters of war and occupation, Le Corbusier returned to his penthouse in Paris to find the roof garden delectably overgrown but the metal frames of the *pan de verre* rusty and deteriorated. He enjoyed the rampant vegetation on the roof and realized that the roofs of his postwar buildings could be places of fantasy and wonder; but the defective metalwork was miserable, and no steel was available to replace it (or is that the last of his apologies?). Forced to replace the window frames with wood, he abandoned the lightness of steel for chunky members, and with some panels of solid and unpainted wood he formed a fourth enclosing wall to the room, making a more private, more relaxed space.

This time there is no apology in the description. Instead he thoughtfully takes a stand different from *Vers une architecture*. "It may be admitted that certain materials are the friends of man. These are stone, wood, terra-cotta, and white chalk or white plaster, while nickeled and chromed metals, polished and brilliant, can only be used in very special circumstances."[15] The long years of hesitation are over; Le Corbusier could face the postwar situation with a consistent approach, very different from that of the twenties.

Not only his own apartment, but his other buildings as well, had suffered neglect during the war. Often they were patched up by unsympathetic hands. The Villa at Vaucresson, which originally had a flat roof, was given a pitched roof; the sloping roofs of the Ozenfant studio were changed to a flat roof. The magnificent villas at Garches and at Poissy were derelict and abandoned. The cladding of the

Figure 89
Relief figure of the
Modulor Man, *Unité
d'habitation,* Marseilles,
1946–1952. Most of the
concrete in the building
is precast, but it was the
rough *in situ* concrete
that attracted attention.
(Photograph by John
Winter.)

Armée du Salut was patched with anything that came to hand. From Stuttgart to Le Pradet large windows were blocked up. Even his mother's house in peaceful Vevey acquired metal siding to keep the water out.

For me, as a student, seeing these houses soon after the war was a powerful architectural experience, combining the emotion of hard geometry blighted with the nostalgia of mighty forms ruined within a generation. Le Corbusier was deeply hurt, but that spurred his efforts to make the new architecture of postwar France into something very different from the precise work of the twenties. The new architecture would have a ruggedness that would make it much less vulnerable to the vagaries of the occupants or the weather.

The *Unité d'habitation* at Marseilles was Le Corbusier's statement of this new architecture and new life style for Europeans. With a commission free of building regulations and restrictions, Le Corbusier had the opportunity for which he had been preparing all his life.

The building was first designed with a steel frame and precast-concrete cladding, reflecting Le Corbusier's previous experience with large buildings and even more so that of his engineer, Vladimir Bodiansky, who had been engineer for the Mopin system of the thirties. This system, as exemplified by the high-rise Drancy scheme of Beaudouin and Lods, consists of a steel frame, very economically used, and a semistructural cladding of pebble-faced precast-concrete panels, with a high degree of repetition. At Marseilles the availability of skills and materials led to the abandonment of steel columns; although steel was retained for internal horizontal structure and precast concrete for cladding, the vertical columns and all special areas of the building were of *in situ* concrete, ruggedly designed and crudely made (Fig. 89). One feels that, whatever Bodiansky may have thought, Le Corbusier was quite content to indulge in the use of primitive materials. Le Corbusier positively reveled in the irregularities of his concrete: "The defects shout at one from all parts of the structure! . . . Faults are human; they are ourselves, our daily lives. What matters is to go further, to live, to be intense, to aim high, and to be loyal!"[16] The contrast between this attitude and *Vers une architecture* is total—then a thousandth of an inch mattered.

It was the *béton brut* at Marseilles that was photographed, written about, and copied, but Le Corbusier had remained thoroughly professional throughout. Most of the concrete is precast, well detailed, and reasonably made; the apartments rest on lead pads on steel beams to give acoustic privacy. The technical know-how is greater than it ever was, but it keeps a low profile; it is the apparently primitive that is glorified.

At the same time as he was designing the massive *piloti* for Marseilles, Le Corbusier was also preparing the designs of Sainte Baume for Edouard Trouin—a world of grottoes, of stabilized earth walls, and of grass on the roof. This was primitivism pushed to the extreme, dear to Le Corbusier's heart. It was never built, but echoes of the Sainte Baume designs run through the Maisons Jaoul in Paris and the Sarabhai house in Ahmedabad, which was built "to reestablish contact with the noble and fundamental materials of architecture; the brick, friend of man, rough concrete, a friend also."[17]

Just as Le Corbusier had used rough stone walls at Poissy and in the Pavillon Suisse during his machine aesthetic period, so during this phase of postwar primitivism he made excursions back into the precise world of metal technology; he patented a quite delicious metal structural system that could build up 2260 cubes for his "Roq et Rob" project, and he designed metal umbrellas for an exhibition at the Porte Maillot. By the midfifties we find him back with his old friend Jean Prouvé, designing fifty metal houses for Lagny, nice designs with steel I-section *piloti*, Prouvé cladding, and sanitary cores, but mercifully free from the A frames that blight typical Prouvé houses.

John Winter 340

"These houses return to the favored graces of the law,"[18] said Le Corbusier, but he was not optimistic about high technology in France at that time and correctly anticipated that the houses would not be built.

The completion in 1952 of the *Unité* at Marseilles and the Lever House in Manhattan, followed in 1958 by the completion of the Seagram Building in New York and the High Court at Chandigarh, revealed the full extent of the deep split within the modern movement. By the fifties American-inspired building technology became a world pace-setter, with Mies van der Rohe, the twentieth-century Palladio, giving it an image and an order. Le Corbusier, hating America, building largely in India, went the primitive way: out of step, lonely, glorious. It was only when glass and metal went out of fashion with the architectural trends in the sixties that Le Corbusier picked it up seriously; as always he was out of line.

The Final Phase

Fame and success brought Le Corbusier work in many parts of the world. In India the construction could be overseen by his colleagues; but in Argentina, in Tokyo, and in Boston, local architects supervised and ran into problems with the *béton brut* approach. It is one thing to accept rough workmanship from Corsican workmen in an impoverished postwar France; it is quite another to require it of a sophisticated American contractor.

The Carrutchet house at La Plata in Argentina was supervised by Amancio Williams; and it was given a smooth stucco covering. In the period 1957 to 1959 the Museum of Western Art in Tokyo was built from Le Corbusier's designs by his former assistants Junzo Sakakura and Kunio Maekawa; as sincere disciples they carried out his designs to the last detail—the workmanship is immaculate, but the visual result is strangely dead. Five years later, in 1964, the Carpenter Center for Visual Arts was completed at Cambridge, Massachusetts, under

Figure 90
The Maison de la Culture at Firminy Vert, 1961–1965, retains the massive concrete form of
Le Corbusier's buildings of the previous decade, but it shows a tendency toward another
technology, with its roof suspended on steel cables. (Photograph by Russell Walden.)

Figure 91
The steel roof of the Heidi Weber Pavilion, Zurich, 1963–1967, stands over the light and
elegant enclosure below. (Photograph by Russell Walden.)

the direction of Le Corbusier's CIAM friend José Luis Sert, and reportedly the builders had difficulty getting the formwork rough enough to satisfy the architect.

There was something silly about all this. Le Corbusier may have had only one eye, but it was a damned good one and he could see what was going on. The magnificent rough concrete that seemed so appropriate to India and postwar France became inappropriate in technically abundant cultures. Moreover, leaks in his French buildings and overheating in his Indian ones revealed shortcomings, not too serious perhaps, but worrying nonetheless. Le Corbusier said little, but just as he had reoriented his architecture in the thirties after observing the defects in his early houses, he made another change of direction in the sixties in response to the limitations of his postwar way of building. Already in his seventies, Le Corbusier disregarded the comforts of old age and rethought his architecture, but death cut short this third and last phase before much had been built.

The Youth Center at Firminy (Fig. 90) gives a hint of this new phase of Le Corbusier, with its roof suspended on cables and its shiny metal furniture, but the Heidi Weber Pavilion (Fig. 91) fully reveals the new Le Corbusier of enameled steel and neoprene.

The Heidi Weber Pavilion at Zurich, whose interior "demonstrates the practical, constructive, and plastic capabilities of dry construction,"[19] shows the totality of Le Corbusier's change and also his skillfulness, for this first example of his new approach is put together with a technical sophistication unsurpassed in Europe at the time. Credit must be shared with Jean Prouvé, who gave advice, and with his assistants Robert Rebutato and Alain Tavès, who carried the work through to completion following Le Corbusier's death early in the construction period. The pavilion has a metal parasol roof, which is unduly ponderous and heavy, a hangover from his heavy concrete period; but under its shade is the patent system from "Roq et Rob," where spaces are formed of mild steel angles forming 2260 cubes. In the original patented design the cubes stack up so that the outside corners have just one angle, whereas inside junctions have four angles building up to form a Greek cross. Unfortunately this did not prove workable, as the size of columns cannot be decreased in direct proportion to the load, so all the columns are made Greek crosses and the image of stacked cubes is weakened. The structural members are clearly expressed, however, for the grouped angles show as columns and beams and are painted in contrast to the panels to acknowledge the linear nature of this construction and to emphasize the difference between this cage and the massive solid constructions of the previous years. 2260 may be a basic modulor dimension, but it is a somewhat restricting span within a building; Le Corbusier had to accept a somewhat inhibited arrangement of spaces in order to keep the integrity of the structural discipline he had chosen.

Comparison between early sketches and the final proposals for the pavilion show that, as the design developed and the requirements of metal building became clearer, Le Corbusier abandoned various features that had been dear to him during the previous years. Early designs show *ondulatoires* (floor-to-ceiling mullions of varying spacing) and solid walls seen as planes; later designs have glass unsubdivided, frame revealed, and panels divided into two equal parts—a most unmodulor subdivision. The pressed and enameled panels are secured to the frame with gaskets, but extra metal members are introduced so that the clear outline of the frame is never encroached upon by the gaskets and the construction can be seen as a clear demonstration of frame and fill. The Heidi Weber Pavilion is a splendid construction, showing the way Le Corbusier was developing, but that elephantine roof holds it back to his ideas of the previous decade.

A few weeks before his death he prepared sketches for an extension on top of his Jaoul house (Fig. 92), and this design is being brought to

Figure 92
Design for an extension on top of the Maison Jaoul by Jacques Michel, from sketches by Le Corbusier. The contrast in technologies between the original house and the extension could not be more complete. (Redrawn from the original by John Winter.)

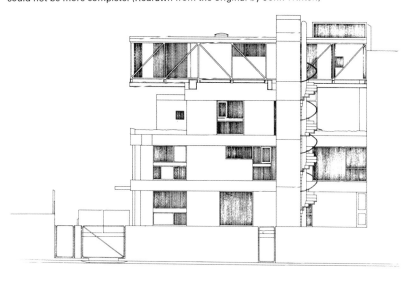

Le Corbusier's Technological Dilemma   345

realization by the architect Jacques Michel. The Jaoul design has no hangovers; it makes its architectural statement with that most metallic of all forms, the Warren truss; and by putting the spaces within the truss, he made sure that the building would be as insistently metal as Marseilles had been insistently concrete.

Seventy-eight is not a young age at which to die. With Le Corbusier it seems that a new creative period was just beginning.

1 Charles Jencks, *Le Corbusier and the Tragic View of Architecture*, London, 1973.

2 Le Corbusier, *Vers une architecture*, Paris, 1923. English translation: *Towards a New Architecture*, 1946 edition, p. 12.

3 Ibid., p. 115.

4 Ibid., p. 121.

5 Ibid., p. 201.

6 Le Corbusier, *Oeuvre complète*, vol. 1, 4th ed., 1946, p. 199.

7 Le Corbusier, *Oeuvre complète 1929–34*, 4th ed., 1947, p. 35. Translated by Helen Walden.

8 Ibid.

9 Ibid., p. 97.

10 Ibid., p. 48.

11 Ibid., p. 119.

12 Le Corbusier, *Oeuvre complète 1938–46*, 3rd ed., 1955, p. 116.

13 Ibid., p. 123. Translated by Helen Walden.

14 Ibid., p. 116.

15 Le Corbusier, *Oeuvre complète 1946–52,* 1st ed., 1953, p. 61.

16 Ibid., p. 191.

17 Le Corbusier, *Oeuvre complète 1952–57*, 1st ed., 1957, p. 115.

18 Ibid., p. 202.

19 Le Corbusier, *Oeuvre complète 1957–65*, 1st ed., 1965, p. 24.

Notes

Part Five

**Chandigarh: Realization, Reminiscences,
and Sociopolitical Realities**

Maxwell Fry **Le Corbusier at Chandigarh**

The city of Chandigarh came first into my recognition in 1948 or 1949 as the whiff of a possible commission wafted via the Royal Institute of British Architects, but remaining without substance. The Punjab Government may have at that time been sending out feelers prior to meeting Albert Mayer, whom they commissioned to make a plan, with the brilliant young architect Matthew Nowicki.

However, the sudden death of Nowicki in 1950 necessitated the selection of a new architect for Chandigarh. When Prem Thapar, of the Indian Civil Service and the administrator of the project, with the chief engineer, P. L. Varma, called upon Jane Drew and myself at our office in the closing months of 1950, a complete plan existed for a city of 150,000 people, along with a detailed budget covering every ascertainable item, including thirteen grades of houses for government officials with the accommodation and the estimated cost set against each.

There was also a generous infrastructure of social and educational services and provision for the supply of water, drainage, and electricity to every level of dwelling provided, so that an examination of the budget and the well-advanced Mayer plan demonstrated the clear intention of the government to construct a modern city on a site selected to serve the state at the highest level of design and execution and set a new standard for India.

The state of the Punjab, truncated by partition, still suffered from the appalling ravages of a bitterly fought war, with millions homeless and landless and refugee camps still in the process of organization. It had lost its beloved capital Lahore to Pakistan; its government was gathered loosely in Simla, a ramshackle affair built only for summer occupation; and it needed a capital city for every practical, political, and spiritual purpose. That it should want and be prepared to build a capital of the first order was the mark of a courage and resolution that never flagged in all our dealings with it.

At our first meeting with Thapar and Varma they asked for two architects to organize and supervise the architectural aspects of the Mayer plan. If Jane Drew and I had been able to drop every other obligation and accept the appointments, Corbusier would not have been approached.

It is no easy decision to drop every other obligation and decamp to India for three years as we were asked to do. I would have continued to decline, had not our chief client, the Inter-Universities Council, urged us to accept and to delegate the bulk of our responsibilities, as we did, to Lindsey Drake and Denys Lasdun who joined the partnership for the purpose.

But Jane Drew, foremost in urging acceptance, felt bound for a few months to her share of the Festival of Britain program, and this put Thapar in the dilemma of having two jobs to offer with only one filled. There would be little difficulty, he said, in fitting Jane Drew in when they returned to India, but they were instructed to fill both posts and meant to obey their instructions.

At this juncture Corbusier was first mentioned. Reflecting on the immensity of the architectural program for a three-year contract, I thought the Capitol group of buildings would be a fitting commission for the great man. "What would be the effect," said Thapar, "of introducing Corbusier to the team?" To which I replied, "Honour and glory for you, and an unpredictable portion of misery for me. But I think it a noble way out of the present difficulties."

So Jane Drew rang Corbusier and we all went to a meeting at his office, very dramatically arranged with a tape recorder that broke down under the pressure of high-minded resolutions. The conditions put forward by Thapar included the acceptance of the Mayer plan and the Project Budget as the working basis of the agreement, but in accepting them Corbusier insisted on the inclusion in the team of his cousin Pierre Jeanneret, from whom he had broken some time earlier.

Maxwell Fry   352

This was inconvenient for the Indians, and we tried to assure Corbusier that our loyalty to the project and to him was beyond doubt, but he persisted, and arrangements were concluded on that understanding.

We returned to London. I reached Simla at the end of 1950 and put up at Clarke's Hotel with Pierre Jeanneret. Both the hotel and the improvised office accommodation were primitive and cold; the Indian staff so far assembled was few in number and only partially trained. We were left much on our own except for a few meetings with the evasive but autocratic chief engineer. Jeanneret was cheerful but narrowly Parisian, with no aptitude for languages; as a consequence my French improved while all else deteriorated.

We had some drawings by Nowicki, which were rather romantically based on Indian idioms. Jeanneret and I started working on housing types while we absorbed the conditions of the Project Budget. I studied the Mayer plan and found by projecting sections along major road lines that the Capitol buildings which he saw enlaced with water were rather like Lutyens' Viceregal Palace at New Delhi, largely eclipsed by the profile of the approach road: they were obviously not well sited. I had doubts also as to the workability of its Radburn-like path system, which seemed to me to be out of scale with the enterprise; and the generally floppy form of its sector planning depressed me in the same way as that of Milton Keynes many years later.

I was at this period taking the appointment on trust but ready to resign if it grew worse. We had laid it down as a condition of our acceptance that we would not work under engineers, as was the custom in the Indian Public Works Department. I was experiencing the onset of a trial of strength with Varma, neglect by Thapar, and a general feeling of lassitude in the organization, the reverse of my experiences in Africa. Not wanting to waste my efforts, I put in a resignation to Thapar that brought him hot foot from his house to tell me that the project would fail without us and that he shared my problem with Varma. So I stayed.

The arrival of Corbusier galvanized the situation. We moved down to the Rest House in the lovely village of Chandigarh on the road to Kalkar, where the mountain railway starts for Simla. Corbusier, Varma, Jeanneret, myself, and intermittently Thapar were there; Albert Mayer was making his way to us from the south.

Without waiting for Mayer to appear, Corbusier started on large sheets of paper to approach a plan by a method of rough and ready analysis familiar to me from the workings of the Congrès Inter-nationaux d'Architecture Moderne (CIAM). First he outlined the main communications with the site on the map of India—air, railway, road (Fig. 93). Then he dealt with the site itself—its immediate background of low foothills rising to the sheer mountains of the Himalaya with the peaks beyond; its gentle plain declining at a fall of one in one hundred; its dry river beds to each side, with a smaller bed inter-mediate to the left; a diagonal road crossing the plan low down, and a loop of railway away on the right (Fig. 94).

It was a difficult situation. My French was unequal to the occasion. Jeanneret was supernumerary, and Thapar only half aware of what was going forward. Corbusier held the crayon and was in his element.

"Voilà la gare," he said, "et voici la rue commerciale," and he drew the first road on the new plan of Chandigarh (Fig. 95). "Voici la tête," he went on, indicating with a smudge the higher ground to the left of Mayer's location, the ill effects of which I had already pointed out to him. "Et voilà l'estomac, le cité-centre." Then he delineated the mas-sive sectors, measuring each half by three-quarters of a mile and filling out the extent of the plain between the river valleys, with exten-sion to the south.

The plan was well advanced by the time the anxious Albert Mayer joined the group. He must have had an unnerving journey, and he was

Figure 93
The broad location of
Chandigarh on the map
of India. (Drawing by
Maxwell Fry.)

Figure 94
The context of the
Chandigarh site.
(Drawing by Maxwell
Fry.)

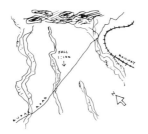

Figure 95
Le Corbusier's emerging
plan for Chandigarh.
(Drawing by Maxwell
Fry.)

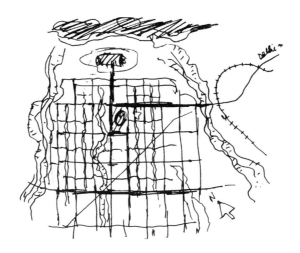

Le Corbusier at Chandigarh   355

too upset to make the most of his entry. I found him a high-minded decent man, a little sentimental in his approach, but good-humored; not in any way was he a match for the enigmatic but determined figure of the prophet.

We sat around after lunch in a deadly silence broken by Jeanneret's saying to Mayer, *"Vous parlez français, monsieur?"* To which Mayer responded, *"Oui, musheer, je parle,"* a polite but ill-fated rejoinder that cut him out of all discussion that followed.

And so we continued, with minor and marginal suggestions from us and a steady flow of exposition from Corbusier, until the plan as we now know it was completed and never again departed from. I stuck out for allowing Mayer to expose his theories in one of the sectors, out of pure *gentillesse* for a displaced person, and I suggested some curvature in the east-west roads to avoid boredom and to mitigate the effects of low sunlight on car drivers. Aside from these considerations, the plan stood, and on my advice Mayer signed it as a participant and later stood by his decision when the new plan was under fire in a cabinet meeting.

In 1950 Corbusier was offered the design of the Capitol buildings on a plan designed by Albert Mayer, and early in 1951 he had redesigned the whole capital plan so that he could turn his undivided attention to the design of a monumental group of buildings forming the culmination of his own plan.

This he could do with a calm mind for, by the time he came to it, he had recognized the existence of a firm and able organization, headed by Prem Thapar, a noble-minded administrator of supreme skill and integrity; a chief engineer of great experience, a man who though evasive and autocratic in his handling of affairs was of elevated mind and indomitable purpose; Jane Drew and I combining energy, creativity, and leadership; and Pierre Jeanneret, not the happiest of collaborators, but a ceaseless worker in the good cause (Fig. 96).

After a time, in addition to Varma, Indian assistants of skill and promise emerged and devoted themselves heart and soul to his work; he came to rely on them with confidence.

Behind this organization stood the government of the state in full support, headed by Trevedi, a governor of some caliber; at Delhi was Jawaharlal Nehru, who valued Corbusier at his full weight and was prepared to pay him what he asked.

A friendship grew between us and Corbusier that lasted, particularly for Jane Drew, until his death. He could turn from his exhausting labors to evenings of ranging talk, with the bottle circulating, in an atmosphere of complete and happy relaxation. Jane Drew gave him colored papers and paste, and with one after another drawing and collage he brought in gestures of gratitude before the evening's talk. *"Pour toi, Jane; et celui-là, c'est pas si bon, pour vous, Maxwell."*

My relations with Corbusier were never intimate. I was never a disciple, as architects such as José Luis Sert was. The authoritative aspect of the Plan Voisin de Paris appalled me when I first saw it, and I preferred the classical clarity of Mies van der Rohe's Turgendhat Haus to the early houses of Corbusier, which I later came to value above most of his later work.

When Jane Drew arrived in Simla, Corbusier was in a huff about a remark I had made concerning a certain theatricality in the High Court design. We had shown Corbusier the Red Fort at Delhi and some of the stupendous Moghul ruins in the vicinity, and we had explained from our experience in West Africa the principle behind the achievement of shade temperature and the cooling effect of moving air under shaded conditions. *"Un parasol, en effet, hein?"* And a parasol he made for the High Court, the greatest of all canopies with just the merest reminiscence of Moghul influence.

At this time he was engrossed by visual effects of buildings in a big space. He had plans of the grand axis from the Louvre to the Arc de Triomphe reduced to appropriate scale and was continually testing his remembered impressions against the terrain upon which he was operating, as though seeking the ultimate possible, the furthest extension of grandeur comprehensible, at a single view, and this with buildings of asymmetrical disposition related only by the imaginary conversation they could maintain with each other across space.

If one compares with this arrangement the nearly instant recognition that perfect symmetry provides even for monuments as distant as the King George V arch and the Viceregal Palace at New Delhi, one may perhaps realize the nature of the struggle that was consuming him at that time, resolved, to the distress of some of his best friends, at the outer, if not beyond the outer limits of the possible.

From the level space between buildings he removed all roads by lowering them, but later allowed little hills to be formed with spoil, which must distract from the aimed-for impression. If in all this one could find cause for frustration, it must be set against the objectives, the first measure of the artist in all works of art.

There was an episode that I have never been able successfully to explain, which concerns the distribution of population over the plan sectors. We had accepted as something unshakable and inevitable the hierarchic disposition of the population from rich to poor, downward from the Capitol, and we could with no great difficulty have distributed the total of 150,000 over the plan. But Corbusier with some secrecy worked feverishly on a sort of computerization, some system he had in his mind, that would present us with the mosaic law of the matter, and somewhere in this computation was the hint of a row of high-rise buildings low down in the plan.

They never rose. Whether Thapar scotched them or not I never knew; I know only that the incomprehensible figures were not to my knowledge applied to the plan, which it was clear from the beginning was to be a poor state's capital in two dimensions, with no two-grade intersections in our lifetime.

Corbusier's sector planning reinforced this idea, with its legally protected boundaries and its strongly internal planning that showed up so well in the first-developed and still most used Sector 22. The sectors with their contrasting bands of daily activity, the cross-threading bazaar streets and cycle paths, and the circumambulatory feeder road to the housing make a pattern that shows him at his grandly logical, for if there were to be both the pressures and the resources of the British New Towns, the scheme would be more workable than it now is, the straight runs of motor road doubled in length, the cycle paths a reality with the aid of underpasses (Fig. 97).

There was a moment when he contemplated a regulatory system of proportion for all the housing of the city (which had hitherto lain outside his control and was the work of Jeanneret and ourselves), together with schools, colleges, hospitals, health centers, local political buildings, and so on, enough in all conscience. It was no more than a gesture of omnipotence or, more charitably, the hope expressed of an overall harmony to be the work of several hands. He did not press it.

More important was the loss of diversity and the small foreground scale of pavement commerce in the city center. I worked with Jane Drew on the shopping center of Sector 22 with its variety of multilevel shopping from closed stores to open booths; we had the direct collaboration of shopkeepers working to our models and giving us back something extra in the shape of connecting covered ways. Thus I was as anxious as Corbusier that the city center should preserve something of the intimacy, even the untidiness, of the typical Indian bazaar.

We both made drawings showing spaces enclosed by blocks of buildings—shops, offices, and residential accommodation—partly filled by booths or stalls, or merely selling space covered by both permanent and temporary canopies. It was not an easy exercise, be-

Figure 96
Le Corbusier's office at Chandigarh. Standing left to right are Pierre Jeanneret, Jane Drew, Le Corbusier, Superintending Engineer G. C. Khanna, Chief Engineer P. L. Varma, and Maxwell Fry. (Photograph by Narindar Lamba, 1952.)

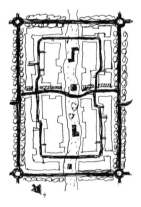

Figure 97
The working sector, as planned by Le Corbusier, with its legally protected boundaries. (Drawing by Maxwell Fry.)

cause the size and actual function of the center was difficult to estimate; its financial practicability was quite indeterminate. Sector 22
was humming as the center of Chandigarh life, but its area was small
when compared with the city center lying up and beyond this first residential sector to be developed.

I had left before it was begun in earnest, and I was taken aback by
its stark brutality when I saw it years later. The scale was gargantuan
but nearly devoid of the sort of surface marking or modeling by
means of which Corbusier established scale, as with the High Court. It
was devoid of intimate street level activity and treeless! What had
happened in the interval? I do not know. There is grandeur in the great
colonnaded blocks. I am not averse to size as an element in urban
composition, but even along the all-purpose entry road I found blocks
of unidentifiable blankness that verged on the vacantly forbidding, a
form of excess to which I was entirely unable to respond. It was one of
the (I fear) vanishing pleasures of New Delhi to come across Lutyens'
influence in the detailing of humble lengths of servants quarters or the
like, and I had hoped to find this element in Chandigarh and sorely
missed it.

Corbusier said to me one day that he was interested only in art. I felt
this in his persistent withdrawal from what might be called vulgar
contact, the ordinariness that makes up the bulk of mankind and is
both its strength and weakness. The loneliness of the great artist shut
off by the mere weight of the concentrated effort of creation has been
spoken of by Conrad and many another. With a writer such as Balzac
or Dickens, contact was the material of the work, but with Corbusier
this was not so. I imagine that he peopled his buildings, where indeed
they gave the appearance of being peopled, by figments of his own
creation, unendowed with normal human attributes; and that as he
grew older and more withdrawn, these counted for less than the ele-
mental forms reaching forward to ultimate ruination.

I would warn those who hope by pecking over the remains of the great—the diairies, letters, reported conversations, photographs, and so on—that they will be permitted to pierce to the heart of the mystery that makes men great. One has only to read the biographies, even the autobiographies, of the grandly creative to find in their contact with the world continuous frustrations, bitternesses, misunderstandings, and rejections, until death ends them—and not these alone, but as often as not, the meannesses, treacheries, and shabbinesses; the envies and vanities, especially the vanities, the defensive vanities that cloud the daily conduct of those otherwise rapt away from the world. It is a dangerous occupation, and few have succeeded in elevating it through some lucky gift of sympathy or from feelings of fellow suffering.

A French critic once said that the beginning of all criticism was contained in the words *Que c'est beau*—how beautiful it is. Without this surely all criticism is vain that seeks to define the exactitude of pleasures that come and go and swell and fade.

Coming to Chandigarh twenty years after I had labored in the field, and with the memory of such criticism in my mind, I went in and about it on a lovely December morning. It was unfinished, poorly maintained, vulgarized in parts, and with standards lowered in large extensions beyond the original plan. Yet I had to say, *"Que c'est beau! How noble a thing this is!"*

I went round with that same engineer with whom I had fought and at whose renewed requests I had come on a sentimental journey to see old friends before we died. And he took me before everything else to see the lake that was in his mind from the beginning, yet had to wait the moment until the tide of recognition and success made it possible, and had to make it then to the limits and to more than the limits of what was possible.

We walked together along the curving sweep of the embankment that was his, not Corbusier's, an embankment he had made ten times wider than was strictly necessary, knowing that it would become the promenade for the city and therefore should be on a scale to match it.

This lake is a contribution to the city that represents for me its soul. It is not less, but differently, the creation of Corbusier's also, for in the association with men of great insight and purpose, works arise of a nature like their own. Since we were not entirely without either of these attributes, we felt the exhilaration and the deep polarization of effort that Corbusier brought to the enterprise, though he barely lifted his head from his work and was only faintly amused by demonstrating it.

This is as I saw him. It seems utterly irrelevant to me how far a man, with the objectives that he had constantly before him, fell below them. The last time we saw him in his apartment in Paris—the place growing old and dusty around him, a sycamore tree bursting the terrace flower box it had seeded itself into—he was all agog with the opportunities enamels presented as an extension of painting. Glasses on his forehead, he groped about in the accumulation of the years to show us his latest experiments in the medium. Gone were the suspicions that clouded the first and fateful meeting many years ago; a simple single-hearted man was sharing his new-found enthusiasm with old friends.

Jane B. Drew   **Le Corbusier as I Knew Him**

I cannot remember when first I met Le Corbusier, but I think it was at the International Congress of Modern Architecture (CIAM) at Bridgewater in 1947, when he made little impression on me.

I was new to CIAM Conferences and realized that there was some kind of political trouble going on between Corb and Cor van Eesteren—I remember Corb being rather dogmatic.

He must have become a friend, for I remember he visited my office in 36 Bedford Square. He was highly excited about the modulor that he produced from his pocket with great pride. It was in a small roll that stretched out for a long way like the roll of his lovers Don Giovanni produces in the opera.

I also remember him trying by some sort of chart at that time to prove he was not Swiss but French.

I saw more of Corb at the CIAM Conference of 1949 at Bergamo. He seemed then to be the most important member of CIAM. He impressed me as having the face of an ascetic with internal force.

The last Congress I attended was in 1954 at Aix-en-Provence, France; there were amusing incidents when the Dutch members walked out because nude French girls appeared on the roof at Marseilles. I remember the CIAM grilles, and Corb talking well, not much more than the others, but with more authority.

Through CIAM a friendship was established, and he sent me a photograph of himself with an affectionate dedication (misspelled) (Fig. 98).

After that Corb seemed to regard me as a special friend and wrote me numerous personal letters. I have kept these letters, but since my life has always been overbusy they will require, like my photographs, a long time to sort out. I remember much of what was in them: "There is no such thing as detail in architecture, everything counts"; his card from Egypt with him (drawn on) sitting on a pyramid, saying, "This time it is not a square peg in a round hole"; his several letters asking me to see Jawaharlal Nehru on points to do with his work, which I did; his letter from America about Costantino Nivola and how happy he was. But I am no historian and one day when I retire I will sort out my letters; meantime I will tell only of those days I remember.

He sent me his Modulor book with an inscription. This inscription was not correct—I did not help him (Fig. 99).

It was when the Indians came to our office about Chandigarh that I first phoned him. I had not yet been to his Paris office. The first visit impressed me—his tiny modulor office and his way of life.

Corb was a very good friend. His numerous letters and postcards and a constant stream of his paintings and drawings, that he sent me until his death, showed me how seriously he treated friendship. He said living was an art.

The drawings and collages, some of which are now in my office, often have two dates. For example, *Woman with Open Hand* (Fig. 100) has two dates on the bottom: Paris 32—when Corb did the preliminary sketches, and Chandigarh 52—where he actually executed it. It is a good illustration of the current themes that appear in his architecture. One can see the acute contrast between the carefully designed curved shapes and rectangles, the combination of architecture in stylized human forms, and few of the very flat triangular forms that he fell in love with after his early visits to Greece and which he used only at points of importance. He very often used as his signature the image of a little crow, which he so much resembled in appearance; and he chose the double dating to indicate when he first started to work on a theme, and when he eventually worked it to completion, in this case twenty years later. The open hand here is part of his lifetime philosophy and implies his idea that one should give, as indeed he did.

I found him a man with a serious purpose, egocentric but also able to appreciate others. He had a great sense of humor and enormous vanity. To go for a walk with him was a revelation, he would notice so

Figure 98
Le Corbusier in his
studio, 24 Rue
Nungesser-et-Coli, Paris
XVIᵉ. ''Pour Jane
Drey [sic], avec mon
amitié,'' signed Le
Corbusier, 12 December
1950. (Photograph by
Maywald, Rue Jacob,
Paris, May 1948.)

Figure 99
Le Corbusier's
inscription to Jane
Drew's copy of *Modulor
2,* January 1956.

Figure 100
Le Corbusier's collage,
Woman with Open Hand,
1952. (Collection of Jane
Drew.)

much. He loved the quiet lines of the green hills and mountains in Chandigarh but he also loved strong colors. His dislike of "sweet pea" colors in buildings (his words) was relevant to his whole wish for a clear definition and drama.

He lived and worked in his own extraordinary way. He painted in the early morning, settled alone at his desk uninterrupted when he wanted to study problems in depth, as he put it, and when he relaxed he liked sport and talk, away from architecture.

He had a lot of the monk in him. His idea was that his painting exercised his imagination. He dated everything he drew. He tried to find logical reasons for all he did and to separate and discover the experiences life could offer, the difference between seeing during night and day, the different experiences possible in daily life, and the maximization of each experience.

I remember visiting him as an old man in his flat. He had taken up enamel work to do the Chandigarh High Court doors. He was determined to get all the virtue out of enamel that was possible and learned when he was seventy how to work with it.

His view of life was moral. He was loyal to mathematics, to order, to living the life he thought worth living. He gave his life to his work; his reason for not having a family was that, like a monk, an artist could not spare the time. He did, however, value affection and women—not in an English way: he spoke to me of his women loves, and although he recognized sex as the force it is and was not respectful of manmade laws, he did respect the women he loved, and his love of his mother was a very great force in his life.

Corb was an extremely witty man. He was not a *raconteur* of others' stories. He possessed a marvelous and original sense of humor. For example, a pompous architect came into my office in Bedford Square while Corb was there. He was a very unbending type and said he had lost his umbrella. Corb murmured to me, *"C'est en dedans."* I remember also when he sent us an invitation to a party in Simla in northern India, where monkeys are sacred. The invitation consisted of a caricature of him and Jeanneret both drawn as monkeys (which they singularly resembled at times!). A further illustration of Corb's humor is a drawing he did in Chandigarh of the "family" responsible for the creation of Chandigarh—a sort of caricature of us all (Fig. 101). This shows Corb as a crow, looking in the opposite direction. Jeanneret is shown as a cock with his head in the sand. I am shown as a goat and Max as a dog. I asked Corb to scrub out the names because I thought Jeanneret, in particular, might take offence, but it was a good illustration of his kind of humor.

Corb's judgment of men was also good. He despised the American scene, the waste of materials, the wrong direction in life. He used to say Paris could live for a month on the waste New York made in a day. He disliked the slick smooth finishes of the expensive American offices; equally the way of life of the business men as he saw it.

I remember him admiring Edwin Lutyens' work greatly; he was too big a man for style in itself to prejudice him—proportions and forms were what mattered.

He did not bother much about cost or what he had told his clients. It was almost irrelevant to him; although he was anxious to do good cheap housing, he was even more anxious to make major works. He did not like anonymous artifacts. He liked a world where bosses, for example in the Secretariat building in Chandigarh, could visibly be made important. Where station in life was defined, he had no intention of wasting his own efforts on anything irrelevant, but he did regret that sometimes he put himself and his own work so much in front of doing things that mattered for others.

He has written so much that his views about architecture must be known, but to be with him was to find him always discovering (Fig. 102). Discovering why Moghul forms look right in the Indian light, dis-

Figure 101
The Chandigarh
"Family," as depicted by
Le Corbusier, 8 April
1952. (Collection of Jane
Drew.)

Figure 102
Le Corbusier and Jane
Drew on the grass at
Chandigarh, 1951.
(Photograph by Eulie
Chowdbury.)

covering why saris might be a better solution to heighten the attraction of women than French fashions. Discovering how underarm hair is beautiful and to him added to a woman's attractiveness. Discovering the mood of the late afternoon and night in India. Not for him were the views of the fashion merchants and depilatory salesmen.

I am not saying that I agree with all Le Corbusier's views; I am trying to describe how I found him as a person. His manner to reporters was offhand because he thought them unserious about architecture and untrustworthy; also because he did not wish to waste his time, for he cared much about whom he was with.

His life was, in a way, a battle. He recognized that authorities with their by-laws about, for example, heights of rooms were not concerned with proportion; such laws were pointless to him. All proportions must be related to man and to geometry.

He was able to tell Nehru that he had put more thought into the High Court in Chandigarh than he had envisaged and so his fees must be higher—I was with him and translated this to Nehru. For him a formal contract regarding fees was irrelevant. Luckily Nehru was another big man who also saw that a contract was not important in such a work.

Le Corbusier was so egocentric that I once teased him about the fact he could not talk for ten minutes without bringing himself into the conversation! He realized this was true. I also said to him that he was too selfish, and he must go and thank the Indian young men who had worked so hard for him. He had not wanted even to go and see them; however, he did go and agreed it was right to do so. He was both selfish and unselfish. His kindness and unselfishness to me may well have been partly or largely due to my being a woman, but he continued it when our work association was over.

Le Corbusier, with all his maximizing of drama, was also delicate and refined. I do not know if I have given the full picture of this man who was thrilled to be receiving our architect's Gold Medal from the Queen of England and who argued with Jeanneret for the virtues of royalty versus democracy because it was more poetic and detached. I am writing of a man whom I greatly admire, but I recognize that I also am very attached to him.

I think of Le Corbusier as the architect from whom I have learned most. I am sympathetic to him for his primary allegiance to his own vision of the truth and his life spent in trying to affirm it.

Madhu Sarin   **Chandigarh as a Place to Live in**

The following is a personal introduction to Chandigarh in Le Corbusier's own words:

City of Chandigarh

I Definition of use of Chandigarh

(i) Chandigarh is a city offering all amenities to the poorest of the poor of its citizens to lead a dignified life.
(ii) Chandigarh is a Government city with a precise function and, consequently, a precise quality of inhabitants.

On this presumption, the city is not to be a big city (metropolis)—it must not lose its definition. Some people say that life must come in the city from other sources of activity, especially industry—but an industrial city is not the same as an administrative city. One must not mix the two. It seems that the complement of the original definition should be the invitation of forces which can reinforce the functions of the city and not open a conflict or rivalry. We must take care that any temptations do not kill the goal which was foreseen at the time the city was founded. Therefore, naturally, old doors must be opened to unknown initiatives. It appears that the future of Chandigarh will be open to all cultural factors in different manifestations:

Teaching (schools, university, new science of teaching, audiovisual training, etc.—in one word all kinds of knowledge)

Means to express and disperse thought (editions: books, magazines, and, eventually, their printing, etc.)

Modes of expression and dispersion of the arts (in time and space—history and geography)

All kinds of reproduction of art-witnesses (editions: visual means—photographs, diagrams, etc. to different scales)

Diverse kinds of exhibitions, shows, theatre, festivals, creations of the highest modernity, etc.

For the culture of the body, an organism can be created having at its disposition possibilities of meeting for competitions and tournaments.

All this will afford the creation of a "Chandigarh label" which will be the guarantee of quality and will be worth emulation.

II The Four Functions

The CIAM "Charter of Athens."

The force of this charter lies in giving the first place to the dwelling:

the environment of living—the family under the rule of "24 Solar Hours."

The second place is given to "Working" which is the daily act of human obligation.

The third is the culture of body and spirit on the one hand and an intellectual leisure on the other.

When all these goals have received their definite containers, it is possible to give to each of them its respective rightful place and at this moment can occur the problem of realizing the contacts: that is circulation.

III

With this line of conduct, the urbanism of Chandigarh emerged.[1]

Ever since the day Le Corbusier's name was associated with the Chandigarh project, Chandigarh has received a tremendous amount of publicity, propaganda, and documentation. Certainly in the fields of planning and architecture, Chandigarh was seen by many as a landmark in the present epoch, and, inevitably, it has been watched with keen interest through all its life of twenty-three years. Writing about Chandigarh has been largely confined to three broad categories: first, a pure description of the planning doctrine with details about the "sector," the 7V's (*les sept voies*), the Capitol complex, and so on; second, a flowery applause of the marvels of Chandigarh and its modern architecture; or third, an outright criticism of the project on the basis of its "non-Indian" character, an importation of Western ideas into an alien milieu, usually followed by statements announcing the failure of Chandigarh on these grounds.

Cities, however, are complex phenomena. Much as architects and planners may like to think about the importance of their concepts, visions, aesthetics, or planning, these remain only partial aspects of a much greater totality. And, once a city starts growing, whether due to social, economic, political, or geographic reasons, it becomes increasingly difficult to control its growth or to be selective about the quality of inhabitants it attracts. If the rate of growth of a city, particularly a new city, is any measure of its success, then Chandigarh is indeed a phenomenal success. In the last decade, from 1961 to 1971, Chandigarh registered a growth of 144 percent, having increased its population from 89,000 to 219,000. Although the planning process is essentially concerned with both anticipating future growth and regulating its development, the Chandigarh label of planning has resulted in a somewhat bizarre situation. For, today, there are virtually two separate faces of Chandigarh: the planned and the nonplanned. What Chandigarh is like as a place to live in depends largely on which of the two one belongs to.

The planned Chandigarh is the city of Le Corbusier's vision, first consolidated in the document of the Chandigarh master plan over the period of less than a month in March 1951. Most of the fundamental aspects of the physical plan have been implemented with almost religious devotion. The concept of the sector, the circulation network on the basis of the 7V's, the linear V4 bazaar streets, the leisure valley, and the green belts running from the northeast to the southwest in continuous bands, the industrial area located on one side, the university on the other, the Capitol complex towering in its magnificent aloofness outside the rest of the city, against the background of the mountains, and the city center, with all its frame control and *béton brut* located in Sector 17.

Vast areas of future commercial belts have been retained as reservations for big business yet to come. All the roads have been meticulously planted with various exotic trees and bushes that burst into bloom at different times of the year, producing startling effects with splendid color. A large chunk of the leisure valley has been developed into a vast rose garden, with literally hundreds of different varieties. The green belts, at least in the wealthier and more developed sectors, are now grassed, although almost invariably surrounded by barbed wire fences. The roads are well maintained and the V2's now even have separate side lanes. Chandigarh can rightly boast of the most elaborate urban road network in India (Fig. 103).

All the buildings have been built strictly according to the building bylaws specially framed by Jane Drew and Maxwell Fry with Le Corbusier's approval. Their masses, volumes, building lines, and architectural features rigidly follow the zoning plans prepared individually for each sector. Chandigarh zoning plans are among the most carefully detailed documents anywhere in the world. Not only do they contain stringent limitations on how and where to build, but they also give instructions about the permissible shapes and sizes of windows, the heights and materials of boundary walls, and the two or three different designs of compound gates that must be used (Fig. 104).

Each sector is fully serviced with water-borne sewerage, electricity, and piped water supply. When Chandigarh was first planned, not a single city in the Punjab had water-borne sewerage; in this aspect, Chandigarh is a substantial landmark in the development of Indian cities, with its commitment to better environmental and service standards.

Physical planning, however, cannot be an end in itself. Eventually, it serves little more than the purpose of defining shapes and locations of containers of various activities. Where many assumptions are made regarding the way life is to function within these containers, it is essential to keep a vigilant check on how they actually perform and whether the original assumptions have proved correct. Unfortunately, Chandigarh is showing signs of becoming a monument to one man's preconceived vision of a tidied up society, dwarfing the need for cross-checking, experimentation, or the evolution of more relevant solutions.

Figure 103
An aerial view of the V2 Capitol with rush hour traffic at 5 P.M. To the left is a segment of the Leisure Valley, to the right a commercial belt reserved for big offices, hotels, and so on, and in the background is Le Corbusier's Capitol complex against the backdrop of the hills. (Photograph by Madhu Sarin.)

Figure 104
An illustration of private housing conforming to "frame control" in Sector 22. In front is an unauthorized market, and under the tree a collection of cycle-rickshaw pullers awaiting customers. (Photograph by Madhu Sarin.)

Chandigarh as a Place to Live In   379

The Sector

As explained by Le Corbusier: "The plan is based on the main features of the '7V Rule' determining an essential function: the creation of 'sectors.' The 'sector' *is the container of family life* (the 24 Solar Hours cycle which must be fulfilled in perfect harmony)."[2] Its dimensions are based on the Spanish *cuadra* of 110 to 100 meters square.

A useful reclassification of them [*cuadras*] led me to adopt a ratio of harmonious dimensions and productive combinations: seven to eight *cuadras* on one side, ten to twelve *cuadras* on the other side, that is to say 800m × 1200m. And this was the "sector" issued from an ancestral and valid geometry established in the past on the stride of a man, an ox or a horse, but henceforth adapted to mechanical speeds.
... The entrance of the cars *into the sectors of 800m × 1200m which are exclusively reserved to family life* can take place on four points only in the middle of the 1200m (= two times 600m); in the middle of the 800m (= two times 400m). All stoppage of the circulation shall be prohibited at the four circuses, at the angles of the sectors. The bus stops are provided each time at 200m from the circus so as to serve the entrances of the pedestrians into a sector.[3]

Each sector was further visualized as a fairly self-contained subunit of the city, with its own schools, community centers, daily shopping facilities along the V4's, and well-defined residential areas. Detailed allocation of land use for each of these functions was laid down in the zoning plans. No fast traffic was ever to enter any sector, and buses were to have only limited access to the V4's. Shopping and commercial activity on the V4's was to be restricted only on the south side of the streets to prevent frequent crossing of traffic and the consequent danger to pedestrians. Children were to be able to walk to school in a pedestrian's paradise, on the V7's through the green belts, never having to cross a single fast traffic road. Slums were not supposed to be possible in the new city.

What are Chandigarh's sectors like today? First, sector populations display a glaring disparity. It had been arbitrarily decided to house a minimum of 5,000 to a maximum of 20,000 persons per sector for the same total area of approximately 240 acres. Today sectors 9, 10, or 11 have total populations of just over 2,000 to 3,500 each, while other sectors such as 20 and 22 already have populations of 25,600 and 23,320. The total amount of public open space per sector being almost the same, the per head variation is from 1:12 or even more. The green spaces, although grassed and watered now, remain more like spaces to look at than the centers of healthy activities, of sports, or even walking (Fig. 105).

Population growth in some high-density sectors, much beyond planned population figures, has been the result of multiple occupation caused by an acute housing shortage in the city. There are up to ten families living in a house on a 250-square-yard plot designed for only two families. With families of six to ten persons often living in one room without a kitchen and sharing toilet facilities with others, some Chandigarh sectors are already beginning to display all the characteristics of overcrowding and lack of privacy that is such a common malaise of other Indian cities.

The V4's are slowly filling up with shops, showrooms, offices, printing presses, and private practitioners on the residential sides of the streets (Fig. 106). They remain far from the planned, slow traffic, hazard-free commercial *rues* initially visualized. Armed with its legal and administrative weapons, Chandigarh Administration has tried its best to stop this affront to the master plan, but to no avail. The ineffectiveness of control is accentuated by the fact that the biggest violator is the government itself. Several large bungalows in low-density sectors are totally occupied by government offices. Housing shortage in the city is made much worse by the shortage of cheap office and commercial accommodations, leading to residential buildings being used for these purposes.

Figure 105
Public open space in an
almost fully developed,
medium-density area of
Sector 18. (Photograph
by Madhu Sarin.)

Figure 106
Several residential units
converted to commercial
and business use, on the
northeastern side of the
V4 (bazaar street) in
Sector 18. (Photograph
by Madhu Sarin.)

Figure 107
One of the many
cycle-rickshaws in
Chandigarh specially
adapted for transporting
mainly primary school
children to and from
school. (Photograph by
Madhu Sarin.)

Do people send their children to schools in their own sector? This has proved to be another myth based on oversimplification. In India today, there is tremendous inequality in access to educational institutions. Committed as the country is to secularism, there are not only government and private schools but, in both, there is a wide range of mediums of instruction and in the general quality of education. Social and economic opportunities are highly dependent upon education. Unequal educational opportunities in different sectors, due to different social levels, reduces the physical proximity of the child to a school to the level of least importance. According to a social survey carried out in 1963 to 1964, "41.7 percent of the households sending children to primary schools sent them outside their own sectors" (Fig. 107).[4]

The 7V's (*les sept voies*)

The following quotation of Le Corbusier explains the basis of the 7V's (Fig. 108):

"The 7V Rule" was studied in 1950 at UNESCO's request. One discovered that with 7 types of roads, the man of the mechanical civilization could:

cross continents: the V1

arrive in town: the V1

go to essential public services: the V2

cross at full speed, without interruption, the territory of the town: the V3

dispose of immediate accesses to daily needs: the V4

reach the door of his dwelling: the V5 and V6

send youth to the green areas of each sector, where schools and sports grounds are located: the V7

But the "7V Rule" was to be the object of an assault: the onrush of bicycles in different countries. The "V8" was subsequently created, the "V8" independent of the others. Effectively, the "two-wheels" have customs which are antagonistic to those of the "four-wheels." At Chandigarh, the "V8" was created a little later on. The matter was then honestly formulated: "The Rule of the 7V's . . . which are 8."[5]

Figure 108
The 7V's at Chandigarh.
(Source: *L'Urbanisme
des trois établissements
humains,* Paris, 1959, p.
44.)

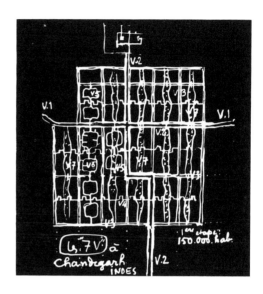

Figure 109
Mixed traffic on the V2 Station/University. The transport of local goods in the city is largely by horse-drawn carts. (Photograph by Madhu Sarin.)

Unfortunately, in Chandigarh, "The Rule of the 7V's . . . which are 8" has remained "The Rule of the 6V's . . . which are not even 7," and that, ironically, when the local transport of the majority of the population remains the bicycle or the feet.

According to a survey carried out from 1963 to 1964, only 3.3 percent of the households owned cars, and as many as 83 percent owned bicycles. More recently, "there were about 10,000 motor vehicles in Chandigarh by the end of 1970. During the succeeding ten years, these vehicles are estimated to increase fivefold to 51,000."[6] The number of bicycles on Chandigarh's roads, however, are already estimated to be over 100,000. The V7—as a continuous tract through green belts, stretching from one end of town to the other, away from the hazards of motorized traffic—is yet to make its appearance. Unpaved sidewalks force pedestrians either to walk on uneven ground or to share the metal roads with the rest of the traffic. Efficient traffic segregation is unlikely to be possible in India for a long time to come yet, for not only are there several motorized speeds to cope with, but also there are horse carts, bullocks, cows, cycle-rickshaws, handcarts, and many other variations (Fig. 109).

Le Corbusier had visualized an efficient system of public transport on the abundant gridiron network of V3's, with three different types of buses stopping every 400 meters. He had consulted the director of the Parisian autobus transport system and drawn up a scheme for Chandigarh on the same basis. The economics of public transport are such, however, that for many years to come there are unlikely to be many buses on Chandigarh's roads. The few buses in the ownership of the Chandigarh transport system wind tedious ways around to collect their passengers. They have found it necessary to break the rules and plough through most of the V4's, because that is where they find their maximum customers. Except for the university and some of the high-density sectors, access to cheap public transport is negligible.

Chandigarh's vast road network remains like an ode to the man of the mechanical civilization. To the common Indian man it must appear rather irrelevant, meaningless, and superfluous. For the small minority of car owners, provided they can afford the fuel, Chandigarh is a true paradise. But this imbalance in priorities has also been instrumental in accentuating visible social and economic inequalities.

The City Center

Sector 17 has been planned as the city center. The commercial center proper

covers an area of 130.09 acres and has buildings four storeys high grouped around a central *chowk* [cross roads]—essentially a traditional Indian feature. The chief amongst these will be the Town Hall, Post and Telegraph Offices, the Chamber of Commerce and a few banks. Of these, the Post and Telegraph office building will be 140 feet high and all of the rest four storeyed rising to a height of 56 feet. The shop office buildings will have exclusive shops or restaurants etc. on the ground and in some cases on the first floor with offices only on the upper three floors. Monsieur Le Corbusier maintains that no residential accommodation should be provided in this area as residences are closely followed by supplementary amenities such as green spaces, educational institutions etc. which take larger spaces. Besides, the commercial centre which would be a very busy area can hardly afford surroundings fit for living.[7]

The very essence of an Indian *chowk* or crossing is its function as a meeting place of various activities. The Sector 17 *chowk* is discernible as a *chowk* only in plans (Fig. 110). On the ground, the scale is so large and the width between meeting streets so great that one sees nothing but vast stretches of concrete paving with a few lone figures here and there. The small-scale street trader, the hawker or the *rehris* (barrows) have been banned from the city center, so that even where sources of interest and activity could be included, if only to reduce the concreted barrenness and austerity of the *chowk,* these are not utilized.

Madhu Sarin 386

Figure 110
One of the ways leading into the *chowk* of the city center. Any sense of enclosure between the two façades is lost, because of the large distance between them. The block containing most of the banks to the left generates little interest on the street level. (Photograph by Madhu Sarin.)

Figure 111
The covered walkway on the vehicular access side of the block of banks in the city center. Although a massive infrastructure for motorized vehicles exists, even parking provision for the bicycles is highly inadequate. (Photograph by Madhu Sarin.)

Banks, post offices, and the like are incapable of generating activity nodes (Fig. 111). As specialized activities, they are of little interest to anybody who does not have business to do there. Then, all banks close early, and shops and big showrooms close by 7:30 P.M. After that, the city center presents a barren, ghostly, and deserted appearance.

One of the things missing terribly in planned Chandigarh is a nucleus, a place to go to when the work of the day has been finished. Immense possibilities exist of making Sector 17 a nucleus of various activities, but they remain unexplored in the fear of upsetting the original vision of the Master.

The Cultural Center and the Leisure Valley

Le Corbusier's views on these are summed up as follows:

The Museum especially concerns mature manifestations; the leisure valley concerns the youth and must be the laboratory of future enrichment of the knowledge and talent of youth. . . . The Cultural Centre and the leisure valley have never to be academic. They are two ways of modern research or of manifestation of the permanent creation through the ages (folklore or outstanding creations).

The equipment of the leisure valley is devoted to the youth (boys and girls). The plays have no need of spectators, but at right times they could offer useful and necessary response or approbation. These spectators will be generally standing and not sitting. They will not necessarily be invited to attend; they could also simply be the walkers through the leisure valley. The tool (the building) does not need a ceiling; stars are enough. Some walls that are well disposed will give many possibilities of:
Plays
Music
Dance
Theatre
Addresses
Variety shows, etc.[8]

Till today, the leisure valley remains far removed from this dream. Armies of labor are leveling, digging, grassing, or planting its vast acres. The part developed so far contains a stadium used periodically and the much treasured rose garden. From the various points of entry to the garden, one is informed about all the things one should not do: "Do not make noise, do not touch the plants, no animals allowed, walk gently on the grass," and so on. About all one can do in the rose garden is walk silently on its twisting paths and look at the roses. There is nothing wrong in having a vast, beautifully manicured rose garden in the city, but it has little to do with constructive and creative canalization of the energy of youth. The *théâtre spontané*, the enacting of live drama, the theater with the ceiling of the stars, remains an elusive idea, unlikely to materialize under present circumstances.

Planned Chandigarh is by no means an undesirable place to live in. The general cleanliness of the city, the pollution-free environment, and the tree-planted roads make it a unique city in India. But the essence of what Le Corbusier had in mind for the quality of life in the city—its function as an intellectual and cultural center with all the accompanying dissemination of creative thought and knowledge—remains a myth.

The nonplanned Chandigarh, on the other hand, is the so-called labor colonies, the squatter markets, the pavement traders, the vast concentrations of *rehri-wallas* (petty traders on barrows), and so on. It contains all the activities and classes of persons for whom there proved to be no comfortable room in the master plan. Disowned, frowned upon, and disliked by the administration responsible for implementing the meticulous details of the architecturally controlled, zoned, frame-controlled, and building-by-lawed Chandigarh, the persons and enterprises falling within nonplanned Chandigarh share one thing in common—the irrelevance of and the inability to pay for all the physical hardware mandatory in the master plan.

The labor colonies of Chandigarh are the slums of the city, where up to 7,000 families or 15 percent of the population live. Outside the framework of the 7V's, there is not a *single* paved street in these areas (Fig. 112). After persistent agitations, demonstrations, and rallies, the inhabitants of the authorized labor colonies have managed to get a few water taps, communal lavatories, and a minimal amount of street lighting. Lacking entirely in drainage facilities, their environment is full of filth, muddy streets, and general insanitation. The maintenance of the communal lavatories is so poor, especially since they are not plugged into Chandigarh's water-borne sewerage system, that a majority of the inhabitants prefer to use open land around. The women complain of the fear of being raped or manhandled there, particularly if the call of nature has to be answered late at night.

Community and educational facilities are also of a minimal kind. In the four authorized labor colonies, the inhabitants have collectively contributed for minimal school buildings where now the government runs the schools. There are a few shops in each of them, also run by colony dwellers, for which the administration promptly auctioned rental leases, thereby extracting rather high rents in return for nothing. There are no green belts or community centers for *les joies essentielles* and, other than the occasional jaunt to the cinema, the only entertainment for these people was claimed to be the family planning films shown there by the government.

The totally unauthorized settlements do not even have absolutely minimal facilities like drinking water. There are no schools, no government dispensaries, no community centers, nothing. Yet, the majority of the workers from these settlements work in Chandigarh, providing essential services. They include construction labor, both skilled and unskilled, buffalo keepers selling milk, cycle-rickshaw pullers, tailors, gardeners, hawkers, petty shopkeepers, potters, industrial labor, cobblers, sweepers, and even many class IV government employees.

The houses in these settlements have been built by the people themselves (Fig. 113). Since three of the major colonies are more than fourteen years old, some houses are no longer *kutcha* (temporary) but *pukka* by now. Slowly, with time and a desire to improve their living environments, the people have invested their meager savings over the years in house building. Their efforts have been met only with threats of impending demolition. To prevent growth of these settlements, the administration has followed a policy of demolishing any new huts that are built. The result of a negative policy of demolition is both ineffective and harassing without simultaneously being complemented by the provision of planned housing within the economic reach of the people.

The labor colony problem has not sprung up overnight, either. Vast numbers of building laborers were among the first migrants to the new city. Many of them are still rotting in the insecurity and stink of the labor colonies. As long ago as 1959, people living in scattered hutments over the city area were temporarily moved to the present sites on the outskirts of the city. Since then a whole generation of children has grown up in these areas, neglected, working at a very early age, and often uneducated, yet Chandigarh's architects and planners are still scratching their heads to find an "architecturally" acceptable solution befitting the standards of the master plan. Also, because of their locations—behind the university compound wall, in the industrial area, or beyond the meticulously cared-for golf club of Chandigarh's elite—a large section of the city's population is not even aware of their existence. They were moved out of the rest of the developed city so that they should not mar its beauty. In the bargain, the labor colonies cannot even benefit from forces of interaction or general public concern.

The other components of nonplanned Chandigarh are closely related to the second function of urbanism of the Congrès International d'Architecture Moderne (CIAM): working. They include street peddlers, *rehri-wallas*, unauthorized markets, and small-scale manufacturing workshops. In the master plan, with all its careful detailing, no room *at all* was provided for open-air markets and street peddlers, which form such an integral part of Indian life. Because of the low initial capital investment required and low overheads, these occupations offer income opportunities to large sections of the Indian urban poor.

Rehris are a very common form of vending for petty traders in India. At the time of Chandigarh's inception, it was *rehri* pullers and squatter shopkeepers who met the basic daily requirements of the early settlers. As the city grew, so did the number of *rehris*. The operation of natural market forces is such that there is mutual benefit in clustering together. Also, since *rehris* can sell their goods at cheaper rates, as well as provide door-to-door service, they are essential and extremely popular (Fig. 114). They could easily have been integrated into the growth of the city by providing minimum facilities like paving, water supply, and drainage at certain locations. Instead, they too have been considered a great nuisance. The threat to the city's jealously guarded clean environment provoked an attempt to actually ban *rehris* in Chandigarh. Today, there are between 2,500 to 3,500 *rehris* operating in the city. The V4's in almost all sectors have their share of a *rehri* market and the *pukka* shops and *rehris* seem to be complementing each other's function (Fig. 115). No satisfactory solution for *rehris* has yet been found, however, and the administration continues to harass them.

The rather inadequate public transport of the city is supplemented mainly by private hired transport of cycle-rickshaws and scooter-rickshaws, both three-wheelers. Clusters of each type are found near specific road junctions, often on V3's, which are ideal locations for collecting potential customers. Not only do they congregate at these points during the day time; they often also sleep there at night, because they cannot afford proper housing. To serve their needs, other

Figure 112
Communal water taps in the labor colony behind the University. Some University housing can be seen in the background, contrasting sharply with the standard of construction in the colony itself. (Photograph by Madhu Sarin.)

Figure 113
A husband and wife build themselves a house in an unauthorized settlement in Sector 32. (Photograph by Madhu Sarin.)

Figure 114
A *rehri-wallah* selling vegetables in front of the door in Sector 18. Another example of private housing built under "frame control." (Photograph by Madhu Sarin.)

Figure 115
V4 shops in Sector 18 with a complementing cluster of *rehris* and open-air stalls. (Photograph by Madhu Sarin.)

services come in like cycle repairers, cobblers, tailors, barbers, and tobacconists. At intervals along the V3's and V4's, cycle repairers have lodged themselves under trees on the sidewalks to serve the thousands of cyclists. All these activities are considered highly undesirable because, in theory at least, the V3's are fast traffic roads and any other activity on them constitutes a potential traffic hazard.

All Chandigarh's land-use planning, based on the CIAM doctrine of separation of functions, considers single-use zones only. India has had a long tradition of multiuse of space, particularly with small-scale enterprises. One common Indian feature is the nucleus of small-scale manufacturing and commercial activities, often part of or close to residential areas where men, women, and children can all be seen participating in productive activity. Because of climate, only a negligible use is made of buildings, as semicovered or open space suffices for most purposes.

The master plan distinctly separated industrial and commercial zones. The only concession is the provision of a number of semi-industrial shops in sector shopping centers. These have proved to be highly inadequate in both numbers and terms of respecting the dynamics of specialized markets. Also, inevitably, any provision in the plan excludes access to those who either do not require or cannot afford the auctioned market price of these buildings and sites.

So, yet another form of nonplanned activity has spontaneously generated at the old location of Bajwara village that was acquired for the creation of the city. Here one can find a large number of blacksmiths, carpenters, rope dealers, cotton processors, quilt makers, and waste dealers trading in and manufacturing some essential and typically Indian items like quilts, charpoys, tin trunks, *chappals*, and so on, with raw material shops in the same location (Fig. 116). Several attempts have already been made to resettle these people in small booths dispersed all over the city; however, the accompanying dis-

Figure 116
A minimal structure suffices for a small furniture workshop in Bajwara. (Photograph by Madhu Sarin.)

persal of complementary activities and the loss of business has brought several persons back to Bajwara illegally. Finding no room for themselves in the master plan, many of these artisans, craftsmen, and traders have devised a solution within their economic reach and supply essential services to the citizens. They do not have much to thank the architects and planners for, because the latter have only displayed an obsessive desire to fit them into the layout of the master plan, irrespective of their needs and priorities.

From all this Chandigarh emerges as a city of dilemmas, of wide disparities in environmental conditions in its planned and nonplanned aspects and in the conflicts faced by Chandigarh administration in dealing with the situation. Although slums, squatting, and a general low standard of living are part of the total Indian picture of economic backwardness and poverty, in Chandigarh they have attained certain peculiar characteristics. In other cities, slums can be seen all over; in Chandigarh, a visitor to the city, even another citizen, can easily be deluded into believing that they have actually been eliminated, while they have only been hidden. Meanwhile other Indian cities like Delhi, Ahmedabad, Calcutta, and Madras have made genuine efforts on the basis of real experiments in devising viable solutions for the urban poor, even if it means only giving the slum dweller the right to live unharassed in his *kutcha* shack, in the absence of anything more positive to offer. Chandigarh has not been willing to give even that much.

It is possible to understand some of Chandigarh's special problems by examining the role of Le Corbusier in the enterprise, the significance of Chandigarh for him and the impact of his personality and fame on the direction the city is taking today.

In spite of his well-known theories on urbanism, a tremendous amount of writing on the subject, and the production of several schemes for cities all over the world, Chandigarh was the only real opportunity Le Corbusier received to put them into practice. The fact that this opportunity came late in his life only increased its value for him. His feelings and thoughts about it are best expressed in his own words at the time when he was first approached to participate in the venture. In a letter addressed to an official of the Indian Embassy in Paris, he wrote in November 1950:

1. I consider myself the only person at the moment, prepared by forty years of experience and study on this theme, capable of usefully helping your Government. I greatly insist on this fact given without modesty.
2. In my participation in this project, I place the pursuit/desire of my career through a work of harmony, of wisdom, of humanity in precise opposition to the chaos generally manifest in urbanism which is only the expression of the chaos reigning in the minds of people on this subject.
   The *raison d'être* of my life is expressed by one word: HARMONY, and this resembles beauty "first above all," order, serenity, effectiveness, economy: in one word wisdom. This wisdom is, alas, a fruit slow in reaching maturity; it is positive if the heart remains young, failing which, it is only a brake.[9]

The Indian Government intended to use Chandigarh as a training ground for Indian architects and planners. With this aim in mind, only four foreigners were employed as senior members of the team: Le Corbusier, Jane Drew, Maxwell Fry, and Pierre Jeanneret. All the rest of the staff consisted of young Indians. The role of a guide or a teacher was much to Le Corbusier's liking:

The Indian youth must take a fundamental part in the enterprise, it is they who will be realizing it in the course of the years; but I shall have been able to provide them with a useful springboard to jump from.
   The young Hindus whom you will gather together from various universities of the old or the new continent need a doctrinal point of view from the outset; in a way they need a friendly shepherd: they are young, consequently they have to grow, to be nourished, to be given strength, to find their direction. You can arouse enthusiasm in them; everything lies there. If you do not succeed in this, your enterprise is lost.[10]

Madhu Sarin   398

Le Corbusier saw himself not only as the *berger amical* of the young Indians but also as the spiritual director of the whole enterprise, including the two English architects recruited by the government. In another document found in the archives of the Fondation Le Corbusier, thinking about the organizational structure of the team, he wrote:

I have qualified this theoretical conception and in practice I have proposed:
1. To assume spiritual and technical direction of the enterprise so as to give it unity.
2. I shall nominate two architects of our spirit, capable and devoted and sufficiently experienced, who would fulfill the functions outlined below.
3. Three Hindu architects would be permanently attached to our *atelier* on the Rue de Sèvres to carry out in turn studies as the work proceeds, in order to give them an education of university type which remains in full contact with the Hindu civilization.[11]

Again, under the subheading "organization," he wrote:

The role of M. Le Corbusier will be that of coordinator and consultant. . . . This contract will be bound to that of the two foreign architects who will be under the control of M. Le Corbusier. He will give them orders of a technical and aesthetic nature.[12]

The extent to which Le Corbusier had seen himself as the spiritual director of the whole enterprise is best illustrated by the diagram that was attached to the document quoted from (Fig. 117). He saw himself as the SOLE supplier of ideas for a city of 500,000 inhabitants.

The reception the Indians gave Le Corbusier was perhaps the best that he ever received. In the postpartition and Independence chaos, his optimism and clarity of purpose were just what the Punjab Government really needed. Besides, in India foreigners have often found a sympathetic and accommodating reception, and the whole team of foreigners benefited from this. The only person who challenged Le Corbusier's desire to totally control the enterprise was Maxwell Fry. Amazed by the extent to which Le Corbusier had assumed responsibil-

Figure 117
Le Corbusier's diagram depicting his role in the team at Chandigarh. (Courtesy of Archives
Fondation Le Corbusier, ref. AW 21-Nov. 50.)

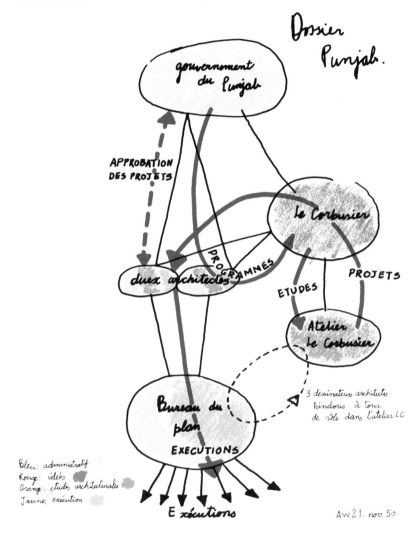

ity for every detailed aspect of design, whether the layout of the sector, the network of roads, the village of 750 inhabitants, or the Capitol complex, as evident from the details he sent back from Paris after his first visit to India, Maxwell Fry protested on the basis of the spirit of teamship upheld by members of CIAM. In a letter dated 11 May 1951, he wrote to Le Corbusier:

Both Jeanneret and I were shocked by the extent to which in your letter of 25 April you had assumed the direction and responsibility for the whole affair, and when I have got over saying all these hard things, which it is necessary for me to say if we are to continue together, I would like to discuss the basis of a *collaboration* which will satisfy us and fit in with the terms of our engagement. . . .
    There is no reason why a group of buildings should not be designed by a group of CIAM architects, but I am opposed to the idea of designing individual buildings in a group or of merely carrying out your designs.[13]

Le Corbusier received Maxwell Fry's letter in Bogota, where his proposals for the city had just been accepted without any modifications. He replied to Fry after a fortnight when back in Paris. In his letter of 13 June 1951, he wrote:

It was in this atmosphere [of success in Bogota] that your letter arrived and caused me dismay, made me feel bad and even made me indignant. From the way I was reading this letter in the Mayor's office, the people present asked me what had happened, I replied to them: "Bad news from Chandigarh."
    I let some days pass; then I spoke openly about it with Sert, the President of CIAM. Finally, the hard experience of life that I have acquired after forty years of struggle restored my optimism and I understood that you were not responsible for this letter because I consider you as the most loyal of companions.[14]

After elaborating on the immensity of the task ahead and the diversity of needs of 150,000 clients to be catered for, he suggested:

Already we have left one or two sectors to Mayer. I propose that you choose from the public buildings those that you would like to execute, that is to invent from A to Z, to create from nothing. Do exactly as you please. This said, I remind you once more of the special contract which binds me to the Punjab Government. This contract is not at all in the sense expressed most impolitely in your letter of 11 May in the 3rd and 4th paragraphs.

... You may depend upon it that I have no intention of changing anything in the very agreeable method of working that we had adopted in March and April in India and we are such good friends, diverse and diversified, and we have before us a task which will be assailed so violently by adverse forces that we will learn to appreciate how good and sweet it is to work among friends.[15]

Even before Le Corbusier had written this letter, however, the matter had been discussed in a meeting held in Simla by the Chief Administrator of the Capital Project, Prem Thapar, Maxwell Fry, and Pierre Jeanneret. Perhaps to avoid disaster, Le Corbusier accepted their proposals. They agreed that the overall plan of the city, the general control of the architectural character of all sectors including landscaping, and the general layout of the city center would be the joint responsibility of all the architects. Le Corbusier was given complete personal responsibility for the whole complex of administrative buildings to which he then gave his whole-hearted attention. A major part of the real spadework essential for the layout of individual sectors and buildings in them, including the thirteen categories of housing, was made the responsibility of the senior architects: Maxwell Fry, Pierre Jeanneret, and later Jane Drew.

Jane Drew's efforts generated a fourteenth and the cheapest category of house in the project program, for the poorest section of the population. Because of this, much credit has since been claimed by the architects for having given the same attention to designing a dwelling for the poorest man as to that of the Chief Minister's house. Unfortunately, only eight hundred cheap houses were built in the early years, and since then no more have been added.

That Le Corbusier had the master plan in almost final form in less than a month is evidence of how much he relied on his doctrinal principles of urbanism, evolved from the early 1920s. But he displayed a tremendous flexibility of mind in accepting a low-density horizontal city, after all his advocacy of the vertical *ville verte*. He was quick to realize and to accept that his cherished *unités* would be both misplaced and irrelevant in the context of Chandigarh. The cost of land at that time was a fraction (1/90) of the cost of construction, and an indigenous life style molded by local climate necessitated access to outdoor space for living, working, and sleeping. A note dated July 1951 in one of his sketchbooks reads: *"La plus petite entité c'est le verandah et le lit sous les étoiles."* [16] A statement a Punjabi will support any day.

After the departure of Jane Drew and Maxwell Fry at the end of their three-year contract, Pierre Jeanneret was made the Chief Architect and Town Planner of Chandigarh. Again, because he was a foreigner, a majority of the proposals sent through him were sanctioned by the government. During his time, even the Indian architects got used to getting away with extravagant proposals on the basis of their architectural merits. The image of the architect as the original designer, each different from the other, was reinforced. Although the architects department itself was responsible for the imposition of stringent rules and controls for anybody desiring to build in the city, this very department became responsible for the major infringements. The architect's role became associated with that of the eccentric, only preoccupied with design considerations, who could waive other equally important matters aside with arrogance. Many complex problems of urban growth were ignored because they interfered with formal and visual matters. Indirectly, this resulted in forcing large numbers of people outside the planned physical boundaries of the city.

The real crisis in leadership and discipline in Chandigarh came after the departure of both Le Corbusier and Pierre Jeanneret. First, Chandigarh architects and planners suddenly lost easy access to higher authority, including the Prime Minister, and second, with the *berger amical* suddenly gone, they were unprepared to take leadership. Accepting orders from foreigners was far easier than from other Indians. The departure of the foreigners was followed by much internal competition and lack of cooperation, to the general frustration of everybody concerned. The maximum that the Indians working on the Chandigarh project seem to have got out of the experience is a conspicuous design consciousness, which, unfortunately, remains irrelevant for the problems of the masses.

Le Corbusier had tried at various times to inform the Indians of his urbanistic doctrines by trying to make them read his books. His sketchbooks contain several indications of a sense of frustration because copies of books he brought personally to the Chandigarh office were not even to be found anywhere, to say nothing of being read and assimilated religiously. *Les Trois Etablissements humains* reached the stage of being translated into English for an Indian edition, but it was never published. Le Corbusier's writing on urbanism is confusing enough for anybody, but only half read and superficially implemented, it can create several distortions in any development. Within the framework of "The Three Human Establishments," Chandigarh was defined as the "radial-concentric city of exchanges." On this basis, a Periphery Control Act, forbidding any development within a radius of ten miles around the planned sectors, was created:

1. Chandigarh is an administrative city and in consequence is a "Radial-Concentric" city. It has never to be an industrial city.
2. The city of Chandigarh is protected by a Periphery Control Act. (No construction in this periphery.)[17]

In the absence of a regional jurisdiction of this Act, the insistent application of this doctrine in the case of Chandigarh has had two grossly distorting effects. First, soon after the political reorganization of Punjab in 1966, a new township was created well within the original periphery control area (Fig. 118). Second, within the area presently

Figure 118
The lighter area represents the limits of the original periphery control zone. The darker patch in the center is the present area left under the control of the Chandigarh Administration. (Photograph by Madhu Sarin. Courtesy of Chandigarh Administration.)

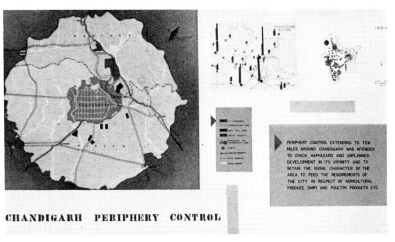

under the jurisdiction of Chandigarh Administration, the Act has been implemented in its negative sense alone. The basis of the Act lay in preventing unplanned development in the immediate vicinity of the city to retain a clear urban/rural dichotomy and to prevent the growth of suburbs, which Le Corbusier saw as an urban malaise. During an early conference he had stated: "To build on open ground, of easy topography, filled with natural beauty, Chandigarh, thanks to its urban and architectural layout, will be sheltered from base speculation and its disastrous corollaries: the suburbs. No suburb is possible at Chandigarh."[18]

The growth of suburbs cannot be prevented by a mere Act of State Legislature, however, particularly when uncomplemented by sufficient development of land and buildings within the planned area of the city. The growth, the changes in occupational structure, and the male-female ratios of surrounding villages indicate that these function as Chandigarh's unofficial suburbs. The labor colonies and other unauthorized settlements are also a direct consequence of this situation.

Urban land policy is central to many urban problems. Rise in land values is a universal result of urban development, and speculation has long been recognized as a major hurdle to planned development. In older cities, the complexity of the problem is magnified by established interests and the owners of land. In the development of a new city, a tremendous opportunity is available for the elimination of several future problems.

In Chandigarh, residential land was initially sold freehold on the basis of development costs by allotment. The cost per square yard was worked out to be a minimum of Rs 4/- for bigger plots to a maximum of Rs 12/- for the smallest plot. After 1960, the administration started *auctioning* residential plots. Today, the small plot fetches an average of Rs 181/- per square yard in open auction, showing a fifteenfold increase in value! At the same time, the release of plots for sale has been restricted further and further, in spite of the phenomenal growth of the city. The result of this attempt to make the city self-financing has been that the administration has taken over the role of a speculator, in the most privileged position of complete monopoly over the land market.

The government provides housing for its employees at a rent fixed at 10 percent of income. In a majority of cases, this falls far below economic rent. In the last several years, the negligible amount of housing built by the government has forced a large number of government employees to seek rented accommodations in the private market. Because private rents are much higher, a further 12½ percent of income is given as a subsidy. This, in turn, has pushed private rents still higher. Altogether, a nongovernment employee or worker with no access to employer's housing or rent subsidy is pushed into an impossible situation, facing two equally undesirable choices—to rent highly inadequate and expensive accommodation, which has resulted in eight to ten families living in a small unit intended for two families, or to squat in an unauthorized settlement and become a violator of the law.

Artificially inflated land values and rents are making adequate housing difficult even for the financially privileged. The government itself, having built approximately ten thousand units, has a waiting list of an equal number, some applications pending since 1957! Ironically, the government is following a policy of allotting two households per unit for the smallest four categories of its houses, including the smallest house type 13, consisting of two tiny rooms, a nook of a kitchen, and a small verandah.

Absurd, indeed, seems the architects' preoccupation with the beauty, aesthetics, or architectural design of the house, for, no matter how well designed a house may be, the sheer stuffing of space with objects and human bodies reduces the design aspect to simple mockery. Remote remains the goal, stated at the beginning of this article, of "Chandigarh—a city offering all amenities to the poorest of the poor of its citizens to lead a dignified life." Dignity seems incompatible with overcrowding and lack of privacy, or simply lack of access to adequate living space.

There is a direct link between the land policy in Chandigarh and Le Corbusier's ideas on the ability of cities to make money. In *The Radiant City,* to the question, "Where is the money to come from?", Le Corbusier replied:

City planning is a way of MAKING money.
City planning is not a way of spending money.
City planning brings in a profit.
City planning is not a waste of money.[19]

In the specific context of Chandigarh, as early as March 1953, Le Corbusier said:

The Authority has the power to give orders, to organize, to value property, and to carry out an effective operation.
For six months, land-purchasing demands have been innumerable at Chandigarh. The Authority is no longer losing money. It is making money, it is selling at a high price. It has created a model city of modern times.[20]

For commercial areas, there may be some logic in publicly auctioning sites, because commerce is essentially a competitive activity and the returns from investment in land and buildings can be very high. But auctioning residential sites in a situation of artificial scarcity creates so many distortions that it can undermine the basic objective of creating a desirable living environment for all citizens. Even in the handling of commercial areas, great care is needed in supplying suitable accommodation within the means of the people. In Chandigarh a great part of the commercial activity on the city scale was visualized in terms of large showrooms and businesses. The needs of the small-scale business man, more representative of the norm in India, seem to have been grossly overlooked.

Recently, when a large unauthorized market, which had slowly grown to almost 450 small shops and repairers, was removed from a V2 commercial reservation in Sector 22, the secretary of the Shastri Market Shopkeepers Union had put a pertinent question to the administration: Were 450 small shopkeepers being evicted from the commercial reservation simply because the master plan visualized a few large showrooms there? How did this comply with the socialistic pattern of society to which India is committed? He has received no reply.

Le Corbusier has written:

One phrase must be affirmed:
  Good urbanism makes money,
  bad urbanism loses money.
The problem is also to be vigilant: one must sell a true merchandise: nothing must be allowed to provoke circumstances which will bring loss to every single inhabitant.
One has the Statute of the land. It is like a seed. What can be grown from the seed? It is in the hands of the administrators.[21]

Despite all the present problems and distortions, a good seed has indeed been sown at Chandigarh, but whether a true merchandise is being sold is doubtful. A clearly defined framework for growth already exists. But it is as if Chandigarh is left with a commitment to build, to the point of minute details, for the hypothetical population that was originally visualized. Twenty-three years of existence have demonstrated glaring disparities between the dream and the reality of present Indian conditions. A city, no matter how magnificent its buildings or roads, is ultimately made by its citizens. Till now, acceptable physical forms have received greater consideration than the people themselves.

Chandigarh has made no effort to build a community. It has not even attempted to inform its citizens of what has been planned for them. Perhaps the most conspicuous lesson staring architects in the face is that people need living space before anything else. Within present Indian conditions of poverty, a *pukka* architecturally designed house will remain irrelevant and beyond the reach of many urban households during their lifetimes. But, sheer physical space for living and working, without constant harassment and insecurity, is a basic minimum need of every human being.

This problem of access has been grossly neglected in Chandigarh. It was never a great problem to build for the rich, for people who have money. The problem of the poor man has received only superficial consideration. As things stand today, Chandigarh is suffering from the *burden* of implementing the master plan. Since the Master himself is no longer around, interpretations have to be made at every juncture of what he would have done in a specific situation. Because of the many intangible aspects of Le Corbusier's writing, only the most tangible parts of the total doctrine are implemented. Since he left detailed designs for many buildings and commercial reservations, only these are followed—the safest and the easiest course available.

Le Corbusier seems to have trained his team marvelously for implementing his words and designs, but he seems to have left them incapable of stepping outside the shadow of his powerful personality.

This paper was written in early 1974.

1 Le Corbusier, "For the Establishment of an Immediate Statute of the Land," Archives Fondation Le Corbusier (hereafter AFLC), 18 December 1959.

2 Le Corbusier, "The Master Plan," in the magazine *Marg,* Bombay, December 1961, vol. 15, no. 1.

3 Ibid.

4 V. S. D'Souza, *Social Structure of a Planned City: Chandigarh,* Delhi, 1968.

5 Le Corbusier, "The Master Plan."

6 Chandigarh Administration, *Draft Proposals, Fifth Five Year Plan, 1974–79.*

7 "Chandigarh City Centre as proposed by the Architectural Adviser Mons. Le Corbusier," AFLC, 13 January 1954.

8 Le Corbusier, A. "Chandigarh Cultural Centre: The Leisure Valley, The Museum and 'School Workshops', Miracle-Box and Itinerant Exhibition." B. "The Leisure Valley," AFLC.

9 Le Corbusier, letter to Madame Lachmanam, Ambassade de l'Inde, 25 November 1950, AFLC, translated by Helen Walden.

10 Ibid.

11 Le Corbusier, AFLC, document ref. AW 21-Nov. 50, translated by Helen Walden.

12 Ibid.

13 Maxwell Fry, letter to Le Corbusier, 11 May 1951, AFLC.

14 Le Corbusier, letter to Maxwell Fry, 13 June 1951, AFLC, translated by Nirupama Rastogi.

15 Ibid.

16 Le Corbusier, Sketchbook E21E, p. 6, 7–14 July 1951, AFLC.

17 Le Corbusier, notes on a copy of "The Master Plan," 18 June 1964, AFLC.

18 Le Corbusier, "Conférence de Propagande pour Chandigarh," 4 May 1951 (Atelier Rue de Sèvres), AFLC, translated by Helen Walden.

19 Le Corbusier, *The Radiant City,* London, 1966, p. 71.

20 Le Corbusier, "Conférence d'Information au Palais de la Découverte," 18 March 1953, AFLC, translated by Helen Walden.

21 Le Corbusier, "For the Establishment of an Immediate Statute of the Land," AFLC, 18 December 1959.

Notes

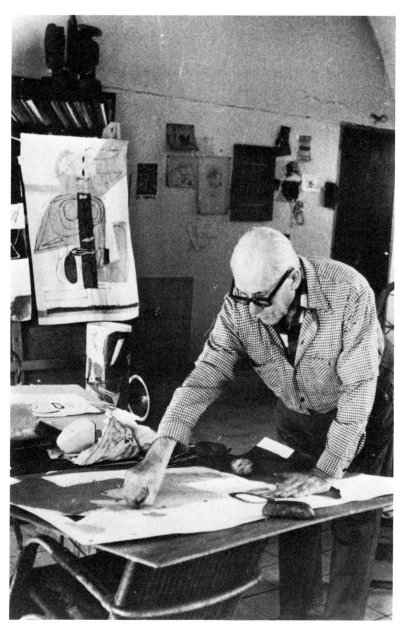

The Politics of the Open Hand:
Stanislaus von Moos **Notes on Le Corbusier and Nehru at Chandigarh**

Chandigarh is not only the best documented urban venture of recent history,[1] it has become a byword. For some, Chandigarh means progressive, socialist planning, crowned by outstanding architectural achievement; for others, it is a symbol for the arrogance of Western planning ideology inflicted upon the Third World. Is it correct to establish the physical form of a city in terms of Western standards of social progress and economic growth, partly, if not totally, at the expense of the traditional way of life of those who have to live in the new environment? Such questions polarize most discussions on Le Corbusier's work in India. They deserve to be pondered, especially if one happens to be an architect or a planner involved in the creation of other Chandigarhs in Asia and elsewhere. As for the historian, it is his job to wonder about the background and the context that made possible such a highly controversial artefact.

It takes a minimum of social awareness, two or three rolls of Kodak film (and possibly an American travel grant) to demonstrate that the physical form of Chandigarh has but little to do with any current notion of "the Indian way of life." But what does such a statement prove? Needless to say, for an enlightened Western commentator of the late sixties and the early seventies, this observation comes close to a diagnosis of failure, the tacit implication usually being that if only the government had appointed a team of up-to-date, progressive sociologists and planners, the situation would probably be all right and nobody would have to suffer.

Description should not be taken for analysis. At this moment in time, barely twenty years after building at Chandigarh has begun, no description of and no judgment on the social quality of the city's equipments can claim to be really conclusive. For, if the people of Chandigarh have been given a physical framework of urban life that is inconsistent with their traditional expectations and immediate needs, one cannot, at least theoretically, exclude the possibility that, in another twenty years, their children might have overcome some of the difficulties of adaptation experienced by their parents. The question is what the critic accepts as the relevant framework of reference: the reality of the *status quo* or the ideal of another improved state of affairs, to be reached some time in the future. It is, indeed, the same dilemma that the planner has to face when he starts to work on his project.[2]

Today, Chandigarh's problem obviously resides in the fact that it has been built on the basis of a prospective utopia that we find increasingly difficult to consider realistic. But who is to blame for this state of affairs? We are frequently given extensive comments on Le Corbusier's authoritarian habits as the city's head planner, and we are given lengthy dissertations on urban "malfunctions" that might have been avoided with the help of more professional goodwill, understanding, and competence of the planners with regard to the people's needs.[3] And so the whole argument comes down to a debate among experts.

Not that all this is irrelevant; but it seems to the outsider, in this case an historian, that the question goes deeper. As long as a plan remains on paper, it can at least partly be judged as a matter of professional expertise. But when, as is the case at Chandigarh, the government and the ruling class of the country decides to realize such a plan in full scale, it does so because it accepts it as the embodiment of its own social and political philosophy. And that is the point where a town-planning policy ceases to be a matter of the professional competence and responsibility of planners and architects alone; it then becomes a means of a society's struggle for images that counterfeit and stabilize its basic beliefs, its ideology.

Thus, Chandigarh's master plan might be appropriately interpreted within the context of Le Corbusier's work; its realization is correctly understood only as a response to the political situation of India at a particular moment of its history: its recent independence from British rule, its subsequent search for national identity, and its struggle with Pakistan. And in such a perspective the current rhetorics (Western, technocratic, and bureaucratic ideals versus Indian way of life) become a weak and hypothetical basis for any serious discussion: for the "Indian way of life" is not a static reality but a dynamic process, whose content and direction are determined not by vernacular traditions alone, and even less by architects and planners, but by the ideology of economic progress, welfare, and social order that the state has adopted as a guideline of action.

Background

When, in July 1947, the Independence Bill was signed, decades of revolutionary struggle, successfully repressed by the British rulers during World War II, finally came to an end. Mahatma Gandhi (1869–1948), head of the "Quit India" movement, was the leading figure and the symbol of that struggle. It is universally known that he attempted to reach the goal of national independence on the basis of nonviolence, but it is not equally well known that he considered a radical change in the economic pattern of his country as the necessary premise for social and political progress.[4] The system established by the East India Company had led to a steady decline of India's traditional economy. The pressures of industrialization in England had given the colony its economic role within the Empire. While the English market was closed to most of the traditional products of Indian manufacture (especially silk and cotton work), it developed a voracity for raw materials, which explains, among other things, the rapid growth of the Indian railway network, efficiently connecting the interior of the subcontinent with the great harbors. The price of this progress is known: the almost total ruin of the traditional agricultural and manufacturing economy of the country.

Gandhi's program—renunciation of advanced technology and capitalist trade, return to agriculture and rural manufacturing—was to resolve the social and cultural crisis created by the colonialist exploitation and the dynamics of industrial growth. "Our concern is to destroy industrialism at any cost," he proclaimed in 1926; "Machinery is the chief symbol of modern civilization. It represents a great sin," he said in 1938.[5] He admitted that industrialism and machinery are not evils in themselves, but only insofar as they were responsible for the impoverishment of India. He never ceased to believe that the self-sufficient village should again become the pivot of Indian economy, that large enterprises such as the cotton mills of Ahmedabad are a potential danger for national economy, since they help concentrate wealth in the hands of the already rich, at the expense of the poor. Rather than to promote industrial growth in the cities, the country should follow his "message of the spinning-wheel" (Khadi) and reestablish the preindustrial equilibrium beneath production of manufactured goods in the villages and their consumption in the cities.

When, however, India gained its political independence (in 1947) and became a sovereign democratic republic (in 1950), things occurred in a slightly different manner. The British, uninterested in the resurrection of a strong and united Indian nation, wanted, as a condition of their departure, the country to be divided into two parts: Pakistan and India. Whatever the reasons given for this decision—among them, the British concern for the Muslim minorities and their potential repression under Indian hinduistic rule—the result was a weakened subcontinent, immersed for many years in ongoing war and bloodshed.[6] Gandhi was radically opposed to that arrangement; but the creation of a Muslim-ruled Pakistan was not the only aspect of the new political reality that was in contradiction to his gospel.

Gandhi's model of socioeconomic reform has only had a limited effect upon the policy of India under its first national government.

"Pandit Nehru wants industrialization because he thinks that, if it is socialized, it would be free from the evils of capitalism. My own view is that the evils are inherent in industrialism, and no amount of socialization can eradicate them." [7] This statement of 1940 anticipates what may have been Gandhi's feelings a few years later, when the new nation established its economic priorities.

"We cannot keep pace with the modern world," Jawaharlal Nehru, India's first prime minister, insisted in a speech, "unless we adopt the latest techniques. We cannot keep pace with the modern world unless we utilize the sources of power that are available to the modern world." [8] Thus, the production of electric power and large-scale industrialization received top priority. Political independence had to be reinforced by a firm position within the international capitalist market: "I shall venture to say that we cannot even maintain our freedom and independence as a nation without the big factory and all that it represents. . . ." [9]

The situation recalls that of Russia around 1921, when the earlier plans for a direct transition to socialist economy, formulated by Nikolai Bukharin and others, had to surrender to the necessity of centralized economic planning and industrialization. What Vladimir Lenin's *New Political Economy* [10] (not to talk about the later five-year plans, 1928 onward) meant for Russia in the twenties, Nehru's and the leading Congress Party's economic policy meant for India in the fifties: the establishment of an economy that would enable the new nation to survive within the given system of the industrialized world. The fifties in India were great days for foreign investment and for an Indian bureaucracy that had been trained under the British rule, if not directly at Oxford and Cambridge.

In any case, Gandhi's dream of a return to a pan-Indian economy based upon agriculture and upon the spinning wheel seems almost forgotten. Gandhi himself remained loyal to the new government and to Nehru, whom he had earlier described as his spiritual heir. Had he not been assassinated in January 1948, it would have appeared to him as if the Indian revolution had been carried through only halfway, allowing a new Indian elite to fill the structures of power and management left behind by the British. He once said that he had purchased a ticket to the holy city of Hardwar, where the Ganges breaks out of the Himalaya, while most others left the train at New Delhi.[11] When asked by the BBC for an interview, he declined: "They should forget that I learned English."[12]

The regime, in turn, considered the "father of the nation" as the hero of Independence, and by making him the object of national worship, it succeeded somehow in removing him from the political discussion. It is interesting to note in Nehru's speeches a subtle criticism of Gandhi's economic thought. While Gandhi's economic policy aimed at providing subsistence for all, but only "at a low level of life," Nehru aimed at higher living standards, with the risk that such progress would only be attainable for few. His declared policy was to achieve both goals,[13] but the latter seems to have preoccupied him most. Thus he tended to explain Gandhi's adherence to "economic or other approaches [which] did not fit in with modern ideas" as the result of his ability to adapt to changing conditions and states of mind of the people.[14]

For Nehru, "the essential and most revolutionary factor in modern life is not a particular ideology, but technological advance."[15] This belief in the pure and salutary nature of technological progress not only brings him in close spiritual neighborhood with other leaders of the Third World, it also illustrates the gap between the now established state ideology and the beliefs of the father of the nation.[16] "Countries of the West may have been colonial powers," Nehru affirmed in another of his speeches. "They may have done injury to us. But the fact is that they have built a great civilization in the last 200 or 400 years.''[17]

In short, the state that made Chandigarh possible is not that which Gandhi had anticipated in his thought. It was a new nation, eager to become a grown-up member within the family of industrialized powers to which it had been attached for so long as a mere servant or slave; a nation whose leaders were waiting for an occasion to create a monument to the new national self-consciousness. And Chandigarh seems to have been this occasion, for the causes and circumstances of the city's foundation were of the highest national significance.

Circumstances

As a result of the 1947 treaty, the Western part of the Punjab, including the old capital of the state, Lahore, was ceded to Pakistan in 1948. This left the Indian part of the Punjab without a capital and millions of refugees from Pakistan without a home. After a few months of hesitation as to whether the state government should be permanently accommodated in one of the existing rural centers, the decision was taken to build a new town. P. L. Varma, chief engineer of the Punjab state, and P. N. Thapar, a former member of the Civil Service and at that time the State Administrator of Public Works, chose the site and the name.[18]

From the beginning, the central government in New Delhi was involved. At the suggestion of Nehru, an American planner was hired to produce a master plan: Albert Mayer, whom Nehru had known and appreciated as a lieutenant-colonel of the American Army in India (Fig. 119).[19] The central government also agreed upon covering one third of the estimated building costs ($34 million) and upon the appointment of the architect Matthew Nowicki, a former coworker of Le Corbusier, who was to be responsible among other things for the design of the government buildings.[20] His sketches show, unlike Mayer's initial plan, a marked interest in a monumental orchestration of the Capitol complex. The Assembly was throned like a mastaba in a ceremonial plaza (Fig. 120), while the Secretariat was to be covered by a shell structure that combined the elegance of Oscar Niemeyer's Pedregulho Chapel with the grandiloquence of the huge exhibition hall in Paris's Quartier de la Défense. In any case, both Mayer's master plan and Nowicki's sketches for the Capitol area illustrate to what degree the general concept and layout of the city was established around 1950—well before Le Corbusier took over the command.

This occurred late in 1950. By then, the planning of Chandigarh had been interrupted by Nowicki's sudden death in a plane crash over Egypt (spring 1950) and by the difficulties incurred in coming to a financial agreement with Albert Mayer. It was then that the two Punjab officials traveled to Europe in search of a new team of planners and architects. Maxwell Fry and Jane Drew were among those they visited first, and they suggested to the Indians that they contact Le Corbusier. His reaction was all but encouraging. Apart from his general skepticism regarding the project's chances of being realized, he considered the proposed honorarium as well as the time allowed for planning "ridiculous."[21] At last though, he yielded to the temptation of the enterprise, but when he was asked to move to India, he answered: "Your capital can be built right here; we, at 35 Rue de Sèvres, are perfectly capable of finding the solution to the problem."[22]

In any case, Le Corbusier finally agreed, at a monthly salary of $420 (and with the injunction to spend four weeks twice a year in Chandigarh during its construction), to become the Architectural Advisor of the Punjab Government for the Creation of its New Capital and, in addition, the architect of the Capitol complex. In February 1951, he flew to India. There he met Pierre Jeanneret and Maxwell Fry and later

Figure 119
Two master plans of Chandigarh: Alfred Mayer's plan of 1950 and Le Corbusier's modified plan of 1951. (Drawing by Narindar Lamba.)

CHANDIGARH — TWO MASTER PLANS.

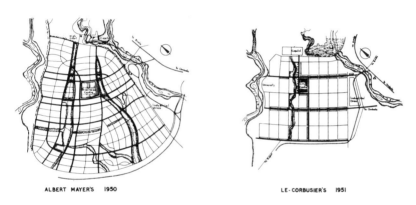

ALBERT MAYER'S 1950

LE-CORBUSIER'S 1951

Figure 120
Matthew Nowicki: sketch for the Secretariats and (in the background) the Assembly in Chandigarh's Capitol complex, circa 1950. (Source: Evenson, *Chandigarh,* plate 6.)

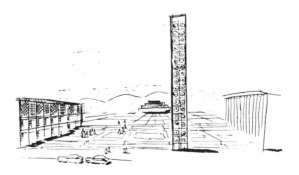

The Politics of the Open Hand   421

Jane Drew. In a small hotel on the road to Simla, the new plan for Chandigarh was drawn up within four days.[23]

The New Imperial City

It was not a new layout but a revised version of the already existing and accepted master plan by Albert Mayer. All the distinctive features of Mayer's plan were carefully taken over: the arrangement of the Government center outside the city, as its "head" (an idea that happened to coincide with earlier town planning concepts of Le Corbusier himself [Fig. 121]); the creation of a business center within the city and the division of the territory into sectors.

The changes to Mayer's concept hardly justify Le Corbusier's implicit claims to be the author of the plan. These changes mainly concerned the size of the neighborhood units, which now received roughly rectangular outlines, measuring about 4000 × 2600 feet: Le Corbusier's "module" of a "sector." The most obvious modification, however, was with regard to roadways. While the Mayer project envisaged them as large curves, Le Corbusier established a system of rectilinear axes. Only the lateral streets that cross the Jan Marg, the grand avenue of the city, are slightly curved for better protection of the traffic from the sun (Fig. 122).

The monumental axis has literally been a central aspect of Le Corbusier's urbanistic proposals ever since the project of a Contemporary City for Three Million Inhabitants (1922), loaded with moral, aesthetic, and functional symbolism (Fig. 123). "Man walks straight ahead because he has a goal; he knows where he is going"—such was the gospel preached in *Urbanisme.*[24] Although Le Corbusier's obsession with monumental axes was rationalized in terms of utilitarian necessities, it was obviously based upon emotional preference. Paris, the Champs-Elysées, Haussmann's breakthroughs are the points of reference, if not, ultimately, La Chaux-de-Fonds, Le Corbusier's home town itself.[25]

Thus, in the Contemporary City and in the Plan Voisin, images and ideals of classical urbanism intermingle with those of the machine age. The city is defined by its traffic pattern; the fast-running traffic is as essential to it as the water to the fountain. One has to consider the quasimagical character that Le Corbusier ascribed to speed. "The city that has speed has success," he claimed.[26] This is a Futurist theme, celebrated, as early as 1914, in Sant'Elia's *Città Nuova* projects (and it is no coincidence that the thirties in Italy produced the most powerful images of the motorized city, based upon the Italian love story with triumphal and imperial *viali* animated by Fiat traffic [Fig. 124]). But I still believe that Italian Futurism was less important for Le Corbusier than more immediate inspirations like the rhetorics of French automobile advertisements and the like.[27]

Be that as it may, for Le Corbusier speed and motorization are factors of the "lyricism of modern times," a lyricism too olympic to be judged on utilitarian grounds. Thus, one of the sketches of the Contemporary City shows how the urban superhighway connects the two triumphal gates; outside the city, where a highway would be justified, the urban axis reverts into a simple cross-country road.

This is the background to Le Corbusier's master plan for Chandigarh. The reality, today, matches the utopia of 1922: after six hours of bumpy country roads, the bus from New Delhi suddenly rolls onto a well-paved highway; the traveler thinks that he is now finally approaching Chandigarh, but he is actually riding through the city's main street (Fig. 125).

Le Corbusier's idea of changing Mayer's original layout seems to have been readily accepted by the Indian officials. Mayer's plan is reminiscent of the organic patterns of the English garden cities and their American descendants (Mayer had played a considerable role in

Figure 121
Le Corbusier, plan for an
organic, extensible city.
(Source: Le Corbusier, *La
Ville radieuse,* 1935,
p. 168.)

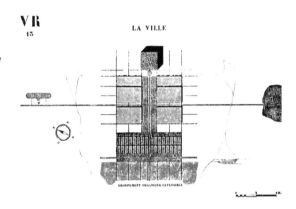

Figure 122
Chandigarh: the Jan
Marg, with brick walls
separating the sectors
from the traffic artery.
(Photograph by S. von
Moos.) Compare with
Figure 127.

Figure 123
Le Corbusier,
Contemporary City for
Three Million
Inhabitants, 1922.
(Source: Le Corbusier,
*Oeuvre complète
1910–29,* p. 35.)

Figure 124
Rome, E.U.R.: master
plan for the Esposizione
Universale, to be held in
1941–1942 (project:
1937). Architects:
Giuseppe Pagano,
Marcello Piacentini, Luigi
Piccinato, Ettore Rossi,
and Luigi Vietti. (Source:
La Casa, no. 6, Milan.)

Figure 125
Chandigarh: view of the
Jan Marg, the city's main
axis. To the right, the
Museum and Art Gallery.
(Photograph by S. von
Moos.)

introducing Ebenezer Howard's ideas to America). Le Corbusier's modification brings the plan back into the tradition of Western pre-Howardian town planning. His project evoked the grandiose urban geometries of L'Enfant's Washington or Haussmann's Paris. Moreover, the axis must have caught the eyes of the Indian officials through its implicit analogy with the plan of New Delhi and its King's Way, India's showpiece of enlightened though colonial planning (Fig. 126).[28]

Through such analogies the plan was able to become a symbol of national self-consciousness. Not that the gridiron plan had been introduced to India by the British Empire. The city of Jaipur dates from the early eighteenth century: it is as Indian an ancestor for Le Corbusier's master plan as one may wish, but its avenues are not traffic arteries alone; they are the multifunctional public spaces that Chandigarh has not created (Fig. 127). The axis, self-sufficient in its declamatory gesture, is a legacy of New Delhi.

Many other monumental aspects of Chandigarh can be understood in terms of their often-concealed analogy with the Indian capital. The vast pedestrian plaza of the City center in Sector 17, stretching out its arms toward the surrounding (empty) traffic arteries, is Le Corbusier's only realization of an enclosed urban space.[29] Its monofunctional character as a mere business district derives from the Charte d'Athènes; its form—the vast open space surrounded by long, arcaded office buildings—reflects Le Corbusier's delight in French squares and Roman fora, a leitmotiv in his sketchbooks and early publications. It is, in short, a colonial variation on the theme of the Venetian Piazza S. Marco: functionally desiccated, dramatically overscaled (the plaza is 1,800 feet long from street to street, while the Piazza S. Marco is "only" 650 feet deep), and lacking the densely packed cluster of the surrounding city, which gives the Italian piazza its meaning as a public amenity and meeting place.

Stanislaus von Moos 426

Figure 126
New Delhi: aerial view of
the King's Way and the
Capitol. (Source: Butler,
*The Architecture of Sir
Edwin Lutyens.*)

Figure 127
Jaipur: typical street scene. (Photograph by S. von Moos.)

The Politics of the Open Hand   427

The core is the opposite of what the Western tourist expects to find in an Indian urban center, the opposite of the bazaar, shaded and noisy, crowding a maximum of people and goods into a minimum of space. And yet, these vast plazas, which become ovens under the glaring sun, are the administration's pride. Many among the Indian visitors from Calcutta and Bombay seem to experience the spaciousness and openness of this plaza as a promise of relief from age-old poverty and overcrowding. And one remembers that the praise of "wide open spaces," of "space, air, and light" and the condemnation of the "horror of slums" is a recurring theme in Nehru's speeches.[30]

The city center, too, has its counterpart in New Delhi: its scale and neoclassical serenity (though stiffened by the narrow-minded repetition of an elevation code, which was meant by Le Corbusier to be used in a varied and flexible fashion)[31] recalls Sir Herbert Baker's Palladian arcades of Connaught Place (Fig. 128).

Finally, in the Capitol lie the palaces of the three powers (Fig. 129). The architecture marks a high point, probably the climax of Le Corbusier's *oeuvre* as a designer—the fulfillment, in many respects, of ideas and concepts developed, questioned, and redefined in a long and partly obscure process, which covers the whole span of the architect's creative lifetime. These palaces have their architectural prehistory in Le Corbusier's previous work, not in an established imagery of monumental building: they are unique in their typological context.[32]

In their uniqueness and bold originality, however, these buildings participate in the great theme of Chandigarh: the old architectural and urbanistic metaphors of rule are appropriated and transformed by the new political establishment. And they even perform this appropriation in terms of architectural ideals that correspond with some of the essential cultural beliefs upon which the new society is built. The Capitol

Figure 128
New Delhi: Connaught Place. Architect: Sir Herbert Baker.
(Photgraph by S. von Moos.) Compare with Figure 110.

Figure 129
Chandigarh: plan of the
Capitol complex.
(Source: Le Corbusier,
*Oeuvre complète
1957–65,* p. 73.)

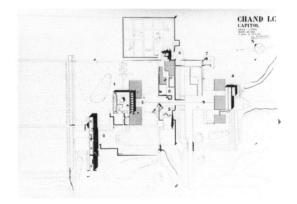

houses the judiciary, legislative, and executive powers of the Punjab. (At least it was designed for this purpose.)[33] But its powerful imagery aims beyond the glorification of a provincial government; it celebrates the recently established independent rule of the young Indian nation.

This theme is not new in Le Corbusier's work. Some of the architect's most spectacular projects grew out of similar programs. His fame in the twenties is intimately connected with his untiring and finally frustrated efforts to become the builder of the League of Nations headquarters in Geneva. Not just the size, but the political significance of this program explains his fanatic struggle to get the commission. Le Corbusier was interested not only in winning an international competition and defeating Academia; he wanted to become the builder of the first world parliament. The solemnity of the task inspired the humanist character of the project, a project whose layout was, despite its avant-garde features, classical enough to serve as the basis for the Beaux-Arts complex that was finally built (Fig. 130).[34]

Creating an acropolis of modern, enlightened mankind was the underlying idea of the Mundaneum complex designed with Paul Otlet in 1928 (and re-elaborated in the following years). On the institutional level the prefiguration of UNESCO was architecturally a clear anticipation of Chandigarh's Capitol. With the Mundaneum, the world was to receive a "sanctuary, inspiring and coordinating great ideas, noble activities."[35] It is no coincidence that some of the Mundaneum's key concepts, such as the Museum of Knowledge, finally found their way into Le Corbusier's Capitol project for Chandigarh. The Soviet Palace (1931) would have been in many ways to the USSR what Chandigarh's Capitol is to India: a grandiloquent symbol to the consolidation of a new technology-oriented, political order. One has to measure the Capitol of Chandigarh against this grandiose sequence of never-realized palaces for the state, a sequence that had its climax of political ambition in Le Corbusier's projects for a World Capital, seat of the United Nations (1946).[36]

From the League of Nations project to the Capitol of Chandigarh Le Corbusier's style has undergone modifications. The basic philosophy, however, has remained the same: an uncorruptible belief in universal salvation through modern technology. In the twenties as well as in the fifties, Le Corbusier's stated intention was to create architectural machines, serving the purpose of government and administration with the greatest efficiency—so much the better if these machines became, as it seems, almost automatically monumental images of their content and function. In Chandigarh's Capitol the form claims to be born out of practical needs. The canopy of the High Court is a colossal shading and cooling device, with its arches, undulating from pillar to pillar, inviting the winds to air the structure. The complicated system of sunbreakers serves not only to perform but also to visualize its essential "biological" function of heat control. It is the manifesto of an architectural language created as an answer to the reality of the subtropical climate: an air-conditioning apparatus defined in structural and architectural terms, with no mechanical help.[37] The same is true of the Assembly, whose Forum is not only a cool and shaded interior, but a cathedral of shade, a celebration of crepuscular relief in the midst of the heat and glare of the surrounding plains.

Le Corbusier's style at Chandigarh is of a strongly (but by no means exclusively) symbolic and declamatory nature—so is its underlying program, inspired by the political background and circumstances. At Chandigarh the purpose of government was one of celebration and persuasion, not just smooth-running administration and bureaucracy. Among the symbols cast in the concrete walls and knit in the tapestries of Chandigarh's palaces, the sign of the sun, determining night and day on earth, plays a central role (Fig. 131). It summarizes the dis-

Figure 130
Geneva: projects for the
Palace of the League of
Nations, 1927–1928;
comparative study
showing the similarity
between Le Corbusier's
project and the finally
chosen plan. (Source: Le
Corbusier, *Oeuvre
complète 1910–29,*
p. 173.)

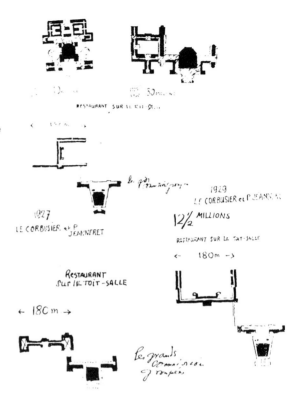

Figure 131
Signs drawn by Le
Corbusier, to be cast in
the concrete walls and
knit in the tapestries of
the palaces in
Chandigarh's Capitol.
(Source: Le Corbusier,
*Oeuvre complète
1957–65,* p. 111.)
Compare these signs
with the detail in
Figure 142.

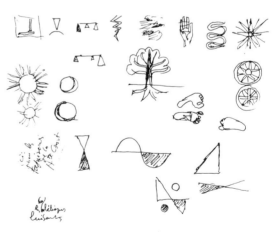

Stanislaus von Moos   432

tribution of light and darkness and heat and coolness, which is the basic theme of Le Corbusier's architecture at Chandigarh. And it gives this theme the irrefutability of a cosmic law.

Not only the architecture, but the society that built it is placed under the sun's ultimate irrefutable command: in the Assembly building Le Corbusier moves his sun symbolism from the area of poetic architectural mythology into the realm of political symbolism. He revives the idea of the *roi soleil.* The sun sign dominates the large enamel door to the Assembly, the ceremonial gate, opened once every year for the Governor of the State (Fig. 132).

The larger of the two chambers of the parliament was to be equipped for a mysterious solar ritual to be held every year (Fig. 133). Its sculptural envelope, the cooling tower-type volume at the center of the building, suspended into the dark space of the Forum like a giant entrail, rising above the roof like a chimney, is topped by an oblique cover. Sculptural forms, reminiscent of the observatories of Jaipur or Delhi, emerge on the slanted surface as a colossal, vaguely cosmological still-life (Fig. 134). "This cap," Le Corbusier explains, ". . . will become a true physics laboratory, equipped to ensure the play of lights. . . . Furthermore, this cork will lend itself to possible solar festivals, reminding man once every year that he is a son of the sun."[38] It is a cosmological sanction of earthly power, like at Abu Simbel, where once every year a sunray reaches into the back of the mortuary cave and touches the forehead of the Pharaoh's effigy. The scientific imagery of Siwai Jai Singh's observatories (Fig. 135) is reinstrumentalized for the celebration of a political myth.

Without the Imperial Capitol of New Delhi in the background, however, Le Corbusier would never have been able to realize at Chandigarh what he had dreamt of ever since 1927: a monument to the machine age, its supposedly universal values and its political institutions. From the beginning, the Capitol was to be the Indian answer to

Figure 132
The Capitol, Chandigarh: view of the Assembly with ceremonial gate.
(Photograph by S. von Moos.)

Figure 133
Le Corbusier, studies for
the light equipment of
the Upper Chamber in
the Assembly, 1954.
(Source: Le Corbusier,
My Work, 1960, p. 210.)

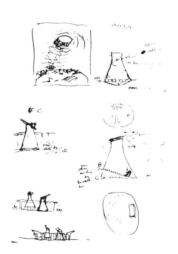

Figure 134
The Capitol, Chandigarh:
view from the High Court
toward the Assembly.
(Photograph by S. von
Moos.)

Figure 135
Jaipur: astronomical observatory, 1718–1734. (Photograph by S. von Moos.)

the Capitol at New Delhi, with its domes and colonnades, its avenues and enormous squares glorifying the British colonial Empire (Fig. 136). Photographs cannot convey the spectacle of grandeur that this complex must have offered to the British visitor of the thirties; what its monumentality may have signified to the Indian people is of course another question. To quote Robert Byron's report in the *Architectural Review* (1931):

The road describes a curve and embarks imperceptibly on a gradient. Suddenly, on the right, a scape of towers and domes is lifted from the horizon, sunlit pink and cream dancing against the blue sky, fresh as a cup of milk, grand as Rome. Close at hand the foreground discloses a white arch. The motor turns off the arterial avenue, and skirting the low red base of the gigantic monument, comes to a stop. The traveller heaves a breath. Before his eyes, sloping gently upward, runs a gravel way of such infinite perspective as to suggest the intervention of a diminishing glass; at whose end, reared above the green tree tops, glitters the seat of government, the eighth Delhi, four square upon an eminence—dome, tower, dome, tower, dome, tower, red, pink, cream, and white-washed gold and flashing in the morning sun.[39]

Twenty years after Byron's visit, Le Corbusier paid his tribute to the work of Sir Edwin Lutyens and Sir Herbert Baker: "New Delhi . . . , the capital of Imperial India, was built more than thirty years ago, with extreme care, great talent, and real success. The critics may say what they want: to do something forces respect (at least my respect)."[40] In fact, as Allan Greenberg has noted, Le Corbusier's early studies for the Chandigarh skyline could easily double as illustrations for Robert Byron's description of Lutyens' palaces and domes: "The essential ingredients are common—the picturesque skyline of government buildings, the flat intervening city, and the monumental connecting axis."[41]

In an early version of the Capitol project, established after that "pathetic soliloquy," that "battle of spaces fought inside the head" which Le Corbusier later described,[42] he seems to have envisaged a complex similar in scale to Delhi's palaces and domes. Later, as the program became more specific, the size was reduced and the symmetries within the complex (especially the axial alignment of the Assembly with the High Court) were modified.

But through all these stages of its elaboration, the complex remained visually dominated by the Governor's Palace (Fig. 137). This building, drastically overscaled in the initial stages of its planning, was designed to "crown the Capital"[43] in a similar way as the Viceroy's House of Lutyens crowns the city of New Delhi. Above the roof, a huge concrete clamp grasps into the sky (Fig. 138), similarly potent in sculptural presence and symbolic if not ritual overtones as the grandiose St. Paul's-type dome of the Viceroy's House (Fig. 139).

There are more analogies. The gardens of the Governor's Palace, extending toward the city and toward the rear, were to be organized in terms of terraces and fountains; the access roadways in terms of depressed channels serving and piercing the building on its cross axis—Lutyens' brilliant and multilevel arrangements at and around the Viceroy's House must have inspired the concept.[44]

The Governor's Palace was not built. Nehru is said to have considered a Governor's Palace within the Capitol area unsuitable for a democracy.[45] Nehru had a lively interest in Chandigarh's Capitol, and his interventions were numerous and decisive, given the central government's important subsidies to the enterprise. Usually, he backed Le Corbusier's proposals against the objections of the local officials; he supported a green carpet in the Upper Chamber, despite the Punjab's desire for a red carpet to correspond with the British House of Lords; he insisted that Le Corbusier's tapestries remain in the High Court, although they seem to have been criticized as aesthetically unacceptable by some judges.[46]

In short, it is through its dialectical commitment to continuity as well as to innovation that Le Corbusier's city, and above all the Capitol, could become, in the eyes of the Indian officials, a symbol of the new state. Or that it could become, as Nehru had said in an ad-

Figure 136
New Delhi: aerial view of the Capitol complex. (Source: Butler, *The Architecture of Sir Edwin Lutyens.*)

Figure 137
The Capitol at New Delhi; Le Corbusier's first project for the Capitol at Chandigarh; Le Corbusier's final project for the Capitol at Chandigarh; all drawn to the same scale. (Source: A. Greenberg, in *Perspecta,* no. 12, 1969.)

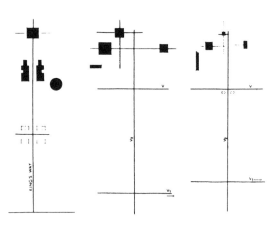

Figure 138
Chandigarh: Le
Corbusier's project for
the Governor's Palace,
"crowning the city," May
1953. (Source: Le
Corbusier, *Oeuvre
complète 1946–52,*
p. 151.)

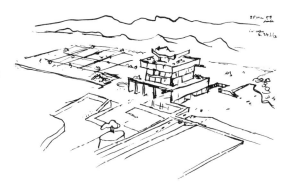

Figure 139
New Delhi: the Viceroy's
House, overlooking the
Capitol. Architect: Sir
Edwin Lutyens. (Source:
Butler, *The Architecture
of Sir Edwin Lutyens.*)

dress at the official Inauguration of Chandigarh (1953), "the first large expression of our creative genius, flowering on our newly earned freedom, . . . unfettered by traditions of the past, . . . reaching beyond the existing encumbrances of old towns and old traditions" and even, finally, the "temple of new India." [47]

Convergence of Ideologies

Thus, besides or rather before being a tool for specific bureaucratic functions, the Capitol is a monumental apparatus, glorifying the two great themes underlying the program of the whole city: first—the establishment of a new, powerful, efficient state order, capable of guaranteeing political stability and independence after the disorders of the Civil War; second—the promotion of modern technology ("the big factory and all that it represents"), as the basis of economic and social progress. It is, of course, no coincidence that Le Corbusier proved to be the right man at the right moment, that his urban imagery and his architecture were capable, more than Mayer's or Nowicki's, of dramatizing the ideas and values that the new Indian elite wanted to celebrate. These values had been central to Le Corbusier's political philosophy since the beginning of his career.

Le Corbusier's enthusiasm for authority—for strong leadership, for great men at the head of important tasks—is proverbial. In the early twenties, Paris confronted him with the deplorable living conditions of the underprivileged, the poor. His commitment to improve their situation was honest and strong. But he perceived their conditions and their problems from above; he thought (as most housing agencies in the industrialized world have ever since) that the solution of the urban crisis is above all a technical, not a political problem. Thus, he addressed himself not to the people, but to those in command. And he recommended his solutions not as the pretext of revolution, but as a means of avoiding it: "Architecture or Revolution. Revolution can be

Avoided" was the slogan in 1922.[48] The call for a strong political authority is a permanent motto in his pamphlets and books. In order to realize the new architecture of collective happiness, society needs a strong, well-informed government with *Pleins Pouvoirs,* to quote the title of a book by Jean Giraudoux (1939) that was highly appreciated by Le Corbusier. Thus his book *La Ville radieuse* of 1935 is dedicated to Authority. He cultivated a paternalistic, more, a patriarchal conception of state rule; he liked to compare it to the authority of the *père de famille* who knows what is best for his children.[49] At the end of *Urbanisme* (1925), he reproduced a print: Louis XIV ordering the construction of the Hôtel des Invalides (Fig. 140). The caption says: "Homage to a great urbanist." Later, he confessed: "I have been haunted for years by the shadow of Colbert."[50]

With that in mind one understands what Nehru must have meant to him. After his frustrated attempts to become a Colbert of the League of Nations, of Joseph Stalin, of Henri Pétain, and of the UN[51] he finally met a political leader whose outlook was in tune with his own architectural philosophy and whose authority was strong enough to put it to work (Fig. 141).

It is easy enough to ridicule Le Corbusier's enthusiasm for authority, this olympic determination to operate *"par-dessus la mêlée."*[52] To judge the ideology in terms of abstract social theory or vaguely anarchist religion is one thing; to ponder its implications within its historical context is another.[53] Le Corbusier's context offered limited alternatives. His alternatives were not between popular self-determination or "freedom now" versus authoritarian "law and order"; they were between the laissez-faire of advanced capitalism and a controlled economic and social progress based upon modern technology put at the service of the masses. He chose the latter alternative.

His insistence upon the nonpolitical, "purely technical" nature of his

Figure 140
Louis XIV ordering the
building of the Hôtel des
Invalides. The caption
reads: "Homage to a
great urbanist." (Source:
Le Corbusier,
Urbanisme, 1925, p. 302.)

Figure 141
Le Corbusier explaining the High Court drawings to Prime Minister Jawaharlal Nehru.
(Photograph by Narindar Lamba, 1952.)

strategy did not prevent him from being judged upon the level of
day-to-day politics. In the twenties and the early thirties his technocratic views placed him, in the eyes of conservative critics, among the
bolsheviks.[54] More recently the same aspect of his work has qualified
him as an accomplice of advanced capitalism; so the themes of conservative and reactionary antimodern propaganda, typical for the late
twenties, have been inherited by the sociological critique of the New
Left.[55]

Le Corbusier was certainly a protagonist of the ideology of the
modern welfare state,[56] and part of his personal drama was that his
early architectural and urbanistic concepts were elaborated some
twenty years before their underlying ideology became universally accepted in the industrialized world. It is interesting to note, in the context of Chandigarh, how he has always naively admired Western col-
onization as a spectacle of *"force morale."* [57] His book *Précisions,* written after his first trip to South America (1929), abounds in sickening
statements about the great effort of investors and industrialists to
"make up America": "In the offices, I have seen that the Germans and
the English had sent technicians in order to equip the country; and
especially I have felt the enormous financial and industrial power of
the USA. From the four corners of the world one comes to Argentina,
for all efforts are useful."[58] It sounds as if he wanted to advertise himself as a new Columbus. And it is no coincidence that, in 1930, a century after the French military takeover of Algeria, he travels to Algiers
in order to announce "the hour of urbanism."

Most of these earlier statements on the salutary nature of modern
technology and industrial development for the well-being of mankind
would probably have found the approval of Prime Minister Nehru. In
India, Le Corbusier was frequently blamed for not having been interested enough in local customs. When an Indian visitor asked him
why he had not stayed longer at Chandigarh, he answered, "I was

frightened of a snake biting me," but he added, "What is the meaning of Indian style in the world of today, when you accept machines and trousers and democracy?"[59]

Machines, trousers and democracy are, however, not the only elements of that universal mythology of which Chandigarh was to be a monument. This mythology has broader outlines, deeper reaching roots. It is based upon Le Corbusier's well-known dogma of *les joies essentielles;* it is inspired by the virtues of simple rural life in preindustrial society;[60] it is oriented toward and qualified by eternal cosmic laws, summed up in the sign of the "solar day of 24 hours." A catalogue of symbols to be cast in the concrete walls of Chandigarh's palaces and to be knit in the tapestries decorating their ceremonial chambers illustrates this cosmology. It is the legacy of an artist who conceives himself as a magician and a prophet of a new myth, if not as a legislator of a new society; of an artist, indeed, who in his youth had read Nietzsche, who had participated in the aesthetic and symbolistic rituals of Art Nouveau, and who dreamed of an integrated society. There is a direct connection between the ornaments of the Villa Fallet at La Chaux-de-Fonds (1906–1907) (Fig. 142) and the decorative program for Chandigarh. Here and there appears the fiction of a state art, elementary and nevertheless occult, because there is no state religion behind it.[61]

There is reasonable hope that the blownup trademarks symbolizing Le Corbusier's architectural mythology (the sign of the Modulor, the harmonic Spiral, the tower of shade, and so on), a rather curious parade of devotional art to be displayed in a "ditch of contemplation" in the Capitol complex, will never be executed.[62] There may even be a fit of uncertainty in Le Corbusier's comments on this pretentiously ritual display: rarely was he so eager to credit one of his collaborators, in this case Jane Drew, with the original idea.[63]

The Open Hand sums it all up. It is no doubt the most powerful,

Figure 142
Detail of the main façade
of the Villa Fallet, La
Chaux-de-Fonds,
1906–1907. Architect:
Charles-Edouard
Jeanneret (Le Corbusier).
(Photograph by S. von
Moos.)

poetic sign among these monuments, for it transcends, in its evocative plainness, the idealistic abstraction of the other elements of this
private decalogue. By its ultimately Ruskin-inspired symbolism of
fraternity, it even brings in a subtle though indirect and certainly unin-
tended allusion to Gandhi's philosophy.

In various letters to Nehru, Le Corbusier comments on the origins
and on the personal implications of this symbol. But he is also eager
to make it acceptable as a metaphor of what Chandigarh, "the temple
of new India," stands for. Thus he reiterates, in one of these letters, a
theme that has always been important equally to him and to Nehru.
The real dilemma in the modern world, he says, is not between the
USA and the USSR, but it is of a more general, human, and technical
nature: "The modern world has made all things interrelated. The relations are continuous and contiguous around the globe, affected by
nuances and diversity. . . . The question is man and his environment,
an event of local as well as of global order."[64]

And in an earlier letter, never published in extenso, he is even more
explicit as to the fundamental role of technology in building up a new
solidarity among men:

India was not forced to live through the century, today gone, of the
troubles of the first machine age. . . .
India might consider precious the idea of raising in the Capitol of
Chandigarh at present under construction, among the palaces which
will house its institutions and its authority, the symbolic and evocative
sign of the "Open Hand":
open to receive the newly created wealth,
open to distribute it to its people and to the others.
The "Open Hand" will assert that the second era of the machine age
has begun: the era of harmony.[65]

Such a commitment to technology as the premise of a new and universal social harmony may have sounded quite familiar to Indian ears.
It corresponds with Nehru's own stated philosophy of progress. The
belief, however, that technology would be able to create a universal

brotherhood of men, that it would enable men at last to understand one another, that it would guarantee once and for all peace on the globe has not been introduced by him. It is at least as old as the Victorian Age, which so deeply shaped the Indian infrastructures. But in the nineteenth century, technology in India turned out to become a servant not to human brotherhood, but to British imperial dominance; it has served as a proof of the gulf existing between Englishmen and Indians, rather than as a means of bridging it.[66]

In fact, Le Corbusier's statement that "India was not forced to live through . . . the troubles of the first machine age" acquires, if seen in the context of economic and political history, an almost cynical meaning. While the country was forced to bleed under the machinery of Western capitalism, it has preserved its older, autocratic, basically feudal power structure and class hierarchy. Almost untouched by the struggles toward democratization, which throughout the nineteenth century changed the political scene in England, India remained, in the eyes of many British conservatives, the model of political order and stability. Thus, it could become, in the twentieth century, the scene of the British Empire's most spectacular building campaign. Chandigarh is unimaginable outside the system of political hierarchy which made New Delhi's Capitol possible; it celebrates the new elite. And thus, even within an independent India, technology and the myth of the Open Hand might well remain an instrument and a symbol of a political strategy, which, up to now, seems to be more successful in keeping people apart than in bringing them together.

Nevertheless, within the "mafia" of Corbusier fans[67] the Open Hand has in fact been able to inspire a sort of universal *camaraderie,* even though it has not been built. Has it perhaps been designed for us?

The present paper is based upon notes for a lecture given at the Carpenter Center for the Visual Arts, Harvard University, April 1973.

1 See Le Corbusier, *Oeuvre complète,* vols. 5–8 passim; Norma Evenson, *Chandigarh,* Berkeley, 1966 (with bibliography up to 1966); David Crane, "Chandigarh Reconsidered," in *Journal of the American Institute of Architects,* May 1960, pp. 32–39; Shedev Kumar Gupta, "Chandigarh: After 20 Years," in *Proceedings of EDRA III,* Los Angeles, 1972; Shedev Kumar Gupta, "Chandigarh. A Study of Sociological Issues and Urban Development in India," in *Occasional Papers No. 9,* edited by the Faculty of Environmental Studies, University of Waterloo, 1973 (with rich bibliography); Sten Nilsson, *The New Capitals of India, Pakistan and Bangladesh,* Lund, 1973; my *Le Corbusier. Elemente einer Synthese,* Frauenfeld and Stuttgart, 1968, pp. 250–265, 307–322 (French edition: *Le Corbusier. L'architecte et son mythe,* Paris, 1971, pp. 180–192, 225–238); and my two articles "Augenschein in Chandigarh," in *Bauwelt,* 1968, no. 30, pp. 931–941 and "Chandigarh—ville morte?" in *L'Architecture d'Aujourd'hui,* no. 146, October–November 1969, pp. 54–61.

2 The planners and the architects of Chandigarh were well aware of the problem's implications—better than their critics. To quote Maxwell Fry: "It so happens that Chandigarh is remote from the industrial centres, and that a fair proportion of its population follow traditions and customs at variance with these ruling ideas, but because it is a function of the architect to interpret change in terms of planning and building, to this extent his work is educative, moulding life by creating new forms for it, and may, therefore, be in advance of its time." "The Architect and the Engineer in India," in *Annual of Architecture, Structure and Town Planning,* vol. 1, 1960, pp. 20–24. See also M. N. Sharma's statement in Le Corbusier's *Oeuvre complète,* vol. 8, p. 49.

3 Sten Nilsson's work, *The New Capitals of India, Pakistan and Bangladesh,* probably the best recent comparative study on new towns in the Third World (Chandigarh, Islamabad, Dacca, and others), is an example of this approach. Planning strategies are aptly interpreted as different professional approaches to urbanization, but only occasionally is there a glimpse into the political context and its possible role in determining the choice of these strategies. Norma Evenson, in *Chandigarh,* is mostly interested in placing Chandigarh's planning strategy and architecture into the universal history of modern architecture and urbanism as professional disciplines, at

Notes

which she admirably succeeds. But, although she realizes that many aspects of Chandigarh are determined by the political character of the campaign, she is not particularly interested in the nature of the political ideas that (implicitly or explicitly) underlie the social and architectural choices of the administration and the designers. The same is true of her more recent, extremely useful study, *Le Corbusier: The Machine and the Grand Design,* New York, 1969. (Compare S. von Moos, "Corbusiana. Zum Stand der Corbusier-Kritik," in *Bauwelt,* January 1972, pp. 8f, 56.)

4   A good recent introduction to Gandhi's political thinking is given by Francis G. Hutchins, *Spontaneous Revolution: The Quit India Movement,* Delhi, 1971. For a collection of Gandhi's writings on economics, see M. K. Gandhi, *Economic and Industrial Life and Relations,* edited by V. B. Kher, 3 vols., Ahmedabad, 1957. Gandhi's first book, *Hind Swaraj (Indian Home Rule),* New Delhi, 1908, is a radical refusal of industrialism and machinery, including railways, doctors, and lawyers, which he considers responsible for the economic and moral degradation of the country. His perception of the socioeconomic reality of India seems to have been influenced by Chunder Dutt, *Economic History of India,* Delhi, 1960.

5   M. K. Gandhi, *Economic and Industrial Life,* Introduction, p. xlvi; also vol. 3, p. 34.

6   According to recent surveys, ½ million people were killed during the Civil War in the Punjab, and 12 million were homeless; see Nilsson, *The New Capitals,* p. 87.

7   Interview with an American, quoted after: M. K. Gandhi, *Socialism of My Conception,* Bombay, 1957, p. 184.

8   Jawaharlal Nehru, *Speeches,* vol. 3, New Delhi, 1958, p. 23.

9   Ibid.

10   Vladimir Lenin, *New Political Economy,* NEP, 1921.

11   Hutchins, *Spontaneous Revolution,* p. 359.

12   Ibid.

13   Gandhi, *Economic and Industrial Life,* Introduction, p. lv.

14   See for example Jawaharlal Nehru, Arnold Toynbee, and Earl C. R. Atlee, *India and the World,* New Delhi, 1962, p. 9.

15   Ibid., p. 19. This lecture gives a good summary of Nehru's political philosophy, for example his belief in the convergence of the capitalist and socialist systems and his idea that the "real difference" lies not in political systems, but in the tension between the industrialized and

the underdeveloped countries in the world.

16 Historically, this outlook has its roots in the Victorian Age and its dreams of universal brotherhood based upon the irrefutable truths of science and technology.

17 Nehru, *Speeches,* vol. 3, p. 422.

18 Varma, incidentally, happened to be in the USA while the Punjab was split—and it is there that he gathered firsthand information on planning and urbanization. See C. Rand, "City on a Tilting Plain," in *The New Yorker,* 30 April 1955; and especially Evenson, *Chandigarh,* pp. 6–11 (with more references).

19 Rand, "City on a Tilting Plain"; Evenson, *Chandigarh*, pp. 12–18.

20 This estimation of the building costs is from Rand, "City on a Tilting Plain." On Nowicki, see Evenson, *Chandigarh,* pp. 19–24.

21 See Evenson, *Chandigarh,* p. 25.

22 According to Le Corbusier's report in *Oeuvre complète 1945–52,* p.112.

23 See Maxwell Fry's report, "A Discursive Commentary," in *Architect's Yearbook,* vol. 6, London, 1955, pp. 7–10.

24 I am quoting from the original edition, Paris, 1925, p. 3. For a more detailed discussion of the urban imagery of the Contemporary City for Three Million Inhabitants and related projects (especially the Plan Voisin), see the forthcoming English version of my Le Corbusier monograph.

25 The town had been heavily damaged by a fire in 1794, and it was then rebuilt according to a *plan américain,* with a grand axis in the middle, the Avenue Léopold Robert, where—incidentally—young Charles-Edouard Jeanneret had spent part of his youth.

26 Le Corbusier, *Urbanisme,* p. 169.

27 In *Urbanisme,* Le Corbusier quotes an article by one of the directors of the Peugeot plant, Philippe Girardet, who saw in automobilism the vigorous and brilliant confirmation of an age-old dream of humanity. Girardet describes man as one of the slowest animals in creation: "A sort of caterpillar dragging himself with difficulty on the surface of the terrestrial crust. The most part of creation moves quicker than this biped so ill-constructed for speed, and if we imagine a race between all the creatures of the globe, man would certainly be among the 'also rans' and would probably tie with the sheep." "Le règne de la vitesse," in *Mercure de France,* 1923; quoted in *Urbanisme,* p. 182.

28 See Evenson, *Chandigarh,* pp. 31–39. The decision to
    move the British administration from Calcutta to Delhi
    had been taken in 1911, and it was then that a planning
    committee was appointed, consisting of Captain Swinton
    (formerly the chairman of the London County Council),
    J. A. Brodie and Sir E. L. Lutyens. It produced the plan of
    New Delhi. The palaces at the Capitol are by Sir Edwin
    Lutyens (Viceroy's house) and Sir Herbert Baker (Sec-
    retariats). See Robert Byron, "New Delhi," in *The Ar-
    chitectural Review,* January 1931, pp. 1–29; A. S. G. But-
    ler (and others), *The Architecture of Sir Edwin Lutyens,*
    vol. 2, London and New York, 1950.

29 Evenson, *Chandigarh,* pp. 64–67; von Moos, *Le Cor-
    busier* (German edition), pp. 258–262.

30 Jawaharlal Nehru, *Speeches,* vol. 3, pp. 25–26 (at the oc-
    casion of the opening of a factory); pp. 466–467 (on
    slums), etc.

31 For Le Corbusier's explanations on this, see Le Cor-
    busier, *Modulor 2,* London, 1958, pp. 210–225.

32 As I try to demonstrate in greater detail in *Le Corbusier,*
    pp. 307–322; compare Evenson, *Chandigarh,* pp. 71–89.

33 In 1966, the Punjab was divided into two separate Indian
    states, Punjab and Hariana, with the result that the capi-
    tal became, to quote the *New York Times,* a "two-
    headed, three-tongued administrative and political
    monstrosity." See J. Anthony Lukas, "Le Corbusier's
    'Organic City' in Punjab Faces Political Surgery," in *New
    York Times,* 27 June 1966.

34 See von Moos, *Le Corbusier,* pp. 272–281; Kenneth
    Frampton has first identified the classicizing aspect of
    the Palace for the League of Nations, see "The Humanist
    versus the Utilitarian Ideal," in *Architectural Design,*
    1967; more recently, Peter Serenyi has pointed out the
    Grand Palais in Paris as a typological source for Le Cor-
    busier's project, see *Journal of the Society of Architec-
    tural Historians,* vol. 3, 1971, p. 258.

35 See Paul Otlet and Le Corbusier, *Mundaneum,* published
    by Union des Associations Internationales, Brussels,
    1928; Le Corbusier, *Oeuvre complète 1910–29,* pp. 190–
    197, 214. See also "Un projet de centre mondial à
    Genève," in *Cahiers d'Art,* 1928, pp. 307–311. The
    Museum of Knowledge at Chandigarh, which was never
    executed, is in many ways a modernized version of the
    Mundaneum; see Le Corbusier's explanations in a letter
    to Mrs. U. E. Chowdhury (Chandigarh) of 29 December
    1960, quoted in U. E. Chowdhury, "Le Corbusier in

Chandigarh, Creator and Generator," in *Architectural Design,* October 1965, pp. 504–513.

36 See Le Corbusier, *UN Headquarters,* New York, 1947.

37 See von Moos, *Le Corbusier,* pp. 152–157, 311–313. We are here at the opposite extreme of Le Corbusier's enthusiasm for the mechanically serviced "maison à respiration exacte," advertised by him around 1930; see Le Corbusier, *Précisions,* Paris, 1930, p. 210; Reyner Banham, *The Architecture of the Well-Tempered Environment,* London, 1969, pp. 143–163. In order to make work possible, however, mechanical air-conditioning had to be provided in some of the Capitol's interiors.

38 Le Corbusier, *Oeuvre complète 1952–57,* p. 94; on Republic Day (26 January) a shaft of sunlight would descend to illuminate a column of Asoka placed on the speaker's rostrum. The idea was rejected after a number of calculations had been made, and today the tower roof contains fixed skylights. See Evenson, *Chandigarh,* p. 82.

39 Byron, "New Delhi," pp. 1–2.

40 Le Corbusier, *Oeuvre complète 1952–57,* p. 50.

41 Allan Greenberg, "Lutyens' Architecture Restudied," in *Perspecta 12,* New Haven, 1969, p. 148.

42 Le Corbusier, *Modulor 2,* pp. 121–225.

43 Le Corbusier, *Oeuvre complète 1952–57,* p. 102; the modifications in the scale of the Governor's Palace are described in *Modulor 2,* pp. 222–223.

44 See Greenberg, "Lutyens' Architecture Restudied," pp. 148–49. Photographs of the gardens of Lutyens' Viceroy's House are in Butler, *The Architecture of Sir Edwin Lutyens,* plates 135–138, 159, 160, 204–213.

45 Evenson, *Chandigarh,* p. 84.

46 Ibid.

47 Quoted in S. K. Gupta, "Chandigarh," p. 6. See also Government of the Punjab, Administration, *Project Estimate of the New Capital of Punjab, Chandigarh,* Chandigarh, 1953.

48 Le Corbusier, *Vers une architecture,* Paris, 1923, p. 243.

49 Le Corbusier, *Quand les cathédrales étaient blanches,* Paris, 1937, re-edited 1965, p. 215; see also p. 222: ". . . il faut le bon plan, le plan totalitaire symphonique, qui réponde aux besoins collectifs et assure le bonheur individuel . . . ici est le rôle tout puissant et bienfaisant de l'autorité: autorité père de famille."

50 *Précisions,* p. 187. See also Le Corbusier, *Une maison, un palais,* Paris, 1928, p. 228: "Colbert?—Qu'il surgisse le nouveau Colbert! . . . un homme de sang froid, mais un

homme qui croit.—Un homme pétri de son temps!" Or the letter to the Governor of Algiers (14 December 1932): "Aujourd'hui, on ne peut rêver qu'à un homme, c'est à Colbert. Agir, entreprendre, réaliser." In Le Corbusier, *La Ville radieuse,* Boulogne-sur-Seine, 1935, p. 249.

Le Corbusier's political philosophy has been discussed by Pierre Francastel, *Art et technique au XIXe et XXe siècles,* Paris, 1956, re-edited 1962, pp. 37–47; Peter Serenyi, "Le Corbusier, Fourier and the Monastery of Ema," in *The Art Bulletin,* 1967, pp. 277–286; Heide Berndt, *Das Gesellschaftsbild bei Stadtplanern,* Stuttgart, 1968, pp. 70–73; S. von Moos, *Le Corbusier. L'architecte et son mythe,* Paris, 1971, pp. 195–201; see also, more recently, Charles Jencks' observations in *Le Corbusier and the Tragic View of Architecture,* London and Cambridge, Mass., 1973, pp. 17–18, 110–133; Manfredo Tafuri, *Progetto e utopia,* Bari, 1973, pp. 115–124.

51 See von Moos, *Le Corbusier* (German edition), pp. 272–299.

52 Le Corbusier, *La Ville radieuse,* p. 222.

53 I am grateful to Marcello Fagiolo for having sent me his mimeographed paper on "Le Corbusier 1930. I progetti per Algeri e l'America Latina" (Politecnico di Milano, Facoltà di Architettura), Milan, 1973. "One will never have elucidated enough," the author insists, "the antidemocratic, authoritarian and substantially archaic and anachronistic role played by Le Corbusier on the two ultimately connected levels of form and ideology" (p. 1). I would not go so far. The moral assumption that authority is by nature antidemocratic may be symptomatic for widely shared feelings in radical architectural circles; in the context of history it seems to me equally mystifying as Le Corbusier's glorification of order and authority. It is a simple truth, after all, that little progress toward democracy is imaginable without the intervention of some sort of political authority.

54 See Alexander von Senger's polemics: *Krisis der Architektur,* Zurich, 1928, *Die Brandfackel Moskaus,* Zurich, 1931, and *Mord an Apollo,* Zurich, 1965. For Le Corbusier's reaction to these and other writings in France (whose protagonists were C. Mauclair and Umdenstock) see Maximilien Gauthier, *Le Corbusier ou l'architecture au service de l'homme,* Paris, 1944, pp. 175–218. Interesting in this context are Hans Sedlmayr's statements on Le Corbusier in *Verlust der Mitte,* Salzburg, 1948: summing up the conservative reservations on Le Corbusier's

technology-oriented architectural philosophy.

55 See von Moos, "Corbusiana."

56 To quote Francastel, *Art et technique,* p. 42: "chacun est
à sa place . . . ; et tout le monde est heureux, heureux
éperdument. Les hommes, régénérés, fondent de
gratitude pour ceux qui leur ont préparé leurs
cadres. . . ."

57 Le Corbusier, *Précisions,* p. 15. Le Corbusier's attitude to
colonialism has been documented and discussed by
Fagiolo, *"Le Corbusier 1930."*

58 Le Corbusier, *Précisions,* p. 201 (my translation).

59 Mulkraj Anand, "Conversation with Le Corbusier," in
Santosh Kumar (editor), *Le Corbusier. 80th Birthday An-
niversary Issue* (published by the International Cultural
Organization), Bombay, 1967, pp. 11–14.

60 It is important to note, at this point, Le Corbusier's interest in native rural houses in India, their scale and their
simple devices of environmental control. It is in comparison with this vernacular tradition that he considered
Chandigarh's housing "un peu oxfordien" (see Le Corbusier, *L'atelier de la recherche patiente,* p. 139). On vernacular building in India see *Modulor 2,* pp. 196–197;
Oeuvre complète, vol. 8, pp. 112–115. Nehru himself
seems to have discovered the virtues of Indian folk architecture through Le Corbusier. In fact, to picture Le
Corbusier as the great designer operating from above,
uninterested in the "real life" of the people is mislead-
ing. See his famous note in *La Ville radieuse,* p. 6: "I am
searching the savage, not in order to find barbarism, but
in order to find a measure of wisdom. America and
Europe, farmers and fishermen"; also see his notes on
the Brazilian favelas in *Précisions,* p. 235.

61 For the iconography of these symbols see my *Le Corbusier* (German edition), pp. 347–362.

62 Le Corbusier, *Oeuvre complète 1946–52,* p. 153; Evenson, *Chandigarh,* pp. 86–89.

63 Ibid., p. 157.

64 Jean Petit, *Le Corbusier lui-même,* Paris, 1970, pp. 116–
117; this part of the letter to Nehru is a quotation from a
manifesto Le Corbusier had sent in 1949 to the Congrès
Mondial des Partisans de la Paix, where, as it seems, he
was asked to come up with a pro-communist declaration—which he was unwilling to produce. There are
numerous other statements by Le Corbusier evoking the
idea of universal harmony based upon modern technol-

ogy. See, in this context, the following statement in *L'atelier de la recherche patiente,* p. 152–153: "Planisphère. La terre désormais est au régime des vingt-quatre heures solaires. Marco Polo prenait son temps. Aujourd'hui, on dit: 'M. le président, ou M. l'ingénieur, etc., voici vos papiers, vos projets de contrats, votre billet d'avion!' . . . *Et le monde entier en est changé!* . . . Les races, les religions, les hégémonies, les hiérarchies . . . , tout est neuf, variable, mobile, flexible. L'echiquier mondial reçoit un coup de balai magistral."

65 I have published a part of this letter in *Le Corbusier* (German edition), p. 359, but it may be useful to reproduce this hitherto unpublished statement *in extenso:*

The world is undergoing a fever of mortal contradictions.

It is agreed: The world may burst! It is possible.

The first machine age, a hundred years of scientific and technical conquest, will shortly bear its fruits. The balance sheet is eloquent.

(a) Science, as it is universally practised and developed, produced an unprecedented technical equipment, revolutionary in human history, capable of producing an unlimited amount of products for fruitful consumption. Thanks to the progress in photography, film and sound recording an extraordinary density of information embraces the total domain between the astronomic spaces and the microcosm. With the help of printing, radio and television this information is spread over the world with the rapidity of lightning. Every day the world is informed about its own palpitation. The science of aeronautics has amplified the means of transportation formerly limited to land and sea. The air route has introduced a major modification in the relations between men. Finally, nuclear energy will create new sources of power and will put industrial production on new grounds. Human pain will then be set aside . . .

(b) Abundance seems to be the sign of the epoch. The open hand to receive, the open hand to give could be chosen as a symbol of these victories: Is it that, today, a contrary destiny will claim to hold us in the terror of possible wars?

India was not forced to live through the century, today gone, of the troubles of the first machine age. On the contrary: she is awakening, intact, at the hour of unlimited possibilities. But India is not a new country. She has lived the highest and the oldest civilizations. She possesses an intelligence, an ethics and a conscience.

India might consider precious the idea of raising in the Capitol of Chandigarh at present under construction, among the palaces which will house its institutions and its authority, the symbolic and evocative sign of the "Open Hand:"

open to receive the newly created wealth,
open to distribute it to its people and to the others.

Stanislaus von Moos 456

The "Open Hand" will assert that the second era of the machine age has begun: the era of harmony.

(I was unable to find the original version of this statement; the present version is based on a bad English translation made available to me by Willy Boesiger, Zurich, whom I would like to thank for permission to publish this document.)

66 See Francis G. Hutchins, *The Illusion of Permanence. British Imperialism in India,* Princeton, N. J., 1967; here pp. 199 ff.

67 It was José Luis Sert, Le Corbusier's close friend, who coined the notion, at the opening of the Le Corbusier section of the library at the Graduate School of Design, Harvard University, spring 1973.

PAUL TURNER, born 1939, in New York. Trained as an architect and architectural historian at Harvard University, graduated Ph.D., M.Arch., and M.A. (Harvard). Architectural experience with Paul Rudolph, and Kallmann and Mckinnell of Boston, and Dmitri Vendenski of San Francisco. Awarded Harvard Travelling Fellowship (France), 1969–1970, to do research on "The Education of Le Corbusier," doctoral dissertation, Harvard, 1971. Currently Assistant Professor of Architectural History at Stanford University, California. Author of *Catalogue de la bibliothèque de Le Corbusier avant 1930,* Fondation Le Corbusier, Paris, 1970 (mimeographed). At present working on "California Architecture," and "F. L. Olmsted's college-campus designs."

MARY PATRICIA MAY SEKLER, art historian. Former Associate, Department of Education, Walters Art Gallery, Baltimore, Maryland, and coproducer of the Gallery's television series "Man the Maker" and "Key to the Ages"; former Teaching Fellow, Harvard College. Collaborator, with Jaqueline Tyrwhitt and Brian Falk, on *Face of the Metropolis,* edited by Martin Meyerson (New York, 1963). Author of "The Early Drawings of Charles-Edouard Jeanneret (Le Corbusier) 1902–1908," doctoral dissertation, Harvard University, 1973. Fellow of the Radcliffe Institute, 1975–1976, for Le Corbusier research.

MAURICE FAVRE, born in 1922. Studied law at Neuchâtel and at Basel and, since 1948, has practised in La Chaux-de-Fonds as a barrister

**Notes on
the Contributors**

and lawyer. Author of various articles and
pamphlets, including a study on La Chaux-de-
Fonds, in *Cahier de l'Institut Neuchâtelois,* no.
7, 1961; "Les Neuchâtelois, recherche d'une
patrie," in *Cahier de l'Institut Neuchâtelois,* no.
13, 1969; also "Le Corbusier à travers un dossier inédit et un roman peu connu," in *Musée
Neuchâtelois,* no. 2. 1974. Since 1963, he has
been on the Editorial Committee of the *Musée
Neuchâtelois.* His parents knew Charles-
Edouard Jeanneret, and as a result he had
heard since his childhood about the legal proceedings of the Villa Schwob.

RUSSELL WALDEN, born 1934, in New Zealand.
Trained as an architect at the University of
Auckland, graduated M.Arch. (Auckland) and
B.Arch. (N.Z.). Awarded Postgraduate
Scholarship in Architecture in 1965 to study
modern European Architecture. Professional
experience in New Zealand 1960–1964, and in
Birmingham on mass housing 1969–1971. Cur-
rently Senior Lecturer in Architecture at the
Birmingham School of Architecture. Editor of
The Open Hand. Essays on Le Corbusier. At
present doing research on "Le Corbusier, ideals
and realities," doctoral dissertation, University
of Birmingham.

BRIAN BRACE TAYLOR, born 1943, in U.S.A. Trained
as an architectural historian at Harvard University, graduated Ph.D. in 1974. Currently Assistant Editor of *L'Architecture d'Aujourd'hui,*

Paris. Architectural experience with Michel
Ecochard, Paris. Awarded Harvard Travelling
Fellowship (France), 1971–1972, to do research
on "Le Corbusier's Prototype Mass Housing,
1914–28," published in condensed form as *Le
Corbusier et Pessac,* La Fondation Le Corbusier,
Paris, 1972; and *Le Corbusier e Pessac,* Officina
edizioni, Rome, 1973. Author of "Sauvage and
Hygienic Housing, or The Cleanliness Revolution in Paris," in *archithese,* no. 12, 1974; and
on CIAM/Team 10: "Songs of Innocence and
Experience," in *L'Architecture d'Aujourd'hui,*
no. 147, January–February 1975.

CHARLES JENCKS, born 1939, in U.S.A. Trained as
an architectural historian at Harvard University,
graduated M.A., B.Eng.Lit., and B.Arch.
Awarded Fulbright Scholarship to do research
at London University, graduating Ph.D. in 1971.
Former editor of *Connection,* 1963–1965, also
member of Cambridge Seven (Mass.) and tutor
at Harvard. Currently Senior Lecturer in Architectural History at the Architectural Association, London. Publications include *Meaning in
Architecture,* edited with George Baird, 1969;
Architecture 2000—Predictions and Methods,
1971; *Adhocism,* with Nathan Silver, 1972;
Modern Movements in Architecture, 1973; and
*Le Corbusier and the Tragic View of Architec-
ture,* 1973. At present working on *Ersatz—The
Phoney in Modern Culture.*

ANTHONY SUTCLIFFE, born 1942, in England. Read

Modern History at Oxford, followed by a Doctorate at the Sorbonne, 1966. Currently Reader in Urban History at Sheffield University. Author of *The Autumn of Central Paris,* London, 1970, and coauthor of *Birmingham 1939–70,* Oxford University Press, 1974; also editor of a symposium on the history of apartment housing in Britain, *Multi-storey Living,* London, 1974. At present working on a comparative study of the development of city planning from 1900 in Britain, Germany, France, and the United States, for publication.

ROBERT FISHMAN, Assistant Professor of History, University College, Rutgers, the State University of New Jersey. Received his Ph.D. from Harvard University in 1974, and has recently completed the manuscript of a book based on his doctoral dissertation, "Ideal Cities: the Social Thought of Ebenezer Howard, Frank Lloyd Wright and Le Corbusier." The book, *Ideal Cities,* will be published in spring 1976, in New York.

MARTIN PURDY, born 1939, in England. Trained as an architect at what is now the Polytechnic of Central London. In 1964, appointed Research Fellow in Church Building at the Birmingham School of Architecture, and studied Liturgy and Architecture, and Town Planning. Currently Senior Lecturer at the Birmingham School of Architecture, and in private practice specializing in ecclesiastical architecture and planning. At present working on a doctoral dissertation concerned with "Architecture and the Urban Church," University of Birmingham.

JOHN WINTER, studied at the Architectural Association, London, and in the Yale Masters' Class under Louis Kahn with a William Bissell McKay Fellowship. Teaching appointments held at Yale University and the Architectural Association, London. Visiting Professor to Toronto University, 1962. Worked as architect in the offices of Stillman and Eastwick-Field, London, Ernö Goldfinger, London, and Skidmore, Owings and Merrill, San Francisco, California. Own practice started in London, 1960. His buildings have been illustrated in various English and French architectural journals. Author of *Modern Buildings,* 1969, and *Industrial Architecture,* 1970. Frequent contributor to the *Architectural Review.*

MAXWELL FRY, C.B.E., R.A., FRIBA, Ll.D. (Ibadan University). Late senior partner, now Consultant to Fry, Drew, Knight and Creamer, architects and planners, London. RIBA Gold Medallist, 1964. In partnership with Walter Gropius 1934–1936. In partnership with Jane Drew since 1945. Senior Architect at Chandigarh in collaboration with Le Corbusier on planning, responsible for five grades of housing, for a range of other buildings, such as colleges for men and women and a printing press, and for much of Sector 22. Publications include: *Fine Building,*

List of Illustrations   467

List of Illustrations   468

Biographical Photos